CourseMate

Engaging. Trackable. Affordable.

CourseMate brings course concepts to life with interactive learning, study, and exam preparation tools that support *TEACH*.

INCLUDES:
Integrated eBook, **Interactive teaching and learning tools,** and **Engagement Tracker**, a first-of-its-kind tool that monitors student engagement in the course.

ON THE WEB

TEACH
Are you in?

ONLINE RESOURCES INCLUDED!

FOR INSTRUCTORS:
• Instructor's Manual
• PowerPoint Slides
• Test Bank
• Instructor Prep Cards
• Student Review Cards
• Engagement Tracker

FOR STUDENTS:
• Interactive eBook
• Interactive Quizzes
• Flashcards
• TeachSource Video Cases
• Portfolio Resources
• Reflection Activities
• Web Links
• Education Standards in the United States and Canada
• Edublog

Students sign in at **login.cengagebrain.com**

WADSWORTH
CENGAGE Learning™

TEACH
Janice Koch

Executive Publisher: Linda Schreiber-Ganster

Executive Editor: Mark D. Kerr

Associate Development Editor: Caitlin Cox

Editorial Assistant: Genevieve Allen

Marketing Manager: Kara Kindstrom

Marketing Assistant: Dimitri Hagnéré

Sr. Marketing Communications Manager:
Tami Strang

Product Development Manager: Steven E. Joos

Developmental Editor: Lachina Publishing
Services

Content Project Manager: Samen Iqbal

Design Director: Rob Hugel

Art Director: Maria Epes

Print Buyer: Rebecca Cross

Rights Acquisitions Specialist: Roberta Broyer

Production Service: Mandy Walden, Lachina
Publishing Services

Photo Researcher: Linda Sykes

Text Researcher: Isabel Saraiva

Copy Editor: Lachina Publishing Services

Cover Designer: Bartay Studio

Cover Image: White apple © Liam Norris/
cultura/Corbis

Compositor: Lachina Publishing Services

For product information and technology assistance, contact us at
Cengage Learning Customer & Sales Support, 1-800-354-9706.

For permission to use material from this text or product,
submit all requests online at **cengage.com/permissions**.
Further permissions questions can be emailed to
permissionrequest@cengage.com.

Library of Congress Control Number: 2010935304

Student Edition:

ISBN-13: 978-1-111-34911-0

ISBN-10: 1-111-34911-8

Wadsworth
20 Davis Drive
Belmont, CA 94002-3098
USA

Cengage Learning is a leading provider of customized learning solutions with office locations around the globe, including Singapore, the United Kingdom, Australia, Mexico, Brazil, and Japan. Locate your local office at **www.cengage.com/global**.

Cengage Learning products are represented in Canada by Nelson Education, Ltd.

To learn more about Wadsworth, visit **www.cengage.com/wadsworth**.

Purchase any of our products at your local college store or at our preferred online store **www.CengageBrain.com**.

Printed in the United States of America
1 2 3 4 5 6 7 14 13 12 11 10

Brief Contents

PART 1   THINKING ABOUT TEACHING: MAKING THE DECISION   2

Chapter 1   Becoming a Teacher: Looking Forward and Backward at the Same Time   4

Chapter 2   Teaching Stories   24

PART 2   THE EVOLUTION OF SCHOOLS AND TEACHING PRACTICES   44

Chapter 3   An Overview of Schooling in America   46

Chapter 4   Principles of Teaching and Learning: Exploring Pedagogy, Curriculum, and Instruction   70

PART 3   LOOKING AT TODAY'S SCHOOLS   92

Chapter 5   Who Are Today's Students?   94

Chapter 6   Contemporary Trends and Pressing Issues in Education   114

Chapter 7   The Information Technology Revolution in the 21st Century   148

Chapter 8   Globalization and Education   164

PART 4   CLASSROOMS, COMMUNITIES, AND YOU   178

Chapter 9   The Classroom as Community   180

Chapter 10   Making the Decision to Become a Teacher   196

GET ONLINE

HE DID

Access CourseMate for **TEACH** at **login.cengagebrain.com**.

You'll find everything you need to succeed in your class.

- Interactive Games
- Quizzes
- Flash Cards
- Videos
- Audio
- And more

www.cengagebrain.com

Contents

PART 1 THINKING ABOUT TEACHING: MAKING THE DECISION 2

CHAPTER 1 BECOMING A TEACHER: LOOKING FORWARD AND BACKWARD AT THE SAME TIME 4

Looking Backward: Talking about Teaching 6

Writing & Reflection: Draw Yourself as a Teacher 6

Your Educational Autobiography 7

What Is Your Metaphor for Teaching? 8

A Favorite Teacher 10

Writing & Reflection: Find Your Favorite Metaphor 10

What Qualities Are Needed to Be a Good Teacher? 11

Attributes of Good Teachers 11

TeachSource Video Case: Advice from the Field 12

Looking Forward: The Profession 12

An Essential Profession 12

A Code of Ethics 13

NEA Code of Ethics of the Education Profession 14

An Organized Profession 16

Honoring Diversity 16

Starting Early 17

NAEYC Standards 18

A National Board 19

More Than a Profession 19

Am I a Professional If I Join a Union? 19

The Workplace: School Climate and School Culture 20

Can You Feel the School Climate? 21

Concluding Thoughts 21

Resources for Further Exploration 22

CHAPTER 2 TEACHING STORIES 24

Who Are Our Teachers? 25

Early-Childhood Education 26

Deciding to Become a Teacher 27

"I Like the Hours" 31

Excitement and Challenges in Teaching 31

What Are the Most Exciting Aspects of Teaching? 31

Rewards of a Teaching Life 32

What Are the Most Difficult Challenges for Teachers? 33

Teaching, Learning, and Burnout 33

Challenges and Opportunities 34

Writing & Reflection: Begin a Teaching Journal 35

Teaching and Vision 37

*TeachSource Video Case: Surprises
of the First Year* 37

Hidden Curriculum 38

Support for Teachers 39

Who Provides the Most Support to Teachers? 39

Mentoring New Teachers 40

Teachers as Lifelong Learners 40

How Do Teachers Continue
Professional Development? 41

Benefits of Lifelong Learning 41

Concluding Thoughts 42

Resources for Further Exploration 42

© Claudia Dewald/iStockphoto

PART 2 THE EVOLUTION OF SCHOOLS AND TEACHING PRACTICES 44

CHAPTER 3 AN OVERVIEW OF SCHOOLING IN AMERICA 46

A Brief History of American Public Education 47

The Colonies 47

Social Capital 48

Latin Grammar Schools 48

Geographical Differences in Colonial Education 49

The Late Colonial Period 49

A New Nation 50

The Academy 50

Rise of the Common School 50

Expansion of Public Schools 52

Teacher Education and the Development of Normal Schools 54

Normal Schools and Female Teachers 54

Gender Roles in Teaching 54

The Tuskegee Normal School and the Education of African Americans 55

Catherine Beecher 55

Competing Visions: Efforts to Rethink and Reform Education   55

   The High School Curriculum   56

   The Emergence of Essentialism   57

   Progressivism and John Dewey   57

   Enduring Ideas: The Influence of Perennialism   58

   Radical Reform Philosophies: Social Reconstructionism, Critical Theory, and Existentialism   59

     TeachSource Video Case: Educational Philosophies in the Classroom   59

   Aesthetics and Maxine Greene   60

     Writing & Reflection: The Pendulum of Educational Reform   62

Federal and State Efforts at Educational Reform: Funding, Priorities, and Standards   62

   Separate but Equal?   63

   The Elementary and Secondary Education Act   64

   Title IX   64

   A Nation at Risk   65

   The Individuals with Disabilities Education Act   65

   Standards-Based Educational Reform   66

Concluding Thoughts   67

Resources for Further Exploration   68

CHAPTER 4   PRINCIPLES OF TEACHING AND LEARNING: EXPLORING PEDAGOGY, CURRICULUM, AND INSTRUCTION   70

Anyone Can Teach?   71

Pedagogy and Instruction   72

Learning Theories   73

   Behaviorism: A Teacher-Centered Approach   73

   Cognitive Learning Theories: The Role of Mental Processing   73

   Social Cognitive Theories: The Role of Social Interactions   75

   Constructivism: Student-Centered Learning   75

     The Essence of Constructivism: Building Mental Schemes   76

      Carl Rogers on Learning   76

     Mental Schemes at Work   77

     Constructivism and Teaching   78

     Perspectives from Neuroscience: The Importance of Context   79

      Cookies and Brain Science   80

     Fish Is Fish   81

     Writing & Reflection: The Context of Learning   81

What Is a Curriculum?   82

     TeachSource Video Case: A High School Debate   82

© murat Sen/iStockphoto

Formal, Informal, and Hidden Curricula   82

The Role of National Standards and State Frameworks   83

The Pressure to "Cover" the Curriculum   *83*

Curriculum and Standardized Assessment   *84*

Curriculum as Window and Mirror   84

Adapting the Curriculum to Your Students   85

Assessment: How Do We Know What They Know?   85

Two Examples of Understanding Performances   *87*

Standardized Testing: A Challenge for Authentic Assessment   88

TeachSource Video Case: Performance Assessment   *89*

Learning to Teach   89

Concluding Thoughts   89

Resources for Further Exploration   90

© Brian Santa Maria/iStockphoto

PART 3   LOOKING AT TODAY'S SCHOOLS   92

CHAPTER 5   WHO ARE TODAY'S STUDENTS?   94

The Students: A Changing Landscape   95

Ethnic Diversity   96

Language-Minority Students   97

Bilingual Education   *97*

TeachSource Video Case: Bilingual Education in Fourth Grade   *98*

Teaching English-Language Learners   *98*

Religious Diversity   99

Sexual Orientation   99

Writing & Reflection: Thinking about Your Own Beliefs and Biases   *100*

Socioeconomic Disparities   100

Overlapping Attributes: The Social Context   101

© Chris Schmidt/iStockphoto

Students Who Are at Risk   101

    Strategies for Reducing High School Dropout Rates   102

Contemporary Issues Relating to Student Diversity   103

  Multicultural Education   104

  Educating Girls and Boys: Separate or Together?   105

  Religion and Schools   107

Multiple Intelligences: What Does It Mean to Be "Smart"?   108

Learning Styles   111

    TeachSource Video Case: Teaching to Students' Strengths   111

Teaching the Broad Range of Diverse Students   112

Concluding Thoughts   112

Resources for Further Exploration   113

CHAPTER 6   CONTEMPORARY TRENDS AND PRESSING ISSUES IN EDUCATION   114

© Ju-Lee/iStockphoto

The Inclusion Classroom   116

    Controversy about Inclusion   117

    TeachSource Video Case: Teaching Strategies for the Inclusion Classroom   117

  Types of Disabilities   118

  Individualized Education Programs   118

  Response to Intervention   118

    TeachSource Video Case: Collaboration between the General Education Teacher and the Inclusion Specialist   118

The Education of Gifted and Talented Students   121

    Who Is Gifted?   123

Differentiated Instruction   123

Social and Emotional Learning   124

The Power of Projects and Problems for Student Learning   125

  Project-Based Learning   125

  Problem-Based Learning   126

    Project-Based Learning in History and Geography   127

No Child Left Behind and Its Successor   129

  Teaching to the Test?   129

    The Main Provisions of NCLB   130

  Does One Size Fit All?   131

  Variation among States: Are the Standards Really Standard?   131

    Authentic Assessment   131

  The Achievement Gap   132

    TeachSource Video Case: Educators Discuss IDEA and NCLB   132

Alternatives to Traditional Schools: More Choices in an Era of Accountability   132

  The Rise of Charter Schools   133

    Who Teaches in Charter Schools?   134

    A Case Study: The Russell Byers Charter School   134

Homeschooling: Another Nontraditional Option   135

Middle School: A Movement in Transition   136

Critiques of the Middle School Model   137

A Framework for Effective Middle Schools   138

**Creating a Safe School Climate: The Concern about Violence
in Schools   139**

Protecting the Rights of Students   139

The Right to Privacy   139

Creating a School Climate That Promotes Safety and Connectedness   140

Recent Challenges to FERPA   141

Students' and Parents' Rights under FERPA   141

Compromises on Privacy   141

First Amendment Rights of Students   142

Writing & Reflection: Prayer at a Football Game   143

The Rights and Responsibilities of Teachers   143

Teachers' Rights   144

Teachers' Rights: A Brief Summary   144

Teachers' Legal Responsibilities   145

*TeachSource Video Case: Teachers Discuss Their Ethical
and Legal Responsibilities   145*

Concluding Thoughts   145

Resources for Further Exploration   146

**CHAPTER 7   THE INFORMATION TECHNOLOGY
REVOLUTION IN THE 21ST CENTURY   148**

What Does Technology Mean for the Classroom?   150

The Flat Classroom   150

The Connected Classroom   150

The Problem of Information Overload   151

Technology and Learning   152

Guidelines for Internet Research   152

© Andrzej Burak/iStockphoto

Ways That Internet Technology Supports Learning   153

    Real-World Problems   *153*

    Simulations and Modeling   *153*

    Communities of Learners   *154*

Web 2.0   155

    **TeachSource Video Case: Integrating Technology to Teach Literacy
in the Middle School**   **155**

    Blogs   *155*

    Wikis   *156*

    Why Use Blogs for Education?   **156**

    Implications of Web 2.0   *157*

    Using Handheld Wireless Devices for Assessment   *157*

    Writing & Reflection: Are Schools Out of Touch with Our Lives?   **157**

Tracking Student Progress from Home   158

Internet Safety   158

The Digital Divide   159

    Learning How to Learn: The $150.00 Laptop Project   **160**

Assistive Technology   161

Concluding Thoughts   162

Resources for Further Exploration   163

CHAPTER 8   GLOBALIZATION AND EDUCATION   164

Education in the Knowledge Economy   165

    The Flat World   165

    The Global Student: Having Information
vs. Constructing Knowledge   166

    Learning How to Learn   *166*

    Global Collaboration   *167*

    TeachSource Video Case: Learning How to Learn   **167**

    Skills for the 21st Century   *167*

Teaching in the Global Classroom   168

    Teaching with Digital Media: Videoconferencing, Games,
and More   170

    Digitally Inclined   172

    Writing & Reflection: The Online Community   **172**

    Virtual Classes in High School   172

    Questions for Teaching an Online Course   **173**

    The Teacher's Role in a Global Classroom   174

Concluding Thoughts   175

Resources for Further Exploration   176

© geopaul/iStockphoto

PART 4 CLASSROOMS, COMMUNITIES, AND YOU 178

CHAPTER 9 THE CLASSROOM AS COMMUNITY 180

Building Community in the Classroom 181

Classroom Management and Classroom Community 181

Rules, Procedures, and Routines:
A Collaborative Effort 184

Is a Well-Managed Classroom Silent? 184

Being Fully Conscious 185

TeachSource Video Case: Teachers Building Community 185

The Classroom as a Safe Place 186

TeachSource Video Case: Using Classroom Meetings to Create Community 187

The Responsive Classroom Approach
to Community Building 187

Tips for Creating a Classroom Community 188

*Classroom Communities: Tips
for Teachers* 189

Community Building in the Secondary
Classroom 189

Consistency 190

Clarity 190

Fairness 190

Foresight 190

Preventing Harassment and Bullying 190

*Writing & Reflection: Establishing
Boundaries* 191

Sexual Harassment in School 191

Bullying and Teasing 192

Types of Sexual Harassment 192

Cyberbullying 193

*Tips for Students Who Are
Cyberbullied* 194

Classroom Community and Goodness of Fit 194

Concluding Thoughts 195

Resources for Further Exploration 195

© Rafa Irusta/iStockphoto

CHAPTER 10   MAKING THE DECISION TO BECOME A TEACHER   196

Goodness of Fit   197

The Importance of Observing in the Field   198

TeachSource Video Case: Effective Teaching   198

The Purposes of Public Education and the Role of the Teacher   199

One Size Does Not Fit All   200

Creating a Culture of Caring   200

Writing & Reflection: Demonstrating Understanding   202

Looking Again at Multiple Ways of Teaching and Learning   202

Using Current Technologies   203

Getting Started in the Teaching Profession   204

Certification and Standards   204

The Praxis Tests   204

The INTASC Standards   205

The National Board for Professional Teaching Standards   205

Teaching Positions Here and Abroad   206

Tips for New Teachers   206

Educational Associations   208

The Vision of the AFT   208

The American Federation of Teachers   208

The National Education Association   208

Build Your Teaching Portfolio   209

A Sample Introductory Essay for a Portfolio   209

Concluding Thoughts   210

Turning to Teaching   210

Passion Quotient   210

Resources for Further Exploration   211

References   213

Index   219

© Joey Boylan/iStockphoto

This book invites you on a personal journey of reflection about education—your own education, the education of people you know, and the education of children who will become America's future. It is a journey of self-exploration, during which you will be asked to look inside your mind and heart and consider what it takes, emotionally and intellectually, to become a teacher who experiences joy and satisfaction through service to others.

The first decade of the 21st century has passed. In this text, we will examine the specific challenges of becoming a teacher in today's social and political context, which raises issues like testing, standards, and the digital revolution. While much about teaching and learning remains the same year after year, technology has significantly changed the ways our students communicate, learn, and spend their time outside of school. As we enter this second decade of the 21st century, compelling truths about our world *must* be considered as you embark on your professional preparation to become a classroom teacher.

- The world is rapidly changing and a far different place than it was only 10 years ago.
- The global economy and the technological innovations of the last decade demand a well-educated citizenry.
- The best teachers grow and change with rapidly changing social and cultural conditions—thereby becoming lifelong learners.
- Online education is a significant presence in K–12 schools all over the country.
- Technology occupies a great deal of time for students of all ages.
- Every single student has the ability to learn, and becoming a teacher means accepting our daily responsibility to take all students, at whatever level and place in their lives they may be, and help them to learn.
- Education provides our students with the opportunity to become productive and contributing members of our society.
- Effective teaching is complex and requires personal reflection.
- The quality of the teacher in the classroom is the most important influence on student achievement.

Part Outline

CHAPTER 1 Becoming a Teacher: Looking Forward and Backward at the Same Time

CHAPTER 2 Teaching Stories

CHAPTER 1

BECOMING A TEACHER:
LOOKING FORWARD AND BACKWARD AT THE SAME TIME

© LWA/Dann Tardif/Getty Images

> *Everyone who remembers his own education remembers teachers, not methods and techniques. The teacher is the heart of the educational system.*
> —Sidney Hook, American philosopher (student of John Dewey), 1902–1989

This book is designed to guide your thinking about entering the field of education. It is about schools and schooling, teachers and teaching, learners and the process of learning. It is also about you. What do you already know about classrooms, and how can you apply that knowledge to the complex experience of being a classroom teacher? Your answers to these questions will play a big role in deciding the kind of teacher you will become. Research has shown that out of all the factors that contribute to a student's school day, the single most important factor in improving students' performance is the effectiveness of the teacher. Yes, the teacher makes all the difference.

You have within you everything you need to enable yourself to become the kind of teacher you want to be. This book challenges you to identify the attitudes, skills, and dispositions that the field of teaching requires. You will need to make a commitment to being a lifelong learner— that is, expanding your ideas by what you learn from your students, your research, and your own personal growth. Donald Schön (1983), an educational researcher, used the term **reflective practitioner** to refer to a teacher who

reflective practitioner
A teacher who consistently reflects on classroom events (both successes and problems) and modifies teaching practices accordingly.

© Brian Powell/iStockphoto

LEARNING OUTCOMES

After reading this chapter, you should be thinking about the following ideas:

LO1 Reflecting on your educational autobiography and teaching metaphor may help to clarify your thinking around what it means to be a teacher. It will also influence your personal philosophy and goals as a future educator.

LO2 A teacher of your own may have had a profound impact on your life and your desire to become a teacher yourself, and may serve as a role model.

LO3 Good teachers usually have common attributes; as you consider becoming a teacher, you must reflect on the goodness of fit between your qualities as a person and the demands of the profession.

LO4 Your understanding of teaching as "the essential profession" will be enhanced by your knowledge of the history and standards of several professional organizations that offer support to educators in settings from early childhood through university-level instruction.

LO5 Teachers must be committed to pursuing a school climate and a school culture that have a positive impact on students' ability to learn; the quality of the teacher in the classroom extends throughout the entire school and makes all the difference.

LO6 Being a reflective practitioner means looking forward and backward and realizing that we teach who we are.

consistently and consciously modifies her or his own teaching practice based on the active consideration of events in her or his classroom. This book invites you to conceptualize teaching as a personal activity requiring a large capacity for reflective thought and deliberate action and experimentation.

The field of teaching, which requires such a heightened sense of self and a commitment to the social good, demands nothing less of its professionals than an ongoing examination of their authentic motives for teaching. Hence, in addition to *knowledge* about schools, curriculum, and instruction, this text provides a *venue* through which you can actively consider your skills, attitudes, and dispositions as they relate to becoming a teacher.

We begin by examining your interest in the field of education. This chapter is subtitled "Looking Forward and Backward at the Same Time" because it will encourage you to reflect on your own educational background as you explore the possibility of forging a career as a teacher.

WRITING & REFLECTION

Draw Yourself as a Teacher

With a pencil and paper, draw a picture of yourself teaching a lesson. You do not have to be an artist; stick figures are fine (see Figure 1.1). Just imagine yourself in a classroom and draw the images you see. Be sure to include the students! This is a way to explore your images of teaching. Close the book while you work! When you finish your drawing, return to this section.

As you analyze your drawing, you may want to reflect on the following questions:

- How is your classroom arranged?
- Are there desks in rows? Or are tables grouped around the room?
- What are you doing? What are your students doing?
- Are you standing in front? In the middle? To the side?
- Are students raising their hands?
- Judging from your drawing, what mental models do you have of yourself as a teacher?

LO1 Looking Backward: Talking about Teaching

When I recently asked a number of new teachers what made them decide to enter teaching, some of them remarked that they had always loved school. School was, for them, the happiest place to be. But several others shared not-so-glorious stories about their experiences. They decided to go into teaching to make a difference, to teach others in ways they wish they themselves had been taught.

Yet other teachers had no specific personal calling to teach. They "fell into" teaching because they needed a job and teaching presented itself. Still others are trying to figure out if teaching is for them. Whichever of these categories you feel you may fit into, this book will help you explore the field of education and discover for yourself if teaching is for you.

Laura and Sharyn pursued teaching careers because they loved school and loved learning. Laura explained that from her earliest years in school, she was excited when the school year began and sad when it ended. School was her happiest place, so she decided to pursue a career that would keep her there. Sharyn described similar feelings:

She remembered how, as a child, she could not wait for summer camp to be over because she wanted to go back to school. In high school, she was part of a peer tutoring program and also privately tutored friends and classmates. When they did well, she was actually happier than when she herself did well because she knew she had helped them to succeed. Sharyn's love for school and learning, combined with the joy she felt when her friends whom she tutored succeeded, led her to want to teach. Sharyn wanted to enable children to love learning as much as she did.

A third teacher I interviewed, Derrick, told me that most of his teachers were female. Not until sixth grade did he experience his first male teacher—the music and he majored in history in college while also pursuing a professional program in elementary education. A kindergarten teacher today, Derrick is firmly convinced

educational auto-biography Your own educational history, told by you.

that men are needed in early-childhood education so children can see that men are able caretakers.

Are you like Laura, Sharyn, or Derrick in your conviction that teaching is a career you clearly want to pursue? Or are you more ambivalent? The "Writing & Reflection" activity will help you think about ways in which your educational past, and your thoughts and feelings about it, may influence your future career.

Your Educational Autobiography

What was school like for you? What kind of a student were you? When you think of teaching, which teacher or teachers do you conjure up?

You may think questions like these are irrelevant at this stage of your life. But examining your early experiences as a student is an important task:

> *Who you are as a person, the kinds of experiences you had inside and outside of school, your values, beliefs and aspirations shape what you will be as a teacher and how you will teach and how you will respond to the changing contexts of teaching. (Bullough & Gitlin, 2001, p. 45)*

Thinking about your own story, and telling it, is an important step in looking backward.

An **educational autobiography** is your own story of your life as a student. It has no definite length but usually responds to the following questions:

- What do you think of when you think of school?
- Where did you attend school?
- When you walked in the building, did you have a sense of comfort? Fear? Anxiety?
- Close your eyes and imagine you are back in elementary, middle, or high school. What was school like for you? Do you remember what school *smells* like? *Sounds* like?
- Try to imagine specific teachers. What grades did they teach? Who were your friends in those grades?

My own first story begins with kindergarten:

I remember starting kindergarten at the age of four years and six months. Arbitrary calendar cutoff dates, typical of many public school districts, allowed me to enter school well before my fifth birthday. Neighbors would say, "She

FIGURE 1.1

Drawing a Teacher
These samples show how three teacher candidates responded to the challenge to draw a teacher. What ideas about teaching do the drawings suggest?

teacher. He gained an appreciation of music from this teacher and started to imagine that he might teach as well. He played school with his younger brother and began to consider a career in education. Later, a male history teacher encouraged him to study that subject,

Think back from your earliest school experiences up to the present—what was going to school like for you?

© Michael Newman/PhotoEdit, Inc.

Christine's first-grade teacher never smiled and often yelled. One day she accused Christine of talking in line, sent her back to the classroom instead of letting her go to art, and then yelled at her. Christine was shy and quiet and never told her parents about the incident. The next day, however, she locked herself in the bathroom of her home and would not go to school.

When she finally did return to school, she was silent for the rest of the school year. It would be years later when her parents learned why she locked herself in the bathroom.

The following year, second grade, turned school around for Christine. She had a second-grade teacher who was loving and nurturing and who took a genuine interest in every child. This teacher developed a classroom environment in which students were encouraged to explore their own interests, and she made a personal connection with each child. From second grade on, Christine loved learning. It was, for her, that love of learning that motivated her to become a teacher.

made the year." That referred to being allowed to commence kindergarten prior to turning five. Other children, born four weeks later, had "missed the year" and began kindergarten after their fifth birthday. They would be the oldest in the grade, while I was the youngest.

I remember being frightened and throwing up every day for the first two months of kindergarten. But I also recall my kindergarten teachers' accepting and welcoming me each day, regardless of my physiological reaction to separating from my home. I was a very "young" four-and-a-half year old and would probably have been better served by "missing the year." How patient and kind my two kindergarten teachers were! They saw me coming and intuitively knew that I was not ready for school. After helping me get over being sick each morning (they

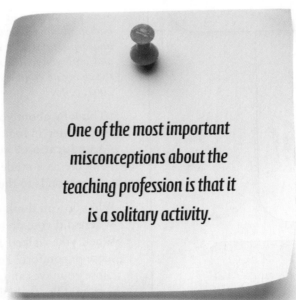

One of the most important misconceptions about the teaching profession is that it is a solitary activity.

had a pail ready), they guided me gently to my seat. Their understanding that I had to become comfortable at my own pace enabled me to make an adjustment without shame and embarrassment.

I shall always remember their acceptance of me and my lack of readiness. How lucky I was to have these two teachers as I acclimated myself to being away from home.

Christine, too, felt some pain in her early school years. Her story begins in first grade:

WHAT IS YOUR METAPHOR FOR TEACHING?

"Being a teacher feels like being a dentist—we are always pulling teeth," a new teacher remarked to me recently. "Ouch," I responded. "Is it that hard?"

"Well," she replied, "when they don't give me what I am looking for, I feel like that."

Aha, I think—some metaphor! One of the most important misconceptions about the teaching profession is that it is a solitary activity—something you do *in order to have control over someone else.* In fact, teaching and learning is an interaction, a conversation, a collaborative process involving you, the teacher, and all of your students. Teaching is about the students, *their* needs, not *your* needs for them. The teacher who feels like a dentist is focusing on what his or her needs are, not on the needs of his or her students.

It is true that sometimes we wish students would respond in certain ways and they just don't. Yet there

Being a **tour guide**

Being a **sailor**

Being a **sculptor**

What is your **metaphor** for teaching?

Climbing a **hill**

Teaching is a **toolbox**

Photos, clockwise from top left: © Ben Blankenburg/iStockphoto; © darren baker/iStockphoto; © Anastasia Pelikh/iStockphoto; © gabyjalbert/iStockphoto; © Vasko Miokovic/iStockphoto; © Alexey Tkachenko/iStockphoto

are much better metaphors than pulling teeth. Much of the time teaching is like:

- **Being a tour guide.** According to one teacher, a good tour guide takes travelers to new places, interprets experiences and sites, helps travelers understand and appreciate these new experiences, and develops a group atmosphere to maximize positive experiences for the travelers. A good tour guide has general goals in mind but is flexible and allows for exploration of ideas that arise from the group.

Indeed, there are many times when teaching is like being a tour guide. The teacher sets the itinerary and takes the students through the lessons to many new places. Yet there are other times when being a teacher is like:

- **Being a sailor.** Sometimes when you go sailing, you think you're going to reach a certain island. You set out for that island, but you find it doesn't have a

dock. The dock is simply not there. So you need to have an alternative plan.

On other days, you have a destination in mind, but the wind is blowing in the wrong direction and the sailboat just will not go there.

Yes, on many days, teaching is like sailing, and the teacher changes course in midstream as he or she determines a better direction and a more feasible destination. Still on most days, teaching is a lot like:

- **Being a sculptor.** Sculptors are fond of saying that they don't "make" their art; they uncover what is already hidden in the material. Similarly, teachers uncover the ideas emerging in the minds of their students.
- **Climbing a hill.** Another teacher explains that teaching is a constant process of ascending an incline. Every once in a while you stop, take a breather, make sure everyone is comfortable, and then you start climbing again.

philosophy of teaching statement A description of your ideas about teaching and learning and how those ideas will influence your practice. It should be based on your knowledge of educational research.

help them enjoy learning on their own. Have *you* ever thought of teaching that way?

When I asked him what would be in this toolbox, Chris gave several examples: the ability to do research, use the Internet to find reliable sources, access data from the library, and make decisions about the information one finds. These indeed are valuable skills. Another skill Chris hopes for is that students will learn to interact with their peers—talking about their ideas and putting information into their own words.

The "Writing & Reflection" activity will help you come up with your own metaphor for teaching. There is an important reason for coming up with and exploring your metaphor: It gets you started on developing your personal philosophy of teaching statement. A **philosophy of teaching statement** outlines your ideas about teaching and learning, sets out techniques for being

As I talked with young teachers, yet another metaphor emerged. Chris imagined teaching as a *thing*: a toolbox. He believed that teaching was about providing students with the tools to be lifelong learners: a set of skills and dispositions to

Q: *What attributes did your favorite teacher possess?*

reflective about your practice, and describes how you will teach. It may also include your goals for yourself as a teacher. If you decide to pursue a career in teaching, your philosophy of teaching statement will form an important part of your teaching portfolio (see the Review Card at the back of the book).

Your teaching philosophy should be backed up by evidence from research. For many decades, educators have studied how people learn and have compiled evidence about successful teaching strategies. As you read this book, you will encounter some of that research; the more you learn about it, the better prepared you will be to state your own teaching philosophy. But it is never too early to begin this kind of thinking. Take a few moments to think about your own teachers.

LO2 A FAVORITE TEACHER

Does one teacher stand out in your mind as having influenced you in a positive way? How did this teacher make an impact, and what was the result of her or his connection to you? Answering these questions is another good way to reflect on your educational past. When I think about these questions I remember junior high school.

I had a seventh-grade teacher, Mrs. Fisher, in JHS 117 in the Bronx, New York. I was, as you read in the early part of my educational autobiography, really young for my grade; I was eleven years old. Mrs. Fisher was my science teacher, and in those days, much of general science revolved around learning how the internal combustion engine of an automobile worked.

I really liked science, but I was shy, young, and from a poor neighborhood. I had little self-confidence. Mrs. Fisher took me aside one day and said, "You know, Janice, you are very good in science; you should go to the Bronx High School of Science." This high school is one of the specialized schools in New York City requiring that students pass an entrance exam. Mrs. Fisher gave me the application and helped me complete it.

I passed the exam, was admitted, and began attending the Bronx High

WRITING & REFLECTION

Find Your Favorite Metaphor

Think of one or more metaphors for teaching. If you need some leads, visit the website "Metaphorically Speaking" from the Annenberg Media Learner Interactive Workshops (http://www.learner.org/channel/workshops/nextmove/metaphor/). You may come up with several metaphors that seem apt. As you choose metaphors, explain why you think each of them is a good description of teaching.

School of Science at the age of twelve. My experience at this distinctive high school changed the course of my future education and career. Years later, I went back to visit Mrs. Fisher and thanked her for having taken an interest in me. I determined that one day I, too, would make a difference for students.

LO3 WHAT QUALITIES ARE NEEDED TO BE A GOOD TEACHER?

After reflecting on your favorite teacher, you may want to compare the attributes of this teacher with a list of some general qualities of good teachers. Read the sidebar "Attributes of Good Teachers." How do these qualities match up with the ones your favorite teacher had?

In making this comparison, think about whether you possess these qualities. As we proceed in this text, we will often return to the concept of **goodness of fit**. This term refers to how good a match there may be between your qualities as a person and the demands of teaching.

Don't be discouraged if you don't find a perfect match between yourself and the ideal characteristics listed in the sidebar. You are always growing and changing as a person, and you certainly may develop qualities you don't have now. When you begin to think about a career in teaching, one of your tasks is to analyze your own strengths and weaknesses. Realizing your strengths allows you to utilize them to the fullest potential, while identifying your weaknesses allows you to work toward improving them or overcoming them.

Q: *What are your strengths and weaknesses as a person? As a student? As a future professional?*

> **goodness of fit** A term generally used in descriptive statistics to describe the match between a theory and a particular set of observations; in this book, it means the match between a teacher candidate's personal attributes, values, and dispositions and the demands of teaching.

ATTRIBUTES OF GOOD TEACHERS

A good teacher needs to be:

Knowledgeable. A sound understanding of the fields of teaching and learning and your own content area is essential. Students know when you are knowledgeable.

Alive! A good teacher has a healthy balance of warmth and strictness and an enthusiasm for being with young people, evidenced by her or his ability to share students' interests. Enthusiasm does not mean boisterousness, but teaching requires a presence in the classroom that is both personal and professional.

Articulate. A good teacher has good communication skills and expresses herself or himself clearly. This includes having a sense of humor.

Innovative. A good teacher constantly seeks new and exciting ways to interest and engage students in the topic at hand. Novel methods and techniques leave a lasting impression on students and demonstrate that the teacher has taken the time to prepare for the lesson.

Patient. A good teacher is not easily overwhelmed or distressed and has the capacity to be a good listener. At times you will need to repeat lessons or remind students of the classroom rules, not to mention the occasions when you will have to help students overcome their doubts and fears. These times require patience and stamina.

Committed. A good teacher is dedicated to furthering the learning experiences of young people and fostering a love of learning. A certain amount of selflessness is required.

Able to find joy in teaching. A good teacher derives a great deal of pleasure from teaching. You cannot make learning a joy for students unless you love the teaching profession and find joy in it.

TEACHSOURCE VIDEO CASE

Advice from the Field

Find the TeachSource Video Case "Becoming a Teacher: Voices and Advice from the Field" on the student website, and you will meet several teachers, some new to the field and some who have been teaching for years. Also view the bonus video called "Essential Qualities That Teachers Must Possess." After watching the videos, consider the following question:

Which of my qualities match the attributes of good teachers?

LO4 Looking Forward: The Profession

Now it's time to begin looking forward. What is special about teaching as a career? What do you need to know about this profession you are considering?

AN ESSENTIAL PROFESSION

"Every child needs—and deserves—dedicated, outstanding teachers who know their subject matter, are effectively trained, and know how to teach to high standards and to make learning come alive for students."
—President Bill Clinton, 1998

In a U.S. Department of Education report, *Promising Practices: New Ways to Improve Teacher Quality* (1998), teaching is referred to as "the essential profession, the one that makes all other professions possible." What do you think that means?

The report further declares that without well-qualified, caring, and committed teachers, neither improved curricula and assessments nor safe schools—not even the highest standards in the world—will ensure that our children are prepared for the challenges and opportunities in America's third century. More than ever before in our history, education will make the difference between those who will prosper in the new economy and those who will be left behind. Teaching is the profession that is shaping this education and therefore America's future—molding the skills of our future workforce and laying the foundation for good citizenship and full participation in community and civic life.

Hence, it is you, the teacher, who will bring to life the ideals, the attitudes, the learning experiences, and the joy that are possible in a classroom. The curriculum, which we will explore later in this text, is a lifeless document in itself. It is the classroom teacher who enables the curriculum materials to have personal meaning for each learner.

Does this sound like a tall order? It is! Because what teachers know and are able to do has such a profound impact on the future of education, you need to understand how people come to learn. You need to spend time in classrooms to become familiar with different contexts for teaching and the diversity of students in our schools.

We would not expect that a future doctor would be able to examine a patient or perform surgery with just a few months' training. Yet we do often expect students to become teachers after a period of only several weeks of in-classroom training. This is why many teacher education programs (and yours may be one) require early field experiences, during which you observe and participate in the life of a classroom at the grade level you are thinking about teaching.

People have debated for years whether teaching is technically a *profession* in the same sense that, say,

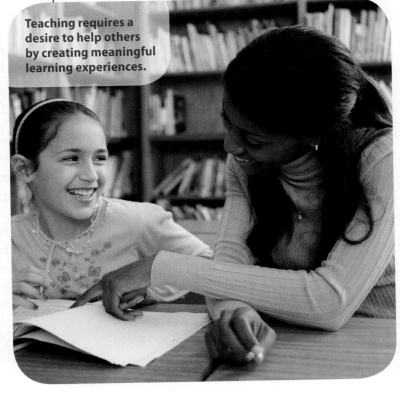

Teaching requires a desire to help others by creating meaningful learning experiences.

© OJOImages/Photolibrary

medicine and law are. On one hand, teachers do not get paid as much as doctors and lawyers, nor is teachers' training as extensive. Also, to many people, the knowledge that teachers possess about teaching and learning does not seem as complicated and technical as what a neurologist knows about the nervous system. On the other hand, teaching does share a number of attributes with other professions. Look at Figure 1.2 and decide for yourself how many of the statements are true about teaching.

A CODE OF ETHICS

The **National Education Association (NEA)** is the nation's largest professional employee organization. It has 2.8 million members who work in

National Education Association (NEA)
The largest organization of teachers and other education professionals, headquartered in Washington, D.C.

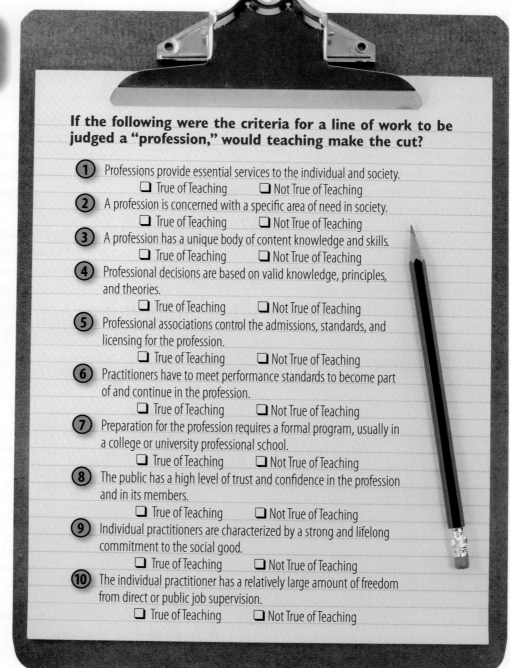

FIGURE 1.2

Is Teaching a Profession?

If the following were the criteria for a line of work to be judged a "profession," would teaching make the cut?

1. Professions provide essential services to the individual and society.
   - ❑ True of Teaching ❑ Not True of Teaching
2. A profession is concerned with a specific area of need in society.
   - ❑ True of Teaching ❑ Not True of Teaching
3. A profession has a unique body of content knowledge and skills.
   - ❑ True of Teaching ❑ Not True of Teaching
4. Professional decisions are based on valid knowledge, principles, and theories.
   - ❑ True of Teaching ❑ Not True of Teaching
5. Professional associations control the admissions, standards, and licensing for the profession.
   - ❑ True of Teaching ❑ Not True of Teaching
6. Practitioners have to meet performance standards to become part of and continue in the profession.
   - ❑ True of Teaching ❑ Not True of Teaching
7. Preparation for the profession requires a formal program, usually in a college or university professional school.
   - ❑ True of Teaching ❑ Not True of Teaching
8. The public has a high level of trust and confidence in the profession and in its members.
   - ❑ True of Teaching ❑ Not True of Teaching
9. Individual practitioners are characterized by a strong and lifelong commitment to the social good.
   - ❑ True of Teaching ❑ Not True of Teaching
10. The individual practitioner has a relatively large amount of freedom from direct or public job supervision.
    - ❑ True of Teaching ❑ Not True of Teaching

Photo: © Feng Yu/iStockphoto

NEA CODE OF ETHICS OF THE EDUCATION PROFESSION

Preamble

The educator, believing in the worth and dignity of each human being, recognizes the supreme importance of the pursuit of truth, devotion to excellence, and the nurture of the democratic principles. Essential to these goals is the protection of freedom to learn and to teach and the guarantee of equal educational opportunity for all. The educator accepts the responsibility to adhere to the highest ethical standards.

The educator recognizes the magnitude of the responsibility inherent in the teaching process. The desire for the respect and confidence of one's colleagues, of students, of parents, and of the members of the community provides the incentive to attain and maintain the highest possible degree of ethical conduct. The Code of Ethics of the Education Profession indicates the aspiration of all educators and provides standards by which to judge conduct.

The remedies specified by the NEA and/or its affiliates for the violation of any provision of this Code shall be exclusive and no such provision shall be enforceable in any form other than the one specifically designated by the NEA or its affiliates.

PRINCIPLE I:
Commitment to the Student

The educator strives to help each student realize his or her potential as a worthy and effective member of society. The educator therefore works to stimulate the spirit of inquiry, the acquisition of knowledge and understanding, and the thoughtful formulation of worthy goals.

In fulfillment of the obligation to the student, the educator—

1. Shall not unreasonably restrain the student from independent action in the pursuit of learning.
2. Shall not unreasonably deny the student's access to varying points of view.
3. Shall not deliberately suppress or distort subject matter relevant to the student's progress.
4. Shall make reasonable effort to protect the student from conditions harmful to learning or to health and safety.
5. Shall not intentionally expose the student to embarrassment or disparagement.
6. Shall not on the basis of race, color, creed, sex, national origin, marital status, political or religious beliefs, family, social or cultural background, or sexual orientation, unfairly—

---

educational settings from preschools through universities. With affiliate organizations in all fifty states and in more than 14,000 U.S. communities, the NEA provides local services such as workshops and collective bargaining for teachers. On a state and national scale, it acts as a lobbying group for educational issues.

Later chapters will have much more to say about professional organizations for teachers. I bring up the

Did You Know?

The NEA was founded in 1857 as the National Teachers Association. (It adopted its present name in 1870.)

NEA here because, as far back as 1929, NEA members adopted a code of ethics for the profession. The most recent revision of the code is shown in the sidebar "Code of Ethics of the Education Profession." Look at the first paragraph of the code's preamble. Let's take this statement apart and see what it means.

- **"Believing in the worth and dignity of each human being"** This phrase

a. Exclude any student from participation in any program
b. Deny benefits to any student.
c. Grant any advantage to any student

7. Shall not use professional relationships with students for private advantage.

8. Shall not disclose information about students obtained in the course of professional service unless disclosure serves a compelling professional purpose or is required by law.

PRINCIPLE II:
Commitment to the Profession

The education profession is vested by the public with a trust and responsibility requiring the highest ideals of professional service.

In the belief that the quality of the services of the education profession directly influences the nation and its citizens, the educator shall exert every effort to raise professional standards, to promote a climate that encourages the exercise of professional judgment, to achieve conditions that attract persons worthy of the trust to careers in education, and to assist in preventing the practice of the profession by unqualified persons.

In fulfillment of the obligation to the profession, the educator—

1. Shall not in an application for a professional position deliberately make a false statement or fail to disclose a material fact related to competency and qualifications.

2. Shall not misrepresent his/her professional qualifications.

3. Shall not assist any entry into the profession of a person known to be unqualified in respect to character, education, or other relevant attribute.

4. Shall not knowingly make a false statement concerning the qualifications of a candidate for a professional position.

5. Shall not assist a noneducator in the unauthorized practice of teaching.

6. Shall not disclose information about colleagues obtained in the course of professional service unless disclosure serves a compelling professional purpose or is required by law.

7. Shall not knowingly make false or malicious statements about a colleague.

8. Shall not accept any gratuity, gift, or favor that might impair or appear to influence professional decisions or action.

SOURCE: National Education Association. (1975). Code of ethics of the education profession. http://www.nea.org/home/30442 .htm; retrieved May 1, 2010.

refers to a teacher's commitment to all of her or his students. A teacher's authentic desire to make a connection with every student and to consider each individual's needs is the essence of good teaching. For some further thoughts about the meaning of this clause in the NEA code of ethics, see the sidebar "Honoring Diversity" on the next page.

- **"Recognizes the supreme importance of the pursuit of truth, devotion to excellence"** This phrase's meaning probably requires even more careful thought in the 21st century than it did in the past. We live in the context of an information technology revolution, a time when the amount of information available to us and to our students is exploding. Teachers must encourage students to embrace the value of examining multiple viewpoints on a topic, but also teach them how to evaluate the validity of information. Hence, our commitment might better be stated as recognizing the importance of *multiple* truths and *multiple expressions* of excellence.

- **"Nurture of the democratic principles"** This phrase reminds us to honor individual expression, capitalize on special student interests, and expand students' abilities to explore and critique multiple ideas and values.

• **"Responsibility to adhere to the highest ethical standards"** Figure 1.3 shows statistics indicating that the public considers teachers to be highly trustworthy. This is positive, as far as it goes. But your ethical responsibility as a teacher goes beyond telling the truth. Your responsibility is to place the needs of students at the center of your work and to give them priority over your own needs. Hence, your constant question is, "What is in the best interests of my students?" This is important as you consider a career in teaching. Many people enter the profession and discover that it is difficult to be as generous of spirit as the profession demands. That would not make you a bad person, but you need to consider how it relates to the "goodness of fit" between this profession and your personal attributes.

AN ORGANIZED PROFESSION

Overall, teaching is a highly organized profession. In addition to the NEA, the **American Federation of Teachers (AFT)**, created in 1916 and affiliated with the American labor movement, boasts more than 1.3 million members. Both the NEA and the AFT provide

HONORING DIVERSITY

Read the following poem by Lew Gardner.

"My Great Uncle's Horse"

My mother's uncle had a horse.
The best time of a deadly relatives' Sunday
was to walk with him to the stable
and watch him feed the quiet animal,
to give it sugar from my own hand
and jump back away
from the big warm tongue,
to smell the hay and manure, to see
the white horse in the next stall,
with tail and mane like yellow silk.

If my mother and I ran into him
as he and the horse were making their rounds,
buying up the wonderful junk
they heaped and hauled in the wagon,
he'd lift me up to the seat
and let me hold the reins and yell "Giddy-up!"

In the spring of 4th grade,
one afternoon of silent division
we heard a clanking and looked outside.
My great-uncle! I could tell them all
how I had held those reins!

But everyone laughed at the hunched old man,
the obsolete wagon and horse,
the silly, clattering junk.
I did not tell them.

Reading this poem, do you see that students, coming as they do from diverse backgrounds and knowledge bases, may be hidden to you unless you create "spaces" for them in the classroom? Respect for diversity must become part of every classroom teacher's agenda, regardless of grade level and subject matter and of whether the teacher looks and sounds like his or her students.

Honoring diversity means accepting that we are all products of our own culture, our own biases, and our own beliefs. You must constantly ask, "Who are my students? What are their lives like? What are their stories? . . . and knowing these things, how can I help them learn?" This is all part of respecting the learner and ultimately respecting ourselves as learners. Chapter 5 addresses the issue of the wide diversity of students in today's schools and its implications for teaching and learning. If we think of diversity as an opportunity, we will grow from the challenge and become better teachers.

SOURCE: "My Great Uncle's Horse" reproduced by permission of Lewis Gardner.

legal services and collective bargaining representation as well as a network of support for teachers, including professional development resources for your growth as a teacher. These large groups also wield a great deal of political influence on behalf of educators and schools.

When you enter the teaching profession, you may decide to join one or both of these organizations. We will visit them again in this book's final chapter, but it is not too early to think about becoming a member.

STARTING EARLY

The **National Association for the Education of Young Children (NAEYC)** is the nation's largest early-learning professional organization. Early-childhood education is recognized as the most critical stage for preparing future learners. The NAEYC has standards for creating the first step in the "cradle to career" educational pipeline. High-quality early-learning programs are the foundation for future success in schools. The NAEYC focuses on the quality of education for all children, birth through age 8. A look at the teaching standards for early-childhood education developed by the NAEYC (see the sidebar on the next page) provides insight into the ways in which teaching very young children could never be considered an afterthought!

National Association for the Education of Young Children (NAEYC) This professional organization is dedicated to improving the quality of education for all children birth to age eight.

© Ekaterina Monakhova/iStockphoto

FIGURE 1.3

Public Trust in Various Professions

Pollsters asked,

"Would you generally trust each of the following types of people to tell the truth, or not?"

The bars show the percentage of respondents who said they would trust each type of person.

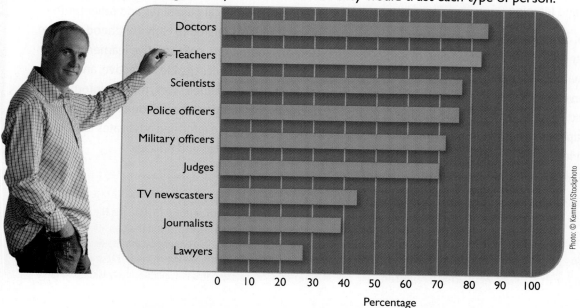

Photo: © Kemter/iStockphoto

SOURCE: Statistics from *The Harris Poll* #61, August 8, 2006; based on telephone interviews of 1,002 U.S. adults, July 10–16, 2006.

NAEYC STANDARDS

Standard 1. Promoting Child Development and Learning

Candidates use their understanding of young children's characteristics and needs, and of multiple interacting influences on children's development and learning, to create environments that are healthy, respectful, supportive, and challenging for all children.

Standard 2. Building Family and Community Relationships

Candidates know about, understand, and value the importance and complex characteristics of children's families and communities. They use this understanding to create respectful, reciprocal relationships that support and empower families, and to involve all families in their children's development and learning.

Standard 3. Observing, Documenting, and Assessing to Support Young Children and Families

Candidates know about and understand the goals, benefits, and uses of assessment. They know about and use systematic observations, documentation, and other effective assessment strategies in a responsible way, in partnership with families and other professionals, to positively influence children's development and learning.

Standard 4. Teaching and Learning

Candidates integrate their understanding of and relationships with children and families; their understanding of developmentally effective approaches to teaching and learning; and their knowledge of academic disciplines to design, implement, and evaluate experiences that promote positive development and learning for all children.

Sub-Standard 4a. Connecting with children and families

Candidates know, understand, and use positive relationships and supportive interactions as the foundation for their work with young children.

Sub-Standard 4b. Using developmentally effective approaches

Candidates know, understand, and use a wide array of effective approaches, strategies, and tools to positively influence children's development and learning.

Sub-Standard 4c. Understanding content knowledge in early education

Candidates understand the importance of each content area in young children's learning. They know the essential concepts, inquiry tools, and structure of content areas including academic subjects and can identify resources to deepen their understanding.

Sub-Standard 4d. Building meaningful curriculum

Candidates use their own knowledge and other resources to design, implement, and evaluate meaningful, challenging curriculum that promotes comprehensive developmental and learning outcomes for all young children.

Standard 5. Becoming a Professional

Candidates identify and conduct themselves as members of the early-childhood profession. They know and use ethical guidelines and other professional standards related to early childhood practice. They are continuous, collaborative learners who demonstrate knowledgeable, reflective, and critical perspectives on their work, making informed decisions that integrate knowledge from a variety of sources. They are informed advocates for sound educational practices and policies.

SOURCE: Excerpted with permission from the National Association of Young Children (NAEYC), from their position statement "NAEYC Standards for Early Childhood Professional Preparation Programs." Copyright © 2009 NAEYC. Full text of all current NAEYC position statements is available at www.naeyc.org.

A NATIONAL BOARD

In 1987 the **National Board for Professional Teaching Standards (NBPTS)** was created to set forth a vision for what accomplished teachers might "look like." These principles were developed in response to the report *A Nation Prepared: Teachers for the 21st Century* (Carnegie Forum on Education and the Economy, 1986). Besides being an advocacy organization, the National Board sets standards for what accomplished teachers should know and be able to do and offers a national system to certify teachers who meet these standards.

The board intends this certification to be a symbol of professional teaching excellence; it is entirely voluntary (National Board for Professional Teaching Standards, 2002). State licensing systems for teachers set entry-level standards, but National Board certification establishes more advanced standards. Out of approximately 2.9 million newly hired teachers in the United States, only about 50,000 will have achieved National Board certification.

Later in this book, we will visit the standards set forth by this National Board as well as some of the components of the certification test. For now, I hope you will see the board and its work as yet another indication of the professionalism of the field of teaching and the exciting prospects you have in entering the field.

> **National Board for Professional Teaching Standards (NBPTS)**
> A nonprofit organization that aims to advance the quality of teaching by developing professional standards for teachers.

MORE THAN A PROFESSION

We have been talking about teaching as a profession, but is that all it is? Carl Jung, the noted Swiss psychiatrist, said:

> *An understanding heart is everything in a teacher. One looks back with appreciation at the brilliant teachers,*

AM I A PROFESSIONAL IF I JOIN A UNION?

Although teachers cannot be forced to join a union, both the NEA and the AFT have local affiliates all over the country, and there are more than 2.5 million people who belong to one or both of them. Because they are labor unions (the NEA became a union in the 1960s, and the AFT was founded as a union in 1912), many individuals challenge the professionalism of teaching, arguing that other professions do not have unions. In fact, many people see the unions' ability to call strikes as a potential means of victimizing the very people teachers serve, students.

Union advocates respond that teachers, unlike members of some of the wealthier professions, need collective bargaining to secure better working conditions and higher salaries. In negotiating contracts on teachers' behalf, unions have certainly helped teachers gain power over their workload expectations, class sizes, pay scales, and benefits.

The unions' role in school reform also provokes debate. As powerful national organizations, the NEA and AFT can lobby for educational improvements. But some people argue that teacher contracts can be so specifically written that it becomes difficult to enact meaningful school reform—that is, the contracts merely serve to maintain the current system.

You will need to form your own opinion about the role of teacher unions and their effect on teachers' professionalism. When you start your first teaching job, you should inquire about the local union affiliation of your school or district and the union's connection to the NEA, AFT, or both. Teachers' unions can provide tremendous support to the new teacher as well as resources for his or her professional development.

but with gratitude to those who touched our human feeling. The curriculum is so much necessary raw material, but warmth is the vital element for the growing plant and for the soul of the child. (McGuire, 1954, paragraph 249)

So much is said about the skills and knowledge that are needed for the profession of teaching. The unspoken requirement, however, has to do with your dispositions, your own ability to understand your students and to connect with them in ways that help them to become better learners.

More than in most other professions, your personality and your belief in yourself shine through the techniques and strategies you employ. Your authentic self—that part of you that wants to make a contribution to the social good—is evident in the way you address the students, in your smile, in your level of preparedness for class, in the questions you ask, and in the respect you demonstrate for students as individuals.

As you work with this text, be sure to explore your innermost hopes and dreams and keep asking yourself, "Is teaching really for me?"

LO5 The Workplace: School Climate and School Culture

The day-to-day workings of a school influence how you enact your philosophy of teaching. Schools are constantly in flux, depending on student enrollment, collaboration among colleagues, pressures from the local community, and the vision of the school leader.

As you think about applying a teacher's professional commitments and values in a particular school setting, there are two terms you should know: **school climate** and **school culture**. These phrases refer to "the sum of the values, cultures, safety practices, and organizational structures within a school

that cause it to function and react in particular ways" (McBrien & Brandt, 1997, p. 87).

Often the two terms are used interchangeably, but some educators make a distinction between them: *school climate* referring to the way students experience the school and *school culture* meaning the way teachers and administrators interact and collaborate.

Still other educators think about *school climate* as the general social atmosphere or environment in a school. This is my preferred way of using the term. The social environment in this sense includes the relationships among students, between students and teachers, among teachers themselves, and between teachers and administrators. Students experience their environment differently depending on the rules and protocols set up by school administrators and teachers. *School climate* also includes the orderliness of the environment, the clarity of the rules, and the strictness of the teachers in enforcing the rules (Moos, 1979, p. 96).

Think back to your educational autobiography. According to the definition of *school climate* as the general social atmosphere, how would you describe the climate of your elementary school, middle school, and high school? A school climate may be described as

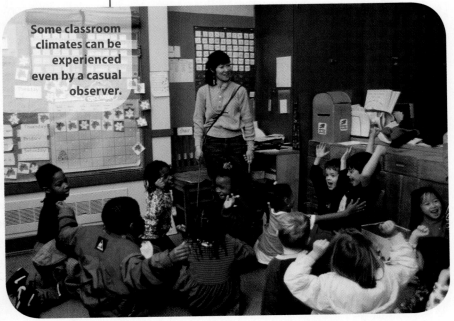

Some classroom climates can be experienced even by a casual observer.

CAN YOU FEEL THE SCHOOL CLIMATE?

Frequently, you can tell if a school's climate is nurturing by the feeling you get in the halls—if the principal and other administrators are readily visible, and if teachers smile and greet students by name. In such a school, students are treated as individuals.

At the other extreme, in a school with an authoritarian climate the halls are very quiet, there are strict "no talking" rules, doors are closed tight, and there is a feeling of tension in the air.

Teaching practices, student and teacher diversity, and the relationships among administrators, teachers, parents, and students all contribute to *school climate.*

Although no single, universally accepted definition of *school culture* has been established, there is general agreement that it involves deep patterns of values, beliefs, and traditions formed over the course of the school's history (Deal & Peterson, 1990). A school culture may have, for instance, a reputation for being very academic. My high school did. The culture of my high school could be described as academically driven, college preparatory, nonathletic,

and very cerebral. We were thought of as "geeks" because we attended this very serious-minded high school whose culture had been forged since its inception. Other high schools in my area had a culture that was more social, athletic, and active in the community, though also academic.

A school's culture is evident in its shared values, heroes, rituals, ceremonies, stories, and cultural networks. For example, if a school's leaders believe that motivation and academic achievement are a definitive part of the school's culture, they communicate and celebrate those values in as many ways as possible. In my high school, students were made to feel proud of the academic productivity of their classmates. Achievement was rewarded in the school newspaper and in organized assemblies.

When you think back to the ways in which the schools you attended functioned, how would you describe the school culture of your elementary, middle, and high schools? What did the schools stand for? How was that communicated?

---

nurturing, *authoritarian*, or somewhere in between. For example, I experienced my high school as nurturing *and* strict, caring *and* rigorous. We can also ask whether a school has a *healthy* climate, one in which students are made aware of expectations for their behavior toward one another and their teachers. In your own elementary school, middle school, and high school, was the student body diverse in terms of ethnicity, race, and social class, and if so, was there evidence of prejudice or racism? How was that expressed? What did school officials do to make students feel like valued members of the educational community?

It is never too soon to consider yourself a reflective practitioner.

LO6 Concluding Thoughts

Although teaching is an important and essential profession, ideas about it are often oversimplified. Our memories of our teachers are sometimes selective and misleading. However, the interpersonal nature of teaching demands that those interested in the profession take account of their own attributes and dispositions, their personal school experiences, and their future goals for themselves as teachers. It is never too soon to consider yourself a reflective practitioner.

Online Resources

American Federation of Teachers

http://www.aft.org/

The AFT's website has news and reports about issues of professional interest, resources for both practicing and aspiring teachers, and a legislative action center.

National Board for Professional Teaching Standards, The Five Core Propositions

http://www.nbpts.org/the_standards/
the_five_core_propositions

Five basic principles, each with several subordinate points, form the foundation of the National Board's mission.

National Education Association

http://www.nea.org/

In addition to the code of ethics reproduced in this chapter, the NEA's website has a wide variety of useful resources and information for teachers.

Donald Schön, Educating the Reflective Practitioner

http://educ.queensu.ca/~ar/ schon87.htm

This article encapsulates some of Schön's thinking about reflective practice in teaching.

Print Resources

Sylvia Ashton-Warner, *Teacher* (New York: Simon & Schuster, 1963).

This is a moving story of a New Zealand teacher's extraordinary work teaching Maori children; it exposes one teacher's thinking processes about placing her students' needs at the center of her practice.

Parker Palmer, *The Courage to Teach: Exploring the Inner Landscape of a Teacher's Life* (San Francisco: Jossey-Bass, 1998).

This exciting book addresses the ways in which teachers' lives, values, personal beliefs, and goals shape their practice.

SPEAK UP!
SHE DID

TEACH was built on a simple principle: to create a new teaching and learning solution that reflects the way today's faculty teach and the way you learn.

Through conversations, focus groups, surveys, and interviews, we collected data that drove the creation of the current version of TEACH that you are using today. But it doesn't stop there – in order to make TEACH an even better learning experience, we'd like you to SPEAK UP and tell us how TEACH worked for you.

What did you like about it? What would you change? Are there additional ideas you have that would help us build a better product for next semester's students?

At **www.cengagebrain.com** you'll find all of the resources you need to succeed – **videos, flash cards, interactive games, quizzes** and more!

Speak Up! Go to **CourseMate** for TEACH. Access at **login.cengagebrain.com**.

CHAPTER 2

TEACHING STORIES

© purestock/Photolibrary

> *Storytelling is the most powerful way to put ideas into the world today.*
> —Robert McAfee Brown, American theologian and teacher, 1920–2001

This chapter gives you a glimpse into the ways teachers from grades pre-K–12 make their decisions to enter the field and what they experience as the most exciting and challenging aspects of teaching. Their stories are designed to help you explore what Parker Palmer (1998) calls the "inner landscape of a teacher's life."

Being a teacher requires an emotional and intellectual commitment. By this I mean that, in a typical school day, teachers can experience excitement and frustration, pleasure and angst, great leaps of joy as well as sadness. How ready you are to navigate these emotions—while at the same time staying focused on your goals for the day—is something only you can know. The stories in this chapter may remind you of yourself or of a teacher you have had. But before we hear the stories of several actual teachers, let's take a brief look at who our teachers are, statistically speaking.

LO1 Who Are Our Teachers?

Figure 2.1 (on the next page) presents various statistics about U.S. public school teachers that give us a glimpse of the teaching workforce.

The majority of public school teachers in the U.S. workforce are over forty years old, with the average age of 46. About 87 percent are white, which is a decline from 90 percent white in 2001 (National Education Association, 2003, 2009). Given the increasing diversity of U.S. students (see Chapter 5), many educators believe that American schools have an urgent need for young teachers from varied ethnic backgrounds.

One figure that has changed in recent decades is the proportion of males in the teaching force. It had declined from 31 percent in 1961 to about 21 percent in 2001, and then by 2006, it increased to 30 percent (Snyder, Tan, & Hoffman, 2006; National Education Association, 2009). Some researchers suspect that the declining number of male teachers had negative consequences for students and for the profession, so it is promising that more men are entering the profession.

LEARNING OUTCOMES

After reading this chapter, you should be thinking about the following ideas:

LO1 Teachers enter the profession for a variety of reasons, but they often cite a love of children and a love of learning as common factors in their decision.

LO2 The nature of teaching makes it both a challenging and rewarding career.

LO3 Teachers reveal themselves in their classrooms; being conscious of this can help you use your strengths to create a hidden curriculum with positive messages for students.

LO4 Many avenues of support will be available to you as a new teacher, such as your colleagues, a mentor, professional organizations, and professional development programs.

Did You Know?

About 87 percent of U.S. public school teachers are white. The majority are over forty and female.

FIGURE 2.1

U.S. Public School Teachers, by the Numbers

SOURCE: Data from National Education Association (2009), *Status of the American Public School Teacher 2005–2006*, Washington, D.C.: Author.

Photo: © Hongqi Zhang/iStockphoto

EARLY-CHILDHOOD EDUCATION

You may recall that we presented the National Association for the Education of Young Children's teaching standards in Chapter 1. A national association dedicated to the early education of children highlights the significance of an auspicious beginning for a child's future learning. You may be wondering why so much attention is given to preschool and kindergarten through second grade.

Just over one million children enrolled in public pre-kindergarten in 2008; that number is projected to reach 1,115,000 by 2012 (Snyder & Dillow, 2010). Preschool, pre-kindergarten, and kindergarten play a vital role in the development of children. What they learn and experience in their early years shapes their views of themselves and the world. Early-learning programs, enrolling children as young as three years old, are seen as the key to closing achievement gaps, which we will examine later. Special sensitivities and skills are required for early-childhood teaching, and they are embodied by the next teacher you will meet.

Q: *Do you have any memories of going to preschool?*

CAROL Carol is in her tenth year as an early-childhood teacher, specializing in young children at the pre-kindergarten level. I once had the opportunity to spend some time in her classroom and was struck by how competent her four-year-old students appeared. They understood the rules of the classroom environment and were encouraged to do things on their own, contributing to the life of the classroom by putting materials away in their proper places, managing their belongings in their cubbies, and much more.

Carol spent her growing up years with a blackboard and chalk, playing school with her younger sister and her friends. But knowing she wanted to be a teacher wasn't enough, and life took her in other directions until, quite by chance, she was asked to assist in a pre-kindergarten classroom in a local private day school in her neighborhood. That was ten years ago, and she has since been a lead teacher for three-, four-, and five-year-olds in two different early-learning environments. Her college education and further courses enabled her to earn the proper early-childhood teaching credential, which she maintains annually by taking courses mandated by her state.

Carol described a major challenge for her work with young children as facilitating their social development. "The most rewarding part of the work is knowing that you are giving the children the tools to appropriately communicate with each other. The proper social development is essential for future learning. I have the opportunity to help the children to begin the process of communicating appropriately and effectively in social situations with other children. I spend a lot of time observing the children's interactions. You have to be able to sit with the child at eye level and discuss alternatives for non-judgmentally helping them to achieve their behavioral goals. It also requires that you understand that whatever the behavioral goals for the young child, they are not going to take place immediately (these are long-term goals that are seeded in the early-childhood classroom and are reinforced through the child's early education)."

When asked what was most stressful about her work, Carol responded by describing the importance of being able to ascertain what acceptable and unacceptable developmental behavior is for a small child. "There are students who require special services that enter school having not been diagnosed; when this happens, the burden is on the early-childhood teacher who must be certain she or he can get the correct services for the child as research on early intervention reveals positive outcomes for children with social and emotional issues. These decisions are not rendered lightly and require thoughtful reflection and expert consultation."

When asked to share the most exciting aspects of her work, Carol responded, "When the kids get it and learn to become comfortable in the classroom—they have learned the routine and the sequence of activities—you can tell they feel safe and competent to carry out routines. These young children are on a journey of self-regulation. My classroom is one step in that journey. It is so exciting to see them grow in this area and see them functioning autonomously. Many people do not recognize how fragile young children are as they develop their own sense of themselves and how terribly important it is to have prepared, informed, and caring professionals with whom they can grow."

Often, early-childhood educators are dismissed by society as glorified "babysitters." This is both incorrect and damaging to the profession and to an understanding of the crucial role that early learning plays in the development of healthy children and productive students. There is consistent controversy over the role of play in early-learning environments. Watching Carol's children at play reminds us of the social skills the students develop through play, like empathy, impulse control, capacity for sharing, communicating, and problem solving. Play-based activities also enhance children's capacity to think creatively, make choices, explore their environment, and develop pre-writing skills and sequencing skills. Carol's emphasis on the children's development of appropriate social interactions is vitally important for how students learn. As we will see in later chapters, learning is an interactive, social experience that requires communication between the learners and their peers as well as their teachers. Perhaps the most dominant misconception about early-childhood education is that it is not as work intensive as teaching in the higher grades. In fact, preparing a curriculum and activities for young children requires many hours of research and careful planning. Like the teachers you will read about in the following section, Carol receives support from her colleagues and the director of the early-learning program.

DECIDING TO BECOME A TEACHER

> "In my entire life as a student, I remember only twice being given the opportunity to come up with my own ideas, a fact I consider typical and terrible." —Eleanor Duckworth, educational researcher (1991)

© Wojciech Gajda/iStockphoto

Over the years, I have often asked elementary, middle, and high school teachers from all backgrounds to talk about themselves and their attitudes toward the profession. We begin with what some of them said about their reasons for becoming teachers.

JESSICA Jessica is a sixth-grade English teacher in a suburban school district on the East Coast. Her first love was dance, and she still teaches dance at a private dance school after regular school hours. She is also a regular choreographer of school plays. She has been teaching for three years. This is how she answers the question about deciding to become a teacher.

I had always wanted to be a teacher. When I was growing up, I loved to play school with the children I babysat, and I would give the neighborhood children free dance lessons. After college, I decided that I didn't want to be a dancer full time, so I turned to my other love—English. From the very first day of my very first graduate class in education, I knew I had chosen the right career.

I attribute my interest in teaching to several things: (1) a lifelong love of learning; (2) I had always loved going to school, even when I wasn't the best student (I did better in school as I got older); and (3) the fact that my mother is also a teacher, and I grew up watching her grade papers and plan her instruction.

AMANDA Amanda is a third-grade teacher in the northwest corner of the country. When I first entered her classroom, I was struck by how quiet it was. She apologized profusely for the silence, remarking that the students were usually noisier and more actively engaged in groups, but this time they were just finishing independent reading. She promised that soon I would see the real class! So often we think of good classes as silent, but learning often happens in social exchanges with others, as we will see in later chapters. When asked why she entered teaching, Amanda said:

Teaching has always been my calling. Ever since my first week of kindergarten, I knew that teaching would be my chosen path. That first day, I came home exclaiming to my mom, "I want to be a teacher just like Mrs. Seguin!" I spent the rest of my elementary school days playing teacher with my sister, my friends, and even my stuffed animals when no one was available. I had grade books, lesson plans, and homemade worksheets, and I made signs for my door that indicated my room was now "Miss Riggs's 1st grade class."

Even though I have always been drawn to the profession, it wasn't until my first year of college when I was taking an education course that I began to fully understand why I wanted to be a part of education. My dad was never what one might call a reader or a writer. The only book that I saw him read was the Bible, and I remember him asking me for help in spelling different words starting in second grade. Yet it was my dad who showed me the responsibility of being an educator. I was talking with him about a literacy lesson that I needed to prepare for class. I shared the many techniques that I had learned and how I was going to have the kids first participate in a hands-on activity and then draw the knowledge out from the activity. My father changed my outlook on education forever when he said, "I would have learned how to read and write if my teachers had taught like you." It was then that I realized I wanted to be a teacher to reach those kids who couldn't learn through traditional teaching methods. I wanted to find a way so that every student "clicked" with literacy and gained the skills to make his or her life one of continuous learning.

JAMES James is in his fourth year of teaching middle school in a midwestern suburban area. He was always involved in sports until he broke his leg in high school and could no longer play football. Many months of physical therapy and then working as an aide to a physical therapist helped him think about those who struggle with adversity. James explains his decision to become a teacher this way:

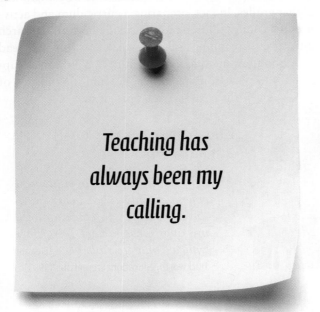

Q: *Why do you want to be a teacher?*

Teaching has always been my calling.

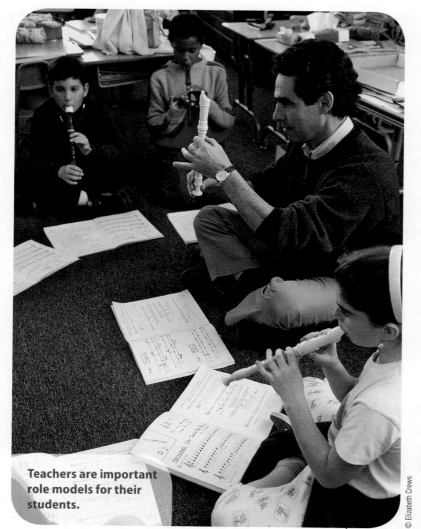
Teachers are important role models for their students.

© Elizabeth Crews

rapport I have with my students more than any other aspect of my teaching life. I attend their sporting events and try to encourage them in the ways that I was encouraged as a youngster. I really enjoy watching the students succeed and helping them overcome personal adversity.

I am very aware of the importance of being a positive role model for kids; they do not always have that at home.

PEARL Pearl is a veteran elementary school teacher of twenty-five years in an urban area of New York City. She has been both the mathematics specialist and the social studies specialist in her school as well as a mentor to countless student teachers. Her intellectual love is mathematics, and she is also committed to issues of social justice. She relentlessly celebrates women and people of color. Pearl's path to teaching went like this:

My parents were immigrants; my mom was born in Russia in 1905. In her little corner of the world, education for girls was not thought of as a necessity. She was never sent to school. When she came to the United States, she worked in sweatshops on the Lower East Side and cooked and cleaned for people to support herself. She cherished the educational opportunities that were afforded to children in this country— "God bless America," she would say. She especially cherished the opportunity afforded me, her daughter, to go to school. In my mother's eyes, teaching was ranked as the most highly important and respected profession.

My paternal grandfather was a theologian and a sought-after teacher in his town, known for his knowledge of religious texts. My father thought the world of him and respected him for his knowledge and ability to communicate ideas. So the teaching profession was well respected in my home.

Then there came Miss Rochford, my sixth-grade teacher. I loved Miss Rochford. She made math fun; she introduced us to musicals; she taught us how to write scripts and then we produced our own play; she showed us slides of her trips to Europe; and she exposed us to poetry. She introduced me to Mark Twain, Shakespeare, and Robert Frost. Miss Geraldine Rochford opened doors for me to a world beyond East New York, Brooklyn. I wanted to do the things she did. I wanted to travel, enjoy

The person who shaped my goal to become a teacher entered my life in the fourth grade. My fourth-grade teacher, a six-foot-four-inch man who was my first male teacher, was also my inspiration to become a learner. I wanted to be just like him, and I saw in him a genuine enthusiasm for teaching and for learning. I began to love school.

As fate would have it, I had him again in the sixth grade and then as the assistant principal of the high school I attended. He had taken me under his wing, and I was always grateful for his guidance. He is currently the assistant superintendent of the school district I attended. I attribute my desire to teach to his model of what that can look like.

My teaching style is derived from a patient mother and a very interested and involved father. Both positive and negative experiences in school shaped my thinking about how to speak sensitively to students. I enjoy the

the arts, and share the wonders of learning with kids like myself. That is why I never wanted to leave the public school system. She was one of the people who made me into a lifelong learner. As early as the sixth grade, I knew that I wanted to teach.

JANE   Jane has been teaching eighth-grade mathematics in an urban area on the East Coast for five years. Her decision to enter teaching came after her own children had gone off to college. The wife of a minister, she had taught religious classes in her church, and she wanted to choose a career she thought she would be good at. Jane is now a mentor teacher and very well thought of by students and faculty. Here's how Jane explains her career choice:

I feel like I entered teaching for all the wrong reasons. I wanted retirement benefits and good working hours, and I wanted to use skills that I believed I had developed as a mother and a minister's wife. I thought you should enter teaching because you had always wanted to be a teacher, but for me, it was really an afterthought that came later in life—that is why I think of it as being for the wrong reasons.

When I self-assessed, though, I recognized that I was a good listener and genuinely excited about math. I had majored in math in college, and I thought that was a good start. I also have a lot of self-knowledge, so I am able to recover from my mistakes. I have the ability to say "I'm sorry" when I have made a mistake, and I have a lot of respect for young people.

I knew when I entered my first education course that I had made the right decision since teaching would ensure that I was a lifelong learner. I am very focused on my own and my students' education. Teaching for me is like water walking; if you keep your eyes on the goals, you will not sink.

ALEX   Alex is in his tenth year of teaching history in a northeastern suburb. He was a perpetual student. He loved learning and loved the study of history, and he decided to get his PhD in history at the ripe old age of twenty-seven. Here is Alex's story:

I entered teaching when my university adviser told me I was ready to defend my dissertation. A perennial student,

I realized I needed a job! My adviser told me of a local college that needed instructors in history, and I started my teaching career with no formal education training.

Once in the classroom, I immediately realized that I really liked making complex concepts understandable to students. I was excited about teaching. I knew that I had a lot to learn, so I entered a program to earn a teaching certificate. I wound up becoming a secondary school history teacher. It gave me the opportunity to connect current events with the history curriculum and to join the faculty of a high-pressured, academically oriented school where we work hard and feel a lot of pressure to meet a high level of quality teaching.

I love it. I could not imagine becoming a high school teacher when I was younger, and now cannot imagine doing anything else with my life's work.

Did You Know?

Teachers work an average of 50 hours per week.

When teachers are asked why they decided to enter the profession, they often say, "I love children" or "I love kids." These answers echo the findings of many formal studies. Another burning reason for deciding to become a teacher is an individual's love of learning (http://www.yic.gov/publications/tenreasons/). The most successful teachers I know—like the ones featured in this chapter—typically talk about how they "loved learning." That is not to say they do not also love children, but teaching is a very complex activity. In the words of educational researcher Jackie Grennon Brooks (2002), from whom we will hear more in a later chapter,

Common thinking is that teaching is simple. But teaching isn't simple. It's a highly sophisticated intellectual activity that requires, among other things, a centered presence in the classroom, good negotiation skills, understandings of pedagogy and psychology that inform one another, and sensitivity to sociological factors in learning.

When beginning education students talk about entering teaching because they love kids, I learn from talking with them that they have been babysitters and camp counselors and that they have enjoyed these responsibilities. That is a fine start, but these informal experiences with children or adolescents are different from the more structured experiences found in classrooms and the demands of teaching. At this point in your reading, you may have already visited one or more classrooms and observed teaching in action, so you are aware of the vast differences between the formal and informal settings in which we interact with youngsters.

In addition to loving learning, people pursuing teaching careers often also loved school. That matches what we heard from Jessica, Amanda, Pearl, and James in this chapter as well as from Laura and Sharyn in Chapter 1. Notice especially what James said about the inspiration provided by a male teacher. Recent research, though controversial, suggests that male teachers may have a significant positive impact on the achievement of male students (Dee, 2005, 2006).

Another major reason secondary teacher candidates cited for becoming educators was prior experiences as a high school tutor or peer teacher. Like Jane, some were motivated to teach because of positive experiences in informal teaching settings. And like Jane, some had early religious training that affected their desire to serve others and teach.

What about Alex's story? His description of what we might call "falling into" teaching may resonate with you if you have just lately considered the idea of becoming a teacher. Not everyone who enters the field has had a lifelong calling to teach. Yet life as a teacher becomes fulfilling when there is a good match between the person and the demands of the profession. This is what I referred to as goodness of fit in Chapter 1. For Alex, teaching offered an excellent fit with his personality and his desire to share knowledge and foster his students' success.

LO2 Excitement and Challenges in Teaching

"Every September, every teacher proceeds into foreign territories." —Maxine Hong Kingston, distinguished writer and professor (1986)

When teachers are asked about the most exciting aspects of their work, invariably their answers relate to student learning. In this section we explore what some teachers say really excites them about their work, and then we examine some difficult challenges.

WHAT ARE THE MOST EXCITING ASPECTS OF TEACHING?

AMANDA Contrary to popular belief, I do not find it exciting when my students get 100 percent on their tests. It is the process that is exciting—the look on a student's face when he or she finally gets it, watching a student move from confusion to understanding, fielding a question you did not expect and do not know the answer to. It has been my greatest joy to see that student who struggled so much in an area work hard and become successful.

© VisualField/iStockphoto

There are many times when I struggle with presenting difficult material so that all students can grasp the "big idea" of the lesson. I can go through four or five activities in my room, and sometimes there are a handful of kids who just cannot make sense of the material. Finally finding a way to reach those kids—now that is exciting.

The classroom is a complex roller-coaster ride in the dark; you never know what will happen next. From scheduling changes to student needs, environmental factors (try teaching about fractions in 90-degree weather!), and even your own moods, no plan is ever left in its original state. An educator must roll with the needs of his or her students, and those needs are ever changing, every day. I find that exciting.

Q: *What do you think will most excite you about teaching?*

JESSICA The most exciting aspects of being a teacher are the possibilities that come with each new day. Of course, school brings a set routine, so I know what to expect in terms of scheduling and planning most of the time. On the other hand, I teach young adolescents, and they truly are different people every day. Watching them change and grow from the first day of sixth grade to the last day of sixth grade is like watching a transformation right in front of your own eyes, and it is very exciting and challenging.

Though it seems like a cliché, the most rewarding part of the day is the "aha" that I see on students' faces when they understand something they didn't understand before. These moments happen daily, but some are bigger than others. The best times are when students uncover new meaning for themselves, because their reactions are so much bigger.

JANE To me, meeting a brand new group of students each year is the most exciting part of teaching. Because every group of students is unique, I am challenged to address my teaching strategies in an entirely new way than I did the previous year. It is like starting a new job

every year. There is so much to learn from each new set of students. It is so exciting and challenging to understand each class's strengths and to tailor your teaching strategies to help them be all they can be in mathematics.

PEARL Teaching has made me a lifelong learner. In order to keep things new and interesting, I am always reading, studying, and thinking of new ways to teach a concept.

As a classroom teacher, I have the opportunity to wear many hats: storyteller, dream weaver, mathematician, scientist, poet, author, playwright, producer, director, choreographer, historian, and social worker—you name it. A classroom teacher has to play each of those roles, and sometimes all in one day. I get so immersed in my work very often that I forget to go to the bathroom until it is time to go home.

Teaching makes you aware of process—for instance, coming up with a rubric for writing a good biographical report and teaching kids how to take notes, organize their materials, and pay attention to the editing and presentation. It is exciting, too, to put together the "problems of the day" for my gifted math class, work on some of the challenging ones myself, and feel my brain churning. There's the frustration in trying to solve a problem and then that satisfaction when you "get it" and then, to top it all off, the opportunity to go through all those feelings again with the students—knowing how to coax them when they are ready to give up and being able to shed some light on a stumbling block so that they can feel that joy of accomplishment when they "get it" themselves.

REWARDS OF A TEACHING LIFE

The following observations about teaching provide an overview of these teachers' beliefs based on their experiences and their hopes for the profession as they continue. You can think of these observations as the "teaching ideas behind their stories."

- For these teachers, the idea of meeting new students every year and, in Jessica's case, feeling like there are new students almost daily, is a stimulating aspect of being a teacher. Each day is different, requiring a sharp and attentive adult presence in the classroom. These teachers enjoy the challenge.

- Amanda notes that the process of teaching is more exciting than the outcomes. Like Amanda, many teachers try different approaches to content material to make sure they reach the various types of learners in their classes.
- Pearl, Amanda, and Jessica talk about the excitement of reaching the children and recognizing that they "got it" as it related to new knowledge construction. Pearl gets so immersed in the activities with her students that she forgets to take a bathroom break.
- These teachers, typical of most, work actively on their teaching preparations and constantly challenge themselves to come up with novel ways to engage students in their own learning. They remind me that "to teach is to learn." Pearl illustrates this idea when she explains her own process in solving a difficult mathematics problem as a learner and then going through it again as a teacher.

WHAT ARE THE MOST DIFFICULT CHALLENGES FOR TEACHERS?

AMANDA   I find that the most difficult challenge is staying focused on my purpose. I am not in the room to raise test scores, to be a child's best friend, or to follow every theory I learned in school. I am there to help students go beyond their potential and gain skill sets needed for a successful, learning life. Many distractions are found in the school environment—often created by those who are well meaning. Stick to what you know is best for your students despite what others around you might think.

This year my room was across the hall from a teacher whom you might refer to as burned out. Every morning she arrived at the same time as the kids. By the time the children began to enter her room, my classroom was busy with morning learning activities. At least four times a week, our classroom was disrupted with her rants of

I find that the most difficult challenge is staying focused on my purpose.

"Why do Mrs. P's students get right to work and you are out here talking! I am tired of my class not being ready for the day!" These outbursts not only damaged her class but mine as well.

A good educator knows how to instruct students about expected behaviors and not shout about bad behaviors. No matter how frustrated, disappointed, or exhausted I become, I am here as a teacher and a learner, and learning happens mostly by my example—a good example or a poor one.

JAMES   If I had one wish about the profession, it would be that it was higher paying—that, for me, is the greatest downside of teaching. To raise a family, I must work a second job, and that is often a burden.

TEACHING, LEARNING, AND BURNOUT

By a "learning life," Amanda refers to a desire to know more and to have the skills to acquire new knowledge when the need and desire arises. Amanda herself has a "learning life," and by example and through practice, she engages her students in what it means to be a learner. Earlier in this chapter, the quote from Jackie Grennon Brooks introduced the concept of the teacher as a "centered presence" in the classroom. Amanda's understanding of her role in the classroom and her goals for her students helps her establish this centered presence. She is prepared and capable and has high expectations for her students. When Amanda says that learning happens by example, she means that she models to her students—demonstrates through her own behavior—what it looks like to be a learner. She learns about the content areas she teaches through her own research; she learns about her students through the interactions she has with them; and she learns about herself as she strives to refine her practice and to discover what works best for her students.

Amanda's teacher neighbor appears to be "burned out," meaning that she has lost the motivation to excel in her work and is no longer able to be an effective teacher. **Teacher burnout**, a reaction to prolonged high stress, commonly results either in withdrawing and caring less, or in working harder, often mechanically, to the point of exhaustion (Farber, 1991). As in any other field, burnout can have serious consequences for the health and happiness of teachers, their students, and the families with which they interact. There are many causes of teacher burnout, the most common being working conditions that are unsupportive and stressful interactions with parents and students. New teachers may experience burnout when the work of teaching requires a different set of skills from what they had anticipated. Teachers who have been in the profession longer and have not taken advantage of opportunities to renew their skills through formal and informal professional development may also experience burnout.

Table 2.1 lists some symptoms of burnout and steps you can take to combat it. One of the most important protections from burnout is being reflective. Remember what Chapter 1 said about being a reflective practitioner. Often a teaching journal—an idea presented in the "Writing & Reflection" activity—is helpful in this respect. Writing in the journal is a way to monitor your work and your emotional availability for the tasks ahead of you.

In a remark not unconnected to the idea of burnout, James complains

Did You Know?

Teachers in elementary and secondary schools have an average annual salary of about $51,000.

about teachers' salaries. Many educators believe that the feminization of the teaching profession—the decline in the percentage of male teachers—has helped reduce the pressure for better pay and benefits. Yet teachers' salaries have, in fact, risen considerably over the past few decades. Elementary and secondary school teachers now make an average of about $51,000 per year. Starting salaries for new teachers average about $34,000 per year. These figures do vary considerably from district to district and state to state. It is important to note that more than half of U.S. public school teachers feel satisfied with their salaries (National Education Association, 2009).

CHALLENGES AND OPPORTUNITIES

JESSICA One of the most difficult challenges for teachers stems from paperwork! I had no idea going into the profession how much paperwork there is to manage. I assumed that lesson plans, student handouts, and student work would be all the paperwork I'd come into

TABLE 2.1	Recognizing and Dealing with Teacher Burnout	
Signs of Burnout	**What Teachers Can Do**	**What Schools Can Do**
Your expectations for becoming a teacher and your experience are in conflict.	Consult with other teachers about your feelings and such matters as curriculum planning.	Create networks for new teachers and set up regular group meetings.
You do not feel like going to work.	Maintain a teacher journal in which you record your experiences and feelings.	Provide adequate resources and facilities to support teachers.
You have difficulty concentrating and feel inadequate in your role as a teacher.	Join new-teacher networks at your school or at the district level. Share your experiences, and keep journaling.	Provide clear job descriptions and expectations for new teachers.
You feel overwhelmed by the paperwork and the workload.	Find a mentor or seek the one to whom you have been assigned. Talk about your feelings!	Establish and maintain open communications between the school administration and the teachers.
You withdraw from your colleagues or enter into conflicts with them.	You may be emotionally exhausted. Find a professional to talk with.	Allow for and encourage professional development activities that help new teachers find mentors and become part of networks.

SOURCES: Adapted from Kyraciou (2001) and Wood & McCarthy (2002).

WRITING & REFLECTION

Begin a Teaching Journal

Start now to keep a professional journal for yourself. If you have not had a lot of practice journaling, starting a reflective journal can be daunting. You may want to begin by inserting the writing activities from Chapter 1: drawing yourself as a teacher and your metaphor for teaching, as well as your educational autobiography and a memory of a favorite teacher. You can keep your journal in a notebook, a blank book, a binder, or digitally on your computer or online—any method that is most comfortable and inspiring to you.

Being a reflective teacher is a theme we will return to again and again in this text. Reflective teachers take careful note of how their teaching practice is going and modify their methods accordingly. Since you are just embarking on teaching, your reflective journal should include how you are experiencing being an education student and what you are learning about teaching and yourself.

You can continue to fill your journal as you read this book, using as inspiration both the guided "Writing & Reflection" activities found in each chapter as well as your own thoughts and ideas on questions and topics presented. As you journal try to let your thoughts flow, without trying to edit them or get them down perfectly, and see where they take you. Your true feelings are more likely to surface this way.

Here are a few questions to help you begin your teaching journal:

- How are you experiencing the introductory education course you are taking?
- What are you discovering about the teaching profession that you did not know previously? Are there any surprises?
- At this point, how do you feel about a career in teaching?

Remember: You are on your own journey of growth and change, and the journal is a good record-keeping device for this process. Getting into the habit of journaling now can serve you well into your future career as a teacher.

of paperwork required for a classroom observation, or a field trip, or a school play, can be mind boggling.

Another major difficulty I didn't anticipate was dealing with parents. Although the majority of parents are on your side because both you and they are trying to achieve the goal of education for their children, there are parents who hold you responsible for things that are out of your control, who will blame you when a child fails even when you've done everything in your power to help the child. When parents see you as the adversary and not as their partner, it can be very painful.

A third difficulty is navigating relationships with in-building and district administration. When you are not tenured, you are advised to walk on eggshells, so to speak. This can create problems when you need assistance or when you disagree with a district policy or with the way a parent issue is being handled. Some administrators are more supportive than others, and it is important to know whom you can go to for help or guidance when you need it.

These things shouldn't dissuade people from becoming teachers. You learn how to deal with them effectively and appropriately soon after you begin teaching. They represent difficulties I didn't know about before I entered teaching, but the benefits of this career far outweigh the challenges in the workplace.

Jessica's comment about paperwork excluded some other areas in the daily life of the classroom where paper needs to be managed. These include attendance reports, progress reports for each student, and evidence of student work. Elementary school teachers often keep work folders for each student, while in the middle and upper grades student work is often handled using computer software programs. Science teachers usually have lengthy lab reports to evaluate, while language arts and social studies teachers evaluate analytical essays, term reports, book responses, and creative writing. In

contact with. In addition to those items, there are constant requests for information from the office, the nurse, the psychologists, special education teachers, parents, administrators, and even people in the community that must be dealt with promptly and regularly. The amount

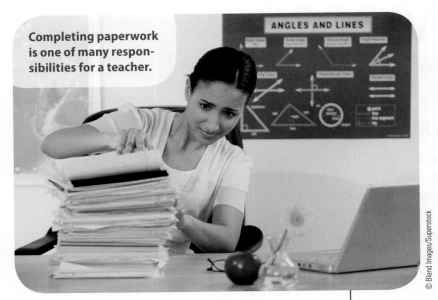

Completing paperwork is one of many responsibilities for a teacher.

ANGLES AND LINES

© Blend Images/Superstock

a 2001 survey, "paperwork" combined with "heavy workload," "extra responsibilities," and "meetings" to form the category that teachers said hurt them the most in their efforts to provide the best service in their teaching positions (National Education Association, 2003, Table 55). Fortunately, there are web-based software products that make handling data for especially large numbers of students much more manageable. We will visit those systems in Chapter 7.

Dealing with parents is part of a teacher's responsibility. We serve the children, but they are not ours. Jessica is conflicted about her communication with parents. Of course, parents are affected by what happens at their child's school and in their child's classroom. Communication between teachers and parents is important, and it is fostered through school practices that we will explore later in this text. Not only can parents influence decisions made about their child's education at school, but they can also contribute to the governance of the school though a parent teacher association (PTA) or similar group. It is always a good idea to reach out to parents and invite them to become part of your classroom community as helpers and contributors. In some school districts, parents are a frequent presence in classrooms. In other communities, parents are not available as often because of work responsibilities, but it is still important to invite them to contribute whenever possible.

Many people experience schools as "little villages," where the principal is the mayor and other individuals have varying amounts of importance or privilege. In all jobs, the politics of the environment can affect each of the workers. It is a good idea to learn about the expectations and norms of the school environment in which you will be working. You may already have had jobs where the politics of the environment affected your work. Although workplace politics may annoy or sometimes discourage you, keep in mind how important it is that schools function as learning communities where all the professionals share a core set of common goals.

JANE For me, the greatest challenge is having to implement the eighth-grade mathematics curriculum at a pace determined by the date of the standardized test. Instead of asking myself, "Should I linger longer on this topic since the students seem to need more time?" I speed along because I know there is so much to cover for the test.

This is a frustration in my teaching career since I am interested in how the students can make their math learning personal and relate it to their lives. This may take time, but it is important, and it always leaves me behind my colleagues in getting the curriculum done. I know that "teaching for the test" does not help the students make personal meaning for themselves.

Jane feels she is constantly challenged to "cover" math topics rapidly to prepare students for the standardized test they must take. With today's emphasis on standards—and on the tests that determine whether students meet those standards—many teachers feel similar pressures. A large number of educators, like Jane, believe that merely "covering" curriculum is the wrong approach. It leads to a shallow form of learning. Instead, these educators say, we need to uncover the curriculum by engaging students in exploring ideas and developing a deeper, more meaningful understanding. Remember what Jessica said earlier in the chapter: "The best times are when students uncover new meaning for themselves."

Q: *What do you think is the biggest challenge you will face as a teacher?*

PEARL As a new elementary school teacher, I found one of the most difficult challenges was engaging with the curriculum. I had to familiarize myself with a lot of topics that I was not sure about. I spent hours each weekend planning for the upcoming weeks by going to the library, finding the right books or the right motivational poems, leafing through magazines for the right pictures to support a lesson or illustrate a word, making visual aids, buying materials, and marking papers. As I became more experienced, I continued to plan on the weekends, but it became more a source of pleasure than of anxiety.

Pearl describes a major challenge for teachers at all levels: the preparation required to engage students in meaningful learning experiences. Many people, like Sam earlier in this chapter, are unaware of the number of hours beyond the school day that teachers spend in preparation. Teachers can never be overprepared. The term *curriculum*, as we will explore later in this text, refers to a plan of studies that includes the ways in which the instructional content is organized and presented at each grade level. Even if you have studied a subject area extensively, you may need to deepen your knowledge of certain topics in the curriculum. Students know when a teacher is prepared for the school day. It is evident in the materials the teacher has assembled and the activities the teacher is ready to implement. It contributes to Brooks's "centered presence" in the classroom.

LO3 Teaching and Vision

Research has found that all teachers carry in their head a vision of what they want to be as a teacher (Hammerness, 2006). That is, all teachers have their own sense of what a classroom should "look like" and how it should function. Yet these visions of teaching are as variable as are the individuals who choose to teach.

Our beliefs and images concerning teaching are often difficult to enact; there is often a disconnect between what we imagine and what we can practice. For example, when I walked into a second-grade classroom early one morning, the teacher had the children in the center of the room and was engaging them in hand motions and movement routines to a popular rock song blasting from her boom box. The children were loving it! When the activity was done, Ms. Outerbridge said, "OK, girls and boys,

TEACHSOURCE VIDEO CASE

Surprises of the First Year

You can find another story about the excitement and challenges of teaching on the student website. Watch the TeachSource Video Case "The First Year of Teaching: One Colleague's Story," in which Will Starner talks about his initial year in a classroom. After watching the video, consider the following question:

What ways did Will find to cope with the challenges of his first year of teaching?

we are now ready to work!" When I asked her about this activity, she said that (like Jessica, whom you met earlier) she had been a dancer, and her life in dance had taught her that releasing the energy in our bodies was an important way to stimulate the thinking in our minds. She worried that when her students came to class, they were too docile, having already learned by grade 2 how to "be quiet." She wanted them to be active in their bodies so they could be active thinkers about the topics of study.

"How wonderful!" I thought. I knew, however, that try as I might, I could never get myself or my youngsters to learn and then enact this intricate movement routine. I do not have that set of skills. I admired Ms. Outerbridge's vision but could not enact it. It is in this way that who we are comes to bear upon what we do with children and how we engage them in learning.

Throughout your teacher education, you will be asked about your personal vision. It is a goal of teacher preparation programs that you develop a personal

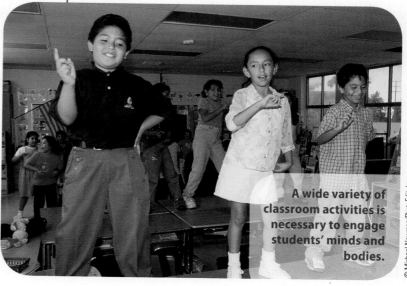

A wide variety of classroom activities is necessary to engage students' minds and bodies.

© Michael Newman/PhotoEdit, Inc.

educational philosophy informed not only by the scholars and research you have learned about in your program but also by your own beliefs, metaphors, personal vision, and values. The combination of self-knowledge and scholarly knowledge will assist you in developing your own philosophy. You started to do this in Chapter 1 when you described your personal metaphor for teaching.

The mantra that "we teach who we are" permeates this text. Ms. Outerbridge is a dancer; that background has served her as a learner, and she shares her passion with her second graders. Similarly, in the story that follows, my life as a scientist found its way into a third-grade classroom not long ago.

Every week, I was visiting a local elementary school classroom and exploring different topics in physical science with them. One weekend prior to a visit, I was in another state celebrating the seventh birthday of my first granddaughter. Her mother, my daughter, discovered that the batteries in her digital camera appeared to be dead and asked if I had batteries in my camera that she could use. We made the switch; I handed the "dead" batteries to my husband, and my daughter was able to use her camera.

Some hours later, when we arrived back home after the party, my husband noticed that his right pocket was very warm—uncomfortably so. "What do you have in there?" I asked. "Just the batteries and my loose change," he replied. Delighted, I shrieked, "The batteries are not dead, and there is an electrical circuit in your pocket. It is generating all this heat!"

It is a family joke now that my thrill at finding "science in our daily life" seemed to overcome my empathy for his discomfort. However, I recognized that this was another opportunity to make the topic relevant to the third graders who were making circuits for an electricity unit. I told the story to them that week and stopped short of an explanation. "If my husband had the dead batteries and some loose coins in his pocket, why would it be warm? Can you draw a picture of the contents of his pocket?" Eagerly students drew coins and batteries and understood that the metal coins acted as a wire and conducted electricity.

This story illustrates how our personal lives meet our professional lives in the classroom. Your students will learn a lot about you, and you will also learn a lot about them.

HIDDEN CURRICULUM

The stories we tell students about our lives and experiences outside of school are one small part of what may be considered the **hidden curriculum**: what students learn as they participate in the act of going to school, being part of a classroom community, and relating to their peers and their teachers. The phrase *hidden curriculum* was coined by the sociologist Phillip Jackson (1968), who described ways in which schools become arenas for socialization and transmit messages to students about how to be in the world. Long before that, educational philosopher John Dewey (1916) explored the hidden curriculum in schools as he examined the social values inherent in the experience of school. Hence, the hidden curriculum includes how we interact with students, how we enact the rules of the school culture, and how we communicate our expectations for student achievement and demeanor and our own passion for teaching and learning.

By telling the batteries-in-the-pocket story to my young students, I gave them a glimpse of what it is like to be an adult with a curious, scientific mind (and a family eager to make fun of my propensities). Perhaps the story helped some students in the class feel that science is fun, interesting, and relevant to daily life—and that certainly matches my vision of what I want to do in the classroom.

Every day, through countless similar incidents, teachers contribute positively to their school's hidden curriculum. However, teachers can also affect the hidden curriculum in negative ways. If you and other teachers are bored and cynical, for instance, you convey those feelings to your students. No matter how dutifully you slog through the subject matter, students will sense that it doesn't interest you, and they will absorb that message.

If you call on boys more than girls, for example, the hidden curriculum of your classroom might include the idea that boys are somehow more important. In early studies of gender and schooling in the 1980s, there were many instances where teachers called on boys more frequently than girls as a way of exercising "control" in the classroom (Sadker & Sadker, 1994; Sadker & Zittleman, 2009). The belief in the latter environment was that if you kept the boys engaged, they would not be apt to "act up." Today, we know that calling on boys and girls in equal numbers is of significant importance.

The hidden curriculum, not a part of public documents, includes messages that deal with attitudes, beliefs, values, and behavior. For example, since 2001, when the No Child Left Behind Act, which will be discussed in later chapters, was passed, regular assessment of mathematics and language arts prompted many elementary school administrators to allocate much more time to these subjects than to science, social studies, art, or music. The tacit message for children is that science is less important than math and reading, for example. A major purpose of the hidden curriculum has been to transmit the cultural and social norms of the school (how things are done, what routines matter, what dress is acceptable, who counts and who does not! When you visit schools and examine their routines and practices, ask yourself what matters to the leaders of this school. By exploring what is displayed in their showcases and on their walls, the hidden curriculum can be revealed.

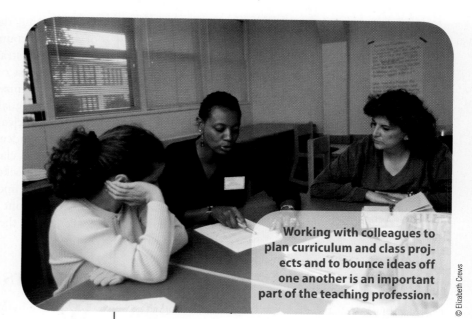

Working with colleagues to plan curriculum and class projects and to bounce ideas off one another is an important part of the teaching profession.

© Elizabeth Crews

LO4 Support for Teachers

When asked who gave them the most support in their teaching careers, Jessica, Amanda, and Jane all agreed that their colleagues were the strongest source of support. This matches the findings of a survey in which teachers rated cooperative and competent colleagues and mentors as the factor that helped them most in their teaching positions (National Education Association, 2003, Table 55). But the teachers I interviewed mentioned other sources of support as well. As you read the following stories, think about how these teachers interacted with their colleagues and others in the school and the community.

WHO PROVIDES THE MOST SUPPORT TO TEACHERS?

AMANDA I have found it supportive to listen to fellow teachers and the administrators, students, parents, and community members. You can learn a vast amount from conversations with others. In a crowded teachers' room, I am the one who is content to sit alone and listen

in on others' conversations. As you listen, you can learn so much about the expectations, the culture, the negatives and the positives, and ways to connect to the school and community in which you teach. I find keeping a teaching journal and jotting down what I discover about the students and the school to be very helpful. I try to make entries at least two or three times a week.

I jumped into school activities when I started and found that others who like to get involved were very supportive. My first year, I became a member of the Staff Development Committee, and I have never regretted that decision. I did not speak up as often as the other members, but I did listen and learn a great deal about the district that I was making my home. I am on various district-wide committees and involved in many school-based activities that have given me insight for understanding the context in which I teach.

JESSICA In the first years of teaching, much of my support came from my fellow teachers in the building. They were the ones who knew the answers to difficult situations and who would give encouraging words. I have found that to be true even now that I am a few years into the profession. Other educators can give you ideas, advice, and a sympathetic ear when needed, and this help can come from other new teachers as well as from veterans in the profession.

I also accessed my education professors, keeping in contact with them through e-mail. I was assigned a mentor at school, and this teacher was very helpful in acclimating me to the routines and procedures that I needed to understand at the very beginning. As time went on, she became an important role model for me.

MENTORING NEW TEACHERS

Many schools and school districts are adopting mentor teacher programs. Mentor teachers are specially trained to work with new teachers and support them in understanding the school culture, the curriculum, and the resources available to them as professionals. You may want to ask if there is a mentor program where you begin teaching. Mentoring has been a trend over the last ten years as the teaching profession has recognized the need to develop a special transition period during which new teachers acclimate to their profession. This period as a whole is often called *induction*. Good mentors have a broad range of skills and are able to help new teachers apply their professional knowledge in the classroom. They are generally master teachers who have demonstrated a love of teaching and learning and are eager to share their experiences with others.

JANE   I gain the most support for my teaching from my colleagues,.the school and district committees on which I serve, communication with my peers and my students, and my church.

Each Sunday, I teach a course in religion to adults, and I am struck by how much the enrollment in this class has increased over time. I employ teaching strategies similar to those I use with my eighth-grade mathematics students. I am organized and prepared, I respect their ideas and who they are, and I try to forge goals with them for our work together.

I also look inward for support. I evaluate my goals and reflect on my week in school and ask myself, "What should I change?"

From Jane's remarks we can see that, once again, teacher peers play an important role

in supporting the work we do in schools. This kind of support, coupled with Jane's capacity to articulate her teaching strategies, has contributed to her success. Notice the list of attributes that Jane uses to describe herself: organized, prepared, respectful of students, establishing goals with students collaboratively. The ability to be clear about your expectations for yourself and your students is key to having a "centered presence" in the classroom. As Jane gains support from peers and weekend teaching experiences, she continues to reflect upon her work and ask herself significant questions about her goals and practices. As mentioned earlier, this is the best prevention against burnout.

Teachers as Lifelong Learners

We are living in a rapidly changing global environment in which youngsters' and adults' lives are drastically different than they were even ten years ago. We are all experiencing the information technology revolution, which has brought access to huge volumes of information—a degree of accessibility never before experienced in human history. This explosion of information, along with the continuous connectedness that we all feel as a result of Internet and cell-phone technology, has changed the pace and progress of our daily lives.

In this ever-changing society, the activities that interest students today are necessarily different from the activities that interested you even just a few years ago. Teachers must constantly adapt and improve their skills as they respond to the recurring question: What works best in the classroom for these particular students at this period of time in our history?

Many educators today like to think of schools as **learning communities**, a term that emphasizes interaction and collaboration in the learning process. The phrase also conveys the idea that all the participants—teachers, students, and administrators—are always learning. Hence, teachers see their own continuing education as part of their work and their lives.

This need for this ongoing **professional development**, as it is called, actually makes many people excited about entering teaching. These individuals understand that to teach is

SUPPORT

professional development

professional organizations

mentors

colleagues

© Ieva Geneviciene/iStockphoto

to learn. To improve our practice requires targeted efforts at our own growth as teachers and learners. Professional development can take many forms. We will learn more about the many ways teachers extend their education in a later chapter. For now, let's hear from Amanda, Jessica, and Jane to learn how they are doing it.

How Do Teachers Continue Professional Development?

AMANDA Alongside life experience, continued schooling is needed. As I conclude my master's degree, I look toward my doctoral studies. Formal education presents important new ideas, strategies, and problems and helps your mind grow in the same way that you want your students' minds to grow.

In addition, formal education puts you in contact with professors who are experts in their fields and classmates who have a wealth of knowledge to add to your own. Being in a formal learning environment gives you a community of peers with whom you can bounce around ideas. Formal education is a wonderful resource for a teacher.

JESSICA I continue my professional development in several ways. The school district in which I teach requires that all teachers take at least fifteen hours of in-district professional development every school year, but I tend to take much more than that because the presenters are fellow teachers or administrators who are well versed in whatever they're teaching. This year we furthered our understanding of differentiated instruction, understanding by design, and brain-based learning.

In addition to attending these courses, I participate in several other professional development opportunities, such as conferences on literacy, standards-based testing, and so on. I belong to a number of professional organizations that offer regular publications to read and conference opportunities. I have begun presenting at conferences; this requires a new level of understanding and preparation for me, so this furthers my professional knowledge.

JANE I am always looking for conferences, classes, workshops, and news that can help me stay on top of the topics at hand. My master's program was extremely helpful in that I learned how to implement project-based learning activities in my class and how to do research on my own practice. It was very exciting, and each year I look for other opportunities to expand what I can offer myself and the students.

CAROL I attend conferences of the NAEYC whenever possible and I participate in meetings arranged by the director of the program where guest speakers address a wide range of topics relevant to working with young children.

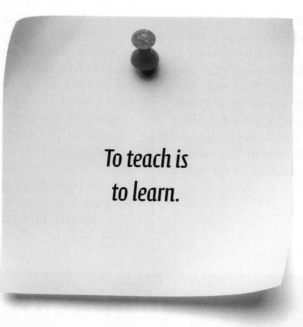

To teach is to learn.

Benefits of Lifelong Learning

Teachers are expected to keep up with the latest developments in education. In many schools and districts, in fact, teachers are offered financial incentives to continue to learn though professional education courses at a college or university or through professional development courses, often referred to as in-service courses, offered by the school district itself. These incentives are based on how many formal graduate school credits or professional development credits a teacher earns in a given academic year. Obviously you'll appreciate the chance to earn a higher salary.

Yet, as the stories you've just read illustrate, there are other incentives for taking professional development courses. Amanda, Jessica, and Jane think of themselves as lifelong learners. They take a genuine interest in expanding their minds and improving their teaching. In fact, all of them have reached the stage of doing their own research or making their own presentations—contributing to the sum of knowledge in the field.

Professional organizations can play a major role in expanding your development as a teacher. The National Education Association, The American Federation of Teachers, and The National Association for the Education of Young Children, discussed in Chapter 1, offer teachers the opportunity to attend conferences, read and contribute to journals, and access professional resources. So do many other organizations; here is just a partial list.

- The National Science Teachers Association (NSTA)
- The National Council of Teachers of Mathematics (NCTM)
- The National Council of Teachers of English (NCTE)
- The National Council for the Social Studies (NCSS)

Many teaching resources are available at no cost online through these professional organizations; see the Resources for Further Exploration section for their websites.

Professional development takes place in informal settings as well, and this is often the most important kind. In one local school district where I have worked, teachers are encouraged to take field trips to local geological formations—by themselves, without their students—even if they do not teach science in a formal way. Imagine you are an elementary school teacher in this district. How might that type of field trip contribute to your professional development? How might it help you interest your young students in the world around them?

Concluding Thoughts

Learning about other teachers' hopes, dreams, and experiences, as you've done in this chapter, gives you a way to consider what teaching might be like for you. Teaching demands so much of the individual teacher. Our emotional sides have to be expressed in order to communicate a sense of warmth and congeniality, while our intellectual selves need to maintain a sense of order, continuity, and consistency. It is a complex endeavor, requiring self-reflection and good analytical skills. One cannot overemphasize the need for personal reflection and the desire to become a lifelong learner. Luckily, teachers receive support from organizations, mentors, preparatory institutions, and sometimes induction programs in their school districts.

Building a personal philosophy of teaching is an important starting point in your development as a teacher. Your teaching philosophy is a work in progress and will most likely change with time and exposure to new ideas about how people learn. In the next two chapters of this book, you will read about important educational philosophies that have influenced American education. Your own thinking should evolve as you engage with these ideas. What remains constant is the fact that teaching is hard work and requires that you be reflective, ever conscious, and well prepared—that you be a "centered presence" in the classroom.

RESOURCES FOR FURTHER EXPLORATION

Online Resource

eduScapes
http://eduscapes.com/
A site for "lifelong learners," eduScapes offers excellent resources for teachers, parents, and students alike.

Print Resources

Jacqueline Grennon Brooks, *Schooling for Life: Reclaiming the Essence of Learning* (Reston, VA: Association for Supervision and Curriculum Development, 2002).
This is a wonderful story about what it means to be a lifelong learner.

Bobbi Fisher, *The Teacher Book: Finding Personal and Professional Balance* (Portsmouth, NH: Heinemann, 2001).
You will want to keep referring to this important book. It shares teachers' stories as well as tips for coping with on-the-job demands.

Sam Intrator, *Tuned In and Fired Up* (New Haven: Yale University Press, 2003).
This book is an inspiration in the ways the author describes ordinary people doing extraordinary teaching.

Judy Logan, *Teaching Stories* (New York: Kodansha America, 1999).
This exciting book relates the adventures and experiences the author shared with her students as a middle school teacher in San Francisco.

David Sadker and Karen Zittleman, *Still Failing at Fairness: How Gender Bias Cheats Girls and Boys and What We Can Do about It* (New York: Scribner, 2009).
This text explores how equitable teaching and learning is compromised with subtle but significant sexism in the classroom that becomes an embedded part of the hidden curriculum.

Professional Organizations

American Federation of Teachers
http://www.aft.org/

National Association for the Education of Young Children
http://www.naeyc.org/

National Council for the Social Studies
http://www.ncss.org/

National Council of Teachers of English
http://www.ncte.org/

National Council of Teachers of Mathematics
http://www.nctm.org/

National Education Association
http://www.nea.org/

National Science Teachers Association
http://www.nsta.org/

W here did we come from? How did we get here? These are questions children often ask their parents about their backgrounds and their beginnings. We might ask similar questions about schools. How did they get here? Why are schools this way? How did elementary, middle, and high schools develop over time? When did schooling become mandatory in America? How is public schooling in America being challenged by reform movements?

In the same way, we might wonder about the thinking behind today's teaching practices. From where did we get our ideas about how to teach? What is really meant by words like pedagogy and curriculum? What does our understanding of how the brain works tells us about how people learn?

These are a few of the questions that the two chapters in Part 2 address as we go back in time to make more sense of the present. Teaching has a long and impassioned history in America. Knowing what and who came before us gives us a deeper understanding of our mission as we move forward.

Part Outline

CHAPTER 3   An Overview of Schooling in America

CHAPTER 4   Principles of Teaching and Learning: Exploring Pedagogy, Curriculum, and Instruction

CHAPTER 3

AN OVERVIEW OF SCHOOLING IN AMERICA

© The Granger Collection

> *Having a history is a prerequisite to claiming a right to shape the future.*
> —Sara Evans, a historian from the University of Minnesota (1989)

Schooling in America has a complex history. As we explore its roots in this chapter, take note of how the educational system has evolved to meet the needs of U.S. citizens. Also think about the descriptions of schooling in earlier times. In what ways do they remind you of teaching and learning in the 21st century? In

LEARNING OUTCOMES

After reading this chapter, you should be thinking about the following ideas:

LO1 The earliest schools in America were both different from and similar to today's schools.

LO2 Early pioneers of public schooling, including Thomas Jefferson, Benjamin Franklin, and Horace Mann, shaped the history of American public education.

LO3 Philosophies influencing education include essentialism, progressivism, perennialism, social reconstructionism, critical theory, and existentialism.

LO4 Public school funding in America has historically been the responsibility of the states (and has fallen to localities), but federal government legislation, publications, and court cases have changed the course of public education.

LO5 Inclusive education integrates students with special needs and general education students in the same blended classroom.

LO6 Standards-based educational reform supports strict benchmarks for student learning that are assessed by state tests in specified content areas.

what ways do these stories sound very different from the schools we know today? Learning about the earliest teachers gives us insight into how far the profession has come and into our own entitlement to consider teaching a highly significant profession.

LO1 A Brief History of American Public Education

As the composition of American citizenry changes over time, so do the perceived goals of schooling. Before we delve into history, consider the following question:

What do you believe to be the goals of American public education?

At different times in the development of our country, answers to that question have varied.

As we explore colonial America, the new nation emerging after the Revolutionary War, and the wave of immigration in the 19th century, you'll see how schools evolved to meet more complex demands. Look for the following themes:

- The role of wealth, privilege, and social capital in emerging systems of education
- The effect of geographic location on access to education
- The meaning of education for a thriving democracy
- The effect of immigration on the emergence of public schools
- The transmission of values and beliefs through public education
- Changes over time in the roles played by local communities, the states, and the federal government

THE COLONIES

Early colonial education began in the home in the 1600s when Puritans[1] established colonies in what is now the northeastern United States. In the early New

---

[1]The Puritans were Protestant dissenters in England who opposed many practices of the established church. When Charles I took the English throne in 1625, government persecution of Puritans increased. Giving up hope of reforming the English church, many Puritans emigrated, among them the early settlers of the Massachusetts Bay Colony (Boston Historical Society and Museum, 2010).

England colonies, education was designed to further Puritan values and ensure that children were well versed in the Bible. The major thrust in early colonial education was the reading and understanding of scripture, so for many early colonists, religious education was synonymous with general education.

The primary responsibility for educating children was placed on the family. You may have heard about the home-schooling movement today in which parents educate their children directly, every day, in the home. We will discuss this current trend later in this text, but you can see that it has very old roots.

Many New England families could also opt to send their children to **dame schools**, which offered education to children six to eight years old. The dame school was like an informal day care center. Parents would leave their children in the home of a neighborhood woman several days a week. The woman would go about her chores while teaching the children their letters, their numbers, and their prayers. Religious teachings, as you can see, were routinely woven into the daily lives of children. These women usually accepted a small fee for each child, and instruction often took place in the kitchen. For the most part, this was the only form of schooling offered to girls, since education was not considered important for their life's work.

Another form of education in the American colonies was apprenticeship. After young boys finished the dame school, they were sometimes apprenticed to craftsmen to learn a trade. Serving an apprenticeship allowed boys to learn a craft they could carry into adulthood. Girls, meanwhile, were usually taught domestic skills at home and learned to stitch letters and sayings onto embroidered samplers. Theirs was a second-rate education compared with what was available for boys.

Latin Grammar Schools

Realizing they needed a way to educate leaders for their communities, the Puritan colonists established **Latin grammar schools**, the first of which opened in Boston

SOCIAL CAPITAL

From the time of the early colonies to the present, Americans have frequently debated the relationship between schools and society and the best way for government to fulfill its responsibility to educate its citizens. Historically, various traditions and forms of schooling have been mediated by the political, economic, and cultural struggles of the people. This means that, for some people, access to education has been easier than for others.

The term *social capital* refers to connections among individuals that give them access to cultural and civic events and institutions. Hence, youngsters from families with social capital are familiar with libraries, museums, and travel. Moreover, parents with social capital know how to get the best education for their children. Social capital generally comes with wealth, privilege, and other marks of social status.

The concept of social capital helps us understand how social issues were addressed as American schools developed. Clearly, our systems of education have become more inclusive; but in the first 150 years of American nationhood, high-quality education was readily available only if you were rich, white, and male.

Do you remember my story about Mrs. Fisher from Chapter 1? She encouraged me to apply to a special high school in my city. Information about special high schools was readily available to families with social capital, but my parents were working-class immigrants who did not fully understand how to negotiate the educational system in New York City. Fortunately, my teacher helped me through the process of applying to take the entrance exam.

The issue of social capital comes up often as we explore the history of schooling in America. There has always been pressure for schools to provide more and better services for an increasingly diverse array of students.

in 1635. Here, the sons of the upper social classes studied Latin and Greek language and literature as well as the Bible. To further extend the boys' education, the Puritans founded Harvard College in 1636. To enter this college, boys had to pass an entrance exam that required reading and speaking Latin and Greek.

In 1647, Massachusetts passed a law requiring formal education. Known as the "Old Deluder Satan" Act, it mandated that every town of 50 households must appoint and pay a teacher of reading and writing, while every town of 100 households must provide a grammar school to prepare youths for university. With the passage of this law, new town schools were established for the youngest students, and Latin grammar schools for older students spread through Massachusetts. Thus began the first education act in America that ensured there would be public schools where children would learn to read and write.

Ultimately the Latin grammar school extended into the other New England colonies and to some extent into the mid-Atlantic colonies as well. These schools were run by an elected board of townspeople and financially supported by the families of the attendees. Under this system, after finishing dame school or town school, wealthy boys could attend a Latin grammar school to prepare for college and a leadership role in society. Girls who finished the dame school or town school would continue to study their letters at home while learning domestic chores. The Latin grammar school is considered one of the forerunners of the American high school.

Geographical Differences in Colonial Education

Educational access in the early American colonies was determined by not only wealth and privilege. Where you lived also had a great impact on the type of education that was available.

In the northern colonies, largely settled by Puritans, people lived in towns and relatively close to one another. Town schools, which principally taught the Bible, became readily available after 1647. In the mid-Atlantic colonies, however, a wide range of European ethnic and religious groups established different types of schools, and various trades established apprenticeship programs. Local control was the norm. Though some Latin grammar schools existed, other private schools developed that were dedicated to job training and practical skills.

The southern colonies, where the population was more rural, had fewer schools during the colonial era. Wealthy plantation owners hired private tutors for their children. Many young gentlemen were sent to Europe for their education.

The Late Colonial Period

By the late colonial era, in addition to the types of schools we have described so far, options for parents included:

- Schools managed by private associations, often devoted to the skills needed for a specific type of job
- Religious schools, sponsored by churches for their members; some churches also established charity schools for the urban poor
- Boarding schools
- A few private academies offering secondary education with a broader curriculum than the early Latin grammar schools (Academies are discussed in the next section.)

Several of these options required tuitions, others were paid for by public funds, and some were funded by a combination of both.

It was still true that most girls received little schooling after the first few years. And if you were Native American or African American, you had practically no chance of formal education. The schools established for the poor typically required a family to sign a "Pauper's Oath," so most poor children did not attend school. Consider how you would

> ### Did You Know?
> The "Old Deluder Satan" Act was so named because the Puritans believed in the presence of evil in the form of Satan; if children studied the Scriptures, they would resist Satan's temptations. Learning to read would thwart evil.

> **Q:** *You had to be wealthy, white, and male to have access to the better forms of education in the early colonies. How has that changed, and why?*

> ### Latin grammar school
> A type of school that flourished in the New England colonies in the 1600s and1700s. It emphasized Latin and Greek to prepare young men for college.

academy A type of private secondary school that arose in the late colonial period and came to dominate American secondary education until the establishment of public high schools. Academies had a more practical curriculum than Latin grammar schools did, and students typically could choose subjects appropriate to their later careers.

common school A public, tax-supported elementary school. Begun in Massachusetts in the 1820s, common schools aimed to provide a common curriculum for children. Horace Mann, an advocate for the common school, is often considered the "father of the public school."

feel if, to send your child to school, you had to sign a public document admitting your poverty. Many families chose to leave their children illiterate rather than suffer the shame of this type of public admission.

LO2 A New Nation

In the late 1700s, after the colonies gained their independence from Great Britain, efforts were made to consolidate schools and mandate education throughout the new nation. Congress enacted the Land Ordinance Act of 1785 and the Northwest Ordinance of 1787. These measures set aside land for public schools. Subsequently, as sending children to school rather than teaching them at home grew in popularity, formal schools were started wherever space could be found.

Schoolhouses of that day were practical shelters: one room with benches and a stove. Desks and blackboards did not appear until many years later. No grades were given in the beginning, and one teacher worked with several age levels at the same time. Children simply learned at their own pace.

The Academy

Thomas Jefferson and Benjamin Franklin, among other founders of the new nation, believed that schools should move beyond the education of wealthy men for the ministry to a more broadly based education. In 1751 Franklin established a new kind of secondary school, one that would eventually replace the Latin grammar school—the **academy**. The Franklin Academy in

Philadelphia offered a variety of subjects, ranging from science and mathematics to athletics, navigation, and bookkeeping. It was open to both girls and boys—if their parents could afford the tuition.

Soon after America's Declaration of Independence, other private academies were established, most of them limited to boys. These included most notably Phillips Academy in Andover, Massachusetts (1778), and Phillips Exeter Academy in Exeter, New Hampshire (1781). Academies changed the model for secondary schools by offering elective as well as required courses. It was still the case, however, that the common denominator for attendance was wealth.

Rise of the Common School

At the turn of the 19th century, education in the new nation was a hodgepodge of schools for basic reading and writing and grammar schools or academies for college preparation and leadership. Many young people still learned through apprenticeships or private tutoring.

Jefferson, Franklin, and others believed that the new democracy required an educated citizenry for its survival. To work properly, they thought, a democracy needs informed citizens, as well as an educational system that allows people to succeed on the basis of their skills and dedication rather than inherited privilege.

These ideas gave rise to the movement for **common schools**—a system of tax-supported elementary schools. The common school is known today as the public elementary school. Horace Mann, an educational historian and reformer who championed the movement, saw common schools as promoting important civic virtues. He criticized private academies because they offered widely different curricula and perpetuated social differences between the privileged classes and ordinary citizens (Wisconsin Education Association Council, 2006).

From their beginnings in Massachusetts in the 1820s, common schools were gradually established in other New England, midwestern, western, and finally southern states. Their spread became more rapid after the Civil War.

Immigration played a key role in the thinking about public education. The 1830s and 1840s brought expansion in manufacturing and transportation. These decades also brought considerable immigration from Europe, especially in the Northeast. Immigrants were becoming an important part of the economy, and factory owners needed a trained, disciplined workforce. At the same time, as population grew in the cities, social tensions rose because of increased poverty, slums, and crime.

Prominent citizens worried about the morals of poor immigrant children and the influence their parents had on them. Many Protestant ministers looked at the rise of Catholic immigrant populations as a possible cause of social problems. Schools, many people believed, could offer a way to address these concerns. By centralizing the control of public education, schools could be used to uplift the poor, spread dominant national values, and assimilate immigrant children into the English-speaking American culture. State authorities, not immigrant parents, would be in control.

However, even though public schools were at this point nonsectarian, they were not necessarily non-religious. Because common schools were seen as responsible, in part, for the moral development of children, it was believed that religion could not be completely separated from the schools. There was much debate about curriculum. Although the main thrust in common schools was the study of the "three Rs" (reading, writing, and arithmetic), history, and science, some schools had regular readings of the King James version of the Bible. Catholic immigrants objected vehemently,

and many church parishes in the late 1800s began their own church schools, known as **parochial schools**. Not until many years later, in 1963, did the Supreme Court rule that prayers and Bible readings could no longer be allowed in public schools.

With tax-supported public education in place, more and more children attended school on a regular basis (see Figure 3.1). However, because of the large size of many immigrant families, parents often needed to send their children into the workforce to help out economically. These poor working families viewed education for their children as a luxury they could not afford. To ensure that children went to school and not to work, compulsory attendance laws came into existence. These laws were adopted by each individual state, beginning with Massachusetts in 1852 and ending with Alaska (then a U.S. territory) in 1929 (Information Please Database, 2006). Eventually, legislation restricting the employment of children in industrial settings was passed by the federal government.

> **parochial school**
> A school operated by a religious group. Today, in the United States, the term most often refers to a school governed by the local Catholic parish or diocese.

Q: *Do you think today's schools still function as institutions for social control?*

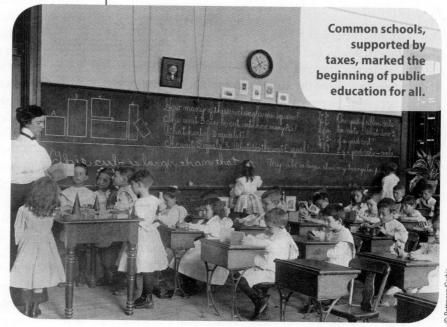

Common schools, supported by taxes, marked the beginning of public education for all.

© Bettmann/Corbis

Photos: © Duncan Walker/iStockphoto (left); © Bonnie Jacobs/iStockphoto (right)

Percentage enrolled

100
80
60
40
20

1850 1870 1890 1910 1930 1950 1970 1990

☐ White enrollment   ■ Minority student enrollment

SOURCE: Data from Snyder, T. D., ed., *120 Years of American Education: A Statistical Portrait* (Washington, D.C.: National Center for Education Statistics, 1993), Table 2, p. 14.

FIGURE 3.1

Rising School Attendance in the 19th and 20th Centuries
This graph shows the percentage of U.S. children (ages 5 to 19) enrolled in school, illustrating the dramatic growth that began in the second half of the 19th century as common schools became well established and compulsory attendance laws were enacted.

Expansion of Public Schools

By the 1870s, there was broad attendance in U.S. public elementary schools, but a large gap in available educational opportunities remained between those schools and universities. Only the wealthy continued their education at private preparatory schools for colleges and universities. Gradually, however, as society became more industrialized and laws were passed to discourage the hiring of teenage workers, parents came to view the high school as the pathway to better jobs for their children. Tax-supported public high schools slowly took hold and became the dominant form of secondary education by 1890.

The rise of the public high school led to the need for a bridge between elementary school and high school. In the early 1900s, the junior high school was established to bridge this gap, concentrating on the emotional and intellectual needs of students in grades 7, 8, and 9. In the 1950s, some middle schools were established for grades 5–8, and by the end of the 20th century, the middle school was gradually replacing the junior high school (Manning, 2000). The emphasis in middle school was on interdisciplinary learning and team teaching, in which groups of students had the same teachers in common.

The timeline in Figure 3.2 summarizes many of the events we have discussed. It is remarkable to consider how many more children were educated as the common school movement took hold and public secondary schools began to flourish. In many areas of America in the early 1800s, school lasted only about 75 to 80 days a year because the entire family was needed to work the farm. By the 1830s, only about half of all children attended school and then only for this short period of time. But as the industrial revolution drew people to the cities for work and common schools flourished, more children began attending school, and by the end of the 1890s, more than 70 percent of children were receiving schooling. There was such a great need for schools between 1890 and 1914 that a new high school was added every day (Krug, 1964; Wisconsin Education Association Council, 2006).

Today we can celebrate the fact that, as our nation grew, more and more people attended public schools. This does not mean, however, that we have now achieved the goal of equal educational opportunity for everyone. Later in this text, as we compare the quality of

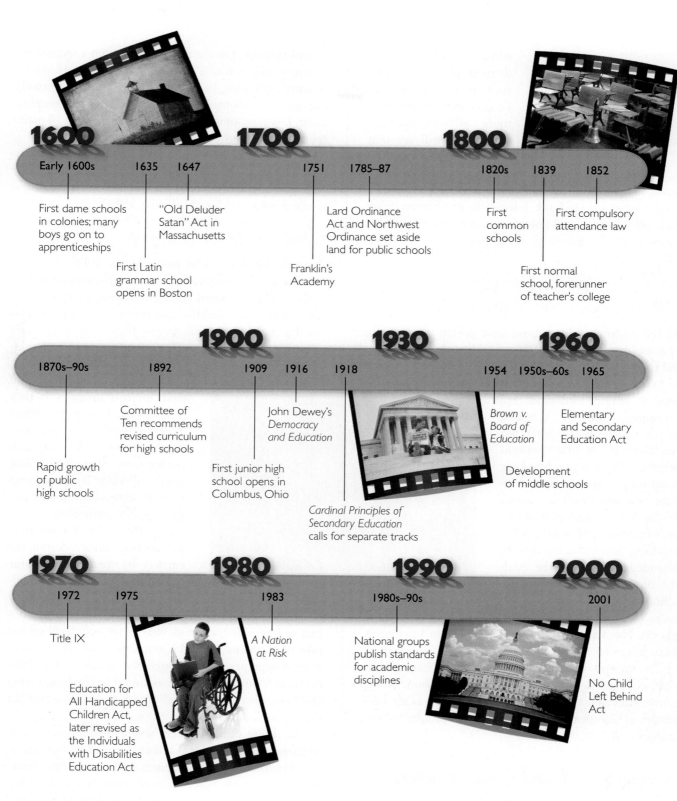

1600 | **1700** | **1800**

Early 1600s | 1635 | 1647 | | 1751 | 1785–87 | | 1820s | 1839 | 1852

First dame schools in colonies; many boys go on to apprenticeships

"Old Deluder Satan" Act in Massachusetts

Lard Ordinance Act and Northwest Ordinance set aside land for public schools

First common schools

First compulsory attendance law

First Latin grammar school opens in Boston

Franklin's Academy

First normal school, forerunner of teacher's college

1900 | **1930** | **1960**

1870s–90s | 1892 | | 1909 | 1916 | 1918 | | 1954 | 1950s–60s | 1965

Committee of Ten recommends revised curriculum for high schools

John Dewey's *Democracy and Education*

Brown v. Board of Education

Elementary and Secondary Education Act

Rapid growth of public high schools

First junior high school opens in Columbus, Ohio

Development of middle schools

Cardinal Principles of Secondary Education calls for separate tracks

1970 | **1980** | **1990** | **2000**

1972 | 1975 | | 1983 | | 1980s–90s | | 2001

Title IX

A Nation at Risk

National groups publish standards for academic disciplines

Education for All Handicapped Children Act, later revised as the Individuals with Disabilities Education Act

No Child Left Behind Act

FIGURE 3.2

Some Important Events in American Education

education offered to students in poor urban and rural areas with the public education available in more affluent communities, you will see that challenges remain. Still, there is no question that more diverse students—including girls and women, people of color, and the poor—are graduating from high school today and going on to postsecondary education than ever before in this country.

TEACHER EDUCATION AND THE DEVELOPMENT OF NORMAL SCHOOLS

As the common school movement gained momentum, you may be wondering: Who were the teachers? Where did they come from and how were they prepared?

Once again, Horace Mann was a major influence. He promoted **normal schools**, which began shortly after the founding of the first common schools. These were two-year institutions designed to prepare teachers through courses in the history and philosophy of education and methods of teaching. Normal schools were intended to improve the quality of the growing common school system by producing more qualified teachers. The first of them, called simply the Normal School, opened in 1839 in Lexington, Massachusetts.

By the end of the 1800s, these schools became four-year colleges dedicated to teacher education. Many universities that are well known today, such as the University of California, Los Angeles, were founded as normal schools.

Normal Schools and Female Teachers

Normal schools played a major role in bringing women into the teaching profession. In the early days of American education, schoolmasters were almost always male. Women, who were mostly uneducated, were not considered suited for the job, even though the prerequisite for teaching consisted of little more than having attended

school yourself. On the rare occasion that a woman did secure a job, it was with young children only. As the country expanded, common schools multiplied rapidly, but women still took a backseat in terms of employment. It was assumed that they were incapable of maintaining the discipline necessary to teach effectively.

Normal schools, however, welcomed female students and made elementary school teaching a career path for many women. By 1900, 71 percent of rural teachers were women (Hoffman, 1981).

Gender Roles in Teaching

After the Civil War and well into the 1900s, teaching became more attractive for women who wanted to find a place of employment outside the domestic sphere. Yet there were considerable constraints on women who became teachers, chief among them that they were not allowed to marry. The stereotype of the "spinster" was often associated with schoolteachers. It was believed that women would have divided loyalties if they were allowed to marry while being employed as teachers. (Can you imagine that happening now?) It was not until after World War II that married women were allowed to enter the teaching profession.

By the 1950s, the teaching profession, once dominated entirely by men, had become a female-dominated, "feminized" profession in many people's eyes. Young men were still attracted to educational administration as well as to secondary school jobs in mathematics and science, however. Here again, a stereotype persisted through the middle to late 20th century: Women were seen as suited to teaching young children, whereas men taught math and science and ran the school.

In recent years, women have gained greater access to careers in educational administration and as teachers of mathematics and science. At the same time, however, the overall percentage of men in teaching has declined significantly since the 1960s, as we mentioned in Chapter 2. Just as it is important to have women teaching math, it is vital to have men represented in early-childhood and elementary education. Breaking down gender stereotypes in schools is important—not only for teachers themselves, but also for the models

> Breaking down gender stereotypes in schools is important—not only for teachers themselves, but also for the models they present to students.

they present to students. We will have more to say about gender and schooling later in this text.

The Tuskegee Normal School and the Education of African Americans

Even after the Civil War, Reconstruction, and the Thirteenth Amendment, which ended slavery in the United States, it took a long time for African Americans to achieve equal opportunity and access to a quality education. Some would argue that appropriate education remains unavailable to minority students today. As we will see in later chapters, our diverse culture and society pose many challenges and opportunities for teachers and students alike. In this respect, we can find inspiration in the story of Booker T. Washington, an African American teacher, who in 1881 became the first head of what was then called the Tuskegee Normal School for Colored Teachers in Tuskegee, Alabama. Later renamed the Tuskegee Institute, the institution today is Tuskegee University.

Q: *What is the history of the college or university where you are studying? When did teacher education programs emerge in your institution?*

Under the leadership of Washington, the Tuskegee Normal School prepared African American teachers to be self-reliant and to acquire practical vocational skills, not only in teaching but in agriculture and other occupations. By the early 20th century, the African American scholar and advocate W.E.B. Du Bois, a graduate of Harvard College and a well-known intellectual, was criticizing Washington's emphasis on vocational training at Tuskegee. Du Bois insisted that formal education in an academically rich course of study was necessary for the African American people. Regardless of these later critiques, however, Washington did a great deal to advance the education of African Americans and their representation in the teaching profession.

Drawing African Americans and other minorities into the teaching force remains an issue today. African Americans make up more than 15 percent of U.S. public school students. So do Hispanics. Yet only about 6 percent of teachers are African American, and only 5 percent are Hispanic. More than one-third of U.S. public schools have no teacher of color on the faculty (National Collaborative on Diversity in the Teaching Force, 2004; Weaver, 2004). To improve this situation, state Departments of Education and many colleges and universities are offering financial incentives to minority students for becoming teachers. An example of such a program, in existence since 1985, is the Minority Teacher Recruitment Project (MTRP) at the University of Louisville (http://louisville.edu/education/research/centers/mtrp/).

CATHERINE BEECHER

Catherine Beecher, who started the Hartford (Connecticut) Female Seminary in 1828, made a major contribution to the professional education of women. Beecher challenged accepted notions of femininity and the education of women in the 19th century.

Born in East Hampton, New York, in 1800, Beecher believed that education should prepare women to assume roles of high responsibility in society. In particular, she thought that women should train to become teachers, a profession that would be a natural extension of their family roles. Along with her famous contemporaries, Elizabeth Cady Stanton and Susan B. Anthony, she promoted educational and political equality for women.

LO3 Competing Visions: Efforts to Rethink and Reform Education

The struggle to change or reform educational practices is as old as organized public schooling. From common school days to present times, the content and processes of education have been under continuous scrutiny. Schools, like other public institutions, are products of their times, politically, socially, and economically. Schools both reflect and influence the societal events of their day.

We are all a part of what we are trying to change. As teachers and future teachers, we seek a profession dedicated to student learning. As citizens, we know that, as Thomas Jefferson observed, it is impossible for a nation to be both free and ignorant. But we are people of diverse regions, ethnicities, and social and economic backgrounds, and to be successful educators we need to make sense of (1) who we are in the world and (2) what conditions we believe are important for learning to occur.

At different periods in our history, different philosophies have dominated our thinking about teaching and learning and about the manner in which education should proceed. In this section, we look at several competing philosophies that have shaped efforts to reform American schools since the late 19th century.

Many classrooms today are hybrids of several of these philosophies of education. As you read this section, think about what is happening in schools today and how the current phase of American public education will be viewed by others fifty years from now.

THE HIGH SCHOOL CURRICULUM

From the end of the Civil War to the late 1800s, the high school curriculum kept expanding as the demand for new courses grew. There was no preset pattern for how the courses being offered should develop; hence the high school curriculum retained old subjects like languages and mathematics and added new ones as demand arose. These new subjects included botany, physiology, anatomy, physics, and astronomy. For those students not interested in pursuing a college education, courses such as commercial arithmetic, banking, business correspondence, stenography, and typewriting were added.

By the late 1800s, opinions about the purpose of high school were sharply divided. Some believed high school should groom students for college. Others thought high school should prepare students for more practical endeavors, serving those who saw high school as the termination of their formal education.

In 1892, the National Education Association addressed this issue by appointing the Committee of Ten, ten scholars led by Harvard University President Charles Eliot, to determine the proper curriculum for high schools. The Committee of Ten recommended eight years of elementary school and four years of high school and proposed a curriculum that was common to both college-bound and terminal students. The new curriculum featured fewer subjects, each of which would be studied for a longer period of time. The courses included foreign languages, history, mathematics, science, and English. Although these subjects offered an alternative to classical Latin and Greek courses, this was a rigorous academic curriculum, and the dominant belief was that the same subjects would be equally beneficial to academic and terminal students.

A generation later, in 1918, the NEA partly reversed course when its Commission on the Reorganization of Secondary Education issued a report called *Cardinal Principles of Secondary Education*. In this report, the commission recommended a differentiated curriculum for the comprehensive high school, offering four different tracks: college preparatory, commercial, industrial, and general academic. The commercial course of study included bookkeeping, shorthand, and typing. The industrial track included preparatory courses for domestic, agricultural, and trade endeavors.

Although high school curricula varied considerably during the rest of the 20th century, some of the ideas set forth by the Committee of Ten and the *Cardinal Principles* continued to be dominant. The core courses—English, foreign language, science, mathematics, and history (which later evolved into social studies)—persisted in the comprehensive high school curriculum. So did the notion that high school should follow a **tracking** system, offering different courses or tracks for students with different academic aspirations.

THE EMERGENCE OF ESSENTIALISM

As you can see from the debate over the high school curriculum, educators in the early 20th century were developing strong opinions about the proper sort of education for contemporary society. In the 1930s, the educator William Bagley coined the term **essentialism** as the name for a philosophy that had a strong impact then and continues to be influential today. According to this view, certain core kinds of knowledge are essential to a person's life in society. Essentialists believe that everyone can and should learn these key elements and therefore that the schools' primary mission is to teach them.

When you hear about teaching the "basics" or about rigorous training in the three Rs, you are listening to an essentialist view of education. The essentials are generally embodied in the standard, time-honored subjects; in other words, essentialists believe that students should take courses in algebra and history, not in ceramics and interpretive dance. In stressing that the curriculum should remain consistent, essentialists tend to assume that a common culture should exist for all Americans. Their vision of the classroom is teacher-centered: Teachers are the dominant figures, transferring their knowledge and wisdom for the good of the students. An essentialist classroom is one in which the teacher knows best. Students listen to their teacher and learn what is taught.

To many educators in the early 20th century, essentialism made good common sense. It was soon challenged, however, by the progressivism of thinkers like John Dewey.

PROGRESSIVISM AND JOHN DEWEY

Probably the most influential educator of the 20th century, John Dewey (1859–1952) was an educational philosopher and a professor at the University of Chicago and Columbia University in New York. He participated in a variety of political causes, such as women's rights and the unionization of teachers, and he contributed frequently to popular magazines and journals in which he connected social action in democracy with educational principles.

In Dewey's view, students should be active participants in their own learning; they learn by doing, and their interests must be a driving force behind curriculum and classroom experiences. His educational philosophy has been referred to as **progressivism** and as *pragmatism*. It was progressive because it gave more responsibility to students and pragmatic (practical) because it embedded teaching and learning in the context of daily living. This approach contradicted the strict, top-down, authoritarian model of education that had thrived from colonial times into the 19th century and that continued to be reflected in essentialist approaches.

Dewey thought that schools should help children learn how to live and work cooperatively with others. Consequently, he believed that students needed to participate in decisions that affected their learning and that they should be guided by academically autonomous teachers—that is, teachers who were not bound by rigid rules about what and how to teach and who were able to build on students' strengths and talents. Dewey and his followers viewed the school as a laboratory in which the purpose of the curriculum was to integrate education with real-life experiences and a child's curiosity defined the process of learning just as much as the subject matter being taught.

John Dewey, and the progressive movement that he helped found, had a profound influence on educational thought in the United States. Progressives advocated a vibrant school setting with a curriculum that followed the interests and needs of students, encouraged active learning and problem solving, fostered deep understanding of concepts through experimentation, and supported assessment of students through close observation by well-prepared and caring teachers.

> **essentialism** An educational philosophy holding that the purpose of education is to learn specific knowledge provided by core academic disciplines such as mathematics, science, literature, and history. Teachers must impart the key elements of these subjects so that all students have access to this basic or "essential" knowledge.
>
> **progressivism** An educational philosophy that stresses active learning through problem solving, projects, and hands-on experiences.

Did You Know?

John Dewey (1859–1952), an educational philosopher and professor, was probably the most influential educator of the 20th century.

perennialism An educational philosophy that emphasizes enduring ideas conveyed through the study of great works of literature and art. Perennialists believe in a single core curriculum for everyone.

Dewey's progressivism fell out of favor, however, when it was deemed necessary that America foster stricter teaching methods during the Cold War following World War II. The Soviet Union's launch of the satellite Sputnik in 1957—making that nation the first in space—became a symbol of what American public education had failed to achieve. Progressivism lost ground as American educators shifted again toward a more authoritarian approach and a strict adherence to lecture and rote learning. A new wave of essentialism took over, and schools focused on the task of preparing students for the technological and engineering challenges of the time.

Educational progressivism revived in the 1960s as the "child-centered" movement gained popularity in America. In the years since, various groups of educators have revisited the ideas of Dewey and his followers and revised them to address the changing needs of schools, children, and society. The philosophical influence of progressive ideas in education can be seen today in "whole language" reading programs, multi-age approaches, experiential education, problem-based learning, and student-centered instruction.

Q: *What are some examples of Dewey's progressivism in classrooms today?*

ENDURING IDEAS: THE INFLUENCE OF PERENNIALISM

An educational philosophy related to essentialism, **perennialism** stresses the belief that all knowledge or wisdom has been accumulated over time and is represented by the great works of literature and art as well as religious texts. This educational philosophy found a strong expression in the 1980s with the *Paideia Proposal* by Mortimer Adler. In this influential call for school reform, Adler proposed one universal curriculum for elementary and secondary students, allowing for no electives. Everyone would take the same courses, and the curriculum would reflect the enduring ideas found in the works of history's finest thinkers and writers.

Like essentialism, perennialism holds that one type of education is good for all students. It differs from essentialism by placing greater emphasis on classic works of literature, history, art, and philosophy (including works of the ancient Greeks and Romans) and on the teaching of values and moral character. Essentialism can include practical, vocation-oriented courses—a class in computer skills, for instance—but perennialism leaves little room for such frivolity.

The perennialist approach has found a home at several U.S. colleges, such as St. John's College in Maryland and New Mexico, and its influence shows in the core curricula at some larger universities, including the University of Chicago and Columbia University. Threads of the perennialist philosophy are present in many parochial schools as well. Whenever you hear about a program centered on "great ideas" or "great books," it most likely reflects perennialist ideas.

Adler emphasized the Socratic method, a type of teaching based on extensive discussion with students. In this respect he was somewhat less teacher-centered than many essentialists. His perennialism does, however, leave little room for flexibility in the curriculum and little opportunity to reflect the changing demographics of our times.

Progressivism asserted that students learned by doing and that their interests had to be a driving force of the learning experience.

© Bettmann/Corbis

Radical Reform Philosophies: Social Reconstructionism, Critical Theory, and Existentialism

Alongside essentialism, perennialism, and progressivism, the 20th century gave rise to some radical reform philosophies that proposed a fundamental rethinking of the nature of schooling. Among these are social reconstructionism, critical theory, and existentialism.

Social reconstructionism is an educational philosophy that emphasizes social justice and a curriculum promoting social reform. Responding to the vast inequities in society and recognizing the plight of the poor, social reconstructionists believe that schools must produce an agenda for social change. Linked with social reconstructionism is *critical theory* or *critical pedagogy*, which stresses that students should learn to challenge oppression. In this view, education should tackle the real-world problems of hunger, violence, poverty, and inequality. Clearly, students are at the center of this curriculum, with teachers advocating involvement in social reform. The focus of critical theorists and social reconstructionists is the transformation of systems of oppression through education in order to improve the human condition.

Among critical theorists, Paulo Freire (1921–1997), a Brazilian whose experiences living in poverty led him to champion education and literacy as the vehicle for social change, has had a particularly profound impact on the thinking of many educators. His most influential work was *Pedagogy of the Oppressed*, published in English in 1970.

Another philosophy that proposes fundamental changes in education is *existentialism*, which takes student-centered learning to an extreme. Rooted

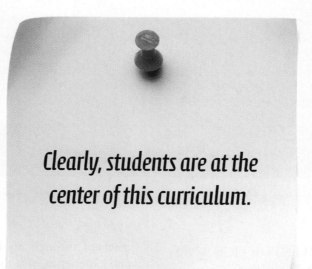

Clearly, students are at the center of this curriculum.

in the thinking of 19th-century philosophers like Søren Kierkegaard, existentialism gained popular notice in the mid-20th century through the works of Jean Paul Sartre and others. According to this philosophy, the only authoritative truth lies within the individual. Existentialism is defined by what it rejects—namely, the existence of any source of objective truth other than the individual person, who must seek the meaning of his or her own existence.

Applied to education, existentialism proposes that students make all decisions about their choice of subject matter and activities as they seek to make meaning of their place in the world. This philosophy has not had as profound an impact on American schools as the other philosophies described in this chapter have, but you can find elements of it in classrooms where teachers insist that students make their own decisions about what is important for them to know. The best-known model of existentialism is Summerhill, a school founded in England by A. S. Neill in 1921.

Table 3.1 summarizes some key features of the educational philosophies we have discussed, and the TeachSource Video Case will help you explore how these ways of thinking translate into practice in actual classrooms.

TEACHSOURCE VIDEO CASE

Educational Philosophies in the Classroom

Find the TeachSource Video Case "Philosophical Foundations of American Education: Four Philosophies in Action" on the student website to see different philosophies at work in a classroom setting. The philosophies shown are essentialism, progressivism, perennialism, and critical theory. After watching the video, consider the following question:

If I followed this philosophy strictly in the classroom, what would my pedagogy look like?

TABLE 3.1 Key Elements of Five Educational Philosophies

Philosophy	Focus of Study	Teacher's Role
Essentialism	Core knowledge that students need to be educated citizens; this knowledge is embodied in traditional academic disciplines such as history and mathematics	Teachers are the central figures in the classroom, transferring their knowledge to students
Perennialism	Enduring ideas found in the great works of literature and art	Teachers engage in extended dialogue with students, discussing and reasoning about the great ideas
Progressivism	Integration of study with real-life experiences through active learning, problem solving, and experimentation	Teachers structure the learning activities and encourage students to explore the ideas that arise; teachers can vary the curriculum to match the needs and interests of students
Social reconstructionism/ critical theory	Schooling promotes social and political reform by focusing on social problems and the need for change	Teachers guide students to think critically about social injustice and challenge oppression
Existentialism	Students choose their own course of study as part of their effort to figure out their place in the world and the meaning of their lives	Teachers support students in exploring their own interests

aesthetic education
Traditionally, this term referred merely to education in the fine arts, such as painting and music. In the broader view of Maxine Greene and other recent philosophers, however, it means education that enables students to use artistic forms and imagination to approach all fields of learning, including the sciences, and to share their perspectives with others.

AESTHETICS AND MAXINE GREENE

❝We want to expand the range of literacy, offering the young new ways of symbolizing, new ways of structuring their experience, so they can see more, hear more, make more connections, embark on unfamiliar adventures into meaning.❞
—**Maxine Greene (2002)**

In this era of global interdependence and multicultural diversity, educators continue to develop their ideas about the purposes of education and the best ways to reform American schools. One influential contemporary thinker is Maxine Greene, an American philosopher, social activist, and teacher who has been an active scholar and educator at Teachers College, Columbia University, since 1965. Her belief is that the role of education is to create meaning in the lives of students and

teachers through an interaction between knowledge and experience with the world.

Greene's educational philosophy is rooted in Dewey's ideas about art and aesthetics. Dewey's democratic view of education suggested that when children are able to approach problem-solving artistically and imaginatively, they grow socially and culturally through their shared experiences, insights, and understandings. Therefore, the arts are an essential part of the human experience.

Building on Dewey, Greene has contributed to the growth of a paradigm known as **aesthetic education**. She believes that the goal of education is to help students realize that they are responsible not merely for their own individual experiences; rather, they have a deep connection to, and responsibility for, other human beings who share this world. Her philosophy asks us to consider how being able to express oneself in a number of different "languages"—including imagery, music, and dance—helps us make meaning of ideas (Greene, 1995). Greene also believes that education must lead students and teachers to the discovery of their own truths and that the arts promote a type of consciousness or "wide-awakeness" (1978) in service to this process. She stresses the importance of shared perspectives in looking at the world and a respect for differences in experience.

In connection with her work at the Lincoln Center Institute for the Arts in Education in New York City, of which she was a founding member, Greene began the Maxine Greene Foundation for Social Imagination, the Arts, and Education, which prepares teachers to guide students in merging artistic expression with social justice. Its tenets focus on equity issues, quality of experiences in school, and the uses of imagination as a means of breaking down the barriers of diversity that children encounter in their daily lives. This perspective values the personal liberty of children and celebrates the imagination for its ability to open a child's mind to different possibilities and alternative solutions. An underlying assumption is that the humanities can serve as a catalyst enabling teachers and students to explore ideas more deeply and be more critically engaged with the world.

How do Maxine Greene's ideas work in an actual classroom? Consider this story:

In a sixth-grade class, Ms. Nelson is interested in her students' capacity for careful observation. She is a great admirer of many types of artists, and decorating her room are poster reproductions of famous paintings. The students move their chairs to position themselves by the poster of van Gogh's *The Starry Night* (see Figure 3.3), and Ms. Nelson asks, "What do you think van Gogh was thinking about when he painted this?"

"Circles" one student responds. Another says, "dreams," and still another student offers "motion." Then Ms. Nelson asks, "What do *you* think of when you look at this painting?" Students respond with phrases like "wind blowing," "scary dreams," "day and night," and "church spires." The students really seem to like the painting, and Ms. Nelson urges them on. She asks, "What is the organizing principle behind this painting?" (This is a question she asks often when the class looks at collections of objects: what principle did the collector use to gather these objects together?)

The students decide that van Gogh was looking for images that used circles and pointy spires. Those were his organizing principles.

Asked about her goals for *The Starry Night* lesson, Ms. Nelson explains, "I am interested in getting students ready to make careful observations. We are doing a science unit on mystery powders, and I want them to think about properties that objects have in common."

Can you see how this lesson represents Maxine Greene's philosophy of integrating the arts into education?

The progressive philosophies of John Dewey and Maxine Greene share a number of fundamental views:

- Making connections with social issues should be central to school curricula.
- The arts are creative tools that can expose children to new perspectives and new ways of communicating.

The Starry Night, June 1889 (oil on canvas) by Vincent van Gogh (1853–90) © Museum of Modern Art, New York, USA/The Bridgeman Art Library

FIGURE 3.3

The Starry Night (1889) by Vincent van Gogh
Starry Night is one of the most well-known paintings in modern culture.

inquiry A multifaceted activity that involves making observations, posing questions about the subject matter, and conducting research or investigations to develop answers. Inquiry is common to scientific learning but also relevant to other fields.

- Learning is an experiential process. Students learn by interacting with material in intellectual and sometimes manipulative ways; that is what "learning by doing" means.
- All forms of education should emphasize learning by **inquiry**— a process in which students ask meaningful questions and then seek their own answers.

Maxine Greene believes that people who choose to become teachers should ideally be "those who have learned the importance of becoming reflective enough to think about their own thinking and become conscious of their own consciousness" (Greene, 1995). What do you think that means?

WRITING & REFLECTION

The Pendulum of Educational Reform

To understand the ways American public schooling has shifted emphases over the last century, imagine the swings of a pendulum. Education swung from early, rigorous, authoritarian emphasis on transmission of facts to the progressive philosophies of Dewey and others who believed in the importance of learning by doing and the interplay between experience and education. Then the pendulum swung back to a more rigid view of how schools should function. Then, once more, the rigor lessened, then it tightened again, and so on. Reflect on how the pendulum is continually on the move by thinking about the following questions.

- Which period of educational reform do you believe us to be in today and why?
- Where is the pendulum now, and which way is it moving? Think about the Race to the Top competition from the federal government! (Race to the Top is a federal fund for competitive grants. It awards states money based on their approved plans for educational reform.)

LO4 Federal and State Efforts at Educational Reform: Funding, Priorities, and Standards

Although education of the citizenry was very important to the founders of the United States, there is no mention of education for all in the Constitution. Hence, schooling became the domain and responsibility of the states, which left most of the control of schools to local communities.

Thus American schools have traditionally been run by local school boards, and the bulk of the money they need has been raised through local taxes, especially the property tax. Many critics have argued that the reliance on local property taxes is unfair, since it means that wealthier districts can raise more money for schools than poorer districts can. Yet Americans have long been reluctant to give up local funding and the control that goes with it.

As we noted earlier, however, the Soviet Union's launch of *Sputnik* in 1957 prompted a rethinking of American educational priorities. Federal and state governments increasingly began to intervene in educational matters, setting priorities and (at least sometimes) providing funds to make sure those priorities were met. The overall result of these changes is that local school districts now supply less than half of the funding for public schools, as shown in Figure 3.4. Although local schools are happy to receive government money, they are not always pleased that the funds come with strings attached, reducing local control over the way schools operate.

The following sections introduce you to several ways in which government legislation, publications, and court cases have changed the course of American public education. The "Writing & Reflection" activity will help you think about how these changes affect students and teachers as you continue to read about past and current educational reform movements.

© murat Sen/iStockphoto

Separate but Equal?

Earlier in this chapter, we discussed the fact that African Americans were denied the right to an education when this country was new and evolving. Even after the Civil War, schools were slow to develop for African Americans, and when they did, they were separate schools, only for black children. According to an 1896 Supreme Court ruling in *Plessy v. Ferguson*, "separate but equal" public facilities for different races were legal. But in time, during the first half of the 1900s, the schools serving African Americans were found *not* to be equal. They did not share equally in the resources available for public schooling; in most locations, they had fewer tax dollars and inferior conditions.

The situation came to a head in 1954 with the case of ***Brown v. Board of Education of Topeka, Kansas***. In this landmark case, the Supreme Court of the United States ruled unanimously that separate schools for whites and blacks were inherently unequal because the effects of such separate schooling are likely to be different. Because of this inequality, the Court decided, schools could not remain segregated.

Initially, the *Brown* decision had particular impact in the South, where schools were segregated by law (*de jure* segregation). But many northern schools were segregated informally because of separate living patterns for whites and blacks (*de facto* segregation). Over the following decades, many school systems and various court cases dealt with the challenge of eliminating *de facto* segregation, with mixed success. The efforts toward integration had a significant impact, but there was much turmoil and resistance. Numerous educators argue that *de facto* segregation still exists today in many cities and especially in suburban America.

Federal legislation, including the Civil Rights Act (1964), reinforced the importance of creating educational opportunities for all Americans regardless of race, gender, or ethnicity. The Bilingual Education Acts of 1968 and 1974 provided supplemental funding for school districts to establish programs for large numbers of children with limited English-language ability. Similarly, the Equal Educational Opportunities Act of 1974 provided specific definitions of what constituted denial of equal educational opportunity. These included "failure to take the appropriate action to overcome

> ***Brown v. Board of Education of Topeka, Kansas*** A 1954 case in which the U.S. Supreme Court outlawed segregation in public education.

FIGURE 3.4

Percentage of School Funds Derived from Local, State, and Federal Sources
Notice how the percentage of school funds raised by local governments has decreased since the early 1900s, while the proportion contributed by federal and state governments has grown.

SOURCES: Data from National Center for Education Statistics. (2006). *The Condition of Education 2006* (NCES 2006-071). Washington, D.C.: U.S. Government Printing Office; National Education Association. (2006). *Rankings and Estimates: Rankings of the States 2005 and Estimates of School Statistics 2006.* Washington, D.C.: Author.

Photo: © Alex Slobodkin/iStockphoto

Title 1 The section of federal education law that provides funds for compensatory education.

Title IX Part of the federal Educational Amendments of 1972, Title IX states that "No person in the United States shall, on the basis of sex, be excluded from participation in, be denied the benefits of, or be subjected to discrimination under any education program or activity receiving Federal financial assistance."

language barriers that impede equal participation by all students in an instructional program."

THE ELEMENTARY AND SECONDARY EDUCATION ACT

The most extensive federal financing of schools in America was made possible in 1965 when Congress passed the Elementary and Secondary Education Act (ESEA). At that time, this legislation was seen as part of President Lyndon Johnson's War on Poverty because it ensured that federal assistance would be sent to the poorest schools and communities in the nation. Its immediate impact was to provide one billion dollars to improve the education of students from families living below the poverty line.

Every five years since its enactment, ESEA has been reauthorized; it is the single largest source of federal support for K–12 education. The federal government distributes the funds to the states, and it is the states' responsibility to identify the schools and districts to receive the funds. This legislation, particularly the section known as **Title 1**, has led to many important programs that fall into the general category of compensatory education—educational services designed specifically to create better opportunities for students with disadvantages, such as those from high-poverty neighborhoods. Examples include:

- Early-childhood education: Head Start, the most well-known national early-childhood program, helps prepare preschool children for school, focusing not just on academic skills but also on nutrition, health, and the family environment.
- Tutoring and other supplemental academic instruction
- After-school centers
- Computer labs for poor schools
- Dropout prevention services
- Job training
- Parental education
- Professional development for teachers

The No Child Left Behind Act (NCLB) of 2001 revised the ESEA and called for states to develop

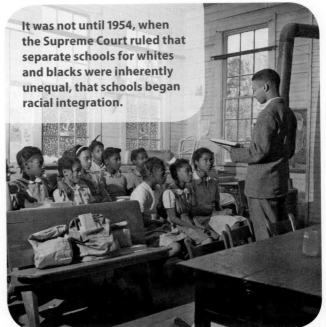

It was not until 1954, when the Supreme Court ruled that separate schools for whites and blacks were inherently unequal, that schools began racial integration.

© Bettmann/Corbis

content-area standards and annual testing of math and reading in grades 3 to 8. Schools with poor test results face the possibility of being closed. This revision also gives parents greater choice about where their children go to school. We discuss the implications of this act in Chapter 6 when we explore contemporary trends in education.

TITLE IX

Title IX, part of the Education Amendments of 1972, is a federal law that prohibits discrimination on the basis of sex in any federally funded education program or activity. The main objective of Title IX is to avoid the use of federal money to support sexually discriminating practices.

Title IX was modeled on Title VI of the Civil Rights Act of 1964, which prohibits discrimination based on race, color, and national origin. However, unlike Title VI, which applies to all federal financial assistance, Title IX is limited to *education* programs or activities that receive federal financial assistance.

Title IX protects the rights of both males and females from pre-kindergarten through graduate school—in sports, financial aid, employment, counseling, and school regulations and policies. One impact of Title IX has been on girls' sports activities and facilities; it requires that schools provide equal opportunities, funding, and facilities for boys' and girls' teams. Unfortunately, Title IX enforcement has been fairly lax, so it is not entirely unusual to find schools in apparent violation of part of the regulation.

What has been your own experience of the effect of gender on educational opportunities? Many studies have explored the ways in which some girls and boys experience school differently. Many students, for example, who have attended single-sex private schools have had very positive experiences. In fact, some public schools, for a wide range of reasons, have offered single-sex classes as well. In one public school I encountered, an all-girls physics class was thought to be a good way to engage more young women in physics. Success was measured by the achievement of the young women in the class. Similarly, in Queensland, Australia, several high schools are experimenting with all-boys English literature and writing classes. They also are meeting with successful outcomes in terms of achievement. Do these examples show that "separate but equal" can be a useful principle when it comes to segregation by sex? There is a great deal of controversy over this issue in education today.

Two other sections of the 1964 Civil Rights Act relate to education as well, and they can be used in conjunction with Title IX to challenge discriminatory practices:

- Title IV authorizes federal assistance to prohibit discrimination in education on the basis of sex, race, and national origin.
- Title VII prohibits sex discrimination and other types of employment discrimination both in and outside of education contexts (Klein et al., 2002).

A NATION AT RISK

In 1983, the National Commission on Excellence in Education, a group of scholars and educators convened by the U.S. Department of Education, issued a report in the form of an open letter to the American people. Called *A Nation at Risk: The Imperative for Educational Reform*, this document showed deep concern about the educational system in America:

Our society and its educational institutions seem to have lost sight of the basic purposes of schooling, and of the high expectations and disciplined effort needed to attain them. This report, the result of 18 months of study, seeks to generate reform of our educational

system in fundamental ways and to renew the Nation's commitment to schools and colleges of high quality throughout the length and breadth of our land. (National Commission on Excellence in Education, 1983)

The report called for tougher standards for graduation, increases in the required number of mathematics and science courses, higher college entrance requirements, and a return to what was called "academic basics." It also defined "computer skills" as a new basic.

The report further recommended an increase in the amount of homework given, a longer school day, more rigorous requirements for teachers, and updated textbooks. *A Nation at Risk* inaugurated a new period of academic rigor, with increased attention to skills and standards and less emphasis on progressive concerns such as schools' role in building social understanding. The "at risk" wording implied that the United States would lose its global competitive edge if the reforms were not carried out. Even though these recommendations came from the federal government, they were implemented (or sometimes ignored) in different ways at the local, state, and district levels.

A Nation at Risk: The Imperative for Educational Reform A 1983 federal report that found U.S. schools in serious trouble and inaugurated a new wave of school reform focused on academic basics and higher standards for student achievement.

Individuals with Disabilities Education Act (IDEA) The federal law that guarantees that all children with disabilities receive free, appropriate public education.

Q: *Do you remember ways in which your educational experience differed from that of your female or male peers?*

LO5 THE INDIVIDUALS WITH DISABILITIES EDUCATION ACT

In 1975, Congress passed the Education for All Handicapped Children Act (Public Law 94-142) to ensure that all children with disabilities could receive free, appropriate public education, just like other children. This law was revised in 1990, in 1997, and most recently in 2004. It is now known as the **Individuals with Disabilities Education Act (IDEA)**.

What is so important about this act? Before 1975, there was no organized, equitable way of addressing the needs of disabled students in the public school system. Often they were marginalized, taught in separate classrooms, and provided with watered-down curricula.

As a result of the federal legislation, however, strong efforts have been made to include students with disabilities in regular classrooms. This reform, known as **inclusion**, has been implemented to greater or lesser degrees in different school districts. In some classrooms, students with learning disabilities are integrated with general education students as much as possible. In other classrooms, students with special educational needs are included in the general education classroom some of the time; this arrangement is called *partial inclusion*. Some districts have a *self-contained* class as well, for students with special needs (who are often called *special education* students). Often, depending on the needs of the student population, all three models exist in the

same school district. Reform movements on behalf of children with disabilities have dominated special education programs for the past thirty years. Much educational research suggests that inclusion benefits both special education students and students from the general population. We will return to the subject of inclusion in Chapter 6.

LO6 STANDARDS-BASED EDUCATIONAL REFORM

As a response to *A Nation at Risk* and similar publications that followed, groups of scholars from content area associations developed standards for their disciplines, beginning with the National Council of Teachers of Mathematics. The first version of *Principles and Standards for School Mathematics* appeared in 1989. Language arts, science, social studies, and foreign languages followed in the 1990s, developing standards for what children at each grade level from pre-kindergarten to grade 12 should know and be able to do in each of the content areas. States were asked to prepare content standards based on these national guidelines and to create assessments to match the standards.

Hence the era in which we are presently living—and in which you are preparing to teach—is dominated by standards-based school reform and assessments. Many of you went to school as the standards-based movement was getting under way. Standards in the academic area were developed by professional organizations in concert with scholars and teachers in the field. Standards-based educational reform refers to clear, measurable, academic standards for all school students in all academic areas.

National standards and the testing that assesses whether students are meeting those standards is a policy issue that has supporters and critics. This movement, supported in part by the No Child Left Behind Act of 2001, is a model of considerable rigor, accountability, and strict benchmarks for student learning. Supporters of the movement contend that this reform movement encourages schools to set higher standards for their students and to find ways in which their students can meet those standards. Critics insist that curriculum needs to be connected to the students' lived

Strong efforts are made to include students with disabilities in regular classrooms.

© Richard Hutchings/Corbis

experiences and that standards will stifle innovation and creativity in the classroom.

Today, teachers and school administrators often find that they have relatively little freedom to vary the curriculum or even the order in which topics are taught. Yet local control still predominates in some places, as the following story demonstrates:

© doram/iStockphoto

Ms. Bennett is the principal of a public elementary school in Maryland, where children in grades 1 through 5 explore a different human-made artifact each year. The first grade studies bridges, the second grade studies elevators, the third grade investigates escalators, the fourth grade focuses on airplanes, and fifth-grade students explore the automobile. These various products of engineering design form themes that are addressed during the entire school year, regardless of what other topics are studied in that year.

How did this unusual curriculum come about? Few elementary schools have a mandate to teach students about such inventions in a formal way. When you meet Ms. Bennett, however, you learn that she entered the field of education after several years as a civil engineer. One of the first women in her college class to excel in civil engineering, she brought her passion for the work to her elementary school students. As a principal, Ms. Bennett enlisted her faculty's help to make learning about engineering design part of the school's curriculum.

In the current era of standards-driven school reform, do you think the curriculum in Ms. Bennett's school would win enthusiastic approval from the state or federal government? Later chapters will go deeper into the implications of the standards-based movement for teaching and learning.

Concluding Thoughts

As you think about the history of American public education, consider all the factors that contribute to the structure and design of schooling today. In addition to geography, acts of Congress, immigration, and educational movements, we now have international events, global challenges, and a technology revolution shaping and reshaping the landscape of public education.

Today we are faced with unprecedented cultural, ethnic, and racial diversity in our schools. Further, as young people spend more time online, texting, twittering, and seeking information, the nature of teaching and learning in the classroom is undergoing a transformation, reflecting these modes of communication. Although there are many local and national academic standards, *there is no standard student!* In this respect, we live in an unusual period in American education. Yet our long educational history, and the philosophies and debates that have emerged during that time, continue to influence our choices.

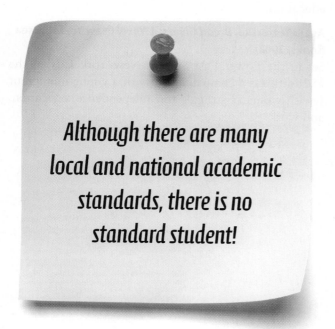

Although there are many local and national academic standards, there is no standard student!

Online Resources

The Informal Education Archives
http://www.infed.org/archives/

A wide-ranging collection, this site offers works by John Dewey and many other writers on educational philosophy and practice.

National Dissemination Center for Children with Disabilities
http://www.nichcy.org/

This website provides data and research related to children with disabilities, explains various iterations of the IDEA, and offers helpful suggestions for teachers of students with disabilities.

School: The Story of American Public Education
http://www.pbs.org/kcet/publicschool/roots_in_history/index.html

In addition to providing a survey of famous innovators in American education, this site explores the historical roots of current educational controversies.

Title IX of the Education Amendments of 1972
http://www.usdoj.gov/crt/cor/coord/titleix.htm

Explore this website, sponsored by the Civil Rights Division of the U.S. Department of Justice, for further information about Title IX.

Print Resources

Mortimer J. Adler, *The Paideia Proposal: An Educational Manifesto* (New York: Simon & Schuster, 1998).
This is a now-classic statement of perennialist philosophy.

Lawrence Cremin (ed.), *The Republic and the School: Horace Mann on the Education of Free Men* (New York: Teachers College Press, 1957).
This book provides original speeches and documentation exploring the contributions of Horace Mann, commonly known as the "Father of American Public Education."

John Dewey, *Democracy and Education: An Introduction to the Philosophy of Education* (Carbondale: Board of Trustees of Southern Illinois University, 1985; originally published in 1916).
Dewey describes the challenges of providing quality public education in a democratic society. He argues for the necessity of universal education for the advancement of the individual and of society.

Paulo Freire, *Pedagogy of the Oppressed,* 30th anniversary edition, trans. by Myra Bergman Ramos (New York: Continuum, 1970).
This book presents an impassioned argument for education in the service of social change.

Maxine Greene, *Variations on a Blue Guitar: The Lincoln Center Institute Lectures on Aesthetic Education* (New York: Teachers College Press, 2001).
This collection, which brings together lectures given over a period of 25 years, reflects a growing urgency for aesthetic education.

Nancy Hoffman, *Woman's "True" Profession: Voices from the History of Teaching* (Cambridge, MA: Harvard Education Press, 2003).
In addition to essays by Hoffman, this volume includes writings by women teachers who practiced between 1830 and 1920. The book gives terrific insight into the lives of teachers who built and transformed public education.

Anzia Yezierska, *Bread Givers: A Novel* (New York: Persea Books, 2003).
Set in the Lower East Side of New York City in the 1920s, this is a compelling story of a young immigrant Jewish woman's struggle for independence, education, and work.

LISTEN UP!

SHE DID

TEACH was designed for students just like you – busy people who want choices, flexibility, and multiple learning options.

TEACH delivers concise, focused information in a fresh and contemporary format. And…
TEACH gives you a variety of online learning materials designed with you in mind.

Through **CourseMate** for **TEACH**, you'll find electronic resources such as **videos** and **interactive games** for each chapter, as well as downloadable audio that explores and reviews chapter themes. Access at **login.cengage.com**.

These resources will help supplement your understanding of core concepts in a format that fits your busy lifestyle. Visit **www.cengagebrain.com** to learn more about the multiple resources available to help you succeed!

CHAPTER 4

PRINCIPLES OF TEACHING AND LEARNING:
EXPLORING PEDAGOGY, CURRICULUM, AND INSTRUCTION

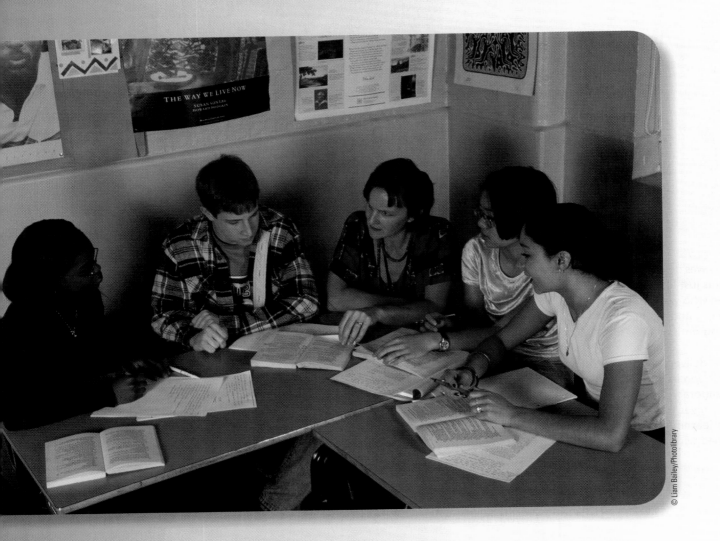

© Liam Bailey/Photolibrary

> *If a doctor, lawyer, or dentist had 40 people in his office at one time, all of whom had different needs, and some of whom did not want to be there and were causing trouble, and the doctor, lawyer, or dentist, without assistance, had to treat them all with professional excellence for nine months, then he [or she] might have some conception of the classroom teacher's job.*
> —Donald D. Quinn

LEARNING OUTCOMES

After reading this chapter, you should be thinking about the following ideas:

LO1 Many people think that they can teach because they have spent many years in classrooms.

LO2 Pedagogy is both an art and a science and is expressed through instructional practice.

LO3 By studying the human brain and development, scientists and educators have acquired a lot of knowledge about how people learn; it makes sense to use this understanding of how people learn as we think about how to become better teachers.

LO4 While the term "curriculum" is used often in schools, most people do not recognize that a curriculum is a course of study in a given subject area. National and state standards define topics to be addressed in a given subject area at each grade level.

LO5 Evidence of learning takes many forms, but the best way to understand what students know may be to ask them.

LO6 The expression "one size fits all" does not apply to teaching—teachers must learn about their students and find ways to teach to their special needs and talents.

As you consider a teaching career, you will frequently hear the terms *pedagogy* and *instruction*. How do they relate to teaching and learning? What does Donald Quinn mean when he speaks of "different needs"? How can we define professional excellence so that we can imagine what it might look like in ourselves?

In this chapter we examine the meaning of teaching and learning through an exploration of learning theories. Currently, the field of neuroscience—the study of the structure, function, development, and physiology of the brain and the nervous system—is at the forefront of understanding how people perceive and interact with the external world. Other important approaches have also contributed to the way educators think about learning today. We will explore what we teach—the school's curriculum—as well as how the content of a school's curriculum is shaped by not only national standards but also states, local school districts, local school boards, school curriculum committees, and teachers themselves.

At several points in the chapter, we will encounter parts of an interview with Dr. Jacqueline (Jackie) Grennon Brooks, a cognitive scientist and an expert in the area of learning theory. First, however, let's deal with the nature of teaching and whether it does, indeed, require special knowledge or whether it is a job anyone can do.

LO1 Anyone Can Teach?

Most people have spent much of their lives as students in classrooms. Add up the years of schooling you have had up to this time—the number is certainly considerable, isn't it? Because people have been in classrooms for so much of their lives, there exists a common myth that "anyone can teach."

As a new teacher just starting out, I confided my nervousness about my first day of teaching to a friend, and he said to me, "Teaching is easy. You just stand up there and talk—and you like to talk." For me, that was the first of several experiences with people who *think* they know what being a teacher is all about.

pedagogy The art and science of teaching; all that you know and believe about teaching.

instruction The act or process of teaching; the way your pedagogy becomes enacted in practice.

pedagogical content knowledge (PCK) The understanding of how particular topics, problems, or issues can be adapted and presented to match the diverse interests and abilities of learners.

As you are probably discovering for yourself, teaching and learning are complex activities. They are far from easy and automatic. As we explore the ways a teacher fosters learning, you will see that there is a lot to know about the principles behind what a teacher does. Remember, too, that the process is a dialectic. That is, it requires communication with your students, and it demands that you be an active listener, not just a talker. (My friend was right, however: I *do* like to talk.) As you will see, teaching is not "telling," and in addition to what you have to *know* to be able to teach, there are many things you have to *do* to create the opportunities for students to learn.

LO2 Pedagogy and Instruction

In Chapter 2, we discussed how *who we are* comes to bear on *what we do* with our students and how we engage them in learning. In fact, who we are has everything to do with how we teach.

Pedagogy is commonly thought of today as the art or science of being a teacher. I like to think of this modern interpretation as the art *and* science of being a teacher. What makes pedagogy an art? It is a personal creative expression of oneself. I am reminded of the French philosopher and essayist Joseph Joubert (1754–1824), who said, "To teach is to learn something twice." As a teacher, you explore ways to create a lesson that will help your students understand something you already understand; this is like learning the concept again!

Yet pedagogy is more than an art. It is also a science because it relies on careful observations of (1) students' dispositions, (2) students' prior knowledge, and (3) students' responses to the activities and questions in which they are engaged. Scientists have helped us understand more clearly how students learn and how we can best promote that learning.

Q: *Do you remember any teachers who relied on external rewards or punishments?*

How, then, does *instruction* differ from pedagogy? In a conversation I had with Jackie Grennon Brooks, which I will quote from later in the chapter, she helped clarify the distinction between the two words. As Jackie explained, the root of the word *pedagogy* is the Greek stem *paid-*, meaning "the child." Pedagogy began as the study of the child, and the term morphed to mean the study of teaching and learning.

In formal terms, therefore, **pedagogy** can be thought of as the belief system and the orientation that you bring to your instructional practice. **Instruction** emerges from that on a daily basis. Your pedagogy is the subtext beneath the instruction you provide in your classroom. For example, if you believe that you need to understand students' ideas and beliefs to help them gain new understanding, then that is part of your pedagogy. Your instructional decisions will emerge from that pedagogy. As teachers gain new ideas about how people learn, their pedagogical stance can shift in response to those ideas.

People often use the terms *instructional methods* and *pedagogy* interchangeably, but understanding the difference helps teachers reflect on their practice. Pedagogy is the personal teaching philosophy that gets expressed through instructional practice. It informs all the methods of instruction and decision making in the classroom. Keeping the meaning of the terms separate is important because it reminds us to revisit our personal teaching philosophy every time we plan for instruction.

Many special subject area teachers—such as math, science, social studies, language arts, and foreign language teachers—believe that they need merely to be experts in their particular areas. However, even if you are a subject area expert, becoming an expert *teacher* in your subject area requires special professional understanding. Teachers must integrate, transform, and represent subject matter knowledge in ways that are understandable to students (Toh et al., 2003). This special type of knowledge is referred to as **pedagogical content knowledge**, or **PCK** for short. Being subject-specific, PCK refers to the ways particular subject matter material is best represented and communicated to make it accessible to students (Shulman, 1987, p. 4).

Now that we have clarified our terms, let's look at what some major investigators of the past century have discovered about the learning process. As you'll see, their work has led to competing theories about the way learning occurs.

LO3 Learning Theories

The growth of the field of psychology in the 20th century and recent advances in neuroscience have formed the foundation for learning theories that are reflected to a greater or lesser extent in schools across the country. **Learning theories** are formal ideas about how learning may happen.

There are many ways to think about learning. For some people, learning is a process; for others, it is a product; and for most people, it is both. Over the past hundred years or so, psychologists and others have used the developmental theories of their time to describe conditions that they have considered optimal for learning.

BEHAVIORISM: A TEACHER-CENTERED APPROACH

In the mid-1900s, Harvard psychologist B. F. Skinner pioneered a theory of how people learn that still has followers today. Skinner's theory of *operant conditioning* viewed learning as a response to external stimuli in the environment. For Skinner, learning was a product that could be promoted by teachers who provided the right incentives and motivation. This general approach came to be known as **behaviorism**. Behaviorists believe that all learning is shaped by the stimuli in the environment and that free will plays no role in the process.

Using the behaviorist approach, teachers structured their lessons around clear objectives that stated what students would be able to do by the end of the lesson. The desired behaviors were regulated by carefully planned reinforcements and punishments. The external rewards could include good grades, increased privileges, or a special smile from the teacher. Students were seen as passive participants in the classroom who responded to the teacher's direct rewards and punishments.

Behaviorist ideas still form a backdrop for many techniques used to establish classroom discipline. For instance, teachers rely on behaviorist principles when they set up specific rewards for good behavior. Behaviorism asserts that students will modify their behavior in response to consistent delivery of rewards and punishments.

Yet there are many critics of behaviorist techniques today. Some argue that behaviorist teachers exercise too much control over their students, with the result that students tend to learn facts rather than deep concepts. Others remind teachers that rewards and punishments do not help students develop their own internal mechanisms for doing quality work and that students eventually lose interest in what they are essentially being "bribed" to do (Kohn, 1999).

COGNITIVE LEARNING THEORIES: THE ROLE OF MENTAL PROCESSING

As behaviorists focused solely on students' observable behaviors as the indicators of learning, many educators and psychologists began to resist this view and suggested that the learner was not a passive recipient of new concepts but rather played a more active role in the learning process. **Cognitive learning theories** emerged to describe students' mental development. Cognitive

learning theory
An explanation of how learning typically occurs and about conditions that favor learning.

behaviorism The theory that learning takes place in response to reinforcements (for instance, rewards or punishments) from the outside environment.

cognitive learning theories Explanations of the mental processes that occur during learning.

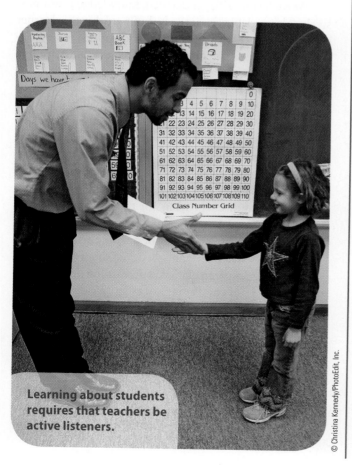

Learning about students requires that teachers be active listeners.

© Christina Kennedy/PhotoEdit, Inc.

learning theorists went "inside the head of the learner" to discover and model the thought processes that occur during learning.

A key figure in cognitive learning theory was the Swiss scholar and scientist Jean Piaget, who began conducting interviews and research studies with children in the 1920s. From these investigations, he developed the idea of *stages of cognitive development*. According to Piaget, at certain times in a child's intellectual growth, different mental structures begin to emerge. He believed that most children between birth and two years of age are in the sensorimotor stage, in which learning occurs mainly through sensory impressions and movement. The child learns that he is separate from his environment and that aspects of his environment—his parents or favorite toy—continue to exist even though they may be outside the reach of his senses.

Later, children begin to learn words and other symbols (the preoperational stage, ages two to seven). In this stage, a child's thinking is influenced by fantasy—the way the child would like things to be—and he or she assumes that others see situations from his or her viewpoint. The child takes in information and then changes it in her mind to fit her ideas.

In the next stage, from age seven to eleven, the child develops the ability to generalize concepts from concrete experiences (the concrete operational stage). In this stage, the child makes rational judgments about concrete or observable phenomena, which in the past he or she needed to manipulate physically to understand.

Finally, the child develops the ability to manipulate abstractions (the formal operational stage, ages eleven and older). In this stage, the learner no longer requires concrete objects to make rational judgments.

Piaget argued that at each of these stages of maturation, a child is ready for a different type of learning. The discrete boundaries of Piaget's stages of development came under scrutiny as researchers learned that children can be in several stages at once and that the stages cannot easily be linked to predetermined ages. In other words, as significant as Piaget's work is, we now understand that there are not clear demarcations of mental development from one stage to the next; as the learner progresses from one stage to the next, there is an overlap. For example, many children handle concrete operations earlier than Piaget thought.

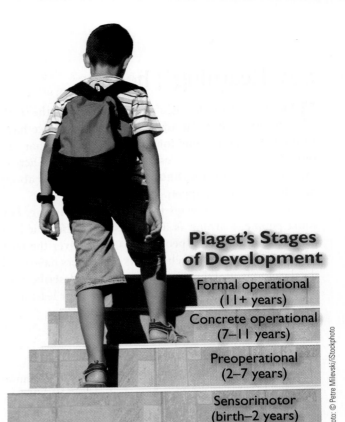

Piaget's Stages of Development

Formal operational (11+ years)

Concrete operational (7–11 years)

Preoperational (2–7 years)

Sensorimotor (birth–2 years)

Photo: © Petre Milevski/iStockphoto

At each stage, Piaget decided, knowledge is not passively received but is actively built up by the learner through a process of invention or creation, not reception. This gives a great deal of responsibility to the learner.

Jerome Bruner (1960, 1966), another cognitive learning theorist, took Piaget's ideas a step further by arguing that at any stage of cognitive development, teachers should allow children to discover ideas for themselves. He was a leading supporter of Piaget's work, but he suggested that at *any* given stage of cognitive development, teaching should proceed in a way that allows children to discover ideas for themselves. His work became known as *discovery learning*. He differed from Piaget in one important respect. Whereas Piaget believed that readiness for a particular type of learning depended on a child's stage of cognitive development, Bruner noticed that children are always ready to learn a concept at *some level*. Realizing this, Bruner emphasized the importance of returning to curriculum topics at various ages, revisiting them at different stages of the child's development (Bruner, 1960). This produces a *spiraling* of curriculum topics, as the same

© Eugene Junying Sim/iStockphoto

broad topics are revisited at higher grade levels. This practice has become an important part of curriculum planning. Discovery learning remains influential today and has much in common with constructivism, which we will come to in a moment.

SOCIAL COGNITIVE THEORIES: THE ROLE OF SOCIAL INTERACTIONS

Piaget's work was soon criticized for not taking into account the learner's social contexts. After all, when children develop their understanding of the world, they do not do so in a social or cultural vacuum. Some of Piaget's critics developed forms of *social learning theory*; these over time were extended into **social cognitive learning theories**, which take into account both the learner's own mental processes and the social environment in which the learning occurs.

One important social cognitive theorist, the Russian psychologist Lev Vygotsky (1962), showed how social contexts influence the ideas that people develop. As one example, the teacher and students in a classroom use language that is socially and culturally accepted in that specific environment. The ideas that children develop in the classroom conform to these socially accepted usages and meanings. When students work in groups and read each other's writing in order to critique it, for example, one student says of the other's work, "This is so cool." The meaning is that this student peer really liked the story, and the comment is readily understood. Clearly, different cultures, neighborhoods, and parts of the world would have different ways of expressing the same meaning. Since students do not learn in a cultural vacuum, studying how people learn requires consideration of the context.

Many social cognitivists stress the importance of *modeling*. For instance, if you were teaching young students how to add columns of numbers, you would probably model the process of exchanging ten ones for one ten. According to social cognitivists, students would learn, in part, by observing you; then they would learn more by doing a similar problem themselves; and they would be further served by using manipulative materials and working on exchanging units with their peers in a group.

Thinking about modeling reminds us that teachers are not the only important social influence on learning. Parents, other adults, siblings, and peers have major effects on a child's intellectual development as well. A young person learns a great deal by observing various other people, communicating with them, and solving problems with them.

CONSTRUCTIVISM: STUDENT-CENTERED LEARNING

The work of Piaget, Bruner, Vygotsky, and others have paved the way for understanding in greater depth how people learn. The accumulated research has shown that the essence of learning is the constant effort to assimilate new information. As Carl Rogers (1983) explained, you don't merely draw in new information from the outside. For real learning to occur, you also have to make that information your own so that it becomes significant to you and you can use it for your own purposes. These ideas form the basis of a group of learning theories called **constructivism**. The constructivist

social cognitive learning theories Explanations that describe how learning involves interactions between the learner and the social environment.

constructivism A group of theories about knowledge and learning whose basic tenet is that all knowledge is constructed by synthesizing new ideas with prior knowledge. Constructivism holds that knowledge is not passively received; rather, it is actively built by the learner as he or she experiences the world.

Helping students work with others to meet common goals is an important part of teaching.

© Mark Garten/Corbis

mental scheme An organizational structure in the brain; a group of foundational concepts that help the individual make sense of the world.

approach builds on cognitive and social cognitive theories but goes further by considering how new information becomes meaningful to the learner.

The Essence of Constructivism: Building Mental Schemes

Since constructivism is the learning theory most closely related to what we currently understand about how people learn, I sought an expert in the field, cognitive psychologist Jackie Grennon Brooks, to answer some questions.

JK: You have written a great deal about the learning theory called constructivism. How do you describe it?

JGB: Constructivism is a learning theory, and it is also an epistemology.[1] It is the study of how people learn in various contexts. It is the exploration of how people create their own knowledge using the social context around them. Learners interact with people, objects, and ideas to construct their understanding of what is happening around them.

JK: What is the main premise of constructivism?

JGB: Constructivism postulates mental schemes that change both incrementally and through big leaps. Learners see the outside world through their mental schemes. When the learner is interacting with new data and the information does not fit [an existing scheme], the learner uses what does not fit to reformulate the scheme. The learner then goes on to use this reconstructed scheme to make sense of the new information.

Let's pause a moment to examine this idea of **mental schemes**. A scheme is a sort of organizer in the brain. As the result of all your experiences during your lifetime, you have formed these organizing structures in your mind that help you make sense of the world. As Jackie notes, when you encounter new information, you try to fit it into your existing schemes. Sometimes it fits easily, but when it doesn't fit, you have to revise your existing mental scheme (see Figure 4.1).

When new information fails to match your existing schemes—when it doesn't fit your picture of the world—you have a choice. You can ignore the new

[1]*Epistemology* is a branch of philosophy devoted to the study of knowledge. It examines the nature and scope of knowledge and philosophical questions such as: "What is knowledge?" "How is knowledge acquired?" and "What do people know?"

CARL ROGERS ON LEARNING

The well-known psychologist Carl Rogers (1983) had this to say about the learning process:

> I want to talk about learning. But not the lifeless, sterile, futile, quickly forgotten stuff that is crammed into the mind of the poor helpless individual tied into his seat by ironclad bonds of conformity! I am talking about LEARNING—the insatiable curiosity that drives the adolescent boy [and girl] to absorb everything he [or she] can see or hear or read about gasoline engines in order to improve the efficiency and speed of his [or her]"cruiser." I am talking about the student who says, "I am discovering, drawing in from the outside, and making that which is drawn in a real part of me." I am talking about any learning in which the experience of the learner progresses along this line: "No, no, that's not what I want"; "Wait! This is closer to what I am interested in, what I need"; "Ah, here it is! Now I'm grasping and comprehending what I need and what I want to know!"

I especially like the part of this quotation that talks about "drawing in from the outside, and making that which is drawn in a real part of me." That would omit the types of "learning" that include memorizing for tests!

information—in a sense, reject it. In that case, we can say that no new learning has occurred. Or you can remake your set of schemes to accommodate the new data—a process of truly making new information your own. That is what happens when we learn something.

To explain how people make meaning of new ideas, Jackie Grennon Brooks uses the metaphor of a "grand dance." This phrase refers to the ways each of us makes sense of the world. The "dance" involves synthesizing new experiences with what we have previously come to understand. We achieve this synthesis either by interpreting the new idea or event through our existing set

FIGURE 4.1

The Role of Mental Schemes in Learning
In this *Peanuts* cartoon, Linus learns from Charlie Brown that his ambition to become a doctor requires eight extra years of school. Being admired is not sufficient compensation for this, and Linus revises his mental scheme.

of schemes about the world or by creating new schemes that better take into account the new experience, idea, or concept.

For a concrete instance of mental schemes at work, consider the following teaching story, which is not about a classroom but about an earlier context in which teaching occurs—a mother dealing with a puzzled young child.

Mental Schemes at Work

I grew up in an inner-city apartment building with six floors and twenty apartments on each floor. When I was six years old, I was allowed to use the small key to open the mailbox assigned to my family and "take out the mail." This was my daily job after school.

I had my own personal theory about mail delivery. I imagined that, when the envelope was dropped in the public mailbox on the corner, a tube carried it through underground chutes to its destination in my little mailbox. Even at the age of six, however, I was troubled by not being able to explain how the letter knew how to get to my mailbox.

One day, when walking with my mother, I bent down to look under the mailbox on the corner. "What are you looking for?" she asked. "I was wondering where the tubes were," I responded. "What tubes?" she asked, and I then proceeded to share my theory. Nodding, she said that she could not explain right then how the mail got to the mailbox but she would arrange a way for me to find out.

Shortly thereafter, I was home ill from school, in the care of my grandmother. My mother called from work and asked Grandma to take me down to the mailboxes at the precise time that Artie, our mailman, would arrive. She bundled me up and I was able to witness the mailman, with his special key, open the portal to all of the mailboxes in the building. One box at a time, he inserted the mail in the various boxes.

He allowed me to help him, thrilled with my curiosity about how mail "knows" where to go. He also invited me and my family to the local post office for a view of how the postal workers sort the mail for the various neighborhood routes.

I shall never forget this experience. It demonstrates, for me, what it means to reorganize my mental schemes as I set about understanding more of my external world.

It would have been easy for my mother to say, "No, Janice, mail does not travel through tubes in the ground." Instead, she honored my theory, found it quite interesting, and arranged for me to have an experience that would challenge my beliefs about underground tubes and mail delivery. By observing how the mailman opened all the mailboxes simultaneously with his large master key, I saw people as an intricate part of the mail delivery process. I began to expand my thinking and accommodate this new experience into my mental scheme.

Constructivist instruction begins with close attention to students' existing ideas, knowledge, skills, and attitudes. Just as my mother realized, these are the foundation on which new learning builds (Bransford & Donovan, 2004). Learning as much as we can about students' existing mental schemes is important if we hope to help them learn. Constructivist teachers try to activate students' prior knowledge so that, in the course of the lesson, students can build on what they already know, challenge it, rethink it, and refine it.

Because constructivists pay so much attention to students' preexisting ideas, they often face a situation similar to the one my mother encountered: the student reveals ideas that are plainly "wrong." What should a teacher do when a student has such misconceptions?

Many educators believe that if a teacher merely corrects a student's erroneous ideas verbally, those ideas may go underground—they may linger in the student's mind, unrefuted. Instead, the teacher should treat the misconceptions with respect and guide the student in confronting new information that contradicts them. In wrestling with the contradiction, the teacher hopes, the student will modify old mental schemes or create new ones, and in this way genuine learning will occur.

There will be many times when you will be tempted to refute a student's idea or explanation. It's certainly true that you should not allow your student to harbor misconceptions for a long time. But try to find a way to provide convincing evidence for the alternative, more accurate explanation.

Perhaps you can remember a personal theory that you held onto when you were young. How did you eventually learn, through experience and interaction with the material, that you had to adjust your thinking?

Constructivism and Teaching

❝*A teacher's purpose is not to create students in his [or her] own image, but to develop students who can create their own image.*❞ —**Anonymous**

In my interview with Jackie Grennon Brooks, she went on to explain how teachers demonstrate the constructivist approach when they help students build ideas for themselves.

JK: OK, what does this notion of mental schemes say to us about teaching?

JGB: It says a lot about teaching. If we can offer opportunities for students to work iteratively[2] on big concepts, the students can address those concepts over time until they can construct those concepts for themselves.

Here is an example: understanding that the order of the digits in a number tells you the value of the digits. Place value is a huge idea! Students cannot understand place value by having it explained, but when they have the opportunity to exchange bundles of units and bundle the bundles and then represent the bundles in some numerical form, then they can come to make sense of numbers.

Representing numbers as numerals is part of the convention we establish. We talk in code to one another, and students need to reinvent that code for themselves. Then the ones, tens, and hundreds columns have meaning, and the number really represents a quantity.

This may seem like a radical idea—that individual students need to "reinvent" a basic operation we use for arithmetic. But think about what happens if students learn only the mechanical processes of mathematics. When young children are adding numbers, they can learn to "carry a 1" from one column to the next, but if they do not get the *meaning* of this procedure, they will have only a shallow and fragile understanding of what they are doing. Later on in their mathematical education, they will likely get confused because they don't fully grasp what is happening.

JK: What is the most important message of constructivism for teachers?

JGB: That the child's changing understandings of the world are the centerpiece, and the teacher is always trying to maximize the likelihood of that child's intellectual transformatio n by offering multiple learning opportunities.

By now you must see that constructivism is a very student-centered approach to teaching and learning.

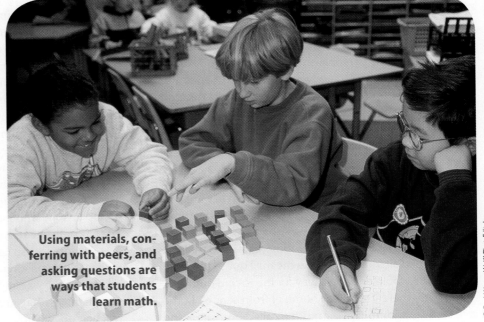

Using materials, conferring with peers, and asking questions are ways that students learn math.

© David Young-Wolff/PhotoEdit, Inc.

[2]*Iteratively* means repeatedly, on multiple occasions.

(See Table 4.1, which compares constructivism with behaviorism, cognitive learning theories, and social cognitive learning theories.) In this respect, John Dewey's progressive philosophy of education, which we examined in Chapter 3, provides fertile ground for teaching and learning. I asked Jackie about the link between constructivism and progressivism.

JK: In what ways, if any, did John Dewey's theories and the progressive era in American education anticipate current theories about how people learn?

JGB: The progressive era was consistent with current learning theories because it invited children into a learning environment that was their life. Progressives did not talk about mental schemes, but they talked about opportunities to create a mind free to think for itself.

There was an inaccurate perception of progressivism—that it merely meant doing something physically, like a hands-on experience. Instead, Dewey referred to an active *mental* engagement. This can occur while students are listening, but it needs an attentive teacher.

Perspectives from Neuroscience: The Importance of Context

As my conversation with Jackie continued, we began to explore the ways that recent discoveries in neuroscience support what we know about learning.

JK: How do theories about how people learn help us teach?

JGB: Theories of learning become the data on which we base our practices of teaching. The theories of how people learn are changing. For a long time, methods of schooling were based on the behavioral theories that included stimulus-response iterations. What we know now is based on the emerging relationship between neuroscience and teaching.

The more we learn about how the brain cognitively processes, the more we realize that the way our mind works is dependent upon how the neurons in our brain are fired, and that is very dependent on the context that is created for learning. The progressive era had the right idea when it encouraged the active participation of students in their own learning.

TABLE 4.1	Learning Theories Compared
Learning Theory	**Key Elements**
Behaviorism	• Teacher-centered • Students respond to external stimuli and learn the correct responses through rewards and punishments, eventually internalizing rewards and punishments • Teachers are in absolute control through the stimuli they present in the classroom
Cognitive learning theories	• Somewhat learner-centered • Learning is active, not merely passive • Symbolic mental constructions in the minds of learners help them process information
Social cognitive learning theories	• Somewhat learner-centered • Internal mental processes are important, but we also learn through experiences shared with others; learning is as much social as it is individual
Constructivism	• Learner-centered • We all construct our own perspective of the world, based on individual experiences and personal schemes, which are internal knowledge structures • A person adjusts his or her mental model to incorporate new experiences and make sense of new information

COOKIES AND BRAIN SCIENCE

For perspective on the evolving understanding of learning, consider the effect of cookies and milk. We have always known that cookies and milk help you sleep; your great-grandmother understood that without any deep scientific exploration. More recently, though, science has added to our understanding. We now know that milk has tryptophan in it. Tryptophan is an essential amino acid and the precursor the body uses to metabolize serotonin, a neurotransmitter that regulates sleep, mood, and other physical processes. The sugar in the cookies helps catalyze the metabolism. Hence, when you have milk and cookies, your serotonin level increases and you fall asleep. Science has provided a justification for a common practice as well as a better understanding of why it works.

Similarly, we learned many years ago that when students are actively engaged in their own learning, they understand it better. More recently, as science was able to explore neural pathways in the brain, we came to understand the physiology at work, and we see that there is a scientific reason why active engagement of the learner results in better learning. Actively engaged students have more neurons firing, allowing them to use more parts of the brain, connect with prior knowledge, and build upon what they already know.

JK: How has neuroscience helped us guide our instruction?

JGB: Problem solving involves the firing of neurons in different regions of the brain. A problem-solving event requires that multiple areas of the brain connect with each other to produce solution sets. This is why many scientists and educators see problem solving as a good way to learn.

The Chicago Mastery Learning Program [implemented in the early 1980s] divided the process of reading into hundreds of different operations. What we found out was that students could decode [words] more accurately with this process than before it was broken down into hundreds of different operations, but the students were not reading or wanting to read books. We know now that there has to be a conceptual framework on which to build the parts. There needs to be a context—a reason to do the decoding. Yes, more and more data are important, but the learner still needs to construct the knowledge. In order to do this, he or she must have the palette on which to put the ideas. The palette must have space for mixing the colors as you need them.

Years ago we taught children that the brain is not a muscle—you cannot exercise it in order to grow. We know differently now. The brain is an organ that actually controls all of our muscles, and there are different learning opportunities that do create different types of neural network firing that allow the brain to expand its capacities.

When Jackie talks about a "palette," she refers to the context in which the concept being learned occurs. I am reminded of a story in my own third-grade class when we were learning about the sun.

My teacher, Ms. Schultz, walked us outside our large brick building in an urban area into the schoolyard and asked us to feel the sun's warmth. It was an autumn day and the air was cool, but the sun felt warm against our faces. Then she asked us to move about and explore our shadows.

Something Ms. Schultz said in the midst of this experience has stayed with me forever: "Isn't it amazing, girls and boys, that this sun is 93 million miles away and it still has the power to warm us up?" I remember thinking that the sun must be very, very hot if, after traveling all those miles, it still warmed my skin. I have thought about the sun in that way ever since.

On the next sunny day, we returned early to the schoolyard and explored our shadows again, noticing how their length changed with the time of day. Experiencing the sunlight in the context of learning about shadows made a big difference to me. I was taken with how different the size of my shadow was at noon, compared with early morning. Experiencing myself in space, responding to the sun's warmth on my body, joining with my classmates in measuring our shadows—all these activities created a palette on which my learning about the sun and shadows occurred. I have always remembered the distance of the sun from the Earth and that when the sun is overhead, around noon, my shadow is the shortest.

In these simple ways, Ms. Schultz helped create a context that shaped my learning.

Fish Is Fish

One of my favorite children's stories illustrates the role that prior and current knowledge plays in student learning. *Fish is Fish* by Leo Lionni (1970) is the story of a young minnow and a tadpole who become friends when they meet underwater in a pond. But the tadpole soon grows legs and explores the world beyond the pond and then returns to tell his fish friend about the new creatures he sees, such as birds, cows, and people. As the illustrations demonstrate, the fish imagines these creatures as bird-fish, cow-fish, and people-fish and is eager to join them. The minnow learns the limits of life beyond the safety of the water environment to which he is adapted, but not before we get to see the images of

WRITING & REFLECTION

The Context of Learning

Specific school memories or anecdotes often stay with us as we grow older. Can you recall an experience in which the context of a lesson or activity became attached to the memory of the lasting idea or concept you learned? Describe that experience and indicate how you think the context—or, as Jackie refers to it, the "palette"—made a difference.

What Makes a Fire Burn?

Read the following poem by Judy Brown (2000). Think about it as a metaphor for teaching and learning.

Fire

What makes a fire burn
is space between the logs,
a breathing space.
Too much of a good thing,
too many logs
packed in too tight
can douse the flames
almost as surely as a pail of
    water would.

So building fires
requires attention
to the spaces in between,
as much as to the wood.

When we are able to build
open spaces

in the same way
we have learned
to pile on the logs,
then we can come to see how
it is fuel, and absence of the fuel
together, that make fire possible.

We only need to lay a log
lightly from time to time.
A fire
grows
simply because the space is there,
with openings
in which the flame
that knows just how it wants to burn
can find a way.

How does this poem relate to constructivism as a theory of how people learn? What do the spaces between the logs represent to you?

SOURCE: Poem excerpted from *The Sea Accepts All Rivers & Other Poems* by Judy Sorum Brown, Miles River Press, 2000. Available from Judy Brown, 3907 Calverton Drive, Hyattsville, MD 20782.

creatures as bird-fish, cow-fish, and people-fish and is eager to join them. The minnow learns the limits of life beyond the safety of the water environment to which he is adapted, but not before we get to see the images of fish with wings as he hears about birds, fish with udders as he hears about cows, and fish walking on their tail-fins as he hears about people. You may be wondering what this has to do with learning theories. In fact, it is a wonderful illustration of how learners process new material through their prior and current conceptions. Unless those ideas are acknowledged, learners create mental images that are quite different from those that are intended—in this case, by the minnow's friend, the frog. The implications for teaching are clear: Access students' existing understandings and experiences and draw attention to the kinds of knowledge that help students to learn with understanding (Bransford et al., 2000).

Hence, if the frog had provided more details about birds, cows, and people, it would have helped the fish to understand that their body parts have functions that these animals need for survival. Of course, the fish in Lionni's story is endowed with human capacities for thought, but he does make a good illustration of why it is so important for teachers to understand how people learn.

LO4 What Is a Curriculum?

You have read in this chapter a lot about theories of learning and instruction, but what about the actual material you will be required to teach? Educators refer to this as the **curriculum**. Who determines the curriculum, and how can teachers express their personal and creative selves when handed a list of topics they must address? Think about these questions as you read the following sections.

FORMAL, INFORMAL, AND HIDDEN CURRICULA

The word *curriculum* derives from the Latin term meaning "running course." It is the overall plan that includes what you will teach and how the material should be arranged and presented. A curriculum may be thought of as an organizing tool for the myriad topics that are

"Cows," said the frog. "Cows! They have four legs, horns, eat grass, and carry pink bags of milk."

addressed at each grade level. Curricula are typically organized by content area. There are language arts, mathematics, social studies, foreign language, and science curricula. There is a curriculum associated with any subject matter taught at a given school.

Sometimes you will hear the official plan of studies referred to as the *formal curriculum*. There is also an **informal curriculum**, which includes all the things you do in the classroom that are not part of the official, prescribed plan. For example, you might use an important local event or news story to create a learning experience closely linked to the students' own lives. In a high school earth science class, the teacher might address an earthquake that was in the news that week and explore

TEACHSOURCE VIDEO CASE

A High School Debate

Constructivist teaching places much responsibility for learning on the students by asking them to actively create meaning through their experiences. View the TeachSource Video Case "Constructivist Teaching in Action: A High School Classroom Debate" on the student website. After watching the video, consider the following question:

How are the students taking charge of their own learning?

the causes for earthquakes, even if this was not the formal topic of study at that moment. Local news events often become the centerpiece of social studies lessons because of their relevance. Although not written into the preplanned curriculum, these informal events bring meaning to the formal curriculum and deepen students' understanding of the concepts they are learning.

In speaking of the informal curriculum, educators often include the concept of the hidden curriculum, mentioned earlier in this book. The *hidden curriculum* consists of the social rules and values schools and teachers transmit to students. Hidden curricula are communicated through the rules of conduct, dress codes, social atmosphere, and relationships among teachers, administration, and students in a given school environment. They are hidden in the sense that they are not written down, or at least not presented as part of the subject matter to be learned; but they are very much part of the school experience for both students and teachers. For example, when I was growing up in the middle of the last century, it was customary for the girls in the elementary school that I attended to erase and wash the blackboards, also called chalkboards, which are not very common in modern classrooms. It was also usual for boys to march in the assemblies carrying the flags in what was called a color guard. I always wanted to carry the flag; however, I knew that I dare not ask. The hidden curriculum dictated what girls and boys would and would not have permission for in this school.

The Role of National Standards and State Frameworks

In the United States, the formal curriculum in public schools is established by each state, with individual school districts adjusting it to a greater or lesser degree. Each state, however, relies heavily on the input of national groups that have been actively involved in establishing standards for their discipline. For example, the National Council of Teachers of Mathematics has a great influence on mathematics curricula throughout the country.

As we explored in Chapter 3, the standards movement has dominated public education since the early 1990s. This movement has prompted subject-area associations to state explicitly what students should know and be able to do at each grade level from kindergarten

through twelfth grade, resulting in national standards for each subject. Hence, there are national standards for science, language arts, foreign languages, social studies, mathematics, technology, health, and physical education.

Many states assign statewide committees or task forces to construct curriculum frameworks based on these guidelines. The state frameworks are then adapted by the local school or district and used to develop the school-based curriculum in each subject area. Does this sound complicated? It is! But the key feature here is local control.

Local schools' control of their curricula in each area was quite broad until the federal No Child Left Behind Act was passed in 2001. The act requires that students be held accountable by means of statewide exams that assess their knowledge at various grade levels, often beginning in

Did You Know?

The standards movement has dominated public education since the early 1990s, with the No Child Left Behind Act being passed in 2001.

THE PRESSURE TO "COVER" THE CURRICULUM

Educators often talk about "covering the curriculum." You may hear them say, "There is so much to cover; I can never find enough time." Because of the importance of standards-based assessments, today's teachers do indeed have a great deal of material to address with their students.

In this context, it's important to remember that to "cover" can also mean to "hide." Instead of covering curriculum, constructivists would rather see teachers "uncover" it—that is, guide students to engage with the material in ways that help them reveal the key ideas and construct new understanding. Unfortunately, significant time pressure means that curricula often do get covered instead of revealed. We will discuss this matter further in Chapter 6.

third grade. That change reduced local schools' control over their curricula. The statewide assessment is often thought of as a "one-size-fits-all" process because it demands a uniform statewide curriculum if students are to be successful on the tests.

Curriculum and Standardized Assessment

Sometimes, do local schools' curricula suffer as a result of the inflexibility imposed by standardized assessment? Consider this story of a project in an elementary school where the teachers and administrators had the idea and the funding to build a pond on the school property.

Several years ago, an elementary school in a northeastern suburb began an initiative to build a pond on its school property. The pond would attract birds and insects, the teachers and administrators thought, and they could build an elementary science curriculum around it. They had the pond installed and "seeded" it with a few small koi (similar to goldfish) and water plants.

Grade-level classes took responsibility for monitoring the temperature and turbidity of the pond as well as carefully noticing the life in and around it. The science curriculum in that school grew, with exploration of the properties of the pond being the centerpiece.

CURRICULUM AS WINDOW AND MIRROR

Ideally, curriculum should be both a window and a mirror. This metaphor, suggested by Emily Style in a 1996 essay (http://www.wcwonline.org/seed/curriculum.html), implies that:

1. Curriculum must provide windows for students into the worlds of others. That is, it should help students learn about other people, other cultures, other realities.
2. Curriculum must also offer mirrors of students' own reality. It should be connected to their lives in ways that help them see the subject matter as meaningful.

I am reminded of how I felt growing up in an inner-city environment and reading *Dick and Jane* basal readers. You are probably

Q: *Do you think a curriculum can be both innovative and standards-based?*

familiar with *basal readers*, which are textbooks used to teach reading. The *McGuffey Readers* are an early example; *The Alice and Jerry Books* are another. Typically, basal readers are published as a series of books, with each book in the series designed for a particular reading level. Dick and Jane were the main characters in basal readers used to teach reading from the 1930s to the 1970s. Figure 4.2 shows a typical page from a basal reader.

Dick and Jane lived in their own house with a white picket fence and a lawn sprinkler. They had a cute dog and a little red wagon. There is nothing wrong with those things, of course, but I used to ask my mother, "Where do Dick and Jane live?" I did not recognize the surroundings, and I wondered where they could be found. Certainly the private house and lawn sprinkler were not found on my block!

For me, the reading curriculum that relied on *Dick and Jane* may have been a window, but it was not at all

FIGURE 4.2

A Page from a Basal Reader

Alice and Jerry

© Mabel O'Donnel/HarperCollins Publishers. Reproduced with permission of HarperCollins.

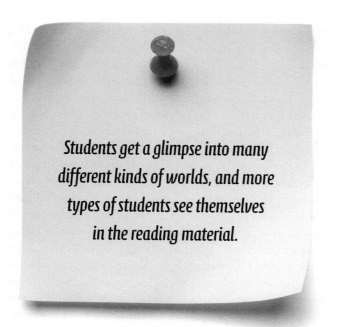

Students get a glimpse into many different kinds of worlds, and more types of students see themselves in the reading material.

a mirror. Many students in other areas of the United States had similar experiences with basal readers. The use of basal readers waned during the 1980s and 1990s because their stories and images did not reflect the diversity of students in classrooms across the country. Basal readers were also thought to be less authentic than other forms of writing, such as regular children's literature. Many states and local districts opted for authentic early-childhood literature as a way to teach reading.

In many places today, schools use basal readers *and* authentic children's literature, offering students a language arts curriculum that includes both formats. Often, local district committees select the required literature for each grade level, and this, in conjunction with a basal reader, forms the backbone of the language arts curriculum. Many of the newer basal readers include some combination of nonfiction, biographies, adaptations of original children's books, condensations of classic children's literature, and original stories. They also feature students of many origins, not only Caucasians.

In this way, the typical language arts curriculum has evolved to function better as both a window and a mirror. Students get a glimpse into many different kinds of worlds, and more types of students see themselves in the reading material.

ADAPTING THE CURRICULUM TO YOUR STUDENTS

assessment Collecting information to determine the progress of students' learning.

One implication of what we have been saying is that you should evaluate the curriculum in light of who your students are. When presented with a curriculum in a subject area, ask yourself, "How can I make this curriculum more relevant to the students in this classroom at this time in their lives?" If we think of learning as a process of re-forming mental schemes, then teachers need to begin to understand their students' mental schemes in order to be successful.

This is a challenging task. One way to accomplish it is to pay careful attention to the experiences of your students. Through discussion and writing assignments, you can invite the students' authentic selves into the classroom and learn much more about them. Table 4.2 lists some questions that can help you explore the world of your students.

LO5 Assessment: How Do We Know What They Know?

Closely linked to curriculum and instruction is **assessment**, the process of collecting information to find out what students are learning. As teachers, we are always asking, "What do my students know? How are they able to demonstrate that knowledge?"

Evidence of student learning, like learning itself, is complex and takes many forms. You are probably

TABLE 4.2	Questions to Ask about Your Students
Who are my students?
What are their interests, concerns, hobbies, beliefs, and feelings about themselves and others?
Where do they live? Do they have siblings? Do they have both parents at home? Do both parents work outside the home? What do the students do after school?
How can I adapt the formal curriculum to the experiences that the students encounter every day? How can I provide students with a mirror so they will understand that their lives are part of the school curriculum?

embedded assessments Classroom-based assessments that make use of the actual assignments that students are given as a unit is being taught. These can be used to evaluate developmental stages of student learning.

authentic (performance) assessment An assessment that asks students to perform a task relating what they have learned to some real-world problem or example.

accustomed to traditional assessments, such as paper-and-pencil tests with multiple-choice, true/false, fill-in-the-blank, and essay questions, used to evaluate students' understanding of the subject matter being taught. Typically, except for the essay questions, these tests are thought of as a measure of what students can recall at the moment, not necessarily what they have incorporated into an existing or new mental scheme.

Many students think of assessments as tests of this traditional type, given at the end of a unit. However, the more we understand about how people learn, the more we realize that an assessment is like a good instructional task and should be part of every lesson, providing feedback to both the teacher and the students about how the students are developing their understanding of the concepts in a unit. Assessments of this type are often called **embedded assessments**.

Many of the questions in the "Writing & Reflection" sections of this text are examples of embedded assessments. These questions are tools for reflection on the current instruction, as you are reading the text. Embedded assessments feel like a natural part of the instruction, so you may not be aware you are being assessed!

When we ask students to maintain a journal, write a research report, engage in a debate, design a project, or write an essay explaining a phenomenon, we are using embedded assessments. When these assessments relate directly to tasks or examples in the "real world" outside the classroom, they are also thought of as **authentic assessments**. Activities of this type ask students to perform tasks

through which they can express their own ideas. You can see how different these are from tests in which students check true or false, circle a correct choice, or guess at a word for a fill-in question, relying on their recall abilities instead of demonstrating understanding.

Authentic assessment often involves some kind of student *performance*; hence, this type of assessment is also called *performance assessment*. One type of performance assessment was pioneered by a group of scholars at Harvard University's Graduate School of Education. In an effort called Project Zero, the educators and psychologists were interested in teaching for understanding and in designing assessment tasks called *understanding performances* or *performances of understanding* (Perkins, 1993). Understanding performances are activities that require students to use what they know in new ways or in ways that build their understanding of unit topics. In these performances, students publicly demonstrate their understanding by reshaping, expanding on, extrapolating from, and applying what they already know. See the sidebar for examples of understanding performances.

Your teaching portfolio is another example of an authentic or performance assessment. The "Building Your Portfolio" card in the back of the book guides you in developing your portfolio, using the information you are exploring in your course and in this text to present concepts and challenges that represent your view of teaching and learning. The portfolio reflects the

Q: *How did your teachers grade you in school?*

A student makes a presentation to her class, demonstrating her understanding of a particular topic. Then classmates ask questions.

© moodboard/Photolibrary

Your teaching portfolio is an example of an authentic or performance assessment.

rubrics specify the level of performance expected for several levels of quality. These levels of quality may be written as ratings (for example, Excellent, Good, Needs Improvement) or as numerical scores (such as 4, 3, 2, 1). Numerical scores can be added up to form a total score, which is then associated with a grade (A, B, C, and so forth).

Imagine you are assessing student understanding of two sides of a contentious issue, such as the trial of Dr. Jack Kevorkian, who was found guilty of assisting people in committing suicide. (This lesson is described in Chapter 6.) You decide to engage the students in a high school history class in a debate on the issue. Table 4.3 shows a rubric you might use. Notice that there are specific ways to describe student effectiveness and achievement. The highest score a student can achieve on this rubric is 24, indicating that she or he scored a 4 for each category described.

sense-making in which you are engaged as you prepare to teach, and it also contains examples of plans and projects that you create for your students as you practice teaching in the schools.

Because of the open-ended nature of authentic assessments and performance-based assessments, guidelines for evaluating the final performance are important. These guidelines take the form of a checklist or rubric. A **rubric** defines the expected qualities of student performance and establishes a rating scale. Generally,

TWO EXAMPLES OF UNDERSTANDING PERFORMANCES

For a social studies unit with the understanding goal "Students will understand that history is always told from a particular perspective and that understanding a historical text means understanding who wrote it":

Students compare two accounts of the beginning of the Revolutionary War, one claiming the British fired the first shot and one claiming the colonists did. They then discuss why the two reports might be different and how they could find out what really happened. They use some of these strategies to figure out which (if either) of these accounts is the more plausible; then they present their explanation to the class.

For a mathematics unit with the understanding goals "Students will understand how percentages can be used to describe real-world happenings" and "Students will understand how to represent numerical information in clear graphs":

In small groups, students collect and compile data about school attendance over the course of two weeks. They calculate the percentage of students who fit various categories (percentage of students absent, percentage present, percentage tardy, and so on). They then create graphs to represent their data visually, collect feedback from the class, and revise their graphs in accordance with the feedback.

SOURCE: From Tina Blythe and Associates, *The Teaching for Understanding Guide*, Copyright ©1998 by Jossey-Bass, San Francisco.

TABLE 4.3	A Sample Rubric for a High School Class Debate			
	Score			
Category	**4**	**3**	**2**	**1**
Understanding of topic	The team clearly understood the topic in depth and presented its information forcefully and convincingly.	The team clearly understood the topic in depth and presented its information with ease.	The team seemed to understand the main points of the topic and presented those with ease.	The team did not show an adequate understanding of the topic.
Presentation style	The team consistently used gestures, eye contact, tone of voice, and a level of enthusiasm in a way that kept the attention of the audience.	The team usually used gestures, eye contact, tone of voice, and a level of enthusiasm in a way that kept the attention of the audience.	The team sometimes used gestures, eye contact, tone of voice, and a level of enthusiasm in a way that kept the attention of the audience.	One or more members of the team had a presentation style that did not keep the attention of the audience.
Information	All information presented in the debate was clear, accurate, and thorough.	Most information presented in the debate was clear, accurate, and thorough.	Most information presented in the debate was clear and accurate, but usually was not thorough.	The information had several inaccuracies or was usually not clear.
Organization	All arguments were clearly tied to an idea (premise) and organized in a tight, logical fashion.	Most arguments were clearly tied to an idea (premise) and organized in a tight, logical fashion.	All arguments were clearly tied to an idea (premise), but the organization was sometimes not clear or logical.	The arguments were not clearly tied to an idea (premise).
Rebuttal	All counterarguments were accurate, relevant, and strong.	Most counter-arguments were accurate, relevant, and strong.	Most counter-arguments were accurate and relevant, but several were weak.	The counterarguments were not accurate and/or relevant.
Use of facts/ statistics	Every major point was well supported with several relevant facts, statistics, and/or examples.	Every major point was adequately supported with relevant facts, statistics, and/or examples.	Every major point was supported with facts, statistics, and/or examples, but the relevance of some was questionable.	Not every point was supported.

SOURCE: Developed with RubiStar, a free online rubric tool at http://rubistar.4teachers.org/. Reprinted by permission of Advanced Learning Technologies in Education Consortia.

Standardized Testing: A Challenge for Authentic Assessment

As we noted earlier, the No Child Left Behind Act mandates large-scale, standardized assessments in each state and requires that they address mathematics and language arts at varying grade levels. These are traditional-style assessments that may not have any particular relevance to the nature of the instruction in a given class in a specific school. Because of this, critics argue that the data gathered from these large-scale assessments are not that reliable. In any case, these tests tell you only a little of what you need to know about your students' learning. Good teaching requires that we seek multiple ways to find out what students know and are able to do in a given area of content.

Because standardized tests are given to broad populations of students, it is often difficult for test makers to consider the variations in students' geography and learning experiences. As a result, standardized tests, often criticized by educators because one size does not fit all, usually represent a small sample of what is important in a subject area. They also represent a single assessment experience, which can result in getting an incomplete measure of students' understanding.

Many educators fear that teachers "teach to the test." This is because in many schools and districts, raising test scores has become the most important indicator of school improvement. As a result, teachers and administrators feel enormous pressure to ensure that test scores go up. Some schools narrow and change the curriculum to match the test. Teachers teach only what is covered on the test. Methods of teaching conform to the multiple-choice format of the many standardized tests. Teaching more and more resembles testing (http://fairtest.org/). If however, the standardized test had many modalities and offered different types of assessment formats, matching instruction to the assessment would not be as problematic. Earlier in this chapter, you read the description of the beginnings of a pond curriculum for an elementary school in the northeast. If the standardized test did not address the science ideas behind freshwater ponds, it is doubtful that the students in that school would have that experience. This has serious implications for standardized curricula in all the subject areas. We will return to "teaching to the test" in Chapter 6.

LO6 Learning to Teach

There is often a disconnect between what we learn about teaching and what we are able to enact in an actual classroom. One reason is that teaching, like many other endeavors, requires practice. Another reason is that we need to examine our beliefs and become comfortable with ourselves as learners as we embark on becoming teachers.

There are no quick and easy ways to make the transition into teaching. But here are some ideas to keep in mind as you consider joining the profession:

- Be comfortable with yourself as a person and feel secure in who you are.
- Wherever possible, give students opportunities to express their own ideas and to be active thinkers.
- Interrogate your students about their thinking. That is, ask them where their ideas come from.
- Make connections between what you are teaching and the students' lived experiences.
- Gain an understanding *for yourself* of the material you will teach. Using that knowledge, construct activities and opportunities that lead students to engage with the materials *for themselves*.
- Preparation is a prerequisite for successful teaching!

Concluding Thoughts

Is your head spinning from all the theories, philosophies, and movements in American public education you have read about? If so, it is important to remember that your approach to teaching should never be "all or nothing." The boundaries between movements and learning theories can overlap and become blurred.

Understanding more about how people learn helps us know that exploring students' preconceived ideas is essential to planning for instruction. Your plan may borrow principles from learning theories other than constructivism. Naming your personal approach is less important than understanding that it is subject to revision as you grow and learn and enter classrooms in a more formal role. Your present style of teaching and learning is the result of all that came before you historically and all that you personally have experienced in school. Developing consciousness about the role of the teacher and the responsibilities you will have toward your students is important preparation for your future work.

By discussing pedagogy, curriculum, instruction, and assessment, this chapter has provided perspective on part of a big question that all teachers face: Who are my students, and how can I best teach them? In the next chapter, we will explore in detail the nature and diversity of today's students. We will examine demographic trends in the country and consider the ways your pedagogy may be informed by who your students are.

RESOURCES FOR FURTHER EXPLORATION

Online Resources

FairTest: The National Center for Fair and Open Testing
http://fairtest.org/
This grant-funded organization promotes fair, open, valid, and educationally beneficial evaluations of students, teachers, and schools.

Rubistar
http://rubistar.4teachers.org/
This website offers a free tool to help teachers construct rubrics for all types of performance assessments. You may edit the suggestions and create your own; however, the starting points provided here can produce quality rubrics.

Print Resources

John Bransford, Ann L. Brown, and Rodney Cocking (eds.), *How People Learn: Brain, Mind, Experience, and School* (Washington, D.C.: National Academy Press, 2003).
This is a good introduction to new research about the way the brain works—and the relevance of this research for teaching and learning.

Jacqueline Grennon Brooks, *Schooling for Life: Reclaiming the Essence of Learning* (Reston, VA: Association for Supervision and Curriculum Development, 2002).
Inspiring stories of teachers, students, and parents provide a vision of what authentically respectful and meaningful learning looks like.

Jacqueline Grennon Brooks and Martin Brooks, *In Search of Understanding: The Case for Constructivist Classrooms*, revised edition (Reston, VA: Association for Supervision and Curriculum Development, 1999).
If you liked what you heard from Jackie Grennon Brooks in this chapter, read this book, which is already a classic.

Suzanne Carothers, "Taking Teaching Seriously," in William Ayers (ed.), *To Become a Teacher: Making a Difference in Children's Lives* (New York: Teachers College Press, 1995).
In this essay, Suzanne Carothers captures the essence of the complexity of teaching.

John Dewey, *How We Think: A Restatement of the Relation of Reflective Thinking to the Educative Process* (Boston: Houghton Mifflin, 1998; originally published in 1933).
This classic work by the great progressive philosopher is still highly relevant today.

Sam M. Intrator and Megan Scribner (eds.), *Teaching with Fire: Poetry That Sustains the Courage to Teach* (San Francisco: Jossey-Bass, 2003).
Do you sometimes find poetry inspiring? Each poem in this collection is accompanied by a story from a teacher explaining how the poem provided encouragement and insight.

Eric Jensen, *Teaching with the Brain in Mind*, 2nd edition (Alexandria, VA: Association for Supervision and Curriculum Development, 2005).
This book provides a multidisciplinary approach to teaching and learning, using research about what happens in the brain when we learn.

Alfie Kohn, *Punished by Rewards: The Trouble with Gold Stars, incentive Plans, A's, Praise, and Other Bribes* (Boston: Houghton Mifflin, 1999).
Warning! Before reading this book, be prepared to suspend your beliefs about rewards and punishments and to learn the truth about how harmful incentives can be to students' full development.

Mel Levine, *A Mind at a Time* (New York: Simon & Schuster, 2002).
This important book, written by a pediatrician and an education expert, explains how each student is "wired" differently and that learning is an individual and unique experience for every child.

Barbara L. McCombs and Lynda Miller, *Learner-Centered Classroom Practices and Assessments: Maximizing Student Motivation, Learning, and Achievement* (Thousand Oaks, CA: Corwin Press, 2007).
This book offers a wide range of teaching and assessment strategies, including self-assessments and personal reflection devices.

REVIEW

HE DID

TEACH puts a multitude of study aids at your fingertips.
After reading the chapters, check out these resources for further help:

- **Chapter in Review cards**, found in the back of your book, include all learning outcomes with summaries, definitions, and review questions for each chapter.

- **Online printable flash cards** give you three additional ways to check your comprehension of key concepts.

Other great ways to help you study include **interactive games** and **online tutorial quizzes with feedback**.

You can find it all at **CourseMate**. Login at **login.cengagebrain.com**.

Here you are, considering a career in education in the second decade of a new millennium, one that has already brought a host of major events and transformations. Historians will have much to say about the years you are living through. The ways in which we communicate and access information are very different from just a decade ago. Because schools reflect society, we need to examine the ways schools and schooling have been transformed by the vast social, political, and technological changes that have accompanied this new century.

The following chapters look at phenomena like the enormous influx of immigrant families from various parts of the world, and the Internet and smart phone technology revolution that has blossomed into a way of life. Furthermore, the increased role of federal and state governments in setting standards to measure the performance of students and teachers has led to routine standardized testing with varied results. As you read, think about questions like these:

- What is the composition of the student body? In what ways does its great diversity pose both challenges and opportunities?
- What contemporary educational trends are visible in today's classrooms, and how has access to the Internet both enhanced and posed difficulties for education?
- In what ways has standards-based assessment affected the lives of teachers and students?

As you continue your journey toward becoming a teacher, I hope you will remember that "goodness of fit" remains an underlying principle of this text. Keep asking yourself: Am I selecting a career path for which I am uniquely well suited?

Part Outline

CHAPTER 5   Who Are Today's Students?

CHAPTER 6   Contemporary Trends and Pressing Issues in Education

CHAPTER 7   The Information Technology Revolution in the 21st Century

CHAPTER 8   Globalization and Education

CHAPTER 5

WHO ARE TODAY'S STUDENTS?

© moodboard/Corbis

> *A person's a person no matter how small . . .*
> —Theodor Geisel (a.k.a. Dr. Seuss),
> *Horton Hears a Who!* (1954)

This chapter looks at the students in contemporary U.S. schools—children between the ages of five and eighteen. As the quotation from Dr. Seuss indicates, our schoolchildren are important people; their education is vital not only to their own future but also to the future of our country.

You may be familiar with the Dr. Seuss books—the often silly, rhyming, outrageous stories that delight many children from preschool through graduation from high school. Often they have deep meaning. In a commentary on Dr. Seuss and his influence, A.O. Scott of the *New York Times* had the following to say:

> *Rather than describe the mental world of children, Seuss labored over his verses and sketches in the hopes of replicating it. His guiding insight was that some version of his words and stories was there to begin with, and that children, in discovering his work, would recognize in it what they already knew. (Scott, 2000)*

The significance of these comments is that the students we meet and greet in the classroom come to us with their own stories, backgrounds, and experiences. It is your task to learn about your students; what their lives are like; and what hobbies, interests, talents, and challenges they bring to the classroom. Respecting and understanding them as people with their own ideas and experiences is the first step toward becoming an effective educator. In this chapter, we address the nature of the learner, today, in the second decade of the 21st century.

LEARNING OUTCOMES

After reading this chapter, you should be thinking about the following ideas:

LO1 Your own elementary, middle, and high schools may have undergone a shift in student population and a major change in curriculum.

LO2 Today's classrooms may be multi-ethnic and multi-lingual.

LO3 Students arrive at the classroom door from a wide range of social, economic, and emotional contexts.

LO4 Teachers must recognize the importance of understanding their students' cultural experiences.

LO5 Students have a large variety of learning styles.

LO6 The mental image you have of yourself as a teacher is frequently based on your own experiences as a student.

LO7 Honoring the learner is the primary task of the teacher.

LO1 The Students: A Changing Landscape

Since the mid-1990s, student enrollment in American schools has mushroomed. In fact, when the estimated population of the country surpassed 300 million people in 2006, roughly one-quarter were children under the age of eighteen (Annie E. Casey Foundation, 2006a).

Total public school enrollment reached an earlier peak in 1971, when the youngest members of the baby boom generation[1] arrived in school (Fry, 2006). Enrollment then dropped off considerably in the 1970s, but it began to climb again in the late 1980s and early 1990s. By the second half of the 1990s, enrollment passed the 1971 mark, and the number of students in school has continued to rise. Between 1985 and 2005, enrollment in public elementary and secondary schools increased by more than one-fifth, and by 2010 public school

[1]*Baby boom generation* refers to those Americans born in the quarter-century following World War II, roughly from 1946 to 1964. Some experts use slightly different dates.

TABLE 5.1 American Public and Private School Enrollment

ENROLLMENT IN ELEMENTARY AND SECONDARY SCHOOLS, BY LEVEL AND CONTROL OF INSTITUTION: SELECTED YEARS, FALL 1970 THROUGH FALL 2009 (IN THOUSANDS)

Year	Total	Public			Private		
		Total	Grades Pre-K–8	Grades 9–12	Total	Grades Pre-K–8	Grades 9–12
1970	51,257	45,894	32,558	13,336	5,363	4,052	1,311
1980	46,208	40,877	27,647	13,231	5,331	3,992	1,339
1985	44,979	39,422	27,034	12,388	5,557	4,195	1,362
1990	46,864	41,217	29,878	11,338	5,648	4,514	1,134
1995	50,759	44,840	32,341	12,500	5,918	4,756	1,163
2000	53,373	47,204	33,688	13,515	6,169	4,906	1,264
2001	53,992	47,672	33,938	13,734	6,320	5,023	1,296
2002	54,403	48,183	34,116	14,067	6,220	4,915	1,306
2003	54,639	48,540	34,202	14,338	6,099	4,788	1,311
2004	54,882	48,795	34,179	14,617	6,087	4,756	1,331
2005	55,187	49,113	34,205	14,908	6,073	4,723	1,350
2006	55,394	49,299	34,221	15,078	6,095	4,711	1,384
2007	55,710	49,644	34,589	15,055	6,066	4,681	1,385
2008	55,879	49,825	34,903	14,922	6,054	4,681	1,372
2009	56,116	50,067	35,240	14,826	6,049	4,695	1,355

SOURCES: U.S. Department of Education (2009) and National Center for Education Statistics (2009).

enrollments are estimated to be more than fifty million students in grades pre-K–12 and more than six million students in pre-K–12 private schools, as shown in Table 5.1 (National Center for Education Statistics, 2009).

Clearly, the number of students in our schools has been rising rapidly. But who exactly are our students?

LO2 ETHNIC DIVERSITY

Our era of expanding school enrollment has been marked by a significant rise in minority students, driven mainly by an extraordinary influx of Hispanic[2] students, who account for more than 64 percent of the increase in student enrollment.

By 2010, 43 percent of public school students were considered to be part of a racial or ethnic minority group. The distribution of minority students in public schools differs across regions of the country, but minority enrollment grew in all regions between 1972 and 2007. In comparison, the number of white students decreased from 78 to 57 percent of public school enrollment during this same period (U.S. Department of Education, 2009).

Immigration accounts for a large part of the diversity among today's students. About one-fifth of youngsters under the age of eighteen are part of immigrant families. States with the highest percentage of immigrant families are New York, New Jersey, California, Texas, and Nevada—states that attract the largest number of Hispanic immigrants (Annie E. Casey Foundation, 2006b, 2007).

Although ethnic diversity is increasing overall, recent decades have seen a new rise in *de facto segregation*—that is, whites living in different neighborhoods than minorities. Neighborhoods that are primarily white naturally have a high concentration of white students in their schools, while neighborhoods that are predominantly minority have a high concentration of minority students in the schools. In some areas, this segregation has reduced the amount of diversity teachers encounter. One report has even found that most white students continue to attend schools populated primarily by other

---

[2]*Hispanic* refers to people whose origin is Spain or any of the Spanish-speaking countries of the Americas.

whites, and relatively few attend schools populated primarily by minorities (Fry, 2006).

As enrollment has expanded, so has the number of schools. About half of the students attending the newer schools are white, while the white enrollment in older schools has dropped. From 1993 to 1994 and 2002 to 2003, more than 65 percent of the increased enrollment in the older schools was accounted for by the rise in Latino[3] enrollment (Fry, 2006). From these statistics, we can see that most of the newer schools are being built in areas that are predominantly white, while the older school buildings are absorbing most of the Hispanic and other minority students.

LANGUAGE-MINORITY STUDENTS

Can you imagine going to school in a place where your own native language is not spoken? If your native language is English, that may seem inconceivable. However, for those of you who are reading these pages and who learned English as your second language, the challenge most likely was great and required understanding teachers and schools. Between 1979 and 2009, the number of school-age children (ages five to seventeen) who spoke a language other than English at home increased from 3.3 million to almost 11 million. In terms of percentages, that is a rise from 9 percent of school-age children to about 20 percent (projection from NCES, 2009).

Among children who speak a language other than English at home, Spanish is the language most frequently spoken. About three-quarters of students who receive special assistance to learn English speak Spanish. Yet hundreds of thousands of students come from homes where other languages are spoken. These include Chinese, Vietnamese, Russian, Arabic, and French Creole. Various reports emphasize that, for most of these *English-language learners* (sometimes called ELLs), success requires targeted and continuing intervention. As one report says,

Children who start school knowing little or no English can learn the basic skills of word recognition quickly—in about two years, if they are carefully taught. They need the same kind of reading instruction that works for native speakers, only more of it, and they need to be monitored carefully so they get help adapted to their language development needs as soon as they run into problems. (American Educational Research Association, 2004)

Did You Know?

By 2010, 43 percent of public school children were considered to be part of a racial or an ethnic minority group.

bilingual education
Educating English-language learners by teaching them at least part of the time in their native language.

Bilingual Education

There has been much debate over how best to boost the academic achievement of English-language learners. **Bilingual education** programs support students with limited English proficiency by teaching them at least part of the time in their native language. Since the early 1970s, these programs have taken many forms. Some teach academic subjects in the students' native language and also provide *English as a Second Language (ESL)* classes to help the students learn English. Other models, known as *two-way* or *dual-language* programs, teach fluency in both languages, so that a class of both language-minority and native English-speaking students becomes fluent in both languages. These approaches have several variations and tend to vary from school district to school

Non-native English-speaking students learn in both languages in bilingual classes.

© Elizabeth Crews

---

[3] *Latino* refers to people whose origin is the Latin American countries of Central and South America. The term is often used interchangeably with *Hispanic*.

district. Meanwhile, other programs *immerse* language-minority students in English-only classes without any native-language communication.

On a recent visit to an elementary school in Queens, New York, I encountered a large sign for parents that read, "We now have a dual-language program in Mandarin." I learned that 87 percent of the students in this K–5 school were from China and that those students who were native English speakers really wanted to learn Mandarin. Hence, the school began a dual-language immersion program with half of the instruction in Mandarin and the other half in English.

There are many other examples of schools that take pride in their bilingual programs. Yet, partly because of the large wave of Latino immigration during the past twenty-five years, the issue of bilingual education has become highly politicized. There are those who believe that only English should be spoken and taught in school. This has prompted some schools to adopt "English-only" programs in which language-minority students have no access to their native language in school. Criticizing this trend, many educators and linguists argue that valuing and honoring new immigrants' native languages enhances their self-esteem and their possibility for academic success.

In 2001, when the No Child Left Behind Act was adopted by Congress, all references to bilingual education as a pedagogical goal were absent. Instead of continuing to fund bilingual initiatives at the federal level, the law turned most of the responsibility over to the states in the form of block grants to assist the academic achievement of language-minority students. The way these state funds are allocated is highly variable.

> Learning something new requires that the learner redesign her or his mental schemes.

TEACHSOURCE VIDEO CASE

Bilingual Education in Fourth Grade

To see how a two-way language immersion program can function, find the TeachSource Video Case "Bilingual Education: An Elementary Two-Way Immersion Program" on the student website. As you begin watching the video, ask yourself if all the students are English-language learners. After watching the video, consider the following questions:

Would you have liked to be a student in this program? Why or why not?

Teaching English-Language Learners

You may well find yourself in a classroom with English-language learners, and it is important to use the most effective strategies to help your students grasp subject matter content while learning English. One current approach is called *Specially Designed Academic Instruction in English (SDAIE)*. Many established teachers have taken workshops devoted to this approach—one example of how being a teacher is a commitment to lifelong learning.

As we explored in Chapter 4, learning something new requires that the learner redesign her or his mental schemes. To do this, the student has to bring his or her existing knowledge into play. SDAIE pedagogy encourages this process by treating the English-language learner as a "knower," a student with lots of ideas that are temporarily inaccessible to the teacher because of the language barrier. Accessing the student's ideas involves teaching strategies like:

- Speaking clearly and at a slower pace
- Using gestures and facial expressions
- Using concrete materials and visuals
- Avoiding idiomatic expressions that are peculiar to English
- Engaging students in group work that is student centered (Kashen, 1994)
- Finding "language buddies" wherever possible—that is, pairing English-language learners with students who are more advanced in English but also fluent in the learner's native language

If you teach a class with both English-language learners and students who are already fluent in English, your task will be to plan for both populations in ways that enrich the environment. Imagine that two students are using a ruler for a lesson. The native English speaker says to the student who is new to this country,

"How do you say 'ruler' in your language?" By sharing in this way, they both become learners. The challenge is to engage all students in helping their classmates overcome barriers to learning.

RELIGIOUS DIVERSITY

As we saw in Chapter 3, religion has always played a large role in American life and American education. The Constitution of the United States guarantees religious freedom to all citizens, and we treasure that right. Yet, as was noted in Chapter 3, Americans are divided about how the principle of "separation of church and state" (a phrase coined by Thomas Jefferson) should apply to public schools.

These matters have taken on more urgency in the past few decades as new strains of religious diversity have arisen in the United States. Christians account for 78.4 percent of the American population, with Protestants accounting for 51.3 percent of that total (http://religions.pewforum.org/reports).

The total number of Americans who identified their religion as something other than Christian increased by more than 32 percent over the last two decades. Religions that barely registered in previous surveys, such as the Wiccan creed, now have a substantial number of adherents. Even the traditional affiliations of Protestant and Catholic contain many subgroups and differences.

With such diversity in the nation's religions, teachers have much to learn about the religious beliefs of their students. Religious beliefs bring with them various expectations for an individual's behavior, including observance of customs and traditions. Remember that culture and religion are linked. Understanding who your students are and the role that religion plays in their lives is significant in helping them to learn and in "honoring" their identities.

sexual orientation An enduring emotional, romantic, sexual, or affectional attraction that a person feels toward people of one or both sexes.

LGBT An acronym used to represent lesbian, gay, bisexual, and transgender individuals.

Q: *How does understanding the ways in which your own religious beliefs have influenced you help you to better serve your students?*

SEXUAL ORIENTATION

Like religion, language, and ethnicity, **sexual orientation** is an important component of a person's identity. Schools are often the places where teens develop social skills and begin to align with peer groups. For adolescents who do not identify as heterosexual in today's culture, this process of social acceptance and approval is fraught with danger and fear of rejection and even physical harm.

Categories applied to sexual orientation typically include heterosexual, homosexual (gay and lesbian), bisexual (sexual attraction toward both sexes), and transgender (having characteristics of the opposite sex). The acronym **LGBT** is sometimes used to refer to lesbian, gay, bisexual, and transgender people as a group. Because sexual orientations are often hidden from view, LGBT individuals are often thought of as the invisible minority. In schools, fear often prevents these students from revealing their sexual identities; it is therefore very important that schools and classrooms provide safe havens for those of our students whose sexual orientation is not aligned with the majority.

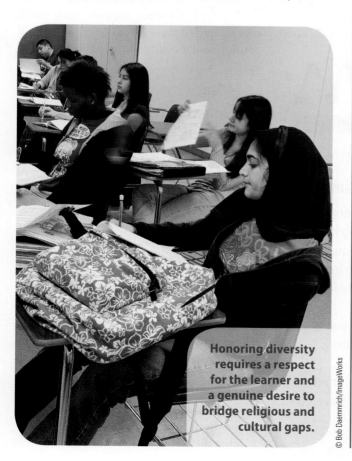

Honoring diversity requires a respect for the learner and a genuine desire to bridge religious and cultural gaps.

© Bob Daemmrich/ImageWorks

socioeconomic status (SES) A person's or family's status in society, usually based on a combination of income, occupation, and education. Though similar to social class, SES puts more emphasis on the way income affects status.

Attitudes about sexual orientation are a product of individual family biases and beliefs. Students bring these to school, and gay, lesbian, bisexual, and transgender youth often have to cope with prejudice and isolation. Lack of family support for these youngsters exacerbates the problem, and there is an enormous fear of stigmatization. These students are at greater risk than others for being harassed and bullied, experiencing depression, and attempting suicide.

How widespread are these problems? The 2007 National School Climate Survey (Kosciw, Diaz, & Greytak, 2008) collected information from more than 6,000 middle and high school students across the country and found that bullying and harassment on the basis of sexual orientation remain common in U.S. schools. Three-quarters of the students reported that they "frequently or often" heard terms like "faggot" and "dyke." Nearly nine-tenths of the students said they frequently or often heard expressions like "that's so gay" or "you're so gay." More than 86 percent of LGBT students said they had been verbally harassed at school in the past

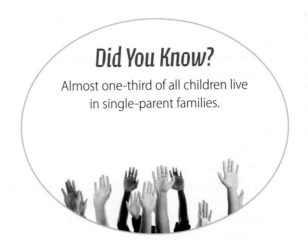

Did You Know?

Almost one-third of all children live in single-parent families.

year, and 44 percent reported physical harassment. In fact, more than 60 percent of the LGBT students surveyed said they felt unsafe at school due to their sexual orientation and another approximately 40 percent felt unsafe because of their gender expression.

Because all students deserve to work in an environment that is both friendly and supportive, student groups have emerged in high schools all over the country to combat LGBT bias and discrimination. These groups or clubs are often called GSAs, for Gay-Straight Alliances; they are student-run organizations that provide a safe place for students to meet, support each other, talk about issues related to their sexual orientation, and work toward ending homophobia.

WRITING & REFLECTION

Thinking about Your Own Beliefs and Biases

Understanding the nature of your own beliefs about people's sexual orientation is a first step toward understanding how you will interact with LGBT students. Reflect on the following questions:

- If you are not LBGT, in what ways, if any, have you been exposed to individuals whose sexual orientation is not heterosexual? What was that experience like for you?
- What do you think contributed to the development of your own attitudes and biases, if any, about people of different sexual orientations?
- As you seek to create a learning environment where all students have the opportunity to grow and learn, how will you deal with your own biases?

SOCIOECONOMIC DISPARITIES

Another way students differ from each other is in their **socioeconomic status (SES)**, a measure of their standard of living that relates to the family's income. According to recent census figures, more than one-fifth of young people under the age of eighteen live in poverty. Table 5.2 shows the official definition of poverty as related to family size. You may be surprised to see how much a family must earn to avoid being poor in the United States.

Here is another important, related statistic: Almost one-third of all children live in single-parent families (Annie E. Casey Foundation, 2009a). In most cases, obviously, one parent has less earning power than two parents do.

Socioeconomic status relates to the concept of *social capital* that we mentioned earlier in the book. The point is that the students you encounter will come from various socioeconomic backgrounds. The more social capital a child's family has, the greater his or her intellectual and cultural advantages. A child with higher socioeconomic status and more social capital usually performs better than a student with little or no social capital does.

TABLE 5.2	The Poverty Line: Annual Income Levels below Which a Family Is Considered Poor		
Persons in Family Unit	48 Contiguous States and D.C.	Alaska	Hawaii
1	$10,830	$13,530	$12,460
2	$14,570	$18,210	$16,760
3	$18,310	$22,890	$21,060
4	$22,050	$27,570	$25,360
5	$25,790	$32,250	$29,660
6	$29,530	$36,930	$33,960
7	$33,270	$41,610	$38,260
8	$37,010	$46,290	$42,560
For each additional person, add	$3,740	$4,680	$4,300

SOURCE: Data from *Federal Register*, Vol. 74, No. 14, January 23, 2009, pp. 4199–4201.

OVERLAPPING ATTRIBUTES: THE SOCIAL CONTEXT

The aspects of student diversity we have been considering are not isolated and independent. Often they overlap. Consider, for instance, what happens when poverty intersects with the need to learn a new language. The reality of many English-language learners is that they also represent our poorest children: They live in crowded housing environments where transportation and employment opportunities are limited and where schools are old and overcrowded. In fact, of all students who live in poverty, more than 28 percent are Latino (Aleman, 2006). Conditions of this sort cannot help but affect the students' achievement in school, putting many of these students at risk for educational failure. In the next section we will consider the term "at risk" and its full implications.

Many analysts express concern that educational policy too often ignores such individual social contexts. One criticism of the federal No Child Left Behind Act (2001), for example, is that the law's mandated standards and assessments pay little attention to ethnic- and language-minority students.

Differences do not mean deficits; they just mean differences from the norms in public education that were once thought to be white and middle class. The norms are shifting, and it is very important that we never think of students who are different in any way as lesser. As future teachers, the guiding question must be: How can I help each child feel successful in school?

LO3 Students Who Are at Risk

"National research has shown that children living in poor, tough neighborhoods are much more likely to drop out of school, become pregnant as teens, get in trouble with the law as juveniles, and live in poverty as adults, with their own children struggling to succeed. They are much more likely to go to prison and suffer from debilitating health conditions that further limit their ability to provide support for their children."
—Annie E. Casey Foundation (2001)

When we examine all the ways our students can differ from each other, we need to ask ourselves what combination of factors might hinder a child's becoming a successful student, graduating from high school, and pursuing further education or vocational training. The term **students at risk** came into widespread use after the 1983 national report *A Nation at Risk*, described in Chapter 3. This report warned that U.S. schools were becoming mediocre and that significant changes had to occur to keep the nation as a whole from declining.

Critics of this report noted that there was little mention of the role of poverty in the life of children. Many

dropout rate The percentage of students who fail to complete high school or earn an equivalency degree.

reacted to the report by citing glaring social inadequacies and saying that schools could not make up for these deficiencies. There was a "blame the victim" mentality, critics complained, in which students and parents were held to be the culprits. Indeed, schools cannot make up for many of the problems of poverty and degradation, but in turn educators must not blame their own inadequacies on the students. Both points are at work when we examine who is "at risk."

The precise definition of the term *student at risk* varies. Here are three samples:

- One who is in danger of failing to complete her or his education with an adequate level of skills (Slavin & Madden, 2006).
- One who is judged as not having the potential to participate in society in ways that are meaningful and purposeful for themselves or for society in general (McGuirk, 2001).
- [A student] judged to be in serious jeopardy of not completing school or not succeeding in school (Ryan & Cooper, 2007).

As two of these definitions suggest, failing to complete high school is a key problem. The **dropout rate** in the United States, though it has declined recently, is still around 9 percent, meaning that one out of every eleven U.S. students fails to get a high school diploma or an alternative credential U.S. Department of Education, National Center for Education Statistics (2009). (The dropout rate refers to the percentage of 16- through 24-year-olds who are not enrolled in school and have not earned a high school credential.) What puts a student at risk of dropping out or of not getting an adequate education? Social problems in our society make it difficult for even high-ability students to be successful. The greatest social risk factors include substance abuse, child abuse, poverty, homelessness, hunger, depression, and teen pregnancy. For teachers from stable homes and environments, it is often difficult to relate to these problems that affect the lives of some of America's students every day. Hence, it is essential to learn as much as possible about your students' lives.

To make the concept of risk more specific, a *family risk index* (Annie E. Casey Foundation, 2009b) identifies a "high-risk child" as one who lives in a family with four or more of these risk factors:

1. Child is not living with two parents.
2. Household head is a high school dropout.
3. Family income is below the poverty line.
4. Child is living with parent(s) who is (are) underemployed.
5. Family is receiving welfare benefits.
6. Child does not have health insurance.

Further statistics about risk factors come from the National Youth Risk Behavior Survey (YRBS), which monitors behaviors that contribute to death, disability, and social problems among youth and adults in the United States. Conducted every two years during the spring semester, the YRBS provides data representative of ninth- through twelfth-grade students in public and private schools throughout the United States. Factors that have been worrying educators and parents for several decades include drugs, sex, and violence. Recent surveys indicate that the percentage of students in grades 9 through 12 who have seriously considered suicide in the course of one year has gone down from more than 17 percent in 2005 to less than 15 percent in 2009. Rates for having sexual intercourse have remained

STRATEGIES FOR REDUCING HIGH SCHOOL DROPOUT RATES

- Adopt a long-term approach that begins with strengthening school readiness.
- Enhance the holding power of schools, with an intensive focus on ninth grade.
- Focus on the forces outside of school that contribute to dropping out.
- Address the needs of those groups at highest risk of dropping out.
- Build on the skills and understanding of the adults who affect teens' motivation and ability to stay in school.

SOURCE: Adapted from Annie E. Casey Foundation. (2009). *Kids Count Indicator Brief: Reducing the High School Dropout Rate.* Baltimore, MD: Author. Reprinted by permission of the Annie E. Casey Foundation.

steady at about 47 percent of ninth to twelfth graders. For the same group of students, alcohol use remains at 44 percent; marijuana use at 38 percent, and cocaine use at 8 percent of the student population. The percentage of students in this group who have been engaged in a physical fight on school grounds has remained the same at 12 percent (CDC, 2010).

The U.S. teen pregnancy rate has gone down in recent years, but it remains the highest of any industrialized nation in the world. For young women, teen pregnancy is the major contributor to high school dropout rates. Substance abuse is a serious problem that crosses all socioeconomic classes. The importance of sex education and drug abuse counseling programs in the schools cannot be overstated. Internet chat rooms, social networking sites, and informative websites have given teens better access to information on safe sex and the dangers of substance abuse. This has contributed to lowering the rate of teen pregnancy. Teachers and students can explore useful websites together.

Recent studies have outlined several broad approaches for reducing high school dropout rates for all teens. These reports call for prevention strategies that address community and school collaborations. The recommendations are summarized in the sidebar "Strategies for Reducing High School Dropout Rates."

In this light, think about the ways in which a high school could focus on students at risk and help them to succeed.

Chana High School is a small "continuation" school in Auburn, California. A continuation school is designed to meet the needs of young adult students who were not successful in completing traditional high school; it has an enrollment of 250. In 2009, all of the students passed the California state exit exam, enabling them to earn a high school diploma. On its website (http://www.puhsd.k12.ca.us/chana/), Chana Continuation High School states that it is committed to developing

Q: *Do you identify with any of the risk factors that could lead to* dropping out*?*

individuals who value themselves, others, and the environment, and who possess the skills necessary to succeed in a changing world (2010). The school has a wealth of services to support these youngsters, including teen parenting classes, substance abuse counseling, anger management intervention, and mental health counseling. The dedicated teachers at Chana work diligently to bolster students' academic achievement while also supporting them emotionally. The school offers five vocational programs funded by the state (including computer technology and electronics), and partnerships with technical colleges and local community colleges allow the students to earn college credit while completing their high school work.

LO4 Contemporary Issues Relating to Student Diversity

As you might guess, the increasing diversity of American students has led to controversy about educational priorities. In this section, we focus on three areas that have provoked much recent discussion: multicultural education, gender-fair education, and the role of religion in the schools.

© Chris Schmidt/iStockphoto

multicultural education Education that aims to create equal opportunities for students from diverse racial, ethnic, social class, and cultural groups.

culturally relevant pedagogy Teaching practices that place the culture of the learner at the center of instruction. Cultural referents become aspects of the formal curriculum.

MULTICULTURAL EDUCATION

You may be feeling dizzy from all the data and statistics you have read in this chapter. Why are these details about students important? As we seek to become better teachers, we must understand the origins of our students and the ways their needs can be met in the classroom. If you are not of the same culture, race, ethnicity, or social class as your students, you should make a special effort to understand their needs. You can also turn the diversity of your students into an advantage—an opportunity to share identities and cultures as you create community in your classroom. It is a way to broaden our understanding of the human condition and reminds us that the informal curriculum can be both window and mirror!

If you pursue a career in teaching, you will hear a lot about **multicultural education**, a broad term for many approaches that recognize and celebrate the variety of cultures and ethnic backgrounds found in U.S. schools. Students from groups that have traditionally been underrepresented in the school population—ethnic and racial minorities—have also been understudied. That is, until recently, most educators have not focused on what

these students need to succeed in school. We now realize that these students will not be served well and will even become marginalized unless we seek answers to complex questions like the following:

- Whose stories are told in the classroom?
- How do we build community in a diverse setting?
- What is the role of identity formation in our work?
- What can we learn by hearing the stories of those from traditionally marginalized groups? (Nelson & Wilson, 1998, p. xi)

Diverse learning environments, ones in which students from several racial and ethnic backgrounds come together, offer a wonderful gift. To use Emily Style's metaphor mentioned earlier in the book, diverse learning environments provide "windows" into the worlds of people other than ourselves and create rich experiences for both students and teachers. As a result of these experiences, teachers are encouraged to develop culturally responsive teaching practices, also referred to as **culturally relevant pedagogy**. These teaching practices have several important attributes:

- They use cultural referents—from all the cultures represented in the classroom—to develop students' knowledge, skills, and attitudes.
- They honor the students' life stories and belief systems and find ways to incorporate them into the curriculum and learning context.
- They create classroom community by granting voice and legitimacy to the experiences of students from diverse backgrounds.
  - They encourage all students to achieve academically by acknowledging the students' personal and cultural identities.

As an example of culturally relevant pedagogy, consider a unit in an eighth-grade math classroom in an urban area in the northeast. Ms. Petersen is in an old, overcrowded school building in an urban area. Ms. P. is exploring geometry with a diverse class of students. The topic centers on the different types of symmetry that may be found in shapes using several patterns. About one-third of her students are Latino, and the rest are of many racial and ethnic origins.

This unit in geometry considers what happens to shapes when they are moved through space. Ms. Petersen has examined

A diverse student body provides the opportunity to learn about other ways of being in the world.

© Elizabeth Crews

the basic concepts in many ways with her class, emphasizing that symmetry may be found in patterns in everyday life and having the students create symmetrical patterns with more than one shape. For instance, she brought in men's ties with many patterns on them and asked students to decide what type of symmetry each pattern represented. She then invited them to explore their native countries' flags. The classroom has three networked computers that students used to print pictures of their flags. The flag designs were examined for geometric shapes and symmetry (see Figure 5.1). It was a lesson that engaged all the students.

After the students had experience with several types of symmetry, Ms. Petersen posed a challenge. In groups of two, the students were to design and create a classroom flag incorporating their room number. The flag had to be in the shape of a rectangle, include two types of symmetry, and appropriately represent the students in the classroom. Students were excited about designing patterns, and they selected the colors from the flags of their various countries of origin to represent themselves. Colors from the flags of Colombia, El Salvador, Mexico, Puerto Rico, Guatemala, South Korea, and the United States adorned the design of Room 303's classroom flags.

Q: *How does it help students to learn when you connect to their lived experience?*

What do you think of Ms. Petersen's lesson? Can you imagine how excited the students were that their countries' flags were part of their study of mathematics? The concepts of rotation, reflection, and translation are quite complex in geometry, but by using materials her students could relate to, Ms. Petersen engaged them in a personal way.

We know from research in cognitive science, as reflected by the interview with Dr. Brooks in Chapter 4, that learning occurs best when students are fully invested in the process—when they can interact with the materials, "play" with them, explore and reexamine the concepts, and then individually make those concepts their own. You can see how culturally relevant pedagogy helps make this possible.

EDUCATING GIRLS AND BOYS: SEPARATE OR TOGETHER?

You may recall from Chapter 3 that Title IX, part of the Education Amendments of 1972, prohibits discrimination on the basis of sex in any federally funded education program or activity. That law might seem to discourage single-sex schooling—the practice of educating girls in separate schools from boys—on the grounds

FIGURE 5.1

What Types of Symmetry Are Revealed in These Flags?

Your teaching should incorporate **culturally relevant pedagogy**

Flag of Mexico

Flag of Puerto Rico

Flag of South Korea

Flag of El Salvador

Flag of Guatemala

Flag of Colombia

Photo: © Iuliya Sunagatova/iStockphoto

that separate is inherently unequal. In 2006, however, the U.S. Education Department officially ruled that Title IX does not make single-sex schooling discriminatory as long as it is voluntary and takes place in an environment that also includes comparable coeducational schools and classes. As a result, single-sex schooling is expected to become more prevalent in public schools and public-supported charter schools.

One model for quality single-sex schooling exists in a high-minority area of New York City—the Young Women's Leadership School of East Harlem sent all of its 2006 graduating class to college. Yet there is much debate about single-sex schooling. In the past, all-female schools were typically private schools for the wealthy, and their principles included giving females leadership roles and creating opportunities for them to excel. Many educators feel that if a gender-fair curriculum were commonplace—if it highlighted the lives and accomplishments of women as well as men and used teaching strategies that gave voice to female students as well as to males—the advantages of all-girl environments could be accessible in coeducational environments. That is, females would not need to be separate if indeed they were treated equitably.

Because more single-sex schools will now be available to children from lower socioeconomic classes, many applaud the Department of Education's ruling. Advocates for single-sex schooling argue that girls in these separate schools will have opportunities for leadership and verbal expression often squelched in coeducational environments. Others worry, however, that single-sex environments may promote stereotyping and discrimination. In fact, many advocates for girls and young women believe that same-sex schools for females will be less authentically rigorous.

These are complex problems, at the intersection of gender, race, ethnicity, and social class. Overall, the movement for multicultural education also advocates **gender-fair education**, encouraging teachers to address the needs of females and males in their classrooms in ways that help both genders realize their full

potential. With this concept in mind, consider the following story from Ms. Logan's sixth-grade classroom in an urban area in California.

The students are closing their eyes and thinking back to their earliest memories. Ms. Logan says, "To begin, step out of your body and see yourself at your desk with your head down. Now, travel back in time until you are in fourth grade, then third grade. What are you wearing? Who is your teacher? What are you doing? See yourself at home. What does your room look like? Who are your friends? What do you do after school? Now, see yourself as a kindergartner; see how you are playing. What do you love to do? Travel back again until you are a baby. Look around your room. Notice things around you. Now travel back again and here you are—ready to be born! Everyone is so excited, so happy, waiting for your birth. But this time, imagine you are born as the opposite sex.

"Hence, if you are boy, pretend you are born a girl. If you are a girl, pretend you are born a boy. See yourself as a baby, coming home, learning to walk, starting school, attending elementary school. Look at your room and your friends and your activities. Without talking to anybody, create a list of how your life seems different since you were born a person of the opposite sex."

Ms. Logan really likes this activity because, as the students reveal their beliefs about their lives as a member of the opposite sex, they confront stereotypes. Ultimately they learn that they are really more similar to their classmates of the opposite sex than they are different. As students respond to this exercise, they find they hold various misconceptions: for example, about the paint colors girls or boys would have in their rooms, or how they would have to behave if they were of the opposite sex. The discussion gives students a chance to see the ways they are similar, dispelling stereotypes. *(Reprinted by permission of Kodansha America, Inc. Excerpted from* Teaching Stories *by Judy Logan, published by Kodansha America, Inc. [1999].)*

In Ms. Logan's class, boys said that if they were female, they would have to get up extra early to fix their hair. A few of the girls objected to that remark and pointed out that they never get up early to fuss over their hair. Girls felt that if they were male, they would be able to stay out later—only to learn that the boys in their class also had curfews. Some boys insisted that they would do better in writing if they were female, but

Did You Know?

Title IX prohibits discrimination on the basis of sex in any federally funded education program but does not make voluntary single-sex schooling discriminatory.

other boys argued that they were good writers. In the end, these middle school girls and boys agreed that they both loved sports and a lot of different subjects, and that they were probably more the same than different; however, it was clear that the boys had more personal freedom and privileges than the girls.

Q: *Do you remember being* *treated differently* in *school because of your gender?*

It's important to remember that treating students *equitably* is not the same as treating them *equally*. **Equity** stands for being fair and just. Because students come from such diverse experiences, identities, and backgrounds, you cannot be fair by treating everyone in exactly the same way. To ensure equality in the learning goals we hope to achieve for each student, we need to notice the differences among our students and use strategies to help each student reach maximum success in the classroom. In a science class, equity may mean asking yourself how to encourage more females' interest. One of the many ways may be to post pictures of female as well as male scientists. In a language arts classroom, equity may mean asking yourself how to engage the boys in more reading experiences. One way may be to integrate action heroes into the literature. In each case, the tacit message is: We are here to support all our students, and we will work to counter any stereotyping and biases in the classroom.

RELIGION AND SCHOOLS

In 1995, President Bill Clinton sent material containing guidelines on student religious expression to every school district in the United States. The letter accompanying these guidelines declared:

> *Nothing in the First Amendment converts our public schools into religion-free zones, or requires all religious expression to be left behind at the schoolhouse door. While the government may not use schools to coerce the consciences of our students, or to convey official endorsement of religion, the public schools also may not discriminate against private religious expression during the school day.... Religion is too important in our history and our heritage for us to keep it out of our schools.... [I]t shouldn't be demanded, but as long as it is not sponsored by school officials and doesn't interfere with other children's rights, it mustn't be denied.*

That message seems clear enough. Yet issues concerning religion and the schools continue to cause controversy. If you did the Learning Project on separation of church and state in Chapter 3, you discovered how many arguments there have been regarding prayer, Bible readings, religious displays on school property, and similar matters. Many people want schools to promote religious values more openly, or at least allow students to do so; others, just as vehemently, demand that schools keep strictly out of religious affairs.

One conflict about religious beliefs and the school curriculum involves the teaching of evolution in science classes. A landmark court case (*Tammy Kitzmiller, et al. v. Dover Area School District, et al.*) occurred in the town of Dover, Pennsylvania, where the school board insisted that students be required to hear a statement about intelligent design before ninth-grade biology lessons on evolution. (Proponents of intelligent design believe that the diversity of living things can be explained as the work of a designing intelligence; they do not insist on calling that intelligence God.) The statement

equity The act of treating individuals and groups fairly and justly, free from bias or favoritism. Gender equity means the state of being fair and just toward both males and females, to show preference to neither and concern for both.

© Zurijeta/iStockphoto

read to students said that Darwin's theory is "not a fact" and has inexplicable "gaps." Science teachers objected that science class is not the domain to discuss the presence of an all-powerful being, and some parents brought the case to federal court.

In his ruling in December 2005, Judge John E. Jones asserted that the school board's requirement was unconstitutional. The judge said: "We find that the secular purposes claimed by the board amount to a pretext for the board's real purpose, which was to promote religion in the public school classroom." He said that the policy "singles out the theory of evolution for special treatment, misrepresents its status in the scientific community, causes students to doubt its validity without scientific justification," and "presents students with a religious alternative masquerading as a scientific theory." Hence, he concluded, it was unconstitutional to teach intelligent design as an alternative to evolution in a public school science classroom.

In another recent case in a New Jersey public high school, an eleventh-grade history teacher told his students that evolution and the "Big Bang" theory of the universe's origin were not scientific, that dinosaurs were aboard Noah's Ark, and that only Christians had a place in heaven. The teacher was audiotaped by a student, and the student's family is now considering a lawsuit on the grounds that the teacher promoted religious views in a public school history classroom. The incident has divided and shocked this New Jersey community (Kelley, 2006).

In the midst of such controversies, teachers often receive conflicting messages about what they can and cannot teach regarding religion. The best understanding is to recognize that you cannot teach religion in public schools. Similarly, you *cannot* encourage or participate in student religious activity. However, you can teach *about* religion and can honor the privacy of religious ritual as long as it does not interfere with the functioning of the school or classroom and it is not forced on any other student. The following statement, posted on the website of the First Amendment Center (http://www.firstamendmentcenter.org/), was agreed on by a broad range of religious and educational groups:

Public schools may not inculcate nor inhibit religion. They must be places where religion and religious conviction are treated with fairness and respect. Public schools uphold the First Amendment when they protect the religious liberty rights of students of all faiths and none. Schools demonstrate fairness when they ensure that the curriculum includes study about religion, where appropriate, as an important part of a complete education.

LO5 Multiple Intelligences: What Does It Mean to Be "Smart"?

This section deals with another type of diversity: the variation in intelligence—or perhaps a better way of expressing it, *intelligences*. Until the 1980s, psychologists believed—and many still believe—that intelligence is a fixed and measurable attribute, calculated by an IQ test. Now, though, most experts, drawing on the work of psychologist and neuroscientist Howard Gardner, accept the **theory of multiple intelligences**. That is, instead of having a fixed, single intelligence, each of us is intelligent in several different ways.

From the research of Gardner and others, we now know that babies are born with many capacities. Their intelligences evolve and are expressed in multiple ways. These different ways, or different intelligences, may be more or less dominant in a particular individual. Each individual usually expresses several intelligences, to different degrees. At the beginning of his work, Gardner posited a total of seven intelligences. Later he added an eighth and a ninth, and he has proposed that other types of intelligence may also exist (Gardner, 1993, 2003, 2006). Table 5.3 describes the nine types that he considers definite and two that are tentative.

© Aldo Murillo/iStockphoto

TABLE 5.3	The Multiple Intelligences Proposed by Howard Gardner	
Intelligence	**Explanation**	**Examples of People Who Display This Intelligence**
Linguistic intelligence ("word smart")	Ability to use and manipulate languages	Poets, writers, lawyers, public speakers
Logical-mathematical intelligence ("math/science smart")	Capacity to analyze problems, think logically, and carry out mathematical operations	Mathematicians, scientists
Musical intelligence ("music smart")	Ability to recognize and appreciate musical patterns, pitch, rhythm, and timbre; skill in performing and perhaps composing music	Musicians, composers
Bodily-kinesthetic intelligence ("body smart")	Ability to move one's body and its various parts in a coordinated way and to handle objects skillfully; capacity to use the body to create a performance or solve a problem	Athletes, dancers
Spatial intelligence ("art smart")	Ability to recognize patterns and relationships in physical space and manipulate them mentally	Architects, surgeons, artists
Interpersonal intelligence ("people smart")	Capacity to understand other people's moods, intentions, motivations, and desires	Educators, salespeople, counselors, religious and political leaders
Intrapersonal intelligence ("self smart")	Capacity to understand your own feelings, motivations, strengths, weaknesses	People who are good at regulating their own lives
Naturalist intelligence ("nature smart")	Sensitivity to the natural world; ability to make distinctions among and classify features of plants, animals, and other aspects of the environment	Ecologists, botanists, zoologists
Existential intelligence	Concern with ultimate issues, such as philosophical beliefs about life and death; related to spiritual intelligence	Philosophers and religious leaders
Spiritual intelligence (tentative)*	Capacity to explore the nature of existence in all of its manifestations	Religious leaders
Moral intelligence (tentative)*	Concern with rules, behaviors, and attitudes that govern the sanctity of life; connected to spiritual and existential intelligence	May be present with the other intelligences

*The data for the existence of spiritual and moral intelligence are controversial, and often these are not thought of as separate intelligences

SOURCE: Based on Gardner (2003).

Basketball: © Geoff Black/iStockphoto; Saxophone: © Itzaokas Sapiro/iStockphoto; Paintbox: © Winterling/iStockphoto; Leaf: © Jill Kyle/iStockphoto

intelligence profile An individual's unique combination of relative strengths and weaknesses among all the different intelligences.

According to Gardner, each individual has all of the intelligences, but no two human beings have the same profiles of intelligence. In other words, we all have these different intelligences in differing strengths and capacities for expression. Each learner's **intelligence profile** consists of a combination of relative strengths and weaknesses among the different intelligences. Moreover, intelligences are not isolated; they interact with one another in an individual to yield many types of outcomes (Moran, Kornhaber, & Gardner, 2006).

Gardner's argument leaves educators with an important mission: finding out how to access all the types of intelligences so that all students can learn to their maximum potential. It is clear that schools traditionally have valued the first two of Gardner's categories—linguistic intelligence and logical-mathematical intelligence—and paid little attention to the others. As teachers, we need to change this emphasis; we need to explore topics in multiple ways to reach more students. When schools stress memorization of key terms without exposing students to other ways to learn about a subject, for example, students who are high in linguistic intelligence will grasp the material, but other students may lag behind and be labeled as underachieving—even though these low-achieving students would do much better if they were given the opportunity to learn and express themselves by other means.

One example of a teacher who organizes assignments that have the potential to express multiple learning styles is Mr. Slomin's sixth-grade science class. He includes a unit on the moon in which students study the moon's phases—how it appears from Earth at different times of the month. Here are Mr. Slomin's instructions for this unit:

The students are required to keep a moon-phase journal over a period of five weeks. Each day, they need to record the shape of the moon, the time that they see it, and other information about the moon that can include: how they felt watching the moon, moon poems (original or found), moon facts, or other relevant data about the moon. All these belong in the moon journal. There may be some days, due to weather or other reasons, when the students cannot see the moon. Then, they are asked to develop their own theory about why they cannot see it and keep observing until they see it again. Mr. Slomin's class is accustomed to receiving open-ended assignments. The students trust that he will examine their products as individual creations based on their own interests. At the end of the five weeks, the students are asked to present their moon journals and talk about how they felt during the experience of keeping them. To everyone's surprise and delight, Dan, a shy young man who does not participate much in class, created a beautiful painting on each of the nights he could see the moon. Neither his classmates nor his teacher knew how gifted he was. His entries included a relatively small number of words, but his pictures showed close and accurate observations. Dan's artistic talent was a well-kept secret. This assignment allowed him to express his observations through his artistic designs and keen observations.

Q: *In what ways do you learn best?*

Meeting the needs of students with a wide range of learning styles requires teachers to have more than one way to approach a topic.

© Jose Luis Pelaez/Getty Images

Don't present activities, materials, ideas, and concepts in just one way!

Perhaps you have had interesting assignments like this one. Think about your own response to this type of experience and how it is meaningful to students.

Learning Styles

Gardner's theory of multiple intelligences has had a profound effect on how we think about the ways people perceive the world. A related idea is that people have various **learning styles**. In Chapter 4, we described learning something as a process of drawing it in from the outside and making it your own. *Learning style* refers to the particular way you take in the new idea, event, or concept.

Some people learn best by reading and writing—the traditional approach taken in schools. But researchers (Felder & Silverman, 1988, 2002; Felder & Brent, 2005) have identified other basic learning styles as well:

- *Auditory learners* learn best through verbal lectures, discussions, talking things through, and listening to what others have to say. For these people, written information may

have little meaning until it is heard. Such learners often benefit from reading text aloud and using a tape recorder.

- *Visual learners* need to see the teacher's body language and facial expression to fully understand the content of a lesson. They may think in pictures and learn best from visual displays, including diagrams, illustrated textbooks, overhead transparencies, videos, flipcharts, and handouts.
- *Kinesthetic learners* learn best through a hands-on approach, actively exploring the physical world around them. They may find it hard to sit still for long periods and may become distracted by their need for activity and exploration.

When you study for a test, is reading the book enough for you, or do you have to take notes on what you read to remember the ideas? Most people who need to do something physical in order to make the concepts their own are kinesthetic learners. If you are one, quick—take notes on this chapter! There is so much to know.

Together, the research on learning styles and multiple intelligences has a strong message for teachers: Don't present activities, materials, ideas, and concepts in just one way! Because people learn in different ways and through different personal strengths, it is important to plan your lessons with multiple ways of knowing in mind.

learning style The dominant way in which we process the information around us. Different people have different learning styles.

TEACHSOURCE VIDEO CASE

Teaching to Students' Strengths

To explore how one teacher accounts for his students' varying intelligence profiles and styles of learning, find the TeachSource Video Case "Multiple Intelligences: Elementary School Instruction" on the student website. The video examines a class writing assignment about the passengers' experience during the ocean voyage of the *Mayflower*. After watching the video, consider the following question:

In what ways is this lesson an example of teaching to multiple learning styles?

LO6 Teaching the Broad Range of Diverse Students

"The prevailing question before us is not about what children need to succeed. The research is clear. They need supportive environments that nurture their social, emotional, physical, moral, civic, and cognitive development. Instead, the question becomes, who bears responsibility for creating this environment?"

—**Gene Carter (2006)**

New teachers often draw upon their own experiences as learners, and those experiences become the default mode for what is presumed "normal" or "expected" in the regular classroom. As we have seen, however, students today bring to the classroom a wide range of ethnic backgrounds, languages, religions, sexual orientations, learning styles, and intelligences. All of these are embedded in their culture and upbringing. You also have your own identity, embedded in a particular culture with norms and traditions that are dear to you.

To be a successful teacher, you need to become a *student of your students*. Start to view "difference" from the point of view of a learner and ask yourself, "How am I enriched by learning more about my students? How does that contribute to my understanding of the human condition?" In this way, teaching becomes a never-ending story, a new adventure every year, just as Jane remarked in Chapter 2. Part of your job each year will be to learn about your students and the ways in which they and their backgrounds, languages, learning styles, sexual orientations, and lifestyles prepare them for your classroom.

LO7 Concluding Thoughts

The most important theme of this chapter is that differences among students are a gift to welcome in your classroom, not a barrier to overcome. They are a gift both for you and for your students. Unless we meet and interact with people from many walks of life and with different ways of being in the world, we run the risk of closing our minds to all that is possible in the human condition.

This chapter may leave you with more questions than answers, but you can "live into" the questions.

Ask yourself: Can I do this? Can I examine my pedagogy and develop teaching strategies that help the young girl from the homeless shelter, the boy from Nicaragua with limited English, the suburban youngster who has more than she will ever need, the musically gifted eighth grader who hates history, the logical-mathematical young woman who wants to be a physicist? Can I learn from them and with them and help them be all they can be, as others have helped me?

That is the message of this chapter. In Chapter 6, we explore current trends in education. Some of these trends will feel like stumbling blocks, others like welcome boosts. The following anonymous quotation sums it up:

© William Mahar/iStockphoto

"Teachers who inspire realize there will always be rocks in the road ahead of us. They will be stumbling blocks or stepping stones; it all depends on how we use them."

© Christopher Futcher/iStockphoto

RESOURCES FOR FURTHER EXPLORATION

Film Resources

The Color of Fear

This documentary film, first released in 1994, is a ground-breaking discussion of race relations in America by eight men of different ethnic backgrounds. Directed by Lee Mun Wah, it is used extensively by educators.

Eyes on the Prize

This award-winning documentary film tells the story of the civil rights movement from 1954 to 1965. In fourteen parts, it has been aired over public broadcasting stations since 1987. It has also been used extensively in education to teach students about the civil rights movement and the victories won through nonviolent tactics. A PBS website, http://www.pbs.org/wgbh/amex/eyeson theprize/index.html, provides information about the film and support materials for teachers.

Online Resources

Center for Research on Education, Diversity, and Excellence

http://www.crede.ucsc.edu/

This center at the University of California is a clearinghouse for research reports and briefs about teaching language-minority students.

Language Policy Research Unit

http://www.language-policy.org/

Arizona State University hosts this website that addresses bilingual education and the politics of the English-only movement.

Migration Information Source

http://www.migrationinformation.org/

This website, sponsored by the Migration Policy Institute, offers insights into immigration trends as well as the debate over bilingual education.

NCELA: National Clearinghouse for English Language Acquisition and Language Instruction Educational Programs

http://www.ncela.gwu.edu/

This website provides a comprehensive overview of bilingual education in the United States.

The Pew Forum on Religion and Public Life: Americans' Struggle with Religion's Role at Home and Abroad

http://www.pewforum.org

This downloadable document examines the conflicts surrounding the role of religion in daily life that are encountered by many segments of the American public.

What's YOUR Learning Style?

http://www.usd.edu/trio/tut/ts/style.html

This website allows you to take a survey to reveal your own dominant learning style.

Print Resources

Howard Gardner, *Multiple Intelligences: New Horizons* (New York: Basic Books, 2006).

This is one of Gardner's provocative and influential books.

Laurie Hansen, "Strategies for English-language learning success," *Science and Children*, 43(4) (2006), 23–25.

This article explores how best to engage English-language learners in science learning using the inquiry process.

Judy Logan, *Teaching Stories* (New York: Kodansha Press, 1999).

This book provides detailed and heart-warming stories of life inside an urban California sixth-grade classroom.

Ana Martinez Aleman, "Latino demographic, democratic individuality, and educational accountability: A pragmatist's view," *Educational Researcher*, 35(7) (2006), 25–35.

This is a very important analysis of how Latino students are marginalized by the current accountability systems.

CHAPTER 6

CONTEMPORARY TRENDS AND PRESSING ISSUES IN EDUCATION

© Image Source/Corbis

> *Education is not the piling on of learning, information, data, facts, skills, or abilities . . . but is rather making visible what is hidden as a seed.*
> —Sir Thomas More, 1478–1535

Since schools reflect the culture and politics of contemporary society, there are always many "trends" in education, and we could spend four or five entire books discussing current ones. By "trend" we are referring to a prevailing tendency that has impacted the lives of students and teachers in schools and that seems likely to remain around for the foreseeable future. In this chapter, we will concentrate on several major trends and issues affecting schools across the nation:

- Approaches to teaching students with special needs, including Response to Intervention (RTI), a multi-level teacher response system that identifies students at risk of underachieving and maximizes their chances for success with multiple strategies

- The impact of the No Child Left Behind Act and the emphasis on standards-based testing on teaching practice and the construction of curriculum
- The rising interest in alternative forms of schooling—specifically, public charter schools and homeschooling
- The changing ideas about middle schools and the education of young adolescents
- The influence of students' social and emotional learning (SEL) on their attitudes, behavior, and performance in school
- The significance of teacher professional development that enables teachers to remain current and refine their own thinking about teaching and learning in contemporary culture
- The impact of school violence on students and teachers
- The rights and responsibilities of students and teachers

For you as a prospective teacher, the most significant question behind all these trends and issues is the same one we focused on in Chapter 5: How can the needs of so many different types of learners be met in one classroom in one school? As you can imagine, the

LEARNING OUTCOMES

After reading this chapter, you should be thinking about the following ideas:

LO1 Inclusion classrooms offer all students significant possibilities. They look no different from mainstream classrooms.

LO2 Education for the gifted and talented targets students who give evidence of high achievement in areas such as intellectual, creative, artistic, or leadership capacities. Inclusion students can also be gifted and talented!

LO3 Differentiated instruction requires that teachers learn a great deal about who their students are, what their lives are like, and how they can best learn.

LO4 Problem- and project-based learning experiences engage students in realistic questions that require planning and collaboration before a solution can be found.

LO5 The No Child Left Behind Act has impacted the way teachers design and implement curriculum.

LO6 Many alternative school models have been developed that are unlike traditional public and private schools.

LO7 Teachers and students have legal rights and responsibilities guaranteed by the Family Educational Rights and Privacy Act and the U.S. Constitution.

exceptional learners
Students who require special educational services because of physical, behavioral, or academic needs.

least restrictive A learning environment that, to the maximum extent possible, matches the environment experienced by nondisabled students.

inclusion The practice of educating students with disabilities in regular classrooms alongside nondisabled students.

special education The branch of education that deals with services for students with disabilities or other special needs that cannot be met through traditional means.

answer lies in multiple approaches to implementing the curriculum. It is common to find teachers building a large repertoire of activities and experiences for a given topic. It is, therefore, important to remain professionally active and attend conferences, workshops, and professional development programs well after you have left the formal world of teacher education.

LO1 The Inclusion Classroom

❝*Inclusion involves all kinds of practices that are ultimately practices of good teaching. What good teachers do is to think thoughtfully about children and develop ways to reach all students. . . . Inclusion is providing more options for children as ways to learn. It's structuring schools as community where all children can learn.*❞ —Chris Kliewer, Associate Professor of Special Education, University of Northern Iowa (quoted at http://www.uni.edu/coe/inclusion/philosophy/philosophy.html)

In the preceding chapter, we explored ethnic, social class, and learning profile diversity among students; but those are only a few of the ways students can be classified. In this chapter, we examine the extremes on the spectrum of learning—students with disabilities and students who are considered gifted and talented. Both of these groups of students are considered **exceptional learners**. Teaching exceptional learners requires that teachers

The law guarantees that children with disabilities receive a "free appropriate public education."

stretch themselves and their thinking to consider what works best for these students in their classroom settings.

Earlier in the book, you read about the Individuals with Disabilities Education Act and its various amendments. The law guarantees that children with disabilities receive a "free appropriate public education." But more than just providing access to education for students with disabilities, the law calls for improved results for these students and the implementation of programs to ensure their continuous progress. In fact, guidelines established by the U.S. Department of Education's Office for Special Education Programs call for improved performance

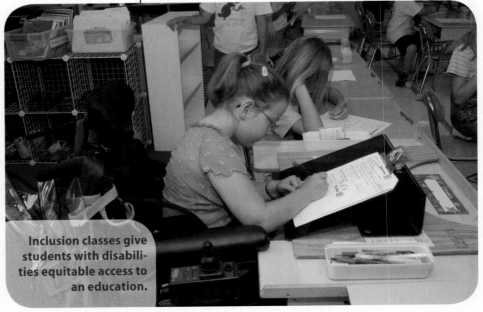

Inclusion classes give students with disabilities equitable access to an education.

of students with disabilities, through an alignment with the No Child Left Behind Act (2001).

The question educators must answer for each student with a disability is: What does free and appropriate public education (FAPE) look like for this child? To comply with the law, this education must take place in the **least restrictive environment** appropriate for each particular student. Hence, to the greatest extent possible, students with disabilities must be educated with children who are not disabled.

Originally, this mandate led to the mainstreaming of students with disabilities. Generally, mainstreaming involved having those students participate in general education classes for part of the school day and spend the remainder of the day in a separate, self-contained classroom for students with disabilities. Today, the prevailing concept is **inclusion**, which goes further than mainstreaming. Inclusion involves a commitment to educate students with disabilities in the general education classroom for the entire school day. Any special services the students need are brought to them in the inclusion classroom. Sometimes this arrangement is called *full inclusion* to emphasize that the students stay in the regular classroom full time. If students spend only

part of the day in the regular classroom, the arrangement is called *partial inclusion*.

The field of **special education** focuses on the services and instructional practices needed by students with disabilities. You may be interested in becoming a special education teacher. Today, because of inclusion, that often means working in tandem with a general education teacher in the same classroom. In addition to having at least two teachers, an inclusion classroom may also have a teacher's aide, who may be specifically assigned to a student in the class with special needs.

The TeachSource Video Case features a general education class that uses the services of an inclusion specialist. Often, an inclusion specialist works with more than one teacher in a school.

TEACHSOURCE VIDEO CASE

Teaching Strategies for the Inclusion Classroom
Find the TeachSource Video Case "Inclusion: Grouping Strategies for Inclusive Classrooms" on the student website. In this classroom, the students are studying the Caribbean, working in groups at different centers. After watching the video, consider the following question:

In what ways do the inclusion teacher and general education teacher function differently in this classroom?

CONTROVERSY ABOUT INCLUSION

There has been a great deal of controversy about inclusion. Parents of general education students worry that their child's education may be compromised by the presence of students with special needs. They fear, for instance, that the teacher may have to spend so much time with the "special" students that "regular" students get less attention. Other people, however, believe that inclusion helps general education students appreciate people who are different from themselves.

On the opposite side of the coin, there are many critiques of self-contained classrooms for students with disabilities. Many educators worry that students in such classrooms are "labeled" for life. Applied at an early age, the disability label persists over time

and limits the students' potential. Other critics point out the disproportionate number of minority boys in self-contained special education classes, especially in urban areas. How do these children get placed in such settings? Why is there a larger number of students from one ethnic group and gender than from others? Who is advocating on behalf of students with special needs?

These and other questions contribute to raging controversies surrounding special education and its implementation in public schools. Wherever you stand on this controversy, the chances are high that you will have an inclusion classroom at some stage in your teaching career.

learning disability (or specific learning disability) A disorder in the basic psychological processes involved in learning and using language; it may lead to difficulties in listening, speaking, reading, writing, reasoning, or mathematical abilities.

individualized education program (IEP) A plan, required for every student covered by the Individuals with Disabilities Education Act, specifying instructional goals, services to be provided, and assessment techniques for evaluating progress.

Response to Intervention (RTI) A service delivery system in schools aimed at preventing academic and behavioral difficulties as well as identifying the best practices for teaching students with disabilities.

TYPES OF DISABILITIES

Approximately half of all students with disabilities—more than 4 percent of U.S. students as a whole—have **learning disabilities** (U.S. Department of Education, 2005). These are students who have difficulty with reading, listening, speaking, writing, reasoning, or mathematical skills. Students with learning disabilities can be good in one subject area but perform poorly in other areas. For students with learning disabilities, hyperactivity and the inability to follow directions are typical problems.

In many cases, students with learning disabilities have social and behavioral problems. Sometimes the learning disability leads to behavioral distress, low self-esteem, and inappropriate behavior in the classroom.

Some other types of disabilities recognized under the IDEA are (in order from most to least frequent):

- Speech or language impairments
- Mental retardation
- Emotional disturbance
- Hearing impairments
- Orthopedic impairments
- Visual impairments
- Autism

(U.S. Department of Education, 2005)

INDIVIDUALIZED EDUCATION PROGRAMS

❝*After my son is out of public school, he'll be living and working with a diverse population of people. I want him to be accepted after he's out of school as much as when he's*

in school. For me, that is why inclusion is a key while he's in school.❞
—**Parent of a child with disabilities, Waverly, IA (quoted at http://www.uni.edu/coe/inclusion/philosophy/philosophy.html)**

© Jon Patton/iStockphoto

Because there are so many types of disabilities with so many different representations among individual children, the IDEA legislation mandates that, in order for each student to have a free and appropriate public education, each student with disabilities be provided with a learning plan. Known as the **individualized education program** or **IEP**, this plan outlines long- and short-range goals for the individual student. It also includes a description of the instructional services that will be provided to meet the goals as well as the assessment techniques that will be used to understand the student's progress.

Figure 6.1 shows a few sections from a sample IEP form. This type of form is usually completed by the general education teacher and the inclusion teacher, working together. In addition to these teachers, other people typically have input into the child's program, including the school psychologist, school administrators, and the student's parents or guardians. A successful inclusion model depends on the collaboration of all these people.

RESPONSE TO INTERVENTION

Response to Intervention (RTI) is a program that enables schools to identify the specific types of support that struggling students need and to provide this support when it is needed. It is a prevention model that

TEACHSOURCE VIDEO CASE

Collaboration between the General Education Teacher and the Inclusion Specialist

Find the TeachSource Video Case "Inclusion: Classroom Implications for the General and Special Educator" on the student website. This video explores a third-grade inclusion class in which several specialists address the needs of students with disabilities. After watching the video, consider the following question:

What interventions do the teachers employ to help all the students in this classroom engage in this reading and writing lesson?

Figure 6.1

Sections from a Sample IEP Form

PRESENT LEVELS OF ACADEMIC ACHIEVEMENT, FUNCTIONAL PERFORMANCE AND INDIVIDUAL NEEDS

Current functioning and individual needs in consideration of:

- the results of the initial or most recent evaluation, the student's strengths, the concerns of the parents, the results of the student's performance on any state or districtwide assessment programs;

- the student's needs related to communication, behavior, use of Braille, assistive technology, limited English proficiency;

- how the student's disability affects involvement and progress in the general education curriculum; and

- the student's needs as they relate to transition from school to post-school activities for students beginning with the first IEP to be in effect when the student turns age 15 (and younger if deemed appropriate).

Academic Achievement, Functional Performance and Learning Characteristics:

Current levels of knowledge and development in subject and skill areas, including activities of daily living, level of intellectual functioning, adaptive behavior, expected rate of progress in acquiring skills and information and learning style.

Social Development:

The degree and quality of the student's relationships with peers and adults, feelings about self and social adjustment to school and community environments.

Photo: © loops7/iStockphoto

SOURCE: Excerpted from New York State Education Department, "School-Age Individualized Education Program (IEP)," Form NYSED-IEP-SA 12-05, http://www.vesid.nysed.gov/specialed/publications/policy/iep/schoolageip.htm.

continued

Figure 6.1: Sections from a Sample IEP Form, *continued*

Physical Development:

The degree or quality of the student's motor and sensory development, health, vitality and physical skills or limitations that pertain to the learning process.

Management Needs:

The nature of and degree to which environmental modifications and human or material resources are required to enable the student to benefit from instruction. Management needs are determined in accordance with the factors identified in the areas of academic achievement, functional performance and learning characteristics, social development and physical development.

MEASURABLE ANNUAL GOALS

Annual Goal: What the student will be expected to be able to do by the end of the year in which the IEP is in effect.

Evaluative Criteria: How well and over what period of time the student must demonstrate performance in order to consider the annual goal to have been met.

Procedures to Evaluate Goal: The method that will be used to measure progress and determine if the student has met the annual goal.

Evaluation Schedule: The dates or intervals of time by which evaluation procedures will be used to measure the student's progress.

Annual Goal:	
Evaluative Criteria:	
Procedures to Evaluate Goal:	
Evaluation Schedule:	

intervenes to identify young students who may be at risk for poor learning outcomes. This organizational framework helps teachers screen all students to determine whether the curriculum and instruction they are implementing is meeting the needs of the majority of students. This screening typically happens for an entire grade and is a means for helping struggling students and preventing them from experiencing academic failure. The RTI program can also identify students with learning difficulties (Brown-Chidsey, 2007).

Q: *What famous people were labeled as having learning, physical, or speech disabilities in school?*

What makes RTI effective is the ways in which it can prevent academic failure and determine whether a student's underachievement is the result of an actual learning disability or the result of inadequate instruction. RTI is a systematic method for instruction and assessment of students that includes a three-tiered approach to intervening on behalf of students with varying instructional needs.

In Tier 1, all students are assessed to determine if they are meeting grade-level standards for the general curriculum. In Tier 2, students who are performing below grade level receive specific instructional activities to help their academic achievement. These are tailored to the individual and require collaboration between general education teachers and the special education teachers. Students in Tier 2 are monitored weekly and, as their skills improve, receive less support until they are fully able to succeed with the general education curriculum as it is implemented in the school. If the Tier 2 students do not make progress in a specified period of time, instruction is modified and they are further monitored. If they need additional support, the students are moved to Tier 3 services, where the school conducts a comprehensive evaluation of a student's skills, including the data from Tiers 1 and 2, to determine why the student's performance is significantly different from that of other students in his or her grade and to decide what instructional support the student needs.

If this sounds complicated, that's because it is! However, outcomes from schools that have practiced RTI for years have shown that it raises the educational attainment of students in general and reduces the number of students who need special education services. One of the reasons for this is that the instructional interventions that are recommended have been validated by research and are not loosely constructed. Think about how wonderful it would be to prevent a child's placement in special education simply because he or she needed specific early-academic support to achieve independently. RTI is a framework in which we think about organizing curriculum and instruction based on students' responses to screening, tiers of instruction, progress monitoring, and understanding of how the intervention was delivered. The National Center on Response to Intervention provides screening tools, case studies, and descriptions of tiered interventions (http://www.rti4success.org).

As we will see in this chapter, RTI is one form of differentiated instruction. In the next section we explore how instruction is differentiated for gifted students.

LO2 The Education of Gifted and Talented Students

"*A teacher asked a class what color apples are. Most of the children said 'Red' . . . a few answered 'Green,' and one child raised his hand with another answer: 'White.' The teacher patiently explained that apples were red or green or yellow but they were never white. The student persisted. Finally, he said, 'Look inside.'***" —Adapted from Tara Bennett-Goleman (2001, p. 43)**

This quotation reminds me of how students with "out-of-the-box" thinking often are not rewarded in school because their ideas are not aligned with conventional questioning or expected answers. Sometimes these thinkers are really gifted or talented students.

Most of us typically have less compassion for gifted and talented students than we do for students with disabilities. Conventional wisdom tells us that gifted students always land on their feet, and some of us even feel jealous of their exceptional skills and abilities. Research, however, indicates that gifted and talented learners are in as much need of special educational services as are students with disabilities (Davis & Rimm, 2004). Often their needs are not met in traditional school settings, and that situation frequently causes depression, lack of interest in school, and underachievement.

> Most of us typically have less compassion for gifted and talented students than we do for students with disabilities.

Further, fewer gifted and talented students are identified from minority groups or groups of low socio-economic status than from white, middle- and upper-middle-class populations. Part of this discrepancy stems from parent advocacy—parents of higher social status are more likely to push for their children to be included in gifted programs. The discrepancy also relates to the issue of social capital introduced earlier in this book. Parents with social capital understand how to get their children into special programs. In addition, social capital exposes the learners themselves to a variety of educational and cultural experiences that poorer students often do not gain access to. That early and consistent cultural exposure outside of school contributes to a sense of "giftedness."

As you might guess, the attempt to define giftedness has led to controversy. For much of the 20th century, giftedness was usually measured by IQ tests: people who scored in the upper 2 percent of the population were considered gifted. Critics pointed out, however, that those tests emphasized a narrow range of skills and tended to discriminate against minority groups. Today, giftedness is defined not so much by test scores as by consistently exceptional performance.

Federal legislation has generally referred to gifted and talented children as those who show high performance capability in specific academic fields or in areas such as creativity and leadership, and who require

special services by the school to develop these capabilities. The schools select students for such services using a variety of measures, including recommendations by teachers; test scores; and an understanding of certain identifying features of gifted and talented students, such as the pace at which they learn and the depth of their understanding (Maker & Nielson, 1996).

Services for the gifted and talented learner can provide enrichment (broadening the curriculum) or acceleration (speeding up the student's progress through the curriculum). Enrichment activities for the gifted are usually classroom-based, while accelerated programs may allow students to skip grades or graduate early from high school. Accelerated programs range from segregated grade-level classes to high school programs such as the International Baccalaureate (IB) program and advanced placement (AP) courses. The IB program is a rigorous course of study concentrating on mathematics, science,

Helen Keller (1880–1968) was deaf and blind; however, despite enormous odds against her, she was able, with the help of her teacher, Anne Sullivan, to graduate from college, become a prolific writer, and tour the world. It would have been infinitely easier for her today.

WHO IS GIFTED?

According to the National Association for Gifted Children (NAGC), there is no universally agreed-upon answer to the question of who is gifted. Nevertheless, the NAGC offers its own definition: A gifted person is "someone who shows, or has the potential for showing, an exceptional level of performance in one or more areas of expression."

Some gifted people have general abilities like leadership skills and the ability to think creatively. Other gifted people have more specific abilities, such as special aptitudes in mathematics, science, or music. By these standards, approximately 6 percent of the student population in the United States is considered gifted (National Association for Gifted Children, 2010).

In many cases, gifted students learn differently from their classmates in at least five important ways:

- They learn new material in much less time.
- They tend to remember what they have learned, making reviews of previously mastered concepts a painful experience.
- They perceive ideas and concepts at more abstract and complex levels than do their peers.
- They become passionately interested in specific topics and have difficulty moving on to other learning tasks.
- They are able to operate on many levels of concentration simultaneously, so they can monitor classroom activities without paying direct or visual attention to them. (Winebrenner, 2000, p. 54)

and foreign language and is internationally recognized. AP courses offer college credit while students are still in high school.

Finally, many people now recommend "gifted inclusion." Can you suppose what that might be? If you think it means designing regular classroom activities that offer gifted and talented students opportunities to expand on the unit of study, you are correct.

differentiated instruction or **differentiation**
The practice of using a variety of instructional strategies to address the different learning needs of students.

LO3 Differentiated Instruction

Thus far in this chapter and in the preceding one, we have been exploring the diversity of students you will find in your classroom. We have focused on students who have exceptional learning needs, special learning profiles, language and ethnic differences, and cultural and socioeconomic differences. Sometimes, strategies for meeting the needs of these learners are developed through collaboration with a specialist, someone who has been trained in a field like special education, gifted education, or bilingual education. The RTI model you read about previously is a good example of how instruction is specifically designed for students with special learning needs. This is a research-based model of differentiation. The various programs for gifted and talented students represent another model of differentiated instruction. As we noted in the previous section, gifted and talented students may require enrichment activities that are often classroom based and frequently designed with a specialist.

Whether in collaboration with a fellow teacher or not, you will be responsible for developing teaching strategies that can accommodate the learning experience to a wide range of student abilities. Teaching to diversity has a name. **Differentiated instruction** or **differentiation** has become an important educational philosophy recognizing students' varying background knowledge, learning profiles, abilities, interests, and language. It is the basis for developing instructional practices that engage all learners through multiple approaches, tasks, and activities.

Differentiated instruction contrasts with the notion that all children should be taught in the same manner. The movement for gender-fair education, for example, identified the different needs of girls and boys in the classroom resulting from the different ways they are socialized (Sadker & Sadker, 1995). The movement first focused on the needs of girls but then went on to consider new ways to help boys succeed. Overall, the important message for teachers is that equality of treatment does not guarantee equity. Equity is what we should strive for, because it provides equal opportunities for all students to succeed.

What we ask our students to do on behalf of their own learning must be geared to their individual needs and strengths. Our approach must be designed to help them achieve to their fullest potential. In other words, one size does not fit all. One type of activity or lesson will probably not reach all of your students. When you approach teaching a topic, ask yourself questions like these:

• In how many different ways can I engage my students in this unit of study?
• How can I support students with learning disabilities and challenge the gifted learner, while at the same time exciting all learners to find their strengths?

According to Carol Tomlinson (2000, p. 6), differentiated instruction is based on the following set of beliefs:

• Students who are the same age differ in their readiness to learn, their interests, their styles of learning, their experiences, and their life circumstances.
• The differences among students are significant enough to make a major impact on what students need to learn, the pace at which they need to learn it, and the support they need from teachers and others to learn it well.
• Students learn best when supportive adults push them slightly beyond where they can work without assistance.
• Students learn best when they can make a connection between the curriculum and their interests and life experiences.
• Students learn best when learning opportunities are natural.
• Students are more effective learners when classrooms and schools create a sense of community in which students feel significant and respected.
• The central job of schools is to maximize the capacity of each student.

Helping students develop a sense of self will ultimately help them to better manage their emotions, communicate, and resolve conflicts nonviolently.
(edutopia.org, 2010)

Social and Emotional Learning

Social and emotional learning refers to individuals' abilities to manage their emotions, develop caring and concern for others, make responsible decisions, establish positive relationships, and handle challenging situations effectively. School programs that help students to develop these skills have been shown to be effective in preventing violence, substance abuse, and related problems, and in helping students succeed academically (Zins et al, 2010). The Collaborative for Academic, Social, and Emotional Learning (CASEL) is a nonprofit organization that was founded by Daniel Goleman, author of *Emotional Intelligence* (2006). It works to advance the evidence-based practices for incorporating SEL into the curriculum in as many schools as possible nationwide.

It comes as no surprise that students' learning is influenced by social and emotional factors and that an anxious, afraid, or alienated student has a diminished capacity for learning. Helping students to communicate, make decisions, and solve problems, increases the likelihood that they can develop a positive attachment to school and experience greater academic success (CASEL, 2010).

SEL skills are explicitly taught through planned, systematic, and evidence-based classroom instruction, and many of the activities that compose an SEL curriculum could be integrated with academic learning areas. These carefully structured learning programs engage students from pre-kindergarten through high school in experiences that build their self-awareness, self-management, social awareness, relationship skills, and responsible decision making. A related component to the SEL approach is the development and maintenance of caring classroom communities. We will explore those types of caring classroom communities further in Chapter 9. Well-managed learning environments are places where students feel safe, respected, and challenged, and where teachers are able to model and provide opportunities for students to practice their social and emotional skills.

LO4 The Power of Projects and Problems for Student Learning

Looking for a history teacher, a suburban high school ran the following advertisement in the local newspaper:

Responsible for implementing curriculum specializing in the time period of 1500–1700 by designing lessons reflecting the theory of multiple intelligences, integrating with other domains using project-based learning and technology.

The phrase toward the end of the ad, "project-based learning," is one you will hear frequently. Both project-based and problem-based learning are contemporary trends aimed at ensuring that students address content areas with depth and skill. Students with diverse needs and learning profiles have been shown to benefit from the use of these strategies.

One major characteristic of both these approaches is that students work in groups, with three to five students organized around a central learning task. This technique had its beginnings in the **cooperative learning** movement, which became popular in the 1990s. Every member of each group is assigned a task, and each task is important for the goal to be reached. The students in the group are responsible for their individual learning as well as the group's learning. They work toward the common goal of promoting each other's and the group's success.

PROJECT-BASED LEARNING

To see what project-based learning looks like, consider a challenging project for a sixth-grade math class in the following story.

In Mr. Roberts's sixth-grade math class in an urban middle school, a visitor is immediately struck by what the students are doing. Students are working in groups of four to construct a model classroom, using cardboard boxes, glue guns, poster board, markers, and construction paper. Centimeter sticks and measuring tapes are scattered around each work station. When asked about their work, students eagerly show their sketches, which indicate the scale of their model and use principles of ratio and proportion. Clearly, this class is learning about mathematical concepts through a design project.

Mr. Roberts is convinced that the students will develop a deeper understanding of the concepts of ratio and proportion as a result of designing and constructing the model classroom. He is preparing a written assessment on this topic in order to more fully understand what the students know.

The *design challenge*, a term from engineering design, began with certain specifications. The ratio was stated in advance, using proportional units of 2 cm = 1 foot. The challenge also specified that the classroom contain (1) seating for 18 students, (2) a teacher's desk, (3) a discussion area with a couch and arm chairs and an area rug, and (4) ample board space. Certain constraints were imposed as well: The students may not use materials other than those supplied by the teacher, and the final model should be no larger than 40 cm long × 40 cm wide × 18 cm high. The materials provided include foam board, cardboard, construction paper, markers, glue guns, cutting tools (handled by the teacher and other adults), and assorted recyclable materials, such as wooden spools from sewing thread, cardboard paper-towel tubes, cereal boxes, and other assorted containers.

cooperative learning
An instructional approach in which students work together in groups to accomplish shared learning goals.

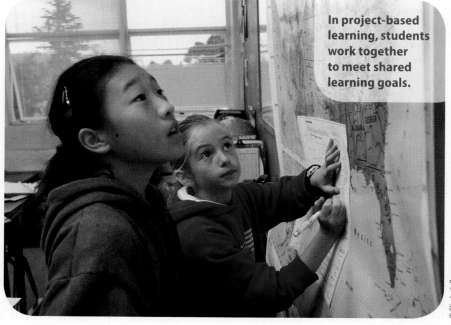

In project-based learning, students work together to meet shared learning goals.

© Elizabeth Crews

project-based learning
A teaching method that engages students in extended inquiry into complex, realistic questions as they work in teams and create presentations to share what they have learned. These presentations may take various forms: an oral or written report, a computer technology-based presentation, a video, the design of a product, and so on.

problem-based learning Focused, experiential learning (minds-on, hands-on) organized around the investigation and resolution of messy, real-world problems.

Working in groups of four, the students present their designs to the entire class after completing their model. They demonstrate how they have met the specifications and constraints of their design challenge and explain why their model classroom contains objects that are in appropriate proportion to the rest of the room. They provide a rationale for the arrangement of the students' and teacher's desks. Throughout this performance, each member of the working group has the opportunity to present his or her understanding of the project and of ratio and proportion. All the students get feedback from their classmates.

This story demonstrates how **project-based learning** adds creativity and depth to a curriculum, promoting more meaningful learning than rote memorization or worksheet activities. Projects can be designed for any subject area, and they often embrace concepts from several disciplines. They also accommodate students with different learning profiles and abilities, helping students work from their own strengths. Everybody becomes engaged in completing the task or constructing the final product. As the newspaper advertisement indicated, projects typically reflect the theory of multiple intelligences and help students integrate knowledge from different domains.

Projects are challenging for teachers because they require more time and more materials than a more traditional lesson does. A project is a carefully planned and organized experience involving thoughtfully selected groups. Although classrooms engaged in projects can be noisy at times, the students are usually self-directed and invested in their work.

PROBLEM-BASED LEARNING

Closely related to project-based learning is **problem-based learning**. Both strategies emphasize connections to real life, but project-based learning usually results in the construction of something, whereas problem-based learning focuses on a problem, the solutions to which may take many different forms. Problem-based learning is often more open-ended. The following story shows problem-based learning in action.

In Ms. Rhodes's fourth-grade Vermont classroom, a unit on recycling and conservation prompted the class to consider the amount of milk wasted in the school cafeteria during lunchtime. Ms. Rhodes introduced the problem by explaining to the class that the custodian had mentioned how many half-full milk cartons were tossed into the trash during lunch. "So many children—wasting so much milk," he said. Ms. Rhodes asked the class to consider the challenge of finding out just how much milk is wasted in a typical day in the cafeteria.

The students' problem was twofold: (1) how to calculate the volume of milk wasted and (2) how to enlist the help of all the students in the school to curb this waste. The class secured the help of the custodian, who brought discarded, but not empty, milk containers to the classroom each day for a week. Working in groups of four and using graduated cylinders, the students measured the amount of milk wasted each day. They constructed a huge bar graph titled "Milk Waste" outside their classroom, labeling the axes with "day of the week" and "liters of milk wasted." Under the graph, they posed the question, "What can YOU do about the amount of milk we waste in our school?"

The students also visited classrooms, talked about the problem, and gathered suggestions. By the end of the school term, there was a 70 percent decrease in the amount of milk wasted!

As this story demonstrates, problem-based learning can help students make connections between school subjects and the world outside of school. Conservation takes on new meaning when students relate it to their own lunchtime habits.

Notice, too, that that the problem the students faced was not a simple one. They were not told how to measure the amount of milk wasted. Instead, they faced

© Ryan Balderas/iStockphoto

an **ill-structured problem**, one for which they had to figure out their own approach to the question. With ill-structured problems, the solutions and the steps for reaching them are not clearly defined. In this way, they resemble real-life problems, which are usually complex and messy and require creative and critical thinking skills. To solve ill-structured problems, students need to make decisions based on the facts they gather and their beliefs about the best way to proceed. Solutions emerge from the process, and there may be more than one solution to a single problem.

Karen Rasmussen (1997) describes how a twelfth-grade geology teacher designed his entire course around six ill-structured problems. Each unit lasted six weeks.

His goal was to teach students that scientific findings have a lot of relevance outside the school building. In one unit, for example, students received a letter stating that a volcano in Yellowstone Park was showing signs of activity. If it erupted, the middle third of the United States could be wiped out. The students were asked what should be done. In response, they worked in groups to study volcanoes, determine the probability that such an event would occur, and describe the effect a major natural disaster would have on jobs and politics in the region. The teacher encouraged his students to

> **ill-structured problem**
> A problem that lacks clear procedures for finding the solution.

PROJECT-BASED LEARNING IN HISTORY AND GEOGRAPHY

Here are two interesting examples of project-based learning.

(1) Third-grade students in northern California take a class trip to nearby Rush Ranch, which includes part of the Suisun Marsh. Once a Native American village, the area was later used for ranching by settler Hiram Rush. Now the remaining buildings have been converted into an information center and blacksmith shop, where students learn about marsh ecosystems, local history, and blacksmithing. Their teacher sees the process as building *geo-literacy*: "an in-depth understanding—or 'literacy'—of geography, geology, and local history."

For this purpose, the students need to do more than simply look and listen. Before the field trip, they established a question to answer, "Why is the preservation of Rush Ranch important?" They formed groups, researched the ranch in books and on the Internet, and planned what they would do on their visit. Once on the site, they take photos and videos as documentation, and they conduct interviews with the docents. Analyzing and distilling the material they have gathered, they will create an informational multimedia website (Ball, 2003).

(2) Working in groups of three, seventh-grade history students design and construct a model for a sarcophagus that would be fitting for an ancient Egyptian ruler. (The sarcophagus was the external tomb for the royal mummy in the coffin inside.) Each group of students is studying a particular ruler, and the students decorate their sarcophagus with symbols and images representing the time in which that ruler lived as well as his or her attributes, likes, and dislikes. Through this design project, students learn a great deal about their specific Egyptian leader and about the culture of the period. Then they present the sarcophagus to the class, explaining what life in Ancient Egypt was like at the time of the ruler's death.

© Michael Utech/iStockphoto

locate information on the Internet. Students prepared a final paper for this unit and also presented oral reports. Their suggestions included:

- Drilling into the volcano to relieve the pressure
- Developing evacuation plans
- Not informing the public at all because, some students reasoned, the volcano was unlikely to erupt, there was no way to predict or prevent an eruption, and widespread panic would lower property values and scare industry away from the area

None of these suggestions was right or wrong, but each had to be supported by the students' research (Rasmussen, 1997).

Again I want to emphasize that project- and problem-based learning can be applied in any subject area. The next story focuses on a high school course in government in which students consider a controversial social and political issue.

In a senior-level high school government course, students are shown a video of the trial of Jack Kevorkian, a doctor who was given a ten- to twenty-five-year prison sentence in Michigan for assisting in the suicide of a terminally ill patient. As is made clear in the video case, Dr. Kevorkian dismissed counsel and represented himself. He had been acquitted of similar charges several times earlier, but in this case, he was found guilty of second-degree murder.

At the point when students are studying the case, Dr. Kevorkian is very ill. After serving less than ten years in jail, he has appealed for parole to the governor of Michigan.

The students are asked to make the case for or against granting Kevorkian parole, using data they collect from news reports, the video case, and their own research.

Students must present an argument with no fewer than five pieces of information to support their claim. Their teacher encourages them to learn as much background information about this case as possible, including the ways this case differs from previous cases in which Kevorkian was brought to trial. Students are also required to understand the parameters of second-degree murder and to decide why or why not they believe the verdict to be just and fair.

In this class of twenty-four high school seniors, opinions are almost evenly spit. Three groups favor granting parole, and three favor refusing parole. Students' arguments cover a wide range of topics, from the techniques for assisted suicide to the actual poisonings Kevorkian helped perform. Although no one is clearly "right or wrong" in the conventional sense, the quality of the problem solving influences some students to reconsider their original decisions when they have heard all the arguments.

In a conversation with the teacher, Alex Winter, I was struck by the following remark: "When students are engaged in determining solutions to problems that exist in their real world, they use all of their mental resources to contribute to the solution. I find that I have to say very little. My role is that of a mediator—organizing presentations and moderating the conversations."

Have you ever thought of teaching in the way that Alex Winter suggests? His technique reminds us, as mentioned earlier in the book, that we may tell our students many things in our classrooms, but teaching is not telling.

To sum up our discussion of project-based and problem-based learning, we can note that these two approaches have several characteristics in common (Torp & Sage, 2002, pp. 15–16):

- Students are engaged problem solvers.
- Students work in groups and collaborate to find the best solution to a problem.
- Teachers are coaches and guides, modeling interest and enthusiasm for learning.

- Projects or problems deal with real-life issues that students care about.
- Students use interdisciplinary resources.
- Students acquire new skills as they work on different tasks.
- Students struggle with ambiguity, complexity, and unpredictability.

Whether project-based or problem-based, however, students are given the opportunity to develop a set of concepts about the topic through their own explorations and collaboration with their peers. Each project-based or problem-based experience has a set of "big ideas" or core concepts that will result from the experience. Those ideas become internalized in a much deeper and meaningful way through the journey the students take to reach those understandings.

LO5 No Child Left Behind and Its Successor

The No Child Left Behind (NCLB) Act of 2001 (actually signed by President George W. Bush in January 2002) was the most dramatic federal education legislation since the 1965 Elementary and Secondary Education Act (ESEA). Although NCLB was a reauthorization and revision of ESEA, it went beyond the earlier act in several important ways. It emphasized increased funding for less wealthy school districts and higher achievement for financially poor and minority students. It also introduced new measures for holding schools accountable for students' progress. Most controversially, NCLB set new rules for standardized testing, requiring that students in grades 3 through 8 be tested every year in mathematics and reading. This requirement had important implications for the way the curriculum was developed and implemented in many elementary schools across the country. Because of the initial push for statewide standardized test in mathematics and reading, elementary students in the first decade of this century received less instruction in science and social studies. For many educators, the promise of the NCLB legislation became a massive testing movement, and there has not been substantial research to demonstrate that these standards-based assessments in each state actually improved student learning.

As the new administration under President Obama overhauls the 2002 No Child Left Behind Act (2010), many things about NCLB will change, including its name. It may revert back to the Elementary and Secondary Education Act, its original name. Whichever name it goes by, however, it will still maintain annual testing for reading and math for students.

TEACHING TO THE TEST?

The most immediate effect of the NCLB legislation has been the emphasis on testing. Although accountability is necessary to assess student, school, and system progress, many argue that a single standardized test in mathematics and reading at each grade level, 3–8, creates a culture of test preparation that often leaves little room for creative and in-depth teaching. Teachers may be pressured, directly or indirectly, to "teach to the test"—that is, to focus narrowly on the precise skills and information students need to do well on the exam. In these circumstances, teachers often resort to old-fashioned drill-and-practice exercises, trying to cram the knowledge into their students. There may be little time left for critical thinking, delving into a subject deeply, or exploring the students' own questions.

Some educators argue that teachers do not have to drill students for the tests. Strategies like problem-based and project-based learning might produce equally good test results. At one middle school in Hahnville, Louisiana, that champions project-based learning, scores have indeed gone up. One teacher states: "Part of [the rise in scores] is probably due to project-based learning, because the knowledge does get across to them. I've had kids come back to me and tell me, 'Remember that project we did?' They have never, ever, come back to me and said, 'Remember that test we did?'" (Ball, 2004).

THE MAIN PROVISIONS OF NCLB

The bold intention of No Child Left Behind was to close the achievement gap between students in poor and minority school districts and those in predominantly white, middle-class school districts by the year 2014. To achieve this goal, the legislation contained four major provisions, summarized as follows by the U.S. Department of Education.

Accountability for Results

Under NCLB, states are working to close the achievement gap and make sure all students, including those who are disadvantaged, achieve academic proficiency. Annual state and school district report cards inform parents and communities about state and school progress. Schools that do not make progress must provide supplemental services, such as free tutoring or after-school assistance; take corrective actions; and, if still not making adequate yearly progress after five years, make dramatic changes to the way the school is run. Under proposed revisions (2010) to NCLB, evaluations of schools would shift, becoming less punitive and offering more rewards. A common complaint of NCLB has been that, based solely on test scores, states have been quick to label schools as "failing." The new system would set forth a multi-tiered system that includes rankings somewhere between passing and failing.

More Freedom for States and Communities

Under NCLB, states and school districts have unprecedented flexibility in how they use federal education funds. For example, it is possible for most school districts to transfer up to 50 percent of the federal formula grant funds they receive under the Improving Teacher Quality State Grants, Educational Technology, Innovative Programs, and Safe and Drug-Free Schools programs to any one of these programs, or to their Title I program, without separate approval. This allows districts to use funds for their particular needs, such as hiring new teachers, increasing teacher pay, and improving teacher training and professional development.

Proven Education Methods

NCLB puts emphasis on determining which educational programs and practices have been proven effective through rigorous scientific research. Federal funding is targeted to support these programs and teaching methods that work to improve student learning and achievement.

More Choices for Parents

Parents of children in low-performing schools have new options under NCLB. In schools that do not meet state standards for at least two consecutive years, parents may transfer their children to a better-performing public school, including a public charter school, within their district. The district must provide transportation, using Title I funds if necessary.

SOURCE: U.S. Department of Education (2006).

However, few educational systems are willing to give up test-driven teaching in favor of more flexible and creative approaches to content. There is too much at stake when the scores of the students are tallied, summarized, and publicly reported. Many educators are concerned that if we value only what the tests measure, then this standards-based movement is ignoring the importance of passion for learning and the celebration of individual talent. As the NCLB legislation comes up for renewal, many educators are concerned that this standards movement has become a testing movement, and there is fear that too many people are using the test scores alone to assess the success of students, teachers, administrators, and schools. As a result, the renewal of NCLB will offer the goal of "college and career readiness" for students by 2020. With this new goal, the new administration is focusing less on grade-level attainment and more on the skills students will need for school or work after high school.

DOES ONE SIZE FIT ALL?

In addition to the problem of teaching to the test, there is a big question about whether one size fits all in educational testing. Under NCLB, a single standardized test is administered to all students in the state, regardless of their individual learning contexts. Many educators believe that stripping away context denies the authenticity of the assessment—that is, it takes away any possible connection to the students' lived experience. Remember what you read in Chapter 4 about authentic assessment. Do test results that are unrelated to students' lives have any real meaning?

Many educators also object to the one-size-fits-all mandate based on what we know about cultural diversity and multiple intelligences. In this view, a single measure of progress is inadequate to evaluate students' understanding of content. Accurate assessments can be achieved only through multiple types of assessments and student performances. Many believe that schools and students are better off when local schools and districts have the "flexibility to create innovative solutions to meet their own unique situations" (Guilfoyle, 2006).

Consider Rhode Island, where annual assessments are only a small part of a student's graduation requirements. Students there demonstrate their proficiency in multiple ways:

- Portfolios, which include selected examples of student work
- Capstone projects, which often involve in-depth research, reports, and oral presentations
- Public exhibitions, such as posters showing the student's accomplishments in a given content area

Imagine what this approach would mean for NCLB. If testing were just one piece of an innovative, comprehensive assessment and accountability system, we would have a more accurate picture of each school's strengths and weaknesses as well as more information to help schools and individual students succeed (Guilfoyle, 2006).

VARIATION AMONG STATES: ARE THE STANDARDS REALLY STANDARD?

Within each state, NCLB mandates standardized tests. Yet as states develop their own standards and tests for subject areas, there is enormous variability from one state to the next. In fact, students in some states perform better on the state standardized tests than they do on national math and reading tests. Some educators

AUTHENTIC ASSESSMENT

In the practice of *authentic assessment*, as we discussed in Chapter 4, students demonstrate their understanding of a content area by performing a task or solving a problem in the real-life context of their classroom or their world. This demonstration often involves some kind of student *performance*; hence, this type of assessment is also called *performance assessment*. The performance can involve anything from conducting an experiment to writing a report to designing a Web-based presentation. The products of project-based and problem-based learning are often used as a form of authentic assessment.

believe these states are setting the achievement bar too low. Because schools—and the states responsible for them—face financial consequences if students fail to show adequate progress, there is some incentive to make the standards easy to meet.

As a result of this problem, a grassroots movement is gathering momentum to coordinate state standards, at least for certain subjects. Nine states (Pennsylvania, New Jersey, Arkansas, Kentucky, Indiana, Maryland, Massachusetts, Ohio, and Rhode Island) have formed a consortium to create a common set of standards and a common test for all their students taking Algebra II (Zuckerbrod, 2007). Proponents argue that standards for a subject like algebra should not vary across state lines. If this effort succeeds, it will be one step toward genuine standardization. In 2010, the Council of Chief State Officers (CCSSO) and the National Governors Association drafted a set of common national standards for mathematics and language arts.

Although the newly revised NCLB Act will retain mathematics and reading tests, schools could also include student performance in other subject areas as part of their overall definition of progress. This is a direct response to critics of NCLB who have said that the tests have narrowed the curriculum for students. The new law asserts that students need a well-rounded education and cites disciplines that include science, history, civics, foreign language, and the arts.

The Achievement Gap

> *"What might happen if we paid less attention to outcomes, as measured by test scores, and more attention to how children learn, which is one of the most important processes of education? . . . Studying the ways in which children learn could help us focus on cultural differences between and among the children who sit in the same classroom, and on how those cultural differences might be used to empower learning rather than to stand in its way."*
> —Ellen Condliffe Lagemann (2007)

Perhaps the most discouraging effect of the NCLB legislation has been its effect on low-achieving schools and districts, precisely the constituents it had hoped to serve. After the first five years under the NCLB legislation, the gap between high- and low-achieving students had actually widened (Tough, 2006). Meanwhile, the law has created a test-preparation culture that narrows the view of knowledge by focusing heavily on reading and mathematics scores (Cawelti, 2006). Although accountability is terribly important, the implementation of one high-stakes test per grade level has forced many teachers to ignore the types of creative, problem-based teaching strategies that we have discussed in this chapter—strategies that engage students in their own learning. Consequently, the very students we are hoping to "hook" become discouraged by a lifeless curriculum.

Moreover, many teachers themselves are discouraged by the effects of high-stakes testing on their teaching. "In a study of 376 elementary and secondary

© Ryan Balderas/iStockphoto

TEACHSOURCE VIDEO CASE

Educators Discuss IDEA and NCLB
Find the TeachSource Video Case "Foundations: Aligning Instruction with Federal Legislation" on the student website. In this video, a school principal, teachers, specialists, and a school intern discuss the challenges and problems of meeting the requirements of IDEA and NCLB. After watching the video, consider the following question:

Why does the principal in this video refer to teaching as the "profession of hope"?

teachers in New Jersey, teachers indicated that they tended to teach to the test, often neglected individual students' needs, . . . had little time to teach creatively, and bored themselves and their students with practice problems as they prepared for standardized testing" (quoted in Cawelti, 2006).

A basic assumption of NCLB was that maintaining high expectations is necessary for improving achievement. This is, however, only one part of a potential solution. Achievement gaps between ethnic groups and groups of differing socioeconomic status are not caused by schools. They are caused by powerful social and family characteristics that affect children long before they start school and continue to operate as they enter school (Hart & Risley, 1995; Brooks-Gunn et al., 2000; Lareau, 2003). This does not mean that social and economic disadvantages—the absence of social capital—cannot be overcome in schools. But NCLB's goals cannot be achieved by enforcing a standardized testing program that few low-income students can become invested in. This is understood as a new administration overhauls the legislation. Further, the new education law will emphasize competition for federal funding through applications that specifically explain the ways in which the individual states will change their laws and rewards to reform their current system of education.

LO6 Alternatives to Traditional Schools: More Choices in an Era of Accountability

Under the NCLB law, if schools do not meet state standards for two consecutive years, parents may move their children into other, higher-performing schools. Essentially, NCLB obligates school districts to replace low-performing schools. Under the new legislation, schools that miss certain targets would not be required to provide students with tutoring or the option to transfer. This requirement had given a boost to charter schools, which are an alternative kind of public school. The new law will still emphasize parental choice in public schooling, however, not as a punitive measure.

Another alternative to traditional schools is home-schooling. More and more parents dissatisfied with public schools have begun to investigate the options for teaching their children at home. What do you think is behind this movement?

As a teacher, you may end up working in a charter school, or you may teach children who have been homeschooled in the past. In this section, we'll take a look at these two alternatives to traditional public and private schools.

THE RISE OF CHARTER SCHOOLS

Since the first charter school opened in Minnesota in 1991, the charter school movement has grown to nearly 4,000 schools with more than 1.15 million children enrolled (Education Commission of the States, 2007a). A **charter school** is a public school that has a specific, written charter from the school district, the state, or another governing agency. The charter typically exempts the school from selected rules and regulations that apply to other schools. In exchange for these exemptions, the school agrees to be accountable for producing certain results, set forth in the charter, in a specified period of time. Every three to five years, a school's status is reviewed; the school's right to exist can be revoked if the school has not met the standards promised in the charter.

By 2007, forty states, the District of Columbia, and Puerto Rico had established charter school laws. This means that concerned citizens, educators, or government officials can bring a plan for a charter school to the local or state education agency and, if the plan meets the established requirements, there is a strong possibility that the school can be established.

The belief is that charter schools have the potential to develop new and creative teaching methods and that these innovations can thrive in a system that is not constrained by the usual rules and regulations. Many

educators also hope that charter schools will foster a positive spirit of competition, encouraging traditional public schools to reform their practices.

What evidence is there that charter schools can fulfill this promise? On the positive side, there is a correlation between states having strong charter school laws and achievement gains for students (Center for Education Reform, 2005). Also, successful charter schools have indeed had a "ripple effect" on the public schools. Increasingly, members of the traditional public school system are turning to successful charter schools for examples of "best practices" regarding everything from curriculum to staffing and teacher retention (Mitchell, 2004).

On the negative side, there is no clear evidence that charter schools as a whole are significantly more successful than traditional public schools. The National Assessment of Educational Progress, for example, found no significant advantages for charter schools in reading or math performance (National Assessment of Educational Progress, 2005; Braun, Jenkins, & Grigg, 2006). For low-performing students in particular—the focus of many reform efforts—no studies definitively suggest that the charter school system is more successful than what is already in place. One of the serious problems associated with charter schools in low-income areas is that they tend to enroll the highest achieving students, leaving the traditional public schools with a less heterogeneous group of students. Consequently, the public schools from which the charter schools' students came usually experience a loss of academic standing. In some cities, those now–low performing schools are shut.

Because many different groups of concerned citizens can start charter schools, often without any prior training in education, professionals who do research in the area of learning and teaching are concerned about the charter school movement. Analyzing the success or failure of charter schools is complicated, however, because there are so many different types serving so many kinds of students. As one team of researchers explains:

> **charter schools** Publicly funded elementary or secondary schools that are granted a special charter by the state or local education agency.

Did You Know?

Since the first charter school opened in Minnesota in 1991, the charter school movement has grown to nearly 4,000 schools with more than 1.15 million children enrolled.

One of the most important difficulties in studying charter schools is that many of them are targeted specifically at particular student populations and thus serve dramatically different kinds of students than regular public schools do. Although most states require charter schools to have open enrollment policies, charter schools can still target specific populations by describing themselves as schools for a particular kind of student or by otherwise encouraging a certain kind of student to apply for admission. A study by the U.S. Department of Education found that one quarter of charter schools are targeted toward certain populations. Many people familiar with charter schools would find this a very conservative estimate. (Greene, Forster, & Winters, 2003)

Similarly, the National Education Association (2007) comments:

It is difficult—not to mention scientifically invalid—to make blanket comparisons of charter schools to traditional public schools. However, because charter schools promise to improve student achievement as a condition of relief from some of the rules and regulations that apply to traditional public schools, it is appropriate to evaluate their effectiveness.

This is a reminder that teaching and learning are highly complex activities and that schools are complicated organizations functioning on behalf of diverse students with a broad range of differences.

Who Teaches in Charter Schools?

Of the forty states with charter school laws, almost half of them stipulate that charter school teachers must be state certified. For the remainder, the requirements vary. In some states, individuals may apply for a waiver to the certification requirement. In the District of Columbia, teachers do not have to be certified at all. In still other states, special guidelines apply. Illinois, for example, requires that charter schools be able to employ noncertified teachers if they have a bachelor's degree, five years' experience in the area of degree, a passing score on state teacher tests, and evidence of professional growth; for all such noncertified

teachers, mentoring must be provided (Education Commission of the States, 2007b).

Most professional educators, like the author of this book, believe that a formal program in learning to become a teacher is vital for anyone who wants to teach. For this reason, we hope that all charter schools will eventually require certification. This will ease some of the doubts about the value of charter schools for American education.

A Case Study: The Russell Byers Charter School

If you have never attended or visited a charter school, a case study may help you understand what the charter school movement is about. Founded in 2001, the Russell Byers Charter School in Philadelphia houses 400 students from kindergarten (including 4K, a kindergarten for four-year-olds) through sixth grade. The school is named after a long-time *Philadelphia Daily News* columnist who devoted much of his writing to the cause of public education and school reform. After he was murdered in a robbery attempt at a convenience store, his widow and their two children spearheaded the effort to open this charter school in his memory.

Open to all children living in Philadelphia, the school draws students from more than thirty-five neighborhoods. Because there is a long waiting list, new students are selected by lottery. The school has committed itself to small class sizes, academic excellence, civic responsibility, and community service.

All classrooms have networked computers and follow Pennsylvania state standards in the various subject areas. However, the school's educational approach, Expeditionary Learning Schools Outward Bound (ELS), based on the Outward Bound model of outdoor education, emphasizes experiential learning. This means that students spend up to twelve weeks studying a single topic both inside and outside the classroom. Located in a downtown area, the school can draw on many nearby cultural resources, such as the Franklin Institute science museum. The cross-disciplinary subjects of study have included insect life, community gardens, the explorers Lewis and Clark, and life in a village in Ghana. When a learning unit is completed, students share their knowledge through performances featuring essays, poems, photos, theater, song, and paintings. Also central to the Byers School experience is a community service project related to the topic of study and selected by the students.

The goals and methods of this school give you some idea of why charter schools have attracted more and more American families. Keep in mind, though, that no one school is typical of this broad-ranging movement in American education.

HOMESCHOOLING: ANOTHER NONTRADITIONAL OPTION

In 1997, a thirteen-year-old named Rebecca Sealfon won the 70th National Spelling Bee. What was remarkable about Rebecca's performance was that she had never gone to school! Having been taught at home exclusively, her performance turned a national spotlight on **homeschooling**.

A few decades ago, homeschooling represented a fringe part of the educational landscape, but currently it is a fast-growing trend. In 1999, an estimated 850,000 U.S. students between the ages of five and seventeen were being homeschooled (Bielick, Chandler, & Broughman, 2001). By 2009, according to some estimates, the number of homeschooled children was expected to have doubled as more families question the efficacy of traditional schools in preparing their children academically and socially for a global economy and a highly competitive marketplace. (In these statistics, students are considered to be homeschooled if their parents report them as being schooled at home for at least part of their education and if their part-time enrollment in public or private schools does not exceed twenty-five hours a week.) At the current time, more than two and a half million students are being homeschooled with a vast number of websites supporting curriculum construction for homeschooled children.

Although many different types of families homeschool their children, the majority tend to be white, middle or upper-middle class, religious, and well educated. Often they select homeschooling primarily for religious and cultural reasons, eager to protect their children from "a popular culture overflowing with images of sexual

Did You Know?

At the current time, more than two and a half million students are being homeschooled.

rebellion and promiscuity" (Anderson, 2000). Figure 6.2 shows statistics from a survey sponsored by the National Center for Education Statistics. In this survey, the most frequent reason parents gave for homeschooling their children was concern about schools' "environment," which included worries about safety, drug use, and peer pressure. Nearly a third of parents mentioned this reason, and almost as many cited a desire to give their children religious or moral instruction. Fewer parents, but still a significant percentage, expressed dissatisfaction with academic instruction in schools (Princiotta & Bielick, 2006).

Clearly, some elements of homeschooling, including the lack of pressure to perform and a freedom of choice concerning the curriculum, are appealing alternatives to mandated curriculum that is based on standardized testing. Schooling children at home also keeps them out of harm's way and, for some parents, allows religious training that, by law, their children would not receive in public school.

Some critics of homeschooling worry that most parents cannot provide the academic support their children need to learn a wide range of subjects. After all, certified teachers are trained in educational methods and in curriculum content areas, and most parents are not. However, a growing number of companies cater to parents who homeschool by providing curriculum materials. In addition, the Internet now offers an abundance of educational resources that were not available a decade ago. Many previously reluctant parents now choose to homeschool their children because of the wealth of materials available online.

Another worry about homeschooling is that students miss the socialization that occurs in schools. The entire experience of "going to school" is composed of much more than lessons, athletics, and theatrical and musical performances. It is a daily and annual ritual event that defines the growth and development of children. As we saw in earlier chapters, many cultural beliefs and social values are transmitted through the "hidden curriculum" of schools. Students meet peers

homeschooling Educating children at home rather than in a school; parents typically serve as teachers.

Figure 6.2

Reasons Parents Give for Homeschooling Their Children

Concern about environment of other schools

To provide religious or moral instruction

Dissatisfaction with academic instruction at other schools

Other reasons

Child has a physical or mental health problem

Child has other special needs

0 10 20 30 40 50

Percentage

Photo: © Barbara Sauder/iStockphoto

SOURCE: Princiotta, D. & Bielick, S. (2006). *Homeschooling in the United States: 2003* (NCES 2006-042). Washington, D.C.: U.S. Department of Education, National Center for Education Statistics.

who represent a cross-section of their community—students with different learning styles, abilities, opinions, strengths, weaknesses, and ways of being in the world. Are homeschooled children denied all these opportunities?

Proponents of homeschooling point out that parents have formed networks to engage their children in social and musical events outside the home. Homeschooling does not mean isolation. Some studies indicate that very few homeschooled children are socially deprived and that homeschooled children in general have a better self-concept than conventionally schooled children do. For instance, a study conducted in 2003 (Ray, 2004) gathered data from more than 5,000 adults who had been homeschooled for more than seven years. The study reported that 71 percent of these graduates were active and involved community members and participated in service activities regularly, as compared with 37 percent of U.S. adults of similar ages from traditional education backgrounds. Further, 76 percent of those surveyed, ages eighteen to twenty-four, reported voting within the last five years, compared with 29 percent for the corresponding U.S. populace.

Most state governments regulate homeschooling to at least some degree. In some of these states, parents merely have to notify the educational authorities that they are schooling their children at home. In other states, parents must submit their children's test scores or other professional evaluations of academic progress. The strictest states have further conditions, such as requiring that parents file a plan or program of study before they can gain permission to homeschool their children.

Middle School: A Movement in Transition

In the early 1900s, the dominant school configuration was eight years of primary school followed by four years of secondary school. This "8–4" model was called into question as more and more students attended public school. In 1899, the National Education Association issued a report calling for secondary school to begin in the seventh grade, citing that time, the beginning of adolescence, as a "natural turning point in a pupil's life" (National Education Association, 1899). Nevertheless, it was another fifteen to twenty years before the junior high school model of grades 7 through 9 emerged and began to proliferate.

Originally, junior high schools were thought of as preparatory grounds for the academic rigor of high school. By the late 1960s and early 1970s, however, various models for reorganization of school district grades were being considered to meet desegregation requirements. Further, many junior high schools were seen as focusing on content mastery rather than on the psychological and emotional needs of early adolescents.

By the 1980s, many school reformers endorsed a new "middle school" concept intended to create an educational experience more appropriate for young adolescents. The goal was to make the old junior high school more developmentally responsive by changing the grade configuration from grades 7–8 or 7–8–9 to grades 6–7–8 and designing new organizational structures such as interdisciplinary teams (Juvonen et al., 2004). The teams would ensure that a group or cluster of students would be taught by the same four or five subject area teachers, thus creating a sense of community and closeness.

In the following decades, many school districts converted their junior highs to middle schools, but the process was far from uniform. As Figure 6.3 shows, there are still several ways of organizing the middle grades.

CRITIQUES OF THE MIDDLE SCHOOL MODEL

Despite well-intentioned and committed educators, middle schools do not yet fully serve the needs of young teens. The history of the middle school movement suggests that

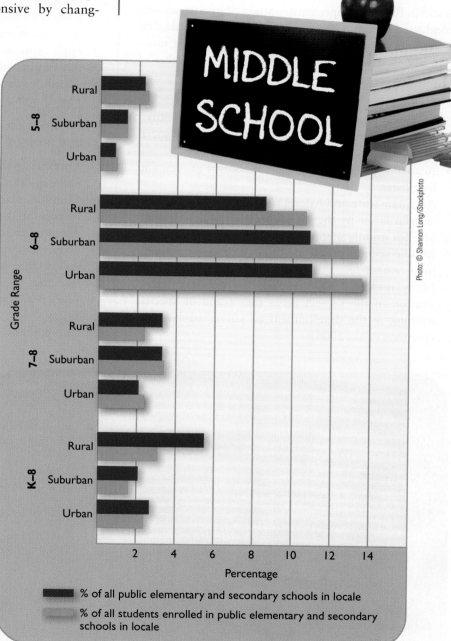

Photo: © Shannon Long/iStockphoto

■ % of all public elementary and secondary schools in locale

■ % of all students enrolled in public elementary and secondary schools in locale

Figure 6.3

Frequency of Different Models for Organizing the Middle Grades

SOURCE: Juvonen, J., Le, V., Kaganoff, T., Augustine, C. H., & Constant, L. (2004). *Focus on the Wonder Years: Challenges Facing the American Middle School.* Santa Monica, CA: Rand Corporation. Figure 1.1, p. 3. Copyright 2004 by Rand Corporation. Reproduced with permission of Rand Corporation in the format Textbook via Copyright Clearance Center.

the middle school became the norm because of societal and demographic pressures and not because of hard evidence to support the need for a separate school for young teens. In fact, research in 1989 showed that seventh and eighth graders schooled in a K–8 model performed better in all areas of achievement and psychological wellness than did their peers at middle school (Eccles & Midgley, 1989; Eccles, Lord, & Midgley, 1991).

For these reasons, organization of the middle grades is still in flux. A comprehensive study of middle schools conducted by the Rand Corporation recommends that states and school districts seek alternatives to the now-typical 6–8 structure of middle school, for a number of significant reasons:

- National school-safety statistics suggest that physical conflict is especially problematic in middle schools.
- Social norms in middle school may foster antisocial behavior.
- Academic progress for middle schools is uneven and lackluster.
- Adequate state and federal supports to meet the new standards set by the NCLB legislation are unavailable for middle schools.
- Middle schools do not do enough to foster parental involvement.
- Many middle school teachers do not have certification in the subject areas they teach or specific training in the development of young adolescents. (Juvonen et al., 2004)

A FRAMEWORK FOR EFFECTIVE MIDDLE SCHOOLS

In the 2003 document *This We Believe: Successful Schools for Young Adolescents*, the National Middle School Association describes eight characteristics of an effective middle school culture:

- Educators who value working with young adolescents
- Courageous, collaborative leadership
- A shared vision
- An inviting, supportive, and safe environment
- High expectations for all
- Active learning by both students and teachers
- An adult advocate for every student
- Family and community partnerships

Further, *This We Believe* identifies and describes six critical program characteristics:

- Curriculum that is relevant, challenging, integrative, and exploratory
- Multiple teaching and learning approaches that respond to students' diversity
- Assessment and evaluation that promote learning
- Organizational structures, such as interdisciplinary teams, that support meaningful relationships and learning
- School-wide policies that foster health, wellness, and safety
- Comprehensive guidance and support services

Reading this list of fourteen characteristics makes us pause and ask: Why can't these characteristics simply be implemented? What does it take? The answers to these questions lie at the heart of every educational reform movement. They are not simple; they require an investment of time and energy on the part of administrators, teachers, parents, school districts, local school boards, and state agencies.

One example of the difficult problems of middle schools is the issue of school safety, which we have mentioned in passing several times in this chapter. When people talk about school safety today, they are referring

Middle schools are being assessed according to how well they meet the needs of preteens and young teens in transition.

© Elizabeth Crews

to the outbreaks of violence that have become all too common in our schools. This is the subject of the next section.

Creating a Safe School Climate: The Concern about Violence in Schools

Although the vast majority of the country's students will never be touched by peer violence in their K–12 school careers, serious isolated incidents of school violence have rocked the headlines and shaken confidence in our schools. In 1999 the Littleton, Colorado, high school, Columbine, was the scene of a violent school attack by two students that claimed the lives of fourteen students and a teacher. This was the most violent school attack in U.S. history until it was eclipsed by the 2007 rampage at Virginia Tech University in Blacksburg, Virginia, which claimed thirty-two lives, including twenty-seven students.

Although these incidents of targeted violence are rare, the highly publicized shootings of the last fifteen years have prompted educators to examine how, if at all, these incidents, and other less serious ones, could have been prevented.

Earlier in this text, we discussed school climate and the ways it is evident when you enter a school as a student or teacher. It may even be evident to a regular visitor. The school climate is a result of the relationships that exist among the students, teachers, parents, and administrators within the school community. In a school with a climate of safety, adults and students respect each other and, importantly, students have a positive connection to at least one adult in authority. When a climate of safety is created, you can sense it in a school; there is a feeling of emotional wellness. In this type of school climate, problems can be raised and addressed in peer groups and with counselors before they escalate. It becomes noticeable when a student is disturbed and in distress. If a member of the school community shows enormous personal pain that could lead to harm—to the student him- or herself or to others—it becomes a cry for help that is answered.

The sidebar "Creating a School Climate That Promotes Safety and Connectedness" (on the next page)

© Ju-Lee/iStockphoto

lists some important factors that help establish a safe school climate. In Chapter 9, we will discuss the classroom community and the ways we can think about teaching as forging relationships with students. On a schoolwide basis, all the participants in the school community—the administrators, parents, school secretaries, custodians, groundskeepers, as well as the teachers and students—must contribute to the establishment of a climate of safety.

LO7 Protecting the Rights of Students

Clearly, students have a right to be safe in school. That is one basic right that cannot be denied. What other rights do students have?

In most states, education of children has been compulsory for more than a century. Children must go to school or (as we discussed earlier in this chapter) to a reasonable home-based alternative to school. Obviously, though, schools cannot do whatever they like with this captive audience. Along with schools' obligation to educate students, students deserve to have certain rights, but exactly what those rights should be isn't always evident. A number of recent laws and court cases have raised serious questions about the subject. Let's explore some of the issues that have come to the fore.

Q: *Do you worry about violence in your school or classroom?*

Before reading further, stop a moment and think: What kinds of student rights do you suppose are covered by law? And how do you suppose the recent concern about school safety has affected students' rights?

THE RIGHT TO PRIVACY

Do you know where all of the information about your educational history is kept? Are your health records in the same place? Does the file contain records of your student loans and other information you might not like to share with everyone? What if you have a learning

CREATING A SCHOOL CLIMATE THAT PROMOTES SAFETY AND CONNECTEDNESS

Working together, the U.S. Department of Education and the Secret Service have produced a guide to help schools create a climate of school safety. According to this document, the major components and tasks for creating a safe school climate include:

Assessing the School's Emotional Climate

- How do the students and teachers experience the daily life of the school?
- Is there a culture of respect?
- Are students' emotional needs being met?
- Is everyday teasing and bullying dealt with immediately?

Creating Connections between Adults and Students

- Do students have a positive relationship with at least one adult?
- Does each student feel there is an adult she or he can talk to about problems and concerns?

Breaking the Code of Silence

- In many schools, students believe that revealing another student's pain or problems breaks a special peer code. This belief often forces troubled students to go it alone.
- In a safe school climate, students are willing to break the code of silence to get help for a peer.

Involving Everyone

- Are all members of the school community involved in creating policy and practices that help each member respond to stressful and potentially harmful events?

SOURCE: Fein, R. A., Vossekuil, B., Pollack, W. S., Borum, R., Modzeleski, W., & Reddy, M. (2002). *Threat Assessment in Schools: A Guide to Managing Threatening Situations and to Creating Safe School Climates*. Washington, D.C.: United States Secret Service and United States Department of Education.

Family Educational Rights and Privacy Act (FERPA) or the Buckley Amendment A federal law requiring educational agencies to protect the confidentiality of students' educational records.

disability—is that documented in your file? Who has access to this file? What are your rights?

The **Family Educational Rights and Privacy Act (FERPA)** of 1974, also known as the **Buckley Amendment**, is a federal law that requires educational agencies and institutions to protect the confidentiality of students' educational records. It applies to all school systems and individual schools, including colleges and universities, receiving federal financial assistance or funding.

FERPA allows students and their parents to have access to the student's records kept by educational institutions. The law also states that no one outside the institution may have access to a student's educational records, nor can the institution disclose any information from the records without the written consent of the student, or for students under the age of eighteen, their parents. The U.S. Congress passed this act in response to instances of parents or students being denied access to their records or information about students being improperly used.

FERPA clearly states that parents of students in attendance at a school have the right to inspect and review the education records of their children. Further, if the parents (or students over the age of eighteen) challenge the contents of the records, they must be given a hearing. At this hearing, the parents and student have the opportunity to insert their own written explanation into the record. The intent is to make sure the records are not inaccurate, misleading, or otherwise in violation of the student's privacy or other rights.

As a college or university undergraduate or graduate student, you should know what is in your personal records at your institution. Once you are eighteen years old, your parents have no inherent right to inspect your educational record; that right becomes yours alone. Parents may, however, gain access to so-called directory information, which includes simple facts that would not compromise a student's privacy, such as enrollment status, major field of study, degrees received, and so on.

Recent Challenges to FERPA

Until 2001, no cases involving violations to FERPA were brought to the U.S. Supreme Court. In 2001, however, the Court heard a case concerning the oral reporting by peers of student grades. In Oklahoma, in the Owassa Independent School District, a mother was disturbed when her son's teacher asked the class to grade each other's quizzes and then had students call out the grades so she could record them. This mother felt that the calling out of grades by her son's peers was a violation of his right to privacy. She lost the case; the Supreme Court ruled that peer grading did not violate FERPA.

A second case was brought to the Supreme Court by a college student at Gonzaga University in Washington state. The teacher certification officer at that university overheard a student discussing a teacher candidate's alleged sexual harassment of another student and proceeded to conduct an investigation, place remarks about it in the student's record, and deny teacher certification to that student. The supposed victim of the sexual harassment denied that it occurred and never pressed charges. The alleged offender sued the university for violating FERPA. This case made its way through various levels of the state court system and finally reached the U.S. Supreme Court in 2002. The Justices ruled that FERPA did not give "enforceable rights" to individuals. Rather, it was up to the Department of Education to enforce FERPA by denying funding to educational institutions that violated the law.

Although this Supreme Court ruling may prevent individual students from collecting damages for violation of their privacy, FERPA still offers protection through the power of the purse. Because educational institutions do not want to lose their federal funding, they will be careful about allowing practices that infringe on rights established by FERPA.

STUDENTS' AND PARENTS' RIGHTS UNDER FERPA

- The right to inspect and review educational records
- The right to request amendment of educational records
- The right to exercise some control over the disclosure of information from educational records
- The right to file a complaint with the U.S. Department of Education if a school or other educational agency fails to comply with the act

Compromises on Privacy

In this age of readily accessible data, it often feels as though anyone can gain access to another person's information just by having Internet access. It is not quite that easy to get educational records. Unfortunately, however, since the Columbine High School shooting in 1999 in Colorado, educators and police agencies have felt an increased need to identify, collect, and share information in a coordinated effort to prevent a recurrence of this type of student violence. Events such as the terrorist attacks at the World Trade Center towers and the Pentagon have also made the sharing of information seem more imperative.

The scope of student data collected has expanded greatly since FERPA was passed in 1974. For example, student records now include data relating to the student's needs for specific educational services. Moreover, requests for student information now come from a growing number of sources inside school systems (including counselors, principals, school social workers, special education personnel, classroom teachers) and outside school systems (military recruiters, university

Q: *Do you think that most teachers consider FERPA when making comments in students' permanent school files?*

CHAPTER 6: CONTEMPORARY TRENDS AND PRESSING ISSUES IN EDUCATION **141** researchers, law enforcement officers, the courts, college admissions personnel, the media, social services agencies, and others).

Some additional laws do help protect the new wealth of information. Individualized education programs are protected under IDEA; parents must have ready access to student IEPs, but the information is considered confidential and schools are restricted from releasing it to people who do not have a legitimate educational interest in the child. Similarly, NCLB ensures the right to privacy of individual students' scores. Nevertheless, the USA PATRIOT Act of 2001 created the possibility that, with a subpoena, authorities could gain access to a student's confidential information without the knowledge of the student or the parents (Vacca, 2004).

Clearly, educational institutions need to exercise careful monitoring of when and to whom student data are released. As a teacher, you, too, should be sensitive to your students' rights to privacy.

FIRST AMENDMENT RIGHTS OF STUDENTS

❝*Congress shall make no law respecting an establishment of religion, or prohibiting the free exercise thereof; or abridging the freedom of speech, or of the press; or the right of the people peaceably to assemble, and to petition the Government for a redress of grievances.***❞**
—The First Amendment to the U.S. Constitution

It is commonly accepted that, in schools and classrooms, the need for legitimate teaching and learning requires rules of behavior that, at times, restrict the speech of students. Yet the Supreme Court tells us in *Tinker v. Des Moines* that "students do not shed their constitutional rights when they enter the schoolhouse door." In this 1969 ruling, the Supreme Court upheld the First Amendment right of high school students to wear black armbands in a public high school as a form of protest against the Vietnam War. Wearing the armband was considered symbolic speech. According to the Court, school administrators could prohibit the armbands only if the administrators showed that the protest would cause a substantial disruption of the school's educational mission. (Do you think the case would have come out differently if school administrators had demonstrated that the armbands caused loud debates to break out in class?)

Similarly, in the 1973 case of *Papish v. the Board of Curators of the University of Missouri*, the Supreme Court ruled in favor of the First Amendment rights of Barbara Papish, a graduate student, after the university expelled her for distributing a controversial leaflet containing profanity and a cartoon of policemen raping the Statue of Liberty.

Other Court decisions, however, have supported schools in their attempts to restrict students' speech. In 1986, the Court ruled in favor of the right of Washington state high school administrators when they disciplined a student for delivering a campaign speech that was full of sexual innuendo at a school assembly. In this case, *Bethel School District No. 403 v. Fraser*, the Court expressed the view that school administrators had the right to punish student speech that violated school rules and that interfered with legitimate educational objectives. As another example, in the 1988 case of the *Hazelwood School District v. Kuhlmeier*, the Court upheld the right of school administrators to censor materials in a student-edited newspaper that concerned sensitive issues such as student pregnancy and that could be considered an invasion of privacy.

Also accepted is the school district's right to impose dress code restrictions on students—and teachers. Schools may require that students wear uniforms,

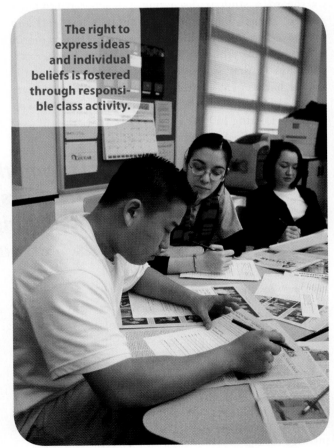

The right to express ideas and individual beliefs is fostered through responsible class activity.

© Elizabeth Crews

and they may also impose reasonable grooming and dress codes for their teachers.

Overall, it seems that the Supreme Court has tried to strike a balance between the right to free expression and schools' need to maintain a productive learning atmosphere. In day-to-day terms, teachers and administrators make their own decisions on the basis of established school policies as well as common sense. Think back to the speech and dress policies of the schools you have attended. Do you think a reasonable balance was struck between individual rights and an orderly learning environment?

The First Amendment also addresses freedom of religion, and here the issues become even thornier and more confusing, as we noted in Chapter 5. There are many legal questions surrounding the separation of church and state and the First Amendment's clause about free exercise of religion. In general terms, public schools must remain neutral about religious beliefs, but does this mean, for instance, that a student-led religious group cannot meet on school grounds? Does it mean that teachers cannot lead their students in reciting the Pledge of Allegiance, which includes the phrase "under God"?

The courts have been actively tackling these issues, and decisions made over the next few years may affect your classroom. Right now, to sum up the impact of various laws, court cases, and federal guidelines, it is fair to say that the following rules apply:

1. Prayer cannot be a regular part of the school day.
2. Worship services, including Bible readings, may not be practiced in public school.
3. Public schools may not intrude on a family's religious beliefs.
4. Teachers and administrators in public schools may not advocate religious beliefs.
5. Extracurricular religious groups may meet on public school grounds as long as they are not led by a teacher or school official.
6. Many states require that schools include the Pledge of Allegiance in their daily schedules, but the practice remains the subject of court challenges. Individual students may not be forced to salute the flag if this conflicts with their religious beliefs.

WRITING & REFLECTION

Prayer at a Football Game

The case of *Santa Fe Independent School District v. Doe* (2000) concerned a group of students at a Texas high school who offered a prayer over the public address system before a football game. The U.S. Supreme Court ruled that this practice constituted a violation of the Establishment Clause and should not be permitted. Reflect on how this case reveals the impact of the law on the educational system as well as decisions you may make as a teacher.

- What is the Establishment Clause? (*Hint*: Look back at the wording of the First Amendment.)
- What do you suppose was the basic reasoning behind the Court's ruling? Think about whether the people who heard the prayer had full choice about whether to participate. Also consider the extent to which football games are sponsored and supported by schools.

The Rights and Responsibilities of Teachers

Like students' rights, teachers' rights are protected by the U.S. Constitution. As agents of the government, public school teachers are protected by state constitutional provisions, statutes, and regulations as well. They are also held accountable to these regulations and may be dismissed if they are not meeting their obligations. This section gives a brief overview of the legal rights and responsibilities attached to the teaching profession.

Like students' rights, teachers' rights are protected by the U.S. Constitution.

due process A formal process, such as a legal or administrative proceeding, that follows established rules designed to protect the rights of the people involved.

tenure A status granted to a teacher, usually after a probationary period, that protects him or her from dismissal except for reasons of incompetence, gross misconduct, or other conditions stipulated by the state.

TEACHERS' RIGHTS

Although private school teachers do not enjoy as much protection as public school teachers, both are protected by the Civil Rights Act of 1964, which prohibits racial, sexual, or religious discrimination in employment. Teachers' employment rights are further protected by the due process clause of the Fourteenth Amendment to the U.S. Constitution, which provides that no state may "deprive any person of life, liberty, or property, without due process of law." This **due process** requirement means that school boards and state agencies must follow established rules when deciding to dismiss or discipline a teacher.

In most states, teachers are also protected by **tenure** statutes. These statutes define a probationary period during which a teacher's performance is evaluated. If the performance is deemed acceptable, a teacher may receive tenure, and then his or her contract is automatically renewed each year unless there is a specified cause for dismissal.

Legitimate causes for dismissal vary from state to state. In Illinois, as one example, a teacher's certificate may be revoked or suspended for immorality, a health condition detrimental to students, incompetence, unprofessional conduct, neglect of duty, willful failure to report child abuse, or "other just cause" (Illinois School Code, section 21–23a).

Teachers have a number of other rights, such as freedom of expression and the right to personal privacy, as outlined in the sidebar "Teachers' Rights: A Brief Summary." All of these are limited, however, by the teacher's responsibility to students. In his book *A Different Kind of Discipline*, Tony Humphreys (1998) talks about the ways teachers must be aware and respectful of students' rights and their own rights. He offers the following list of rights that a teacher should expect and be prepared to uphold when necessary:

- *I have the right to physical, emotional, social, intellectual, creative, and sexual safety.*
- *I have the right to respect from students, colleagues, leaders, and parents.*

TEACHERS' RIGHTS: A BRIEF SUMMARY

Teachers are generally thought to possess all of the following rights. The precise extent of these rights has been the subject of numerous court cases.

Freedom from Discrimination

The Civil Rights Act of 1964 prohibits racial, sexual, or religious discrimination in employment.

Academic Freedom

By tradition, a teacher is reasonably free to teach according to his or her best understanding of subject matter and instructional methods. But the content taught by the teacher must be relevant to and consistent with the teacher's responsibilities; a teacher cannot promote personal or political agendas in the classroom.

Freedom of Expression

Protected by the First Amendment, teachers can express their personal opinions. However, they must not use this freedom to undermine authority and adversely affect the working relationships in a school.

Privacy Rights

Teachers enjoy limited rights to personal privacy. A teacher's personal life may lead to disciplinary action only if it affects the integrity of the school or district and hampers the teacher's effectiveness.

- *I have the right to teach in an atmosphere of order and attention.*
- *I have the right to demand social structures within the school that guarantee respect for my rights.*
- *I have the right to ask for help when needed.*
- *I have the right to fair, just, and effective leadership on the part of the school principal and vice-principal.*
- *I have the right to express any need or grievance I may have.*
- *When any of my rights are violated, I have the right to have recourse to social structures within and outside the school that protect those rights.*

SOURCE: From Dr. Tony Humphreys, *A Different Kind of Discipline*. Copyright © 1998. Reprinted by permission of the author.

TEACHERS' LEGAL RESPONSIBILITIES

Teachers have many ethical and professional responsibilities to their students, the parents, the school, and the district. They also have certain legal responsibilities, established by state law or by court cases.

For example, teachers must take reasonable precautions to keep their students safe. If such precautions are neglected, the teacher or the school may be held legally responsible. Teachers and schools have been sued when students were injured in the classroom, on the playground, or on field trips.

One very important legal requirement is that teachers report child abuse and negligence when they believe they have noticed it in their classrooms. Child abuse is a state crime, and each state has specific reporting guidelines. Consider North Carolina's statute:

> *Any person or institution who has cause to suspect that any juvenile is abused, neglected, . . . or has died as a result of maltreatment, shall report the case of that juvenile to the director of the department of social services in the county where the juvenile resides or is found. The report may be made orally, by telephone, or in writing. The report shall include . . . the name and address of the juvenile . . . ; the nature and extent of any injury or condition resulting from abuse [or] neglect . . . ; and any other information which the reporter believes might be helpful in establishing the need for protective services or court intervention. (quoted in Smith & Lambie, 2005)*

In some states, teacher candidates must complete child abuse seminars in which they learn the symptoms of

TEACHSOURCE VIDEO CASE

Teachers Discuss Their Ethical and Legal Responsibilities

Find the TeachSource Video Case "Legal and Ethical Dimensions of Teaching: Reflections from Today's Educators" on the student website. Think about the discussion of rules and rights. After watching the video, consider the following question:

In what ways are the "rules of the classroom" meant to support students' First Amendment rights?

child abuse, sexual abuse, emotional abuse, and neglect. In many school systems across the country, there are support services to help teachers by providing in-service classes on child, sexual, and emotional abuse and neglect.

Many districts also have specific procedures for reporting bullying and sexual harassment among students. Teachers cannot sweep these incidents "under the rug"; they must report them in a timely fashion. In Chapter 9, we return to this subject because it is a crucial part of building classroom community.

Concluding Thoughts

From inclusion to gifted education, and from problem-based learning to test preparation, public schools in America struggle to find the best way to educate all of their students. Complex, diverse, and challenging are good adjectives to describe our students and the world in which we seek to educate them. Pursuing a career in education requires that you consider all these factors, but it also holds the promise of making a difference for the most vulnerable of our citizens—our children.

There is a strong possibility that the school or district in which you teach will have inclusion classrooms, as nearly 10 percent of all students in public schools (more, by some estimates) have a disability. You will be exposed to approaches like project- and problem-based learning that can make your students' school experience truly challenging and rewarding. At the same time, you will need to deal with the standards-based accountability movement, which is now a dominant trend in American education and is undergoing change as new data is examined. You will also be asked to protect the rights of your students as you seek to contribute to a climate of safety and equity.

You may be drawn to the charter school movement, which seeks alternative ways to educate students who are often ignored by traditional schools. You may be part of an anti-bullying task force in your school. Wherever contemporary trends and pressing issues lead, there will be new ones to catch up to, especially as the technology revolution continues to challenge the way we think about teaching and learning.

There are contradictions here—forces pulling you in different directions. Being a teacher means finding your own way of reconciling these various demands. In the next chapter, we'll explore information technology, no longer a trend, but an integral way of life that must find its place in the world of teaching and learning. It, too, brings both demands and significant benefits for you and your students.

RESOURCES FOR FURTHER EXPLORATION

Online Resources

All Kinds of Minds
http://www.allkindsofminds.org/

This site is designed to help users understand differences in learning. It provides helpful tips and activities to parents and educators on behalf of students with learning differences.

Buck Institute for Education
http://www.bie.org/

The nonprofit Buck Institute is dedicated to improving teaching and learning. Its website offers guidelines and other resources for classroom project-based learning.

Collaborative for Academic, Social, and Emotional Learning
http://www.casel.org/

This site offers resources, articles, stories, tools and specific roadmaps for implementing a social and emotional learning program in schools.

Council for Learning Disabilities
http://www.cldinternational.org/

This site provides explanations of common learning disabilities, an overview of research in this area, and an international perspective on students and learning differences.

First Amendment Center Online
http://www.firstamendmentcenter.org/

This site provides a comprehensive view of First Amendment issues and topics. Featuring daily updates, it offers a wealth of data about challenges to our First Amendment rights.

Keep Schools Safe: The School Safety and Security Resource
http://www.keepschoolssafe.org/

This site provides resources and suggestions for students, schools, and parents to help prevent school violence.

Learn in Freedom!
http://www.learninfreedom.org/

Offers parents links to many resources on homeschooling and provides profiles of famous people who learned without a public school system, including the founders of the United States.

Learning Disabilities Online
http://www.ldonline.org

This website answers frequently asked questions and provides information on a wide range of learning disabilities.

National Association for Gifted Children
http://www.nagc.org/

This website provides information and resources for parents and educators of gifted children.

National Middle School Association
http://www.nmsa.org

This website offers current knowledge, recommended projects, and advice to all who work with youngsters of middle school age.

National Center on Response to Intervention
http://www.rti4success.org/

This website offers tools and screening devices for implementing RTI.

No More "Waiting to Fail"

http://www.ascd.org/publications/educational_
leadership/oct07/vol65/num02/No-More-"Waiting-
to-Fail".aspx

Written by Rachel Brown-Chidsey, this article from
Educational Leadership (October 2007) explores the
Response to Intervention model and the research upon
which it is based.

University of Northern Iowa Inclusion Resources

http://www.uni.edu/coe/inclusion/

Designed for teachers, parents, and school staff, this site
has good suggestions for inclusive classrooms.

Print Resource

**Joseph E. Zins, Roger P. Weissberg, Margaret C. Wang,
and Herbert J. Walberg (eds.), *Building Academic
Success on Social and Emotional Learning: What Does the
Research Say?* (New York: Teachers College Press, 2004).**
This book provides research-based evidence for the
relationship between social-emotional education and
school success.

CHAPTER 7

THE INFORMATION TECHNOLOGY REVOLUTION IN THE 21ST CENTURY

© newscom

The following definitions for the word *revolution* emerge from a quick search on the Internet:

- A drastic and far-reaching change in ways of thinking and behaving
- The overthrow of a government by those who are governed
- Rotation: a single complete turn (axial or orbital) (from WordNet, at http://wordnet. princeton.edu/)

LEARNING OUTCOMES

After reading this chapter, you should be thinking about the following ideas:

LO1 Most school-age children do not know a time when they did not use a computer at least once a week, or even daily, and are engaged by technology in the classroom.

LO2 Because technology is part of many students' daily lives, it makes sense to use it for more than gathering information and social networking—it can be used as a tool that fosters interactive, real-world learning.

LO3 Communication is becoming increasingly open with the rise of Web 2.0; many teachers today participate in blogs or start their own blog as a way to share ideas about teaching and learning.

LO4 Technology in the classroom can benefit disadvantaged and disabled students.

LO5 With so much data available online, teachers have often had to rethink their role because all the information we could ever want to know about a topic is a few mouse clicks away.

It is the first definition, of course, that characterizes the role of computer technology, connectivity, and access to the Internet in the past generation. The information technology revolution has brought about a drastic and far-reaching change in our ways of thinking and behaving, leading us into a period that some are calling the Digital Renaissance (Jukes, 2006). As you might have noticed, I sought the definition of *revolution* on the Internet instead of in a traditional dictionary. When was the last time you went to a printed dictionary? Even your access to the Web-based videos cited in this textbook is testimony to ways in which communication and access to information have changed in the last fifteen years.

One big question for you as a future teacher—for all of us in education—is this: while all aspects of daily life have changed so dramatically, why have the design and conditions of classroom learning and teaching remained somewhat unchanged? I say "somewhat" because we do now find networked computers in many public and private school classrooms, and some teachers do seize the opportunity to engage their students in new learning experiences. Many schools have classrooms using electronic whiteboards, and many teachers use portable wireless devices as part of their daily teaching routines. By and large, however, teaching has lagged far behind the advances in technology.

This chapter addresses the ways information, knowledge, communication, and understanding can be redefined in this Digital Renaissance. It also underscores the fact that the same inequities that have dogged American education since its earliest days persist in the digital age. It is important to keep in mind that even though the Internet holds the promise of infinite knowledge, what gets delivered more often than not is infinite *information* (Orenstein, 2009). Sometimes, when we are inundated with data, it is difficult to make sense of it and connect to that which is most important. It falls to the classroom teacher, in any grade level and in any subject, to ask him- or herself, "What is the best

© ARTqppler/iStockphoto

digital natives People who have grown up using the digital "language" of computers, video, games, and the Internet.

flat classroom A classroom in which students, like the teacher, have ready access to information, so that the teacher is not the lone expert.

way to make use of the electronic resources, videos, and communication tools that are available to my students?" For some teachers, it is overwhelming to answer this question, but to ignore what is available for teaching and learning in any area online is to deny the way your students spend their time outside of school.

LO1 What Does Technology Mean for the Classroom?

Most likely, your future students will spend a good deal of time online. In fact, they will be **digital natives**, a term that commentators like Marc Prensky (2001) coined to refer to people who have used digital technology all their lives. One educator explains the situation this way:

> Adults used to be able to ignore, resist, or fool ourselves about the realities going on in children's lives. Once they reached our classrooms, we paid attention to their engagement with our subject matter and their classmates—the world could and did, for the most part, stay out of school. But now, these digital natives . . . cannot keep their digital selves out of the classroom. . . . The one thing we cannot do is ignore the fact that many kids are playing around creatively, finding friends, watching videos, listening to music, communicating online whether we like it or not, whether we talk about it in school or not. (Ganley, 2009)

Kids, and I suspect, many of you readers, are also creating content and posting it online. Technology is an integral part of our lives, and more and more, it is part of the work teachers do as educators in the 21st century.

THE FLAT CLASSROOM

Despite the fact that many of today's students are digital natives, the structure of most classrooms remains unchanged. A shift has gradually begun, however, in the way we think about teaching and learning. To borrow an idea from Thomas Friedman's bestseller *The World Is Flat* (2006), this shift involves seeing the classroom as "flat."

The term **flat classroom** refers to the ways information access levels the playing field—or should I say learning field?—in the classroom. The teacher no longer must be seen as the keeper of the true truth, the source of all that is valuable to know. A typical student, through the Internet and other digital resources, has virtually limitless access to information on any topic.

If learners are accessing the Internet from home, at night, outside of the school buildings, then it stands to reason that those same learners will ultimately influence the direction of learning at school. Immediately we can see that, in a flat classroom, the teacher must be a filter, a guide, the one who directs the learning events and helps students develop their understanding as they gain access to more and more information. Later in this chapter, you will begin to see how this process works.

THE CONNECTED CLASSROOM

Do you use the Internet every day? Do you check your e-mail? Access a weather site? Shop? Participate in an online discussion? Are you a blogger? Do you own a smartphone? Are you on Facebook? Do you have a Twitter account? Who do you follow? Because our lives have been transformed by the information technology revolution, the life of the classroom is transformed as well.

Although schools often resist change, the past twenty years have brought a significant increase in the use of technology in U.S. schools. In the early 1990s, one networked computer was available for every twenty students. By 2005, U.S. schools as a whole possessed more than one instructional computer with Internet access for every five students in primary and secondary schools (Wells & Lewis, 2006). By 2011, we can expect the data to be more like one networked computer for every two students; in many schools today, there is one laptop for each student. As we will see later in this chapter, though, there are significant disparities in many urban and rural areas.

Did You Know?

The computer in your cell phone is one million times cheaper, one thousand times more powerful, and one hundred thousand times smaller than the one computer in a building at MIT in 1965.

Did You Know? SOURCE: http://thefischbowl.blogspot.com/2009/09/did-you-know-40-economist-media.html, retrieved March 29, 2010.

Imagine you are in a connected classroom—a room with high-speed Internet access for all the students—and your class is doing research in social studies on the causes of the Civil War. Or perhaps students are exploring a science problem related to global warming. Or they may be checking real-time weather all around the world in preparation for a report on climate trends. In a connected classroom, the ease with which students can access a wide variety of information—and the "seamlessness" with which this information gathering can be integrated into the rest of their work—makes it possible for you to be truly creative as a teacher.

THE PROBLEM OF INFORMATION OVERLOAD

Do you ever experience problems with the wealth of information available via the Internet? Is there simply too much of it out there?

Information used to be scarce, and having more of it was considered a good thing. Now it feels as though we are at a saturation point, with more information than we will ever need. One of the disadvantages of this overload is that it is easy for some students to get overwhelmed. Many teachers who use the Internet for

Q: *How was technology used in your elementary, middle, and high schools?*

project- and problem-based learning caution that students need to be taught how to use inquiry-based methods powered by technology.

The following story gives one example of the benefits of a connected classroom; you can also see how the teacher avoids the problem of overloading her students with irrelevant information.

Ms. Frank's inner-city, third-grade class is studying China—a fact evident from the Chinese lanterns hanging along clotheslines overhead. In the current portion of the unit, the students are being challenged to design and construct a model of a Chinese hanging scroll. They must meet certain specifications; for instance, each scroll must provide three pieces of information about the inventions and customs of China. Today the students are beginning the research process for completing this design challenge, and Ms. Frank is discussing how to do research on the Internet.

The students sit at rapt attention and are visibly excited about beginning the project. They listen carefully to the directions for accessing three specific websites they will need to do their research. Ms. Frank has chosen these sites in advance because they provide easy access to the information the students need, they are at the right reading level for her class, and they do not include anything inappropriate or overly distracting.

Ms. Frank announces that students will work in groups of four, and she assigns group names based on the work students have already done on this unit. The groups are called Great Wall, Yeh-Shen, Chinese New Year, Red Envelope, Chinese Lantern, and Dragon. The students nod and smile in recognition of the group names.

From a cabinet in the classroom, the students get their laptop computers, each of which is wirelessly connected to the Internet. There is one laptop for every two students. The groups work well together, carefully accessing the websites Ms. Frank has instructed them to go to. It is clear that they have done this

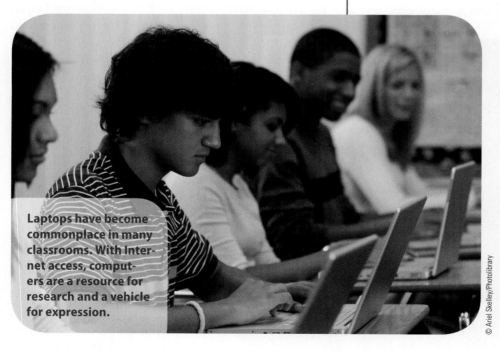

Laptops have become commonplace in many classrooms. With Internet access, computers are a resource for research and a vehicle for expression.

© Ariel Skelley/Photolibrary

kind of work before; using these laptops for research on the Internet is second nature to them. As they gather data, you can hear comments like, "The Chinese invented the compass!" and "Scroll down." Students read aloud statements about the invention of paper money and kites. In each group, the students jointly decide on the information to select from the websites, and they record their data in design portfolios.

Within a few minutes, they have collected plenty of information, and they move on to the next step in designing a hanging scroll.

When a class is researching a topic on the Web, the teacher should filter the websites in advance, as Ms. Frank did, so that students do not waste their time on unproductive sources. In that way, teachers help students manage the information available and avoid problems of information overload. As you prepare units for your students, look for websites with useful links for many different topics or themes. That will make it easier for you to identify good resources for particular units. The sidebar "Guidelines for Internet Research" offers some additional hints for maximizing the Web's potential as an information source for your students.

LO2 Technology and Learning

In Chapter 4, we saw that learning requires the learner to be actively engaged with the material to be learned. Many educators believe that technology encourages this

GUIDELINES FOR INTERNET RESEARCH

- Research is not simply a list of questions for which students find answers. Students' research should focus on finding the information they need to solve a problem or complete a project.
- As they use technology, students need to stay focused on the problem they are trying to solve or the area they are exploring.
- Guide students in interpreting and using the data they find.
- Guide students in finding creative and innovative ways to present their information.
- Encourage students to use the information they gather on the Internet to further other students' understanding of the topic.
- Invite students to collaborate with other students in designing a final product.

process. In fact, in a national survey, more than half of the participating teachers said that technology helped them engage their students in learning, and 75 percent believed that technology use in schoolwork had increased students' achievement (Project Tomorrow, 2007).

But how exactly does technology help get students involved in learning? Entire books have been written on this subject, but here is one key point: Because new technologies are *interactive*, it is easier to create environments in which students can learn by doing, receive feedback, and continually refine their understanding. Through this process, students take charge of their own learning. By integrating technology into the classroom, you promote students' passionate involvement in their own learning,

Computer-based projects can include artifacts downloaded from the Web. The potential to expand upon student learning is part of technology integration.

© Patrick Olear/PhotoEdit, Inc.

allowing them to be adaptable and flexible and to go beyond "education as usual" (Fisch, 2006). Most students are also very familiar with the technologies being employed for classroom learning, and they can bring the skills of their real worlds into their classroom worlds.

WAYS THAT INTERNET TECHNOLOGY SUPPORTS LEARNING

The interactivity of computer-based technologies takes many forms, but from my perspective, there are three paramount ways it supports learning: (1) by allowing students to deal with real-world problems as part of the curriculum, (2) by expanding the possibilities for simulations and modeling, and (3) by creating local and global communities of learners.

Real-World Problems

Technology fosters the use of real-world, exciting problems in the classroom curriculum. Imagine you are working with middle school students on a unit about weather and global warming. Using the Internet, students can find real-time weather data about present conditions as well as archival data showing trends

over time (see Figure 7.1). They can focus on a given part of the world or compare different areas. (See the Resources for Further Exploration section at the end of the chapter for sample websites that offer weather data.)

simulation A computer program or other procedure that imitates a real-world experience.

Now imagine that a high school social studies class is exploring world population, comparing the number of births per day in China, India, and the United States. From the Internet, students gather the most current information related to population growth in these countries—data that have far-reaching implications for consumption of natural resources. This kind of real-world context makes the unit come alive for students. Yet the data retrieval requires only about as much time as it takes to read this paragraph!

Simulations and Modeling

Students can learn a great deal through **simulations**. Often these imitate real-world activities that would be impossible to bring into the classroom. Say you want your students to understand the movements of planets

Figure 7.1

An Interactive Weather Map
Online, interactive maps allow students to study weather developments in real time. This one from the National Weather Service shows a rainstorm in the Midwest.

National Weather Service/NOAA

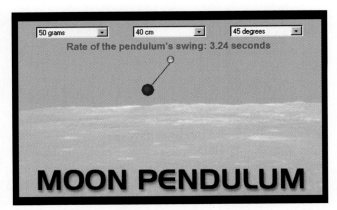

Figure 7.2

A Pendulum Simulation
In this online simulation, students can adjust the pendulum's weight and length and the maximum angle of its swing.

in the solar system. Obviously you can't bring Mars and Venus to class, but you can use simulation software that shows the planets in motion and allows students to view the system from different positions. As another example, if you are teaching biology, your school system may not want to use dead animals, like frogs, for dissections, but you can turn to computer simulations of a frog dissection. In Net Frog (http://frog.edschool.virginia.edu/), one of the most famous such tools, students can perform a simulated dissection online.

Figure 7.2 shows an online simulation of a pendulum that allows students to experiment with the way different factors influence the pendulum's speed. A similar experiment using a real pendulum would be difficult to set up in the classroom, and students' measurements of the speed would be tedious and inexact. With the simulation, they can change the weight, length, and maximum angle of the pendulum and instantly see the effect on the speed.

Similarly, students often learn by creating **models**. For years, science students have created models of atoms and molecules, usually static ones made of plastic or Styrofoam pieces. With a computer, students can create atomic models in which the electrons move in cloud-like orbitals, and the software provides feedback about the correct number of protons and neutrons.

Do you suppose that simulations and models are useful mainly in the physical sciences? That's far from true. In social science, for example, simulations can model social dilemmas and engage students in finding their own creative solutions (see Figure 7.3).

Besides giving immediate feedback to users, many simulation and modeling technologies also provide opportunities for later reflection and discussion—and this point leads us to the third key benefit of technology.

Communities of Learners

Many classes have their own web page, a site where teachers communicate with students and create an online extension of the classroom. The shared class web space has many uses; announcements and schedules can be posted, and areas for more informal communication can be created.

On any given topic, teachers can promote focused discussions online through the use of discussion boards or forums. You may already have participated in such reflective discussions using Blackboard courseware or a similar tool in your college classes. Later in this chapter, we'll discuss the rising use of weblogs, or blogs,

Figure 7.3

Simulating the Writing of the U.S. Constitution
In this simulation from *The Constitution* (part of the *Decisions, Decisions* software series from Tom Snyder Productions), students prepare a constitution for a fictional republic that mimics the United States in the 1780s.

in educational settings. Such technology-supported conversations can help students refine their thinking, and they help build a sense that everyone is working together in a learning community.

In fact, technology can easily extend the learning community beyond the immediate classroom. In Chapter 8, we examine the rise of global networks in which students from around the world collaborate to solve problems and share their cultures. Using technology, students from different places can work on the same projects with multiple solutions and collaborate via shared classroom websites and e-mail. A deep sense of community is created as the groups work toward shared goals and communicate with one another about the strategies needed to solve a mutual problem.

LO3 WEB 2.0

Web 2.0 is a term that loosely refers to a second generation of Internet services that are leading us toward even more open communication. One feature of Web 2.0 that you have probably already experienced is the rise of social networking sites, such as Facebook and Twitter. According to high-tech commentator Dion Hinchcliffe (2006), some of the key aspects of Web 2.0 are:

- Data and software are continuously and seamlessly updated, often very rapidly.
- User interfaces are rich and interactive.
- There is an "architecture of participation" that encourages user contributions.

To put it simply, a fundamental characteristic of Web 2.0 is this: a user can readily input information that then becomes an important source of content for other users. Blogs and wikis are excellent examples of this trend.

Blogs

> **"**Blogging . . . is about reading what is of interest to you: your culture, your community, your ideas.**"**
> —Stephen Downes (2004)

Most likely you're aware of the rapid proliferation of **blogs**, online journals on which a writer posts frequent observations and others respond with their own comments. It seems that everyone, from music fans to politicians, now has a blog. Blogs are becoming increasingly popular with teachers, too, because they offer a forum for expression for students as young as the second grade.

Blogging is not the same as using an online discussion board or discussion forum. Blogs are about "centered communication"—centered on the individual (Ganley, 2009). Blogs require a personal presence, unlike online discussion boards, which can be relatively impersonal as students respond to the questions posed by the teacher. While discussion boards are very directed and require specific, focused postings, blogging is open-ended, allowing users to add content through links called tags. Blogging also invites comments from online users outside of the immediate classroom community.

Blogs can be used for almost any subject. Students write about how they attacked a tough math problem, post observations about their science experiments, or display their latest art projects (Selingo, 2004). For teachers, blogs are attractive because they require little effort to maintain, unlike more elaborate classroom websites. Helped by templates found at a number of online sites (see the Resources for Further Exploration section at the end of this chapter), teachers can build a blog or start a new topic in an existing blog simply by typing text into a box and clicking a button.

Educational blogging, guided and monitored by the teacher, invites students to publish their work on the site.

model A representation of a system or an object, such as a small physical structure that imitates a larger structure or a computer program that parallels the workings of a larger system.

blog (short for weblog) An online journal using software that makes it easy for the user to create frequent entries; typically, visitors can add their own comments and responses.

TEACHSOURCE VIDEO CASE

Integrating Technology to Teach Literacy in the Middle School

Find the TeachSource video case "Middle School Reading Instruction: Integrating Technology" on the student website. In the classroom shown on the video, the teacher is exploring a Greek myth with his inner-city students. After watching the video, consider the following question:

How does the online discussion forum foster literacy skills?

wiki An online site that allows visitors to add, remove, and otherwise edit or change the available content.

A related-comments link allows readers to post comments. Hence educational blogging gives students an opportunity not only to publish their writing but also to receive and respond to comments from their classmates and *the rest of the world!*

Imagine, for example, a fifth-grade class where students are working on writing projects. They publish their writing in online blogs, and teachers link these blogs to other Internet items that relate to the same topic. Students visit each other's blogs and learn more about their classmates, and they also receive comments from a much larger community than their own classroom. Compare this situation to the traditional model in which the audience for students' written work consists only of the teacher.

Students learn from comments on their work and from their own reflection on those comments. Downes (2004) tells the story of students who posted a review of a circus and were amazed when a member of the circus read the review and responded. When the students in this class realized that a lot of people might react and become a part of the conversation, they refined their writing.

Overall, blogging can help students:

- Reflect on their writing and thinking.
- Persist in their writing over time.
- Engage readers of the blog in a sustained conversation that leads to further writing and thinking (Downes, 2004).

Wikis

Wikis are another major feature of Web 2.0. A **wiki** is a website or other online resource that fosters collective authoring by allowing many users to add content or edit the existing content. The most famous example is Wikipedia (http://www.wikipedia.org/), the online encyclopedia that bills itself as "the free encyclopedia that anyone can edit." At the time of this writing, Wikipedia offered more than 13 million articles in more than 200 languages. Theoretically, anyone in the world can contribute his or her expertise to the effort. In case you were not sure about the arrival of "information overload," Wikipedia may convince you that it is here!

For classroom teachers, wikis can provide a forum for student collaboration that even the shiest of students

WHY USE BLOGS FOR EDUCATION?

Charlie Lowe (2002), a professor of writing, made the following observation about blogs in educational settings. (He was writing in his own blog, of course!)

About a year ago, I asked my first-year composition students whether they did much reading and writing outside of class. Most of them said, "No." But when I asked them if they wrote e-mails, used AOL IM, and surfed the Internet, they almost unanimously said, "Yes."

To them, the Internet and other forms of electronic discourse were not associated with their concept of "reading and writing" in the school sort of way. I imagine that this difference might be because one is "fun" and the other is "work." But regardless, I've come to feel that reading and writing on the Web is a way for me to tap into a writing space that students already use—and more importantly, want to use.

contributes to readily. Recently, a sixth-grade language arts teacher used a wiki, a collaborative website that allows students to post work, comment on or critique the work of others, and make revisions in a group setting. In traditional writing instruction, for example, a student writes only for the teacher or another small group of students. But when a student publishes on a wiki, "The audience includes not just the teacher but all of the other students, too, and each student can 'hear' every other student—now there is a symphony" (Bolton, 2009). The teacher expresses it this way: "The wiki is an equalizer in classroom participation; everyone has a role. It's a way to showcase their comments and their give-and-take in a medium they take to like a duck to water." This is because middle school students are texting and using technology on a daily basis. In fact, by 2010, the average number of text messages sent monthly by teenagers was more than 2,000! The collaborative website, or wiki, used in this sixth-grade class requires correct grammar and spelling, a bit different from the "texting language" to which many students are accustomed.

Implications of Web 2.0

Think about the implications of blogs, wikis, and similar developments. In the current wave of wireless communication, handheld devices have implications for teaching and learning and for assessment. The end user of the content or information is also an author of content, along with everyone else who is interested in a given topic. This situation challenges our thinking about information and its reliability and veracity. With Web 2.0 technology, not only "experts" have access to cutting-edge information; there is increasing reliance on communities of "experts" that are redefined to include us all.

This is the flat classroom on a global scale, and it has important implications for the way we teach and learn. Again we are reminded that the most meaningful learning involves inquiry processes, reflection, and active, committed participation by the learner.

Using Handheld Wireless Devices for Assessment

In one school district in Oregon, each elementary school teacher was provided with the iPod touch, a handheld wireless device that, with the proper software, makes it possible for teachers to implement a reading assessment without the customary papers. Using the iPod touch, the teacher listens to a student read aloud from a book while the teacher follows along on the iPod touch and marks common reading mistakes. For each student, the data gets sent and will "sync" to district computers

WRITING & REFLECTION

Are Schools Out of Touch with Our Lives?

Some educators who reflect on the information technology revolution tell the following story:

> Rip Van Winkle awakens in the 21st century after a hundred-year snooze and is, of course, utterly bewildered by what he sees. Men and women dash about, talking to small metal devices pinned to their ears. Young people sit at home on sofas, moving miniature athletes around on electronic screens. Older folk defy death and disability with metronomes in their chests and with hips made of metal and plastic. Airports, hospitals, shopping malls—every place Rip goes just baffles him. But when he finally walks into a schoolroom, the old man knows exactly where he is. "This is a school," he declares. "We used to have these back in 1906. Only now the blackboards are green." (Wallis & Steptoe, 2006)

The authors go on to say that, compared with other institutions, U.S. public schools seem like "throwbacks."

- What do you think of this story?
- Can you imagine starting a blog with students in your classroom? What topics might be discussed? How would it contribute to student learning?

Did You Know?

The number of text messages sent and received by the average teenager monthly is 2,272!

through wireless connections installed by district technology staffers in school libraries. School and district leaders can then look at aggregated data, such as how students are doing in a specific school or across a grade level (Ryan, 2010). Reading samples can be captured and saved for assessment as students speak into the iPod touch, and these files are saved and progress is monitored annually. These devices hold a great deal of promise for more authentic and in-depth assessment than could be attained through traditional paper-and-pencil tests.

Did You Know? SOURCE: http://thefischbowl.blogspot.com/2009/09/did-you-know-40-economist-media.html, retrieved March 29, 2010.

Tracking Student Progress from Home

Parents have new tools with which to track student progress at school. Several companies have developed software products that allow parents to view a password protected web-based grade book that tracks student attendance, homework completion, and grades on tests and projects. The site may also indicate what the homework assignment is for each class, the due dates, and the criteria for the assignment. Many parents and teachers have embraced the use of these software tools because it fosters consistent communication between parents and teachers. While teachers have used e-mail as a form of communication to parents, these secure websites allow parents to intervene early if students need guidance, since they can be updated daily on their child's performance. It allows teachers to communicate with parents on a timely basis.

While teachers and parents have embraced the web-based grade book program in many school districts, some students have been reluctant to have their parents peer into all their grades for all their classes. Since written progress reports often go out quarterly, the web-based grade books are a way to ensure parents keep a watchful eye on their children's attendance and grades on a daily basis. Paper grade books are a thing of the past for many teachers in many school districts across the country. Opinion is mixed on whether the web-based record keeping is more or less work for the classroom teacher. What do *you* think?

Did You Know?

Today, more video is uploaded to YouTube in two months than the three major networks would have produced if they were airing TV 24 hours per day annually since 1948.

Internet Safety

So far in this chapter, we have talked about the many advantages that students can reap from ready access to the Internet and ease of connectivity. But teachers must also consider students' safety in online communication.

Experts agree on several areas of concern (National School Boards Foundation, 2007):

1. Young people may accidentally stumble onto websites that are violent, pornographic, or objectionable due to inappropriate language and content.
2. "Cyberstalking" and threats from online predators pose threats to children's and teenagers' safety. Drawn to social networking, students may reveal personal, identifying information to predators without realizing it.
3. Online marketing aimed directly at children and teens influences young people's decisions about products and brands. This can undermine parental authority in much the same way that television advertising can. The difference is that Internet advertising is not regulated by the government, and exposure is often more intense.
4. The interactive, two-way nature of the Web gives marketers the ability to collect data about individual computer users. Companies collect personal information about children and teens as their websites encourage youngsters to share their hobbies, interests, and other personal preferences. This invasion of privacy is commonplace on the Internet.

Chapter 9 addresses an additional concern, "cyberbullying," which can have devastating consequences for individual students and for which some school districts

Did You Know? SOURCE: http://thefischbowl.blogspot.com/2009/09/did-you-know-40-economist-media.html, retrieved March 29, 2010.

> *In a world that is so information-rich, we have to remember that technology access is not equal.*

are held liable. Cyberbullying refers to willful and repeated harm inflicted through the use of computers, cell phones, and other electronic devices. Cyberbullying often involves peer harassment and has become more prevalent as teens' use of texting on cell phones has skyrocketed in the first decade of the 21st century.

All of these are important issues, and school districts have taken steps to address them. Most school districts and libraries have installed blocking and filtering technologies to safeguard against offensive websites. Schools and districts are also implementing "Net safety" workshops and discussions. As a teacher, you need to be aware of the potential problems in students' Internet and wireless electronics use and make sure sufficient safeguards are in place.

LO4 The Digital Divide

Although all students are expected to develop **technological fluency**, some struggle if they come from schools and home backgrounds in which technology is not widely accessible. Later in life, they will be at a disadvantage for technology-based tasks, and they may even miss out on educational opportunities that involve technological resources (Kim & Bagaka, 2005, p. 319). In a world that is so information-rich, we have to remember that technology access is not equal.

According to Wikipedia, the **digital divide** is "the gap between those with regular, effective access to digital technologies and those without." On one side of the divide, people have easy access to technological resources and know how to use them. On the other side, people have substantially less access, less experience, and correspondingly less knowledge. It was the U.S. Department of Commerce that first coined the term *digital divide*. The distinction is not only between those who have computer access at home and those who do not. The digital divide also refers to the *quality* of hardware, software, and connectivity that is available to users across social classes.

Who are those with less technological access and experience? Students living in poverty are almost twice as likely as other students to access the Internet from school only (DeBell & Chapman, 2003, Table 3). In addition to this gap between social classes, educators worry about a geographical divide: Students in suburban schools spend significantly more time on computers both at home and at school than do rural and urban students.

technological fluency Proficiency in the use of technology, including an understanding of the way technology systems operate and the ability to use technology to access information from a wide variety of sources.

digital divide The division between people who are "rich" in technological access and expertise and those who are "poor" in this respect.

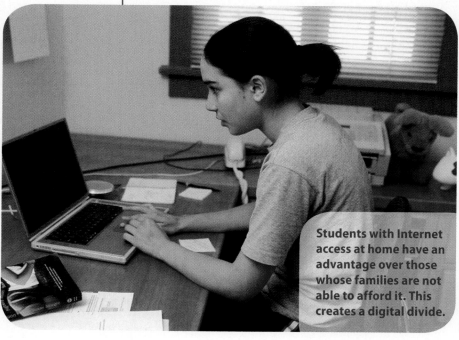

Students with Internet access at home have an advantage over those whose families are not able to afford it. This creates a digital divide.

© Elizabeth Crews

The ratio of students to instructional computers with Internet access is actually higher in schools with the highest poverty concentration than in schools with the lowest poverty concentration (Parsad & Jones, 2005, p. 7), but this abundance of computers at school does not fully make up for less access at home. Access to computers at home has been found to be an important factor in students' ability to use computer resources for word processing, information processing and presenting, and other types of communication (Kim & Bagaka, 2005). For many students in poor urban areas, public libraries provide a free option for Internet access, and Internet cafés may be nearby as well. Still, people are more likely to make regular use of an Internet connection at home than anywhere else. And for students in poor rural areas, Internet-enabled public libraries and coffee shops may be only a rumor.

To help underserved populations develop technological fluency, we must find a means of closing this technology gap caused by lack of access at home. The mere existence of computers in a school does not mean

Q: *In your view, what are the most important reasons for integrating technology in schools?*

$150.00

© CostinT/iStockphoto

LEARNING HOW TO LEARN: THE $150.00 LAPTOP PROJECT

The One Laptop Per Child Project (OLPC)—founded by Nicholas Negroponte, former chairman of the MIT Media Lab, and other faculty members from this lab—is based on the premise that a laptop would be the single most useful learning tool for poor children living in remote places. In addition to providing Internet access, a laptop would enable them to form learning communities. After analyzing what those children most needed from an educational laptop, the group decided to design a new model from scratch, with the goal of making it available for around $150.00. Investment for the project was secured from companies like News Corporation, Google, and eBay. It started as the $100 OLPC project, but the cost rose to somewhat more than that. Now, due to mass production of these little green laptops, the $100 laptop project shipped its first true $100 laptop in 2009. The group has shipped more than 32 million laptops worldwide.

The philosophy behind the project maintains that if young people are given computers and allowed to explore, they will "learn how to learn" (Seymour Papert as quoted by Markoff, 2006). The idea is that each laptop will have wireless capacity, a small 7.5-inch screen, and an external manual generator to recharge the battery. Called the XO, these laptops are a potent learning tool designed and built especially for children in developing countries, living in some of the most remote environments. Each laptop is about the size of a small textbook. It has built-in wireless and a unique screen that is readable under direct sunlight for children who go to school outdoors. It's extremely durable, brilliantly functional, energy-efficient, and fun.

This is a real test of the possibilities of technology itself for closing the digital divide. You can explore OLPC further at http://laptop.org/en/.

they are being used productively. Many educators have pointed out that professional development for teachers is vital in ensuring that computers in schools are used purposefully and with an eye toward improving students' higher-order skills, not just basic skills.

Studies have revealed that when teachers have positive beliefs about technology and their own proficiency in using it, they can better integrate technology tools and practices into their teaching, which results in a narrowing of the digital divide (Kim & Bagaka, 2005). What does this mean for you as a future teacher? You can best serve your students if you make full use of technology; to do that, you need to believe in its potential and in your own comfort and knowledge level. This is a reminder that, as stated earlier in this book, "We teach who we are."

Assistive Technology

A chapter on technology would not be complete without a brief discussion of assistive technology. The term **assistive technology (AT)** refers to devices that promote greater independence for people with disabilities by enabling them to perform tasks that would otherwise be difficult or impossible. AT can take many forms, from simple to complex. For students with visual impairments, for example, a simple type of AT is a keyboard with large symbols that makes it easier for the students to type. A more complex form is speech recognition software that converts the student's spoken words into text on the screen. Similarly, screen reader software can read aloud the information displayed on a computer screen.

In the past, for blind students who read by means of Braille (a writing system that uses raised dots identifiable by touch), curriculum materials were usually converted through a lengthy process that required two to four weeks' lead time. Now, with computer technology, relevant materials can be converted at the time they are needed. With a computer program, text that the teacher types into a word processing document is transformed into Braille and printed on a Braille printer within seconds. This technology makes it possible for the teacher to include blind students in

the same activity as the rest of the class, at the same moment.

For disabled students whose fine motor skills do not allow them to write easily and without pain, note taking is an arduous task. Teachers with interactive whiteboards in their classrooms can save the notes written on the board and print them for these students. An **interactive whiteboard**, typically the size of a regular chalkboard, is linked to a computer. Teachers can project images from the computer onto the board. When a student or the teacher writes on the board with a special marker, the notes can be saved as text in the computer.

In the following story, students with a wide range of learning disabilities experience a lesson on maps using a Smart Board, one brand of interactive whiteboard.

On the day that I visit their classroom, the ten students in Ms. Mandel's self-contained special education second-grade class are learning about maps. Seated on a carpeted area in front of a Smart Board, they tell me that a map is a bird's-eye view of the earth from above.

Ms. Mandel chats with the children about maps that are found on the subway, on trains, in the mall, and at a major sports complex. She uses the Smart Board to display different types of maps. One map has roads, street names, stores, gas stations, and houses. There is a produce map with images relating to fruits and vegetables

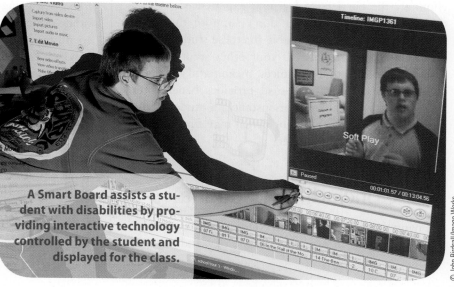

A Smart Board assists a student with disabilities by providing interactive technology controlled by the student and displayed for the class.

© John Birdsall/Image Works

grown in New York state, where the school is located. Still other maps show weather changes, vacation spots, and geographic features.

The children can manipulate a pointer and direct it to different images on the map. By manipulating the image of a car or a plane, they can take a ride from one destination to another. Taking turns with the pointer, the students respond to questions on cards located in a wall "pocket" next to the Smart Board. Each card has a number corresponding to the map type and a question like, "How would you get from Amy's house to The Home Depot?" or "What is the name of the town closest to the dairy farm?"

Deeply engaged in this activity, the students do well manipulating objects and moving them to destinations on the Smart Board. They are using the technology very creatively. One student tells me, "We are having a great time." The questions on the cards involve the class in interpreting symbols, locations, and directions, and I am struck by the way these students with various learning disabilities are making sense of the maps and are developing higher-order thinking skills.

Although we look forward to new ways of teaching our students, many challenges face us as we imagine how the traditional classroom will be transformed to reflect the high-tech world around us.

This story highlights ways technology can reduce or eliminate the barriers to learning experienced by students with disabilities. But don't suppose that only "special" technology is suitable for these students. The technology you use with all your other students—the same technology that enhances meaningful learning, reflection, and discussion—also provides benefits for those who are disabled. For instance, a student who struggles to write with pen or pencil may find it much easier to write on a computer.

LO5 Concluding Thoughts

Living through a social and educational transformation like the information technology and wireless communication revolution is both exciting and challenging. Although we look forward to new ways of teaching our students, many challenges face us as we imagine how the traditional classroom will be transformed to reflect the high-tech world around us.

In the flat classroom, the traditional hierarchy is broken down. Many students can find information as quickly as we can, and that means our role as teachers must change accordingly. We should take full advantage of the ways technology can promote independent learning through real-world projects, simulations, and collaborative investigations. At the same time, we have to guide students in negotiating the overload of information so that they use their time wisely.

We should make sure that students gain the technological fluency they will need in later life. To do so, we need to meet high standards ourselves in our understanding of technology and its uses in education. Further, we need to seek ways to use technology to "level the learning field," so that all of America's students are served equitably by our schools.

Finally, a study from the Kaiser Family Foundation (2010) revealed that the average young American now spends nearly every waking minute, *except for the time in school*, using a smartphone, computer, television, or other electronic device. Those ages eight to eighteen spend more than seven hours a day with such devices, and that does not count the hour and a half that youths spend texting, or the half-hour they talk on their cell phones. It is significant to note that most teachers in most schools in the country ask students to "shut down" their devices when they enter the classroom. While that is certainly appropriate from the standpoint of socializing during teaching and learning time, just think about how empowering it would be for educators and students to use these devices for the very purpose of teaching and learning. Teachers must acknowledge the students' lived experiences and use them as a tool for learning.

RESOURCES FOR FURTHER EXPLORATION

Online Resources

Blogger
http://www.blogger.com/

This website offers easy-to-understand information about blogging and can help you create your own blog in minutes.

Childnet International
http://www.childnet-int.org/safety/teachers.aspx

This kid-friendly site, designed for children and teens, has important tips for Internet safety.

eMINTS
http://www.emints.org/

eMINTS is a professional development site for educators that focuses on engaging students and teachers in meaningful learning experiences using the Internet and wireless technologies.

International Society for Technology and Education: National Educational Technology Standards
http://cnets.iste.org/

This website provides the National Educational Technology Standards for teachers, students, and administrators, combined with a wealth of supporting materials. This will help you understand what it means to learn with technology.

I-SAFE
http://www.isafe.org/

i-SAFE Inc. is a nonprofit foundation dedicated to protecting the online experiences of youth everywhere. i-SAFE incorporates classroom curriculum with dynamic community outreach to empower students, teachers, parents, law enforcement, and concerned adults to make the Internet a safer place.

Kathy Schrock's Guide for Educators
http://school.discovery.com/schrockguide/

This annotated compilation of websites, divided into subject areas, is useful for teachers.

Net Frog
http://frog.edschool.virginia.edu/

This site is a well-known simulation of frog dissection.

NetSafeKids
http://www.nap.edu/netsafekids/

Sponsored by the National Academies, this site is a valuable resource for adults and children who are seeking ways to stay safe in cyberspace.

Teacher's Domain
http://www.teachersdomain.org/

Teachers' Domain is an extensive library of free digital media resources produced by public television, designed for classroom use and professional development.

Twitter
http://www.twitter.com

Twitter is a real-time information network that makes you aware of what is happening now and invites you to share your own "tweets."

tBlog.com
http://www.tblog.com/

This is a website for those who are interested in creating their own blogs or visiting blogs that address a wide range of topics.

Weblogg-ed
http://www.weblogg-ed.com/

Will Richardson introduces the reader to educational blogging via this website.

Wikipedia
http://www.wikipedia.org/

Described as the free encyclopedia that anyone can edit, this website contains entries on events and places that any print encyclopedia would have, but it also includes a related dictionary, thesaurus, and much more.

Print Resource

Will Richardson, *Blogs, Wikis, Podcasts, and Other Powerful Web Tools for Classrooms* (Thousand Oaks, CA: Corwin Press, 2006).
This book has cutting-edge ideas and illustrations for transforming the classroom with Web 2.0 tools.

CHAPTER 8

GLOBALIZATION AND EDUCATION

© Tanya Constantine/Blend Images/Photolibrary

In this chapter, we examine several ways that education is changing in the Information Age. As a result of "seamless" access to the Internet, students and teachers from all over the world can communicate electronically, sharing their cultures, their school lives, and their larger world. Students can work side by side even if they live thousands of miles apart. Let's explore how this interaction occurs and what it means for our students.

LEARNING OUTCOMES

After reading this chapter, you should be thinking about the following ideas:

LO1 The "global" classroom is a reality, with technology making it possible for classrooms all over the world to connect, collaborating on projects and learning from one another.

LO2 Today's students must possess 21st-century skills: to go beyond understanding core concepts and memorizing facts in academic subjects, and to think creatively and critically about a problem, work collaboratively with others to find solutions, and see themselves as problem solvers who communicate their ideas clearly.

LO3 Today's teachers must demonstrate a passion for learning, seek opportunities created by globalization to enhance classroom learning, and help students navigate their ever-expanding world and develop 21st-century skills.

LO1 Education in the Knowledge Economy

We are educating students to become part of an information society in which the creation, distribution, and manipulation of information is a significant economic and cultural activity. The **knowledge economy** is this society's economic counterpart. In the knowledge economy, businesses operate through the collaboration and shared problem solving of people across the globe, transforming information into creative innovations for an ever-changing technological world.

Think about this: one of the most successful recent innovations has been the design and construction of a wireless tablet, about the size of a notebook, that can do everything a laptop can but does not have a keypad! It can surf the Internet, become a book reader, create documents and spreadsheets, presentations, e-mail, and more.

What do such products suggest for education? Innovations like the wireless tablet are complex in their technology, and their success depends on many people from all over the world having access to the technology. Further, people's ability to collaborate ensures that the best design will hit the market. Yet the technological skills and collaboration techniques involved in this kind of product development are not taught in most of today's public schools.

THE FLAT WORLD

In his best-selling book *The World Is Flat*, Thomas Friedman (2006) uses the metaphor of a flat world to describe the leveling of the playing field on which industrialized and emerging-market countries compete. Friedman recounts many examples of **globalization** in which companies in India and China are becoming part of global

knowledge economy
An economic system in which the use and exchange of knowledge plays a dominant role. In this kind of economy, knowledge is both an economic asset and a key product.

globalization The increase of global connectivity, integration, and interdependence in economic, cultural, social, and technological spheres.

supply chains that extend across oceans, providing everything from service representatives and X-ray interpretation to component manufacturing. He also describes how these changes are made possible through intersecting technologies, particularly the Internet.

In a flat world, Friedman explains, the work done by corporations is no longer conducted vertically—that is, in a structure of workers and supervisors with each person at each level having different specific tasks. Rather, much of the work has gone horizontal: corporate analysts examine each step in a process and ask whether the firm is a leader in that step; if not, they determine who in the world can best do that work at the appropriate level of quality and the lowest possible cost. The firm then contracts with providers for each service; the firm itself performs only those functions it does best. This arrangement is known as *outsourcing*, and many functions formerly performed by American workers are now being outsourced to workers in other countries who can do these jobs better, more cheaply, and faster. Remember, one does not have to be in the same geographical location to be a coworker in a company.

Like the flat classroom described in Chapter 7, the flat world creates significant challenges for teaching and learning. We are facing educational decisions that will "ultimately determine not merely whether some of our children get 'left behind' but also whether an entire generation of kids will fail to make the grade in a global economy because they can't think their way through abstract problems, work in teams, distinguish good information from bad or speak a language other than English" (Wallis & Steptoe, 2006). Yet many school classrooms still resemble the ones our grandparents attended—with the teacher front and center and the students listening and writing at their desks. Clearly, our educational system has a lot of adapting to do.

LO2 THE GLOBAL STUDENT: HAVING INFORMATION VS. CONSTRUCTING KNOWLEDGE

"In the flat new world, educational opportunities are limitless, even without help from school, government, churches or business. Much of what you need to know about pretty much everything is out there on the Web somewhere."
—Doc Searls (2005)

One of the first steps in preparing ourselves and our students to function in a data-rich global knowledge economy is to explore the ways in which having a lot of information is different from gaining a lot of knowledge.

In today's **Information Age**, *learning how to learn* becomes more important than *what* we learn. Thus it is the individual with curiosity, imagination, and a passion for learning who will be most successful in the global knowledge economy. Curious students work hard at learning and eagerly find new opportunities to learn. Hence, when we gather information, we reflect on it, apply it to different contexts, examine its meaning, and try to communicate it to others . . . and then we are starting to be knowledgeable.

Learning How to Learn

The kind of information teachers used to ask students to memorize is now available on the Internet, usually just a few keystrokes away. Consider this memorable anecdote:

Learn the names of the rivers in South America. That was the assignment

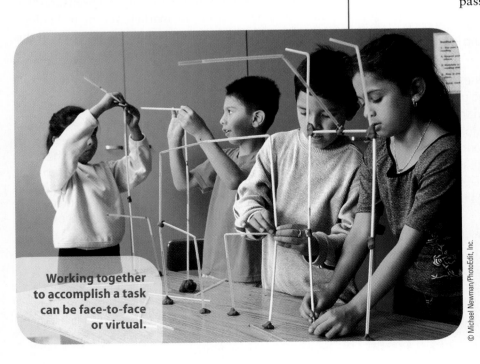

Working together to accomplish a task can be face-to-face or virtual.

© Michael Newman/PhotoEdit, Inc.

given to Deborah Stipek's daughter Meredith in school, and her mom, who's dean of the Stanford University School of Education, was not impressed. "That's silly," Stipek told her daughter. "Tell your teacher that if you need to know anything besides the Amazon, you can look it up on Google." (Wallis and Steptoe, 2006)

Because simple facts are easy to locate, today's students require what educators refer to as more *depth* of understanding and less *breadth*. In other words, key ideas and topics should dominate the curriculum, not lists of facts that can be found easily enough on the Web.

Educators also talk about the importance of **metacognition**, the understanding of one's own learning processes. Students with metacognitive skills know how to approach a learning task. They have good learning strategies. In other words, they have learned how to learn.

The projects and problems described in Chapters 6 and 7 illustrate some ways of developing metacognitive skills and depth of understanding. As students work in teams, both in their classrooms and online, they risk making mistakes on their journey to finding solutions and consensus. They develop critical thinking, making connections between ideas and events, and they learn how to keep on learning.

Global Collaboration

Knowing how to work with others to solve a problem is an essential skill, but knowing how to collaborate across a digital learning environment adds another dimension. In Forsyth County, Ga., a growing number of schools are using desktop **videoconferencing** to collaborate globally. In one current-events class, for example, students exchange information about the political situation, schools, and other issues with students in Greece, Russia, and China.

Students also have the opportunity to connect with professionals. For example, elementary students are learning about insects through a collaborative project with scientists at the University of Chicago. The students send samples of insects to the university, and they can then view those samples on the university's electronic microscope. The images are accessible via computer and projected so the whole class can see them. At one point, a group of third graders asked about a particular part on a ladybug, and the scientists admitted they didn't know what it was and promised to research it for the students (Ashford, 2009).

Collaborative projects not only help teach content but also help students to develop 21st-century skills such as communication, time management, teamwork, and facilitation. These are essential skills, as we will explore in the following section. These skills enable students to function globally and cooperatively, sharing information and ideas and learning how to "to think outside the box"—a necessary skill for promoting innovation.

> **metacognition** The understanding of your own thinking and learning processes.
>
> **videoconferencing** Real-time audio and video communication allowing individuals or groups at different locations to talk in a face-to-face setting.

Skills for the 21st Century

> **"***If you are not prepared to be wrong, you will not come up with anything original.***"**
> —Sir Ken Robinson (2006)

A report by the New Commission on the Skills of the American Workforce (National Center on Education and the Economy, 2006) issues this warning:

> *This is a world in which a very high level of preparation in reading, writing, speaking, mathematics, science, literature, history and the arts will be an indispensable foundation for everything that comes after for most members of the workforce. It is a world in which comfort with ideas and abstractions is the passport to a good job, in which creativity and innovation are the key to a good life, in which high levels of education—a very different kind of education than most of us have had— are going to be the only security there is. (New Commission on the Skills of the American Workforce, 2006)*

TEACHSOURCE VIDEO CASE

Learning How to Learn

Find the TeachSource Video Case "Metacognition: Helping Students Become Strategic Learners" on the student website. This video shows a middle school class trying to make sense of a newspaper article about China. After watching the video, consider the following question:

What metacognitive strategies, if any, do you employ when reading this textbook?

MIVA Acronym for manage, interpret, validate, and act—terms describing what students must learn to do with the vast amount of information they access on a daily basis.

The report goes on to offer a blueprint for rethinking American education to prepare students for the global economy. It describes, among other things, what might be called 21st-century skills important for students as they enter the global marketplace. Let's explore several of these.

Knowing More about the World. Kids are global citizens now. They need to understand the world economy, be able to identify the nations in the developed and developing world, become sensitive to foreign cultures, and learn foreign languages.

Thinking Outside the Box. Students need to think creatively to solve problems, seeing patterns where others may see chaos. As the report confirms, it is interdisciplinary combinations—such as design and technology, mathematics and art, music and science—that spawn really innovative ideas and products for the global economy. Creativity expert Ken Robinson (2006) believes that "we get educated out of creativity" in school. It is essential, therefore, to foster creative problem solving by providing students with challenging problems and guiding them to find solutions.

Managing New Sources of Information. Students need to develop skills that help them manage the vast amount of information to which they are exposed. For one thing, they must learn to distinguish between reliable and unreliable information. Karen Bruett, who serves on the Partnership for 21st-Century Skills, explains that students have to manage, interpret, validate, and act on the overflowing information and the proliferating media that characterize this century (Wallis & Steptoe, 2006). I like to abbreviate these terms as **MIVA**.

Developing Good People Skills. With so much being accomplished online, we can get the mistaken notion that good people-to-people communication is unnecessary in today's marketplace. However, as noted earlier, most recent innovations involve collaboration among teams of people. The ability to work and communicate with others—often people from different cultures—is essential.

You can't expect your students to become curious and inventive if you don't display those qualities yourself.

> "*We've come to realize that knowledge-based content has exploded to such a degree that the ability to find it and use it is more critical than having it archived in our brains. What's clear is that we can't learn all the content. We've got to be sure we're providing learning experiences that give skills for working with the body of content that is expanding so rapidly. We must learn to find it, judge it, and use it.*" —Don Knezek, President of the International Society for Technology in Education (2002)

LO3 Teaching in the Global Classroom

After all that we have said so far about the flat world, the global student, and the needs of a technology-driven world, you must be wondering, "What does this mean for teaching?"

First of all, it means that your job as a teacher is to demonstrate a love and a passion for learning. In the words of Thomas Friedman (2006), "You can't light the fire of passion in someone else if it does not burn in you to begin with" (p. 305). You can't expect your students to become curious and inventive if you don't display those qualities yourself.

Second, it means that you should help students develop the necessary areas of understanding and skills we have mentioned: knowledge of the world; the ability to collaborate; metacognitive skills; the MIVA skills of managing, interpreting, validating, and acting on information; and the willingness to think outside the box to come up with new solutions.

It is an exciting time to be a teacher if you imagine how much you are learning from your status as a digitally connected adult and then imagine what is possible for your soon-to-be-global students.

Students in a fifth-grade class on the eastern shore of Maryland recently used their handheld Palm computers and keyboards to communicate with students in a fifth-grade class in South Africa. Each student e-mailed a message to a student "buddy" in the class in South Africa. The students exchanged information about their personal interests and about what they were learning in mathematics.

Then the teachers set up an international telephone link between the classrooms using Skype, a free Internet phone service. The Maryland students used their math skills to calculate what time it would be in South Africa during their call. In this Skype conversation and in further communications, both classes learned about life and culture in each place, the languages spoken and understood, and the role of homework and studying in their lives.

This story offers a small example of the ways global communication can foster the development of skills necessary for the 21st century. The students develop an awareness of students in another part of the world as well as a sensitivity to another culture and lifestyle. They become better communicators, too, as they adapt to the global terrain. This simple form of globalization can lead to many long-lasting relationships.

A number of websites can help you set up similar "buddy" exchanges with classes from distant countries and cultures. One example, the ePals Global Community (http://www.epals.com/), has linked students in two hundred countries as cross-cultural learning partners and friends. To find partner classes on this site, you can select a country from a map (see Figure 8.1), and then you can specify options such as the type of school, the age range of the students, and the language(s) spoken. Your class may also join any of the global discussion boards and projects hosted by ePals.com.

If you have the resources and opportunity to create this type of global communication, be sure to embed it in a larger learning context. For example, if your middle school class is studying Asia, you can use the ePals site to locate a middle school class in India whose students can become e-mail partners with your students. Guide your students in deciding what types of questions they can ask to learn about their partners' interests, hobbies, lifestyle, and goals. Be sure, too, that your students are aware of their responsibilities in such an exchange, such as responding in a timely manner and using appropriate customs for polite and acceptable communication.

An even more ambitious global collaboration engaged sixth-grade students from several countries in collaborating to design a website that provides information about artificial intelligence.

"Good evening, Earthling!" says the greeting on a website called Artificial Intelligence: Manufactured Minds. This site provides links and animations that address the history and uses of artificial intelligence as well as the ethical questions involved. Its topics range from neural networks to the meaning of consciousness. The site is an impressive achievement, especially when you realize that it was designed by high school students—and that the students are from New Hampshire, South Australia, and India.

You can find this site in the library at ThinkQuest.org (http://library.thinkquest.org/05aug/01158/index.html). For a window into the world of global high school collaboration, look at the Colophon section of the website,

Figure 8.1

The Asia Map from the ePals Site
At the ePals website, clicking on a world map takes you to a regional map like this one. With another mouse click, you choose a country to find a list of schools interested in cross-cultural learning exchanges.

Asia

Please select the country you would like to find classrooms in by clicking on that country below, or use the drop-down menu:

Choose a country:

SOURCE: http://www.epals.com/search/maps/asia/. Reprinted by permission of ePals.

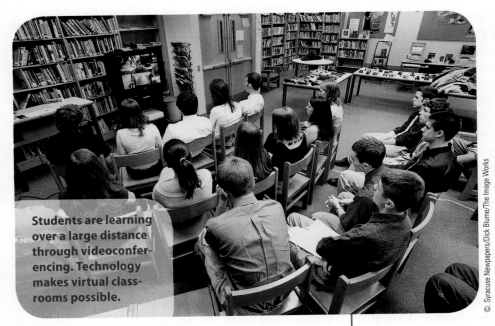

Students are learning over a large distance through videoconferencing. Technology makes virtual classrooms possible.

© Syracuse Newpapers/Dick Blume/The Image Works

In one program from NASA CONNECT, groups of middle school students work together to create a nutrition and exercise plan for a person with particular needs. Each group chooses its subject from the following list:

- A person with hypertension
- A strict vegetarian
- A pregnant woman
- A person who is lactose intolerant
- A diabetic
- An athlete in training
- An astronaut in space

The students begin by watching a video. Sponsored by the National Space and Aeronautics Administration (NASA), the thirty-minute program shows how scientists use mathematics to study astronauts' loss of bone calcium and muscle mass while they live in space. Then students set out to make similar calculations to design the proper diet for their own subject. A NASA website offers links to research information, and another online page provides an exercise-related activity in which students collect and analyze data on heart rate.

In this project, "Better Health from Space to Earth," students in one middle school can collaborate with students from another to create the optimal diet and exercise plan for their chosen person.

NASA CONNECT is another good example of project-based learning that involves collaboration, creative thinking, and problem-solving skills. Notice, too, that each NASA CONNECT project explores an intersection of two or more subject areas. Consider how many subject areas are relevant in creating the nutrition and exercise plans described in the story.

TEACHING WITH DIGITAL MEDIA: VIDEOCONFERENCING, GAMES, AND MORE

Videoconferencing via the Internet, allowing students from one locale to interact with individuals or groups of students from another locale, is a readily available extension of your classroom. Many teachers are already accustomed to "virtual field trips," which use video-conferencing technology to enable students to visit a

where the creators describe their backgrounds and their process of teamwork. I loved reading about the creators and discovering how they learned from each other as they worked on this project. You will, too.

In addition to being an amazing example of cross-cultural collaboration, this story demonstrates the use of project-based learning to foster the type of creative thinking students need in a knowledge economy. Think-Quest (http://www.thinkquest.org), sponsored by the Oracle Education Foundation, offers a project-based learning experience to students and teachers around the world. It is a competition in which nobody loses. The challenge is for students, grades 4 through 12, to work in teams to design and build innovative and educational websites to share with the world. Teachers and students select from a broad range of educational categories and topics. The teams that work on the website collaborate electronically via e-mail, Internet chat, and online forums. Global perspectives are encouraged.

Collaboration of this sort—students from diverse areas of the world working on a project that requires multiple ways of thinking and knowing—can become cumbersome and complex without a well-organized structure. Luckily, in addition to ThinkQuest, other educational foundations, organizations, and corporations have developed websites dedicated to this kind of networked project-based learning. Using programs from NASA CONNECT, students in middle school can make connections to real-life applications of mathematics and science concepts.

museum, zoo, or other remote location. Now, students can use similar technology to "visit" other students and work collaboratively with them. With videoconferencing, students can exchange ideas in face-to-face discussions. Through such interactions, students develop their social and communication skills while preparing and presenting their joint projects.

You may also want to investigate the videoconferencing offered by the NASA Digital Learning Network (http://nasadln.nmsu.edu/dln/). During these videoconferences, teachers and students exchange ideas with NASA experts in science and engineering. Interacting with experts gives students the sense that they are working on real-world questions and that their insights are significant. To help classes make best use of these interactions, NASA provides pre- and post-conference instructional materials that teachers can use to develop and extend the lesson. Videoconferencing is another tool in the quest for real-life collaborative learning among students in different locations.

Gaming has the potential to change education as video games permeate our culture and schools use them for learning. When developed correctly, games can engage players in learning that is specifically applicable to school curriculum (Klopfer et al., 2009). PBS offers educational games for very young learners in content areas including math, reading, science, social studies, music, and art.

Current research suggests that in addition to being motivating, playing video games affects brain function and plasticity (Bavelier, 2009). Some research indicates that playing action video games on a regular basis can alter a player's attention skills. These include low-level vision, monitoring several objects at once, or searching through a cluttered scene; multitasking; task-switching; and a general speeding up of perceptual processing. One researcher sees the next step in education as taking the violence out of the video games and using the same brain-building characteristics in these action videos to make high-quality education games (Stansbury, 2009).

Exploring video games from PBS for primary-grade learners reveals a host of choices where the learners are problem solvers. They acquire understanding through the multistep processes of solving the problems as they play the games. An art education game downloaded from one site contains paintings from great masters belonging to various periods of artistic creation, from the early Renaissance to Surrealism and beyond. As the game unfolds, the paintings are reorganized and some are missing—students need to find the missing works of art and place them in their proper period. All this happens quickly, with fifth graders manipulating the mouse and discovering how to make the best display.

"Business Education" is a set of online high school games that tests students' knowledge of business strategies. Users create their own company and product and participate in simulations, including the Business Game, the Entrepreneurship Game, and the Finance Game. In this high school program, simulations approach reality as students need to apply the principles they have learned in their business education classes. The Business Game gives students the chance to experience a business scenario, in which they develop and market a new product. This provides training in pricing issues, product positioning, sales and marketing budgets, stock levels, and production versus demand. Students build relationships with simulated mentors and coworkers through daily interaction using e-mail and video phone calls (Schaffhauser, 2010).

According to contemporary data, today's high school students take simulations very seriously and do not see them as "second-best" to the real thing. Proponents of simulations suggest that they offer a somewhat risk-free environment, one where learners are free to experiment, make mistakes, and rethink and redesign without fear of destroying something that cannot be easily replenished in a traditional setting. Being able to use technology, work in groups, simulate real-life scenarios, and make and correct mistakes emphasizes the 21st-century skills our students need to survive in a flattened world (O'Neal, 2007).

A report from MIT suggests that, while gaming cannot single-handedly change the way we teach subject matter, it can promote deeper understanding through active engagement. "Games [promote] understanding, motivation, and enjoyment and are terrific at immersing players in complex, feedback-rich problem spaces. And while they are most often not sufficient in and of themselves for a course of study, they can help many students advance beyond the temporary memorization of facts

> **gaming** Used in this context, gaming refers to playing computer and video games. Video game culture is a form of new media that has enormous potential for teaching and learning.

Q: *What are your favorite video games? What have you learned by playing them?*

digital media Web-interactive video games, podcasts, and lesson plans downloaded to digital devices such as laptops, mobile devices, DVDs, and CDs.

and procedures, attainments that are usually lost when classes stop" (Klopfer et al., 2009).

DIGITALLY INCLINED

A 2009 survey, conducted by PBS in conjunction with Grunwald Associates LLC revealed these key findings:

- A majority of teachers are using digital media, with applications including instruction, lesson planning, communications, and professional development.
- Teachers who do use digital media value it and believe that it helps them—and their students—to be more effective.
- Teachers continue to use video, but they increasingly access video online, rather than from broadcast, cable, or videotape. And teachers are becoming more strategic in their media use and savvier about integrating it into their repertoire of instructional strategies and resources.
- Teachers value many different types of digital media, with games and activities for student use in school topping the list.

SOURCE: http://grunwald.com/pdfs/Grunwald_January_2010_ANNUAL_PBS_SURVEY_PUBLIC_REPORT.pdf.

Teachers report that their students prefer **digital media** over other types of instruction and that digital media increases student motivation and stimulates discussions. According to this study, teachers also believe digital media supports their own creativity and student creativity. What is really significant here is acknowledging the many types of digital media to which students are exposed and then asking ourselves, "How can these media serve teaching and learning and extend our understanding of the world?" As you are well aware, ever-increasing numbers of teachers are joining virtual professional communities and many use social networking tools in their personal and professional lives. These technologies, available globally, hold the promise of exciting changes in K–12 education. These include using digital media to foster more engaging, creative, and collaborative learning environments; engaging students in using new tools to produce content and take charge of their learning; and creating more possibilities for real-time cross-cultural conversations with students from all over the world. Taking courses online is another way of becoming a learner in a global marketplace.

VIRTUAL CLASSES IN HIGH SCHOOL

You are probably familiar with online courses at the college or graduate school level. You may be surprised to learn that online courses are growing more and more common at the pre-college level. Online environments in K–12 education have grown from an estimated 45,000 in the year 2000 to more than a million in 2010. Students who are homeschooled or homebound, who live in rural areas where diverse course offerings are scarce, or who are seeking AP courses are the most common online customers.

David, a high school senior in Pennsylvania, has already taken every social science course his small private school can offer. Rather than take electives he does not need, David has enrolled in two Advanced Placement courses online: macroeconomics and microeconomics.

In nearby Collingswood, New Jersey, many such Advanced Placement

WRITING & REFLECTION

The Online Community

To be an effective teacher, you need to build a sense of community in the classroom. Chapter 9 explores the important concept of the classroom as learning community. Take a moment to think about your own experience with online communities, either in coursework or in other areas such as chatrooms, blogs, social networking sites (MySpace, Facebook), and the like.

- What factors help an online group function as a real community?
- In what ways is an online community similar to a classroom community? How is it different?

courses are offered online through the district's virtual high school. Collingswood collaborates with Virtual High School in Massachusetts, a nonprofit organization that offers more than 200 online courses to 7,500 students worldwide in more than 400 participating schools. As part of an online AP course in economics, David can be "in class" with students from all over the country and the world!

Pre-college students who take online courses to supplement traditional courses offered at their brick-and-mortar schools are changing the face of American public education. These virtual classes are becoming more and more popular. In *synchronous* distance learning, students are virtually present through the Internet at the same point in time. More commonly, though, the learning environment is *asynchronous*—that is, students from different geographical areas work at different times.

One of the significant advantages of **virtual schools** is that they can provide courses otherwise unavailable to a local student. This is especially important in rural areas, where one school often serves all students from pre-kindergarten to twelfth grade and the financial resources for extensive enrichment courses are unavailable. Some school districts form partnerships with a distance learning firm that tracks open seats in distance learning courses and offers them to school districts at discounted rates.

In the typical arrangement, students who take courses online communicate daily with the teacher, who may be in some other part of the country or even in another nation. Yet students do much of their course work independently, on their own schedule. Usually a school guidance counselor stays in touch to make sure students are keeping pace with the work required from the online course. Naturally, some students are better at independent work than others; for some students, online courses at the precollege level are not the best choice. The value of an online course depends in part on the individual's maturity, work habits, and motivation.

Online courses can enroll students from many localities and even from many countries. In these situations, collaborative problem solving, as we saw earlier with the ThinkQuest collaborations, entails communication among students from widely different cultures, socioeconomic classes, and geographical regions. Learning to work with such a diverse group enhances precollege students' abilities to be team problem solvers and to appreciate the contributions of people from radically different environments.

What does an online environment mean for teaching? When teachers are asked to develop an online course from a course they are used to teaching face to face, the challenge is often transformative. Imagine that you have developed lesson plans for a unit of study and now you are going to use these lessons online with fifteen to twenty students who are working at different paces and at different times around the globe. To make this leap, you have to ask some soul-searching questions, like the ones listed in the sidebar "Questions for Teaching an Online Course." In fact, research shows that

virtual school An institution that exists in cyberspace, teaching all of its classes online.

© geopaul/iStockphoto

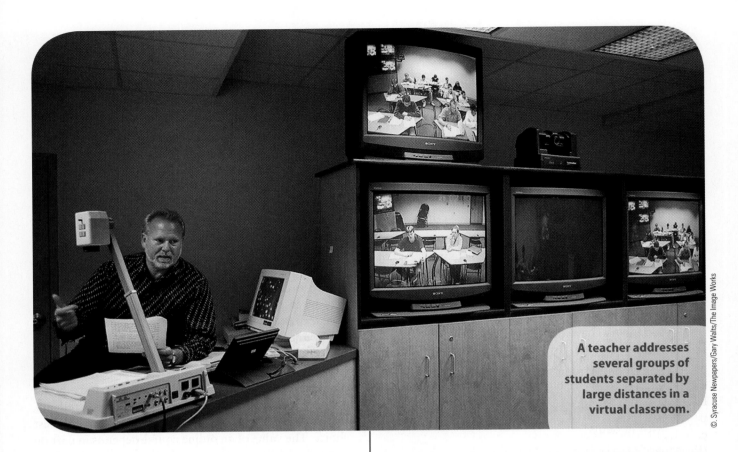

A teacher addresses several groups of students separated by large distances in a virtual classroom.

teaching an online course leads many teachers to reexamine some of their beliefs about teaching and learning. The concepts of teacher-student and student-student communication, as well as student accountability and assessment, change in the online environment. Many teachers improve their skills as they think more deeply about their subject area as well as the nature of communication with and among their students (Lowes, 2005).

Perhaps you will be asked to be part of a virtual high school when you are teaching a face-to-face classroom. You may find it challenging to do both—teach face to face and teach online. The intellectual "space" of the online class requires a different type of preparation. You will be happy to know, however, that most students who take online courses feel like they are part of a learning community and value the experience.

THE TEACHER'S ROLE IN A GLOBAL CLASSROOM

At this point in the chapter you may be wondering, "Why am I going into teaching if students can get so much information elsewhere and connect so readily to the rest of the world?" That is a legitimate question. The answer lies in the importance of your passion, your curiosity, your capacity to listen to and accept students, to gently challenge their ideas and guide them—these are the qualities that will make you a successful teacher.

Your expertise in your content area must be apparent, but it is less important than your ability to help students navigate the flood waters of information available to them. Your challenge is to become a teacher who helps students become discriminating consumers of information, capable of validating data by doing research and formulating well-supported opinions. In other words, your message to students is, "Now that

Who we become as teachers will reflect the times in which we live—our global interconnectivity and our unending access to information and media.

you know what the raw information says, how do you process it?" As a teacher, you will help students make meaning from the data they find; you will help them draw out the big ideas or core concepts in ways that connect to the real world.

Remember as well that you are your students' guide through group learning, collaboration, conflict resolution, and socially acceptable communication. You can help them become lifelong creative learners by challenging them with problems and projects that require them to collaborate and share in this new, open-source world. That sounds like a tall order, but more and more it is how we live our lives. In the words of one student, whose experience with a connected and wired 21st-century teacher was so rewarding, "I think it comes down to either presenting the facts and the rules and getting it over with, or infusing the students with a greater understanding of that era, idea, emotion, equation, etc. . . . How can you expect the students to create a rich, vast knowledge of many different subjects and make great connections to our world . . . if the teachers don't have that themselves and can't present their own knowledge and connections to their students?" (http://thefischbowl.blogspot.com/2007/03/pb-and-j-palm-beach-and-jetlag.html, retrieved April 3, 2010).

Concluding Thoughts

"Why do some things take root and grow while others barely break the surface? How long does something have to be around before we can declare that it's here to stay? What has to happen in order to transform an oasis of change into an entire landscape?" —**Ronald Thorpe (2003)**

The 21st century challenges us to understand more about how people learn, communicate, and do business in a global environment or what Friedman calls the "flat world." Who we become as teachers will reflect the times in which we live—our global interconnectivity and our unending access to information and media.

It is difficult to predict the world in which your students will take part as adults. Think about this: in the years many of today's college-aged students were born, there were hardly any cell phones or digital cameras, no iPods or MP3 players, no iPads, very few Internet sites,

no GPS devices in cars, and no TIVO or Google. Now try to think twenty years into the future. Can you even begin to imagine what further changes will occur?

Connectivity, communication, and collaboration have become this century's reading, 'riting, and 'rithmetic—three Cs to replace the traditional three Rs of the 20th century. Of course, we need the three Rs to become adept at the three Cs. Yet the world into which you must guide your students is more complex and demanding than ever before.

Clearly, to teach in this environment, we must be students of history and of current affairs, and very much able to keep pace with constant change. Further, the global community challenges us to see beyond our own world and into the worlds of others as a way to make the planet a more tolerant, more sustainable, and safer place. As teachers, our personas are revealed in the classroom: how generous of spirit we become, how capable we are of listening to and learning with our students.

With so much information available through such a large variety of media, today's students have become masters of the art of multitasking. Barbara Kurshan, executive director of Curriki, a community of educators, learners, and education experts who are working together to create high-quality online materials for teachers and students, refers to a recent experience she had with a group of middle school students she encountered in a friend's basement. Some students were on the computer, some were sending text messages via their mobile phones, and others were on Facebook. She asked them what they were doing, and they responded, "Studying." They had been given a problem set and were collaborating on how to find the answers, working together and reaching out to other friends to see who had the knowledge they needed.

"That's exactly what goes on in the work world when solving a problem," she says—and too often, "it doesn't go on in the classroom."

Some people believe that when students are multitasking, they are not learning as well. "I disagree," Kurshan says. "I think they're learning the way we work in the business space. If there's something you don't know, you're finding it, and you're doing a lot more critical thinking and problem solving. At the moment, kids may be learning more outside of schools than they are [inside

Did You Know?

When many of today's college-aged students were born, there were hardly any cell phones or digital cameras, no iPods or MP3 players, no iPads, very few Internet sites, no GPS devices in cars, and no TIVO or Google.

them]" (http://www.eschoolnews.com/2010/01/01/esn-special-report-convergent-education/, retrieved April 2, 2010).

Clearly, the experience that students are having in many schools is linear and disconnected, starting from page one and continuing to the end of the book and then being tested on the material. Students must discon-nect from the electronic communities that keep them anchored and keep them learning within their own com-munities. A gap is growing between the way students have begun to learn and the way schools continue to teach. It is the wired, connected, and tech-savvy teacher who can use the language of the Information Age to help students to take charge of their own learning.

RESOURCES FOR FURTHER EXPLORATION

Online Resources

Convergent Education
http://www.eschoolnews.com/2010/01/01/esn-special-report-convergent-education.

Jennifer Nastu reports about how the enormous amount of information available is causing a revolu-tion in education.

Educere
http://www.educere.net/

Educere connects K–12 students and schools with a wide array of distance-learning courses.

ePals Global Community
http://www.epals.com/

This site is a good resource for connecting your class with students in other countries.

Friends across the Sea: Salisbury and Bloemfontein
http://www.wcboe.org/programs/oit/glen/hastings.html

This is a Web record of the exchanges described in this chapter between students in Maryland and South Africa.

The Fischbowl
http://thefischbowl.blogspot.com/

Karl Fisch is the director of technology for Arapahoe High School in Littleton, Colorado. His work on engag-ing teachers in digital media has a large following, and this site yields excellent ideas.

How Online Simulations Work in the Classroom
http://www.edutopia.org/online-simulations-classroom

This article by Chris O'Neal explores the ways in which online simulations are sometimes better than the real thing.

Intercultural E-mail Classroom Connections (IECC)
http://www.iecc.org/

IECC maintains several mailing lists that help teachers link their classes with partners in other countries for e-mail exchanges or collaborative projects.

International Education and Resource Network (iEARN)
http://www.iearn.org/

iEARN connects teachers and students around the world in collaborative projects that emphasize a social justice theme.

Kidlink
http://www.kidlink.org/

This is a global, multilingual e-mail network for young people between the ages of ten and fifteen. Through the associated KIDPROJ, adult mentors organize curricu-lum projects.

Moving Learning Games Forward: Obstacles, Opportunities, and Openness
http://education.mit.edu/papers/MovingLearning-GamesForward_EdArcade.pdf

This Massachusetts Institute of Technology white paper by Eric Klopfer, Scott Osterweil, and Katie Salen describes the promise of using high-quality educational video games for learning.

NASA CONNECT
http://connect.larc.nasa.gov/

This is NASA's series of integrated math, science, and technology programs for middle school students.

NASA Digital Learning Network
http://nasadln.nmsu.edu/dln/

This is NASA's umbrella site linking its many educa-tional programs and activities.

Realityworks Teaches Business Ed with Online Simulation Games

http://thejournal.com/articles/2010/04/02/realityworks-teaches-business-ed-with-online-simulation-games.aspx

This journal article by Dian Schaffhauser describes the ways in which educational simulations work in the context of high school business class video games.

Technology Facilitates Learning in Small Groups

http://www.eschoolnews.com/2009/11/01/esn-special-report-small-group-collaboration/

Ellie Ashford reports on how teachers use technology to help students solve problems together in small groups.

ThinkQuest

http://www.thinkquest.org/

In this project-based learning initiative, students from around the world participate in designing websites that may be used for reference by other students.

Print Resource

D. Bavelier and C.S. Green, "Video game based learning: There is more than meets the eye," *Frontiers in Neuroscience,* **special issue on Augmented Cognition, 3(1) (2009), 109.**

These cognitive scientists report on how video game use affects an individual's abilities in the perceptual domain.

Part 4 addresses the pressing question of how to create classroom environments—real or virtual—that are welcoming, caring, and ultimately effective for teaching and learning. The personal nature of teaching distinguishes it from many other professions. Teaching keeps you on your toes and requires self-awareness and a special mindfulness of your actions and intentions. You need this level of consciousness to become an effective teacher. Remember, teaching is about building relationships.

In this part of the book, we also explore the importance of instilling a sense of belonging among your students—a feeling that everyone in the classroom belongs to the same community. This sense of community not only enhances students' learning experiences; it also acts as a buffer against some of the problems in today's schools, such as bullying and sexual harassment.

Finally, Part 4 offers several tools to assist you in analyzing—once again—whether teaching is the right career for you. Thinking about the "goodness of fit" between yourself and the profession is a crucial step in preparing for a fulfilling and successful teaching life.

Part Outline

CHAPTER 9   The Classroom as Community
CHAPTER 10   Making the Decision to Become a Teacher

CHAPTER 9

THE CLASSROOM AS COMMUNITY

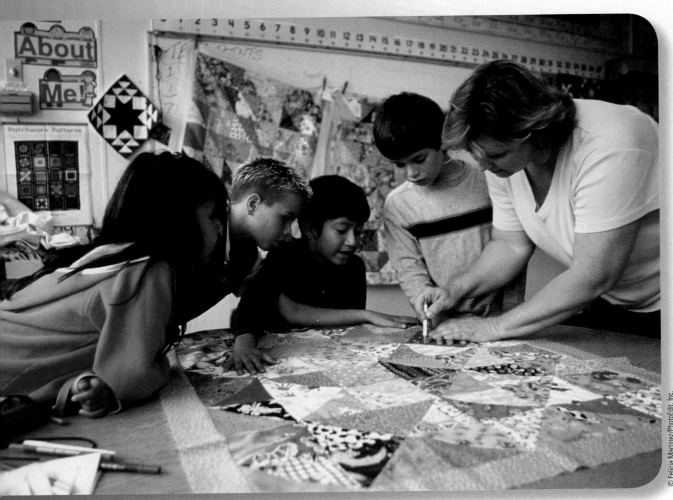

© Felicia Martinez/PhotoEdit, Inc.

> *Children require guidance and sympathy far more than instruction.*
> —Anne Sullivan, American teacher (best known as Helen Keller's tutor), 1866–1936

This chapter considers the issue of "community" in conventional classrooms—where students are gathered, physically face-to-face, with a teacher for a specified period of time. Many of the principles described here also relate to online or virtual classrooms, such as those that were discussed in the previous chapters. Whatever the domain in which you teach, your primary function is to ask, "How do I create an environment in which students have respect for themselves and for the other members of the classroom community?"

In the current era, in which schools focus intensely on the academic proficiency of their students as recorded by standards-based tests, it is important to recognize that academic proficiency is only one of the major goals of education. There are social and emotional goals as well. Students should become learners with the capacity to love, work, and be active community members (Cohen, 2006). Along these lines, the philosopher John Dewey urged educators to have a sympathetic understanding of learners as individuals in order to have an idea of what is actually going on in their minds (1938, p. 39).

classroom management
The ways teachers create an effective classroom environment for learning, including all the rules and conditions they establish.

LEARNING OUTCOMES

After reading this chapter, you should be thinking about the following ideas:

LO1 A classroom becomes a community when the participants share an understanding of the beliefs, values, and goals that form the basis for the group.

LO2 Classroom management is the term typically used when referring to the prevention of disruptive behaviors and the fostering of a smooth-running class.

LO3 Belongingness in school communities refers to the expressed feeling that individuals are part of a group and of something larger than themselves.

LO4 Formal classroom meetings are a venue for sharing feelings and goals and are a way to establish community within a classroom.

LO5 Sexual harassment and bullying, both in class and in cyberspace, refer to abusive behaviors perpetrated by individuals with power over others who feel powerless.

LO1 Building Community in the Classroom

John Dewey (1916–2004) asserted that the aim of education is to support the development of the skills and knowledge needed for responsible and caring participation in a democracy. In a sense, then, the question this chapter seeks to answer is, "How do students become engaged, responsible participants in a democracy, and how does that process start with the environment created in their classrooms?"

LO2 CLASSROOM MANAGEMENT AND CLASSROOM COMMUNITY

New teachers often seek to understand more about what is typically called **classroom management**. By *management*, they mean the ways the teacher can get students to do what the teacher wants them to. Classroom management has been defined as "the set of teacher behaviors that create and maintain conditions in the classroom permitting instruction to take place efficiently and effectively" (Ryan & Cooper, 2007, p. 499). Other educators believe that good classroom managers "carefully arrange their classrooms to minimize disturbances ... and make sure that instruction can proceed efficiently" (Sadker & Zittleman, 2007, pp. 398–399).

Among many progressive educators, though, the term *classroom management* is frowned upon because it can imply that teachers use the power differential between themselves and their students to force students to follow a certain set of rules. Recently, educators interested in classroom management have begun to focus instead on the creation, through various strategies, of a **classroom community** in which each participant is invested in the smooth operation of the whole and all participants have an interest in outcomes. In this viewpoint, rules and conditions are not established by the teacher alone, but by the group as a whole.

Although we do need structures, routines, and class rules to guide the teaching and learning in our classrooms, the way we arrive at these guidelines is crucial. Different teachers have different ways of establishing classroom expectations. When I was chatting with Meredith, who has been in the classroom for two years, we explored her experiences as a first-year teacher in an urban school known for its discipline problems. She taught a second-grade class of thirty students, and she felt her first year had been successful and satisfying. I asked her how she felt before the first day of school.

I was scared. I wanted to meet the children, and I was excited, but before the first day of school, I was told that I had behavior problems in my class. But, after the first five minutes with the class, I was fine. My classroom management skills kicked in, and I was on my way.

When I asked Meredith where she got those skills, she said, "From my mother." I was stunned because I know there are many teaching courses

© Lisa Thornberg/iStockphoto

with the title "Classroom Management." Was her mother wiser than professional educators? She elaborated on what she had learned from her mother:

My mother always expected the best from me, and she was strict and demanding, but I knew she really cared about me and had my best interests at heart. Still, she was a "no-nonsense mom" who set goals with me and had clear expectations. She checked with me to see how I felt about how I was meeting my goals. I do the same thing with the children in my classroom.

I ask them what type of classroom will help them learn. I have strict policies, but we discuss each policy and why it makes sense for their learning environment. I hold out the expectation that they will abide by the rules, and I keep my door open. I explain to them that anyone passing our classroom should be able to see a model of students busy with their work and their class discussions. Of course, when they work in pairs or groups, there is some noise, but that is necessary for them to collaborate with their classmates.

I asked if she used any little tricks to keep students focused and productive. Yes, she said, she had hand signals to get their attention when they were working in pairs or groups; she introduced those signals on the first day of school. Also, during a group conversation, she would quietly walk over to students who were not paying attention, and her body language helped amend their behavior.

Mostly, Meredith explained, she genuinely cares about her students and expects them to be successful. She wants a classroom that works for both the students and the teacher, and sometimes that means she has to alter her plans. For example, if she notices that the second graders are engaged in a topic and working diligently on task, she extends the lesson, altering her own routine to allow them to go further in an area of study that *they* find compelling:

Everything is a collaboration; there is no such thing as "teaching" separate from "learning." It is not always possible to know what curriculum areas will set an entire class on fire—and when one comes up, I hate to let it go just because my plan book says I should.

Good teachers live for those moments when the students are "on fire" (Intrator, 2003), carried away and enthused by a topic, a project, an experience, or a story. It is at these times, when students are fully communicating with each other, responding to peers and to you, that you think, "Wow, this is why I came to this work!" These experiences engage students' thinking and enthusiasm so completely that they "forget" they are supposed to resist school, and they get carried away by the excitement of the moment.

At these moments, you understand that the classroom is "managed" by the quality of the learning experience, the engagement of the students, and the appreciation of the teacher for the intellectual work that is happening. This is a learning community. It is managed by everyone in it. Let's look at another story that can tell us more about the foundations of a classroom community.

In an old school building in the east Bronx in New York City, I am trying to bring eighth-grade physical science to life. As part of a unit on the properties of mixtures, we are studying solutions. For this lesson, I want to show the students that, in a solution with water, even though the particles of a solute (the substance that dissolves) seem to disappear, they can be reclaimed. If you boil off the water, the original solute remains at the bottom of the flask. In fact, if you collect the steam and condense it back into water, you can end up with the solute and the water in separate containers—exactly the way they started before the solution was made.

To do this, I set up an apparatus called a Liebig condenser, made popular by the German chemist Justus Baron von Liebig, which makes it possible to collect vapors and turn them back into a liquid. The condenser has an inner tube and an outer tube. The entire apparatus connects to the lab sink in my classroom.

We start with blue crystals of copper sulfate. We stir them into water, making a copper sulfate solution. Then we try to reverse the process. We place the flask containing the solution on a tripod over a Bunsen burner, connecting the open end of the flask to the Liebig condenser with rubber tubing. When the copper sulfate solution

The classroom is "managed" by the quality of the learning experience, the engagement of the students, and the appreciation of the teacher for the intellectual work that is happening.

boils, the water vapor is collected in the condenser's inner tube, and cold water from the lab sink swirls around the outer tube. Slowly, clear water—the steam turned back into liquid—drips from the condenser into a collecting beaker. The students sit in rapt attention, enthralled.

I ask the class if this process would work if the tube were hooked up to the hot water faucet. All the students shout, "No, it's the cold water that does it!" They seem to understand that the cold turns the steam back into water by removing the heat from the vapor. I do not mind that they are shouting: "Mrs. Koch—look inside the flask—look—the blue crystals are coming back!"

"Yes," I remark, "and how many thought they were gone for good?" Many students raise their hands. They are smiling; they "get it."

They ask if we can try another solution tomorrow. "Sure," I reply, and tomorrow we will try it with salt water. When the students file out at the end of class, some of them call out, "That was so cool, Mrs. K."

I leave the school building elated. I know the students have had a learning experience. They now know more about evaporation, condensation, and the entire process of distillation. As I drive home with a big smile on my face, I am reminded that it is just for days like this that I keep teaching. I say to myself, "It's worth all the preparation!"

Think about what is happening behind the scenes in this eighth-grade classroom. For one thing, the students have learned that I go to a good deal of trouble on their behalf. I have taken the time to set up this complex apparatus and have it ready for their class. They appear to understand that I am deeply invested in their learning and in providing a good science experience. Today will tide us over other days that may not be as exciting, but the students will expect a similarly exciting lab demonstration at some future date.

Over time, as I continued to show my commitment to these students, they never cut science. They were interested. They were well behaved. They managed themselves.

But there are other factors at work here as well. By saying that the students managed themselves, I don't mean that we had no classroom rules. We did in fact have rules in which everyone was invested. This leads us to our next topic.

LO3 RULES, PROCEDURES, AND ROUTINES: A COLLABORATIVE EFFORT

To create classroom community, teachers must provide opportunities and structures that can encourage students to help and support one another. To do so, teachers need to offer explicit instruction so that students learn *how* to support one another (Hittie, 2000).

Rules, procedures, and routines are a good example. Effective teachers use these to manage their classrooms. Too often, however, the decisions are solely in the hands of the teacher, and the students have no voice in, and hence no responsibility for, the way their classroom is managed. To build classroom community, a teacher needs to involve the students in establishing the rules and procedures. Remember what Meredith said: "I ask [my students] what type of classroom will help them learn. I have strict policies, but we discuss each policy and why it makes sense for their learning environment."

Now think about my eighth-grade science classroom. The students were all fired up about the distillation experiment, but their behavior stayed well within the limits of appropriate classroom decorum. What rules do you think the class and I developed?

The students and I developed a chart guiding behavior for watching complex demonstrations. As we made up the chart, the students were creative and inventive, and the result was a true collaborative effort. Rules for observing demonstrations included no crowding around the lab desk; no blocking other students' views; respect everyone's right to see the demo; and so on. As the story reveals, there *was* some calling out, and it was a fitting expression of the students' excitement.

The point is clear. A classroom that functions well allows students to provide input about the ways it should be run. Classroom rules and procedures result from a collaborative effort. Building a community honors all the participants, and the value of creating community is that each participant is invested in the outcomes.

IS A WELL-MANAGED CLASSROOM SILENT?

Many new teachers, and veteran teachers as well, confuse a well-run classroom with pervasive silence. As the distillation experiment reveals, appropriate noise related to the activity or experience in which the students are engaged is a healthy aspect of a well-managed classroom. In fact, classrooms in which teachers insist on quiet all the time run the risk of students becoming

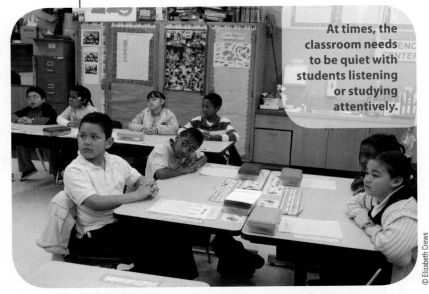

At times, the classroom needs to be quiet with students listening or studying attentively.

© Elizabeth Crews

Good classroom management allows time for the active engagement of students, encouraging the thinking process and creating engaged learners.

© Michael Newman/PhotoEdit, Inc.

disengaged and not really present in the social and emotional ways required for learning.

In Chapter 4 and throughout this text, we describe teaching and learning as active processes requiring thoughtful reflection on challenging ideas and concepts as we make them our own. The best ways to facilitate the process of learning is to engage students in projects and problems related to the conceptual understanding you are hoping to achieve and then invite students to work in small groups to reach consensus. With all that going on, a classroom can be a noisy, not a silent place. This is productive "noise"—communication in the service of learning.

The stereotype of the teacher in the front of a room full of rows of silent children runs counter to everything we know about how people learn. Today, classrooms have many configurations: students may be seated at tables, in groups of desks, or, yes, even in rows. But, however the classroom is arranged, learning cannot happen in silence. The well-managed classroom usually has groups of students communicating, collaborating with other students, working online, and yes, making comments that pierce the silence.

BEING FULLY CONSCIOUS

As a teacher, you are "on" from the moment your school day begins. Everything you say and do may have an effect on your students. For that reason, it's impossible to overstate the importance of being fully aware and in control of your own behavior. As an example, I share the story, as a parent, of an experience my daughter had some years ago. Note the reactions of the student, the teacher, and the parent. What was the effect on classroom community?

TEACHSOURCE VIDEO CASE

Teachers Building Community

To see more examples of how teachers conduct their classrooms, find the TeachSource Video Case "Classroom Management: Best Practices" on the student website. After watching the video, consider the following questions:

In what ways does the elementary teacher's management approach differ from that of the middle school teacher? Why do these different approaches work?

Q: *Has there been a time when you hurt somebody's feelings without realizing it?*

At the end of a school day in third grade, my nine-year-old daughter Robin came off the school bus, made eye contact with me, and started to sob. She had held back tears all afternoon and had to struggle to compose herself to tell me about her humiliation by her third-grade teacher.

It appears that left-handed Robin was holding her pencil in an awkward way. Mrs. Owens held her hand up to the class and said, "Class, do you all see the way Robin is holding her pencil? You must never hold your pencil that way." Well, that was it for Robin for the rest of the school day. Humiliated, she retreated quietly into herself and returned home bruised by this criticism in front of her peers.

I visited Mrs. Owens the following day, and before I could recount the episode, she showered me with compliments about Robin. When I shared my concern about the pencil incident with her, she said, "Oh, that was nothing. I didn't mean anything by it. I just want her to hold her pencil correctly."

The teacher reacted impulsively, without regard for how her words and actions could have affected her student. In fact, her student's feelings were hurt by the exchange, and she didn't even recognize it. Teachers cannot afford to "shoot from the hip." They must be careful to explore ways to change students' habits by engaging in constructive and caring dialogue.

Among the essential qualities teachers need to be successful, one is a clear sense of their own adulthood and a grounded sense of who they are. When you teach, your personality and needs are on display at all times. If you are very needy, your students will sense that. You should make certain that your students' needs come before your own needs.

© Rasmus Rasmussen/iStockphoto

Teachers have different personalities, but what they have in common is that the teacher is usually the responsible adult in the classroom. As the adult, the teacher is obligated to create a safe, secure, and organized learning environment in which routines and expectations are consistent and respectful.

LO4 THE CLASSROOM AS A SAFE PLACE

In Chapter 6, we discussed the importance of creating a safe school climate. In many ways, a classroom community is a microcosm of the larger school climate. You may not be able to control the climate elsewhere in the school, but you can do a lot in your own classroom.

To foster a sense of community in the classroom, teachers must ensure that the classroom is a safe place—not just a physically safe environment, but also an emotionally safe place where students are treated with respect, both by the teacher and by each other. In such a place, everyone is held accountable for what happens. Students come to rely on the teacher's sense of fairness and the consistency with which she or he upholds classroom rules and guidelines.

Some teachers establish a classroom meeting time to help build the sense of community. Teachers may have a "Morning Meeting" every day, or they may have class meetings as needed to discuss a particular event or to handle a problem. Each type of meeting serves a different purpose and contributes to the shared sense of community. The following teaching story illustrates how the meetings work in one fifth-grade classroom.

In a fifth-grade inclusion classroom, Ms. Sanders, who has been teaching for five years, has established the practice of daily Morning Meetings. This is a critical part of the day that fosters relationships among the students. The inclusion students, in particular, comment that this is their favorite part of the day.

The four parts of the Morning Meeting are the greeting, the share, announcements, and the news. The meeting takes place at the beginning of each school day on a rug at the rear of the classroom, where students sit on pillows in a circle facing each other, with the teacher positioned in a prominent spot in the circle.

Ms. Sanders views Morning Meeting as a critical event of the day, a time when students are recognized, life stories are heard, and all individuals are valued. She explains, "I make sure I greet each child, even if he or she is going out to a band lesson or early math. I make sure that I talk to them all, and they are greeted by name. I look at Morning Meeting as a place to talk about what is on the kids' minds and what is going on in their lives. Morning Meeting gives the students a place to share with the whole class, not just me. I love it! It really brings us together as a community, and I learn so much about the students as people from this daily exchange."

The students regard Morning Meeting as an important opportunity to share their life outside of school, learn about their classmates, and celebrate their differences. One boy remarks, "We do Morning Meeting, and I especially like the sharing part when you get to bring in something and share it with the class. I always like to see what other people bring in, and when I bring in something, people always come up to me at snack and want to see it. Then when I have a play date they will ask to see the thing I shared, like my arrowhead or rock collection. It makes me feel good inside and kind of special."

Another student says, "I like Morning Meeting the best because you get to hear about current events and what is going on in the world. You also get to hear what is going on in other people's lives during sharing. I really like that."

Ms. Sanders explains: "I think that the personality of the teacher helps the classroom become a warm and caring atmosphere. I think that I am very easygoing and laid back. I am always happy and smiling, and I try really hard to make the class a fun place for all kids. If I come in and I tell the kids a story that happened to me yesterday or a story about my life, then they will share with me. That creates a nice warm environment in which to learn. I try to make the class like a community. I stress that from day one. I promote an environment where they are free to take risks. They can treat each other like friends, and they can count on each other for help."

The students in this class are aware that they are a part of a special classroom community. Their sense of belongingness is not necessarily the norm outside of their classroom. They talk about bullying, ridicule, and

> To foster a sense of community in the classroom, teachers must ensure the classroom is a safe place.

aggressive behavior by students from other classes—experiences that occur regularly on the playground, in the lunchroom, and on the bus. Some express outrage at the social injustice experienced by their peers. The students in this class feel a sense of responsibility toward each other, reflecting the care and concern embodied by their teacher, Ms. Sanders.

In this classroom, clearly, the management is handled by everyone. *(Reprinted from an unpublished paper by doctoral student Christine Schroder, 2006, Hofstra University, NY).*

Ms. Sanders is quite aware of the various ways she encourages a sense of community. She mentions her easygoing personality; her storytelling, which connects her life experiences with those of the students; and her vigilance in promoting a risk-free environment and a safe place for friendships to grow. All of these are critical components in developing a caring classroom.

Morning Meeting in itself is a structure that can build a sense of community and acceptance among the members of a classroom. The daily exchanges among students allow them (1) to feel validated and an important part of the classroom community, (2) to make meaning out of new concepts, (3) to assist themselves and others in the learning process, and (4) to celebrate personal differences. If you establish a Morning Meeting in your classroom, you may find that students rush to the rug each morning to engage in this community-building ritual.

In this era of high-stakes testing many teachers are preoccupied with students' academic achievements as recorded on standardized tests. This preoccupation sometimes leaves little room for sensing the emotional climate of the class. Research studies have discovered, however, that if students do not feel emotionally and socially safe, the opportunities for them to learn are limited. According to research, a sense of belongingness—of being connected in important ways to others—is one of three basic psychological

TEACHSOURCE VIDEO CASE

Using Classroom Meetings to Create Community
Find the TeachSource Video Case "Elementary Classroom Management: Basic Strategies" on the student website to view an example of the Morning Meeting in the classroom. After watching the video, consider the following question:

How does the teacher engage the students in community problem solving?

needs essential to human growth and development, along with autonomy and competence (Osterman, 2000, p. 325). In simple terms, students' learning improves when teachers *integrate* academic and social learning in the classroom (Bickart et al., 2000; Rimm-Kaufman, 2006). Building classroom community is an intrinsic part of creating academically competent students.

THE RESPONSIVE CLASSROOM APPROACH TO COMMUNITY BUILDING

A group of educators from the Northeast Foundation for Children (NEFC) has developed a program called

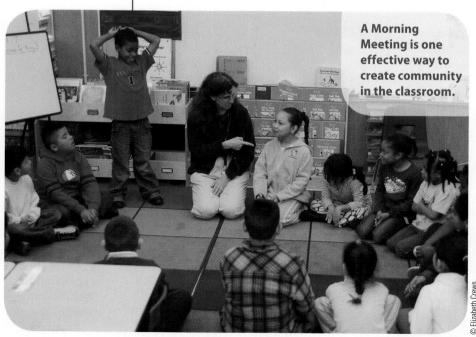

A Morning Meeting is one effective way to create community in the classroom.

© Elizabeth Crews

the **Responsive Classroom**, which introduces teachers to the theory and practice of sound classroom management through democratic principles and practices. The Responsive Classroom approach rests on principles like these (Northeast Foundation for Children, 2007; Rimm-Kaufman, 2006):

- The social curriculum and the academic curriculum are equally important.
- How children learn is as important as what they learn.
- Social interaction facilitates cognitive growth.
- Children need to learn cooperation, assertion, responsibility, empathy, and self-control if they are to be successful socially and academically.
- Knowing children individually, culturally, and developmentally is essential to good teaching.
- Knowing children's families is essential to good teaching.
- The working relationships among the adults in a school are critically important to students' learning.

Notice that many of these principles align with what we have said previously in this book. These ideas rest heavily on the understanding that teaching and learning are about building and fostering relationships—relationships among teachers and students; among students and their peers; and among teachers and other teachers, administrators, and the community at large.

Following these principles, the developers of the Responsive Classroom model recommend a number of specific teaching strategies. They advocate Morning Meeting, for instance. They suggest "guided discovery," an approach to learning similar to the project- and problem-based methods discussed earlier in this text. They also recommend "academic choice," a term that highlights the importance of activities in which students make their own choices, solve problems, and work collaboratively. They even propose strategies for arranging materials, furniture, and displays to encourage independence, promote caring, and maximize learning. You can read more about Responsive Classrooms at http://www.responsiveclassroom.org/.

TIPS FOR CREATING A CLASSROOM COMMUNITY

From what you have read in this chapter, you should already have some good ideas for creating community in your classroom. The most basic suggestion I can offer is to take a genuine interest in your students. Authenticity outs itself. Students can sense when you are honestly interested in them as people as well as learners. Remember, it is often the little things you do that build a sense of trust among your students. For example, elementary school teachers learn quickly that their young students, even in first and second grade, are capable of managing many of the classroom routines—and that doing so gives them a sense of community and responsibility. Giving students classroom jobs facilitates the classroom routines while allowing the students to feel important to the community. These jobs include plant monitor, lunch menu reporter, library helper, whiteboard cleaner, pencil sharpener, and many others. A great deal of psychological research indicates that people, even young children, experience feelings of well-being and happiness when they have a sense of purpose and are of use. Psychologists suggest that this sense

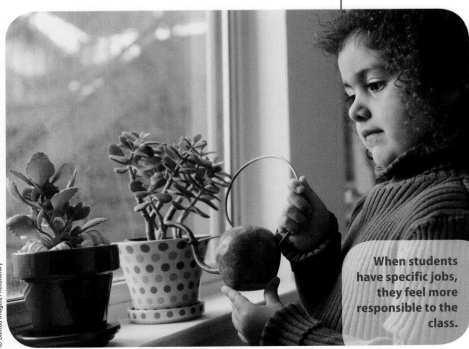

When students have specific jobs, they feel more responsible to the class.

of well-being rests on individuals' ability to use their strengths and virtues in the service of something larger than themselves (Seligman et al., 2005).

Enlisting your students in service to the classroom community gives them a sense of purpose and allows them to make a contribution to the whole. Even in middle and high school, when your time with the students is of shorter duration, you can make this happen.

Beyond the classroom, your students may have the opportunity to engage in **service learning**—that is, community service done in collaboration with a larger project at the school. This type of learning not only connects students with the larger community, but it also forges bonds among the students as they collaborate to make a difference in their own neighborhoods.

COMMUNITY BUILDING IN THE SECONDARY CLASSROOM

Think about a middle school in an urban area, like Los Angeles. In one classroom, students file in, take their seats and immediately begin working on a language arts warm-up exercise. While the teacher takes attendance, the eighth graders silently work. When the short exercise has been completed, students raise their hands and wait for the

service learning
A teaching and learning strategy that integrates meaningful community service with instruction and reflection to enrich the learning experience, teach civic responsibility, and strengthen communities.

CLASSROOM COMMUNITIES: TIPS FOR TEACHERS

- Teachers can never be overprepared. The first key to a successful teaching experience is to plan, plan, and plan!
- Understand your expectations for students' behavior, and share those with them. Show them and tell them what you are hoping for.
- To build a sense of community, develop rules collaboratively with your students, and be very clear about these.
- Be consistent. Have clear consequences when rules are broken, and follow through!
- Be prepared to admit your mistakes. And use humor when appropriate.
- Make respect central to your classroom culture. Make it clear that you care about your students and that your class will lead to real learning that will benefit them.
- Minimize the power differential in everyday communication. Keep calm in all situations. Whenever possible, connect your classroom discussions and curriculum to students' lives, communities, and culture.
- Learn as much as you can about your students and make connections to their lived experiences.
- Build students' confidence in their own intelligence and creativity.

- Talk about multiple intelligences, if appropriate, and how people can be smart and creative in many ways.
- Have engaging activities prepared for the students when they walk into the classroom. Keep lecturing to a minimum.
- Engage students in group projects, centers, presentations, discussions, or role plays.
- Place the students at the center of the learning experience. Make the classroom about them.
- Remember, the best and most appropriate consequences for students are positive ones—the intrinsic joy that comes from success, accomplishment, social approval, good academic performance, and recognition. Create experiences that enable all students to feel good about themselves.

SOURCES: Adapted from Miller, L. (2004). 12 tips for new teachers. In K. D. Salas, R. Tenorio, S. Walters, & D. Weiss (Eds.), *The New Teacher Book: Finding Purpose, Balance, and Hope during Your First Years in the Classroom*. Milwaukee, WI: Rethinking Schools, Ltd.; and from "Tips for creating a peaceful classroom," *Teacher Talk*. http://education.indiana.edu/cas/tt/v2i3/peaceful.html, retrieved May 29, 2007.

teacher to call on them as they go over the answers together.

Down the corridor, seventh graders stream into another classroom and take over. Some sit on table tops; others wander around the room. As the teacher takes attendance, one boy brushes his hair, three girls suck on lollipops, one girl sings, and a boy in the last row unleashes a barrage of spitballs. The day's warm-up is quickly forgotten. Same school, same day, similar students, similar teachers—yet profoundly different behavior (adapted from Mehta, *Los Angeles Times*, December 14, 2009). Educators remind us that the ability to calmly control student behavior so learning can flourish has a huge impact on a teacher's ability to be successful.

Teachers who have good skills in creating an organized classroom community in middle and high school agree on several factors. Most important, an organized teacher who has good communication skills and cares deeply about the students will be able to earn their respect and hence their cooperation. Routines are important, whether in kindergarten or twelfth grade. Students feel safe when they know what to expect. The following attributes are helpful, but so is practice! Learn as much about your students as possible, and demonstrate that you are interested in them as people.

Consistency

Teachers should tell students what to expect and then deliver. This applies to all aspects of the secondary classroom, ranging from identifying test days to delivering instruction. Starting every English class, for example, by posing a question for discussion or written response, helps establish a routine that students can expect.

Clarity

Teachers must clearly explicate their learning objectives for the course as well their expectations for student

Q: *Do you recall having a classroom job?*

behavior. Discuss these topics with students during the first week of class and provide specific examples of what students are expected to accomplish and how they are expected to behave. Practicing classroom rules is not solely reserved for elementary school. By illustrating through role play with students what is considered appropriate and inappropriate behavior, teachers leave no room for student interpretation on these important points.

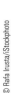

Fairness

This relates to showing respect for your students by setting realistic expectations and offering guidance and support to help students achieve those goals.

Foresight

Map out your class in advance with your students. Spend the first few days of class discussing an overview of what you hope to accomplish as far as content, skill development, student behavior, and class format. If students do not abide by class expectations, they know in advance what repercussions they will face.

LO5 Preventing Harassment and Bullying

Successful teachers invite their students' lives, languages, and cultures into the classroom. They start building a classroom community on the first day of school. They care about their students, and they create

"If you say the next person who talks in class will be set on fire and rolled down the hallway, you're in trouble if someone talks and you don't set them on fire and roll them down the hallway."
—Kendra Wallace, Middle School Principal, Los Angeles, 2009

WRITING & REFLECTION

Establishing Boundaries

Developing good relationships with your students requires setting appropriate boundaries. You want the classroom to belong to everyone; yet, as we noted earlier, you are the adult in the room, and you have a particular responsibility to make sure the environment is conducive to learning. You are not one of the kids. Sometimes new teachers, afraid of becoming their students' "friend," become overly authoritative and defeat their own attempts at creating community. Reflect on your own personality in this respect.

- Are you authoritative, or are you shy?
- Do you anticipate having an easy or difficult time reprimanding students or implementing the rules of the classroom?
- How can you act as the adult in the classroom and at the same time respect your students and make them feel valued and important?

an environment where social justice is both a goal and a reality.

In this type of environment, injustices toward individuals or groups of students become readily apparent. Two prominent examples of social injustice in today's schools are sexual harassment and bullying. This section explores these topics and discusses how you can help prevent them from endangering your classroom community.

SEXUAL HARASSMENT IN SCHOOL

Under the guidelines established by the federal Office for Civil Rights, sexual harassment is considered a form of sex discrimination and is therefore prohibited by Title IX of the Education Amendments of 1972. Generally speaking, **sexual harassment** is any "unwanted and unwelcome sexual behavior" that interferes with a person's life. Sexual harassment does not include "behaviors that you like or want (for example, wanted kissing, touching, or flirting)" (AAUW Educational Foundation, 2004, p. 11).

Sexually harassing behaviors happen in school hallways, stairwells, and classrooms, and they have a negative effect on the emotional and educational lives of students. In a 2000 federal survey, more than 36 percent of U.S. public schools reported at least one incident of sexual harassment (Dinkes et al., 2007, p. 84). Eight in ten students experience some form of sexual harassment during their school lives. Eighty-five percent of students in grades eight through eleven say that students harass other students at their schools, and almost 40 percent of students report that teachers and other school employees sexually harass students in their schools (AAUW Educational Foundation, 2004, 2001).

On May 24, 1999, the Supreme Court ruled that school districts can be liable for damages under federal law for failing to stop a student from subjecting another student to severe and pervasive sexual harassment (Koch, 2002, p. 262). Title IX also guarantees that hostility and ridicule toward gay and lesbian students that is not immediately acted upon by the school or district may be grounds for a lawsuit against that district. See Table 9.1 for a simple checklist to determine what has been done to prevent harassment in the school or district.

As a teacher, you need to learn about your school or district's policies concerning sexual harassment and teach them openly to your students. Make sure students know the sanctioned procedures for reporting abuse so they do not needlessly suffer victimization by others. Many schools use role-playing scenarios or videos to prompt student discussion of sexual harassment issues. Teachers and schools are responsible for creating a harassment-free environment in which all students are safe to learn.

Did You Know?

Eight in ten students experience some form of sexual harassment during their school lives.

TABLE 9.1	Sexual Harassment Checklist for Schools or School Districts
• Does the school/district have a specific policy against sexual harassment?	
• Does the school/district foster an atmosphere of prevention by sensitizing students and staff to issues of sexual harassment?	
• Is the school/district prepared to receive and respond to complaints?	
• Does the school/district have a grievance procedure for sexual harassment?	
• How effective has the school/district been in implementing its antiharassment policy?	

SOURCE: Adapted from AAUW Educational Foundation. (2004). *Harassment-Free Hallways: How to Stop Sexual Harassment in School*. Washington, D.C.: American Association of University Women Educational Foundation.

bullying Repeated cruelty, physical or psychological, by a powerful person toward a less powerful person.

Establishing a sense of community with your students is a vital means of preventing harassment in school. When students feel responsible for one another and care about their learning community, harassing behaviors are less likely to occur—and when they do, they are less likely to persist. If your classroom community fosters an atmosphere of risk-free communication, your students will be better able to talk about alleged harassment and determine what to do.

Beyond the general principle of making respect central to your classroom culture, you should consider specific guidelines for student behavior that will help prevent sexual harassment. Often, well-meaning teachers ignore certain behaviors, especially in middle and high school, as long as they seem socially acceptable to the students themselves. For instance, teachers may decide that name calling and excessive flirting are "normal" for the students' age, when in fact these behaviors can be disruptive to the victim's well-being. It is important to know how to respond to this type of occurrence. There are many surveys and checklists that help teachers and students recognize sexually harassing behavior. A checklist for teens might suggest, for example, that acceptable flirting makes you feel flattered, while harassment makes you feel unattractive or ashamed. The particular guidelines you adopt should take into account your students' age, the cultures represented in your classroom, and your school and district policies. See the Resources for Further Exploration section at the end of the chapter for some useful starting points.

BULLYING AND TEASING

While creating community in the classroom is an important deterrent to negative student behaviors, teachers cannot be everywhere. Let's go back to Ms. Sanders's classroom, described earlier in this chapter. Despite the warm and caring environment promoted by her use of Morning Meeting, one of the students reported bullying and teasing on the playground at lunchtime. Because there is a longstanding tradition of the classroom or school bully, this problem is often overlooked. In fact, half of America's schoolchildren report being bullied at least once a week, and ten thousand children nationwide report staying home from school once a month because of a bully (Corcoran, 2002).

Bullying implies repeated harmful acts and an imbalance of power. It can involve physical, verbal, or psychological attacks or intimidation directed against a victim who cannot properly defend him- or herself because of size or strength or because of being outnumbered or less psychologically resilient. Bullying

TYPES OF SEXUAL HARASSMENT

According to the Office for Civil Rights of the U.S. Department of Education, sexual harassment falls into two basic categories.

Quid pro quo sexual harassment occurs when a school employee causes a student to believe that he or she must submit to unwelcome sexual conduct to participate in a school program or activity. It can also occur when a teacher suggests to a student that educational decisions such as grades will be based on whether the student submits to unwelcome sexual conduct.

Hostile environment harassment occurs when unwelcome verbal or physical conduct is sufficiently severe, persistent, or pervasive that it creates an abusive or hostile environment for the affected student (Office for Civil Rights, 2001, 1997).

includes assault, tripping, intimidation, rumor spreading and isolation, demands for money, destruction of property, theft of valued possessions, destruction of another's work, and name calling (Sampson, 2002). Figure 9.1, which focuses on teenagers, shows statistics about some of the prevalent types of bullying.

The most likely targets of bullies are gay students or students who are perceived to be gay (Corcoran, 2002). As teenagers' sexual identities are beginning to emerge, homophobia, the fear of and intolerance toward homosexuals, is, unfortunately, part of the culture of many secondary schools.

Many antibullying programs have been put in place, including procedures that students can follow if they feel they are being bullied. Most of the time, however, students do not reveal that they are being bullied, and witnesses tend not to come forward. Although there are more male bullies and male victims, the numbers of female bullies and victims are on the rise (Olweus, 2003). Victimization by bullying has been linked to

Q: *How would you recognize sexual harassment or bullying in your own classroom?*

student depression, eating disorders, and even suicidal tendencies (Sears, 1991).

In classes where a strong sense of community has been created, not only is bullying less likely to occur in the first place, but if it does, the bullying victim is more likely to come forward, as are the witnesses. The emphasis is on the common good and on care and respect for one another.

CYBERBULLYING

In Chapter 7, we discussed the concept of Internet safety. Social networking is a way of life for our nation's youth. They are part of myriad online communities, and with all these opportunities to communicate online, there are hidden dangers. In chatrooms, people can pretend to be someone they are not and entice unknowing children and teenagers to meet them. This is a major source of Internet child and teen abuse, and many schools are adopting programs to warn their students about online sexual predators and establishing ways

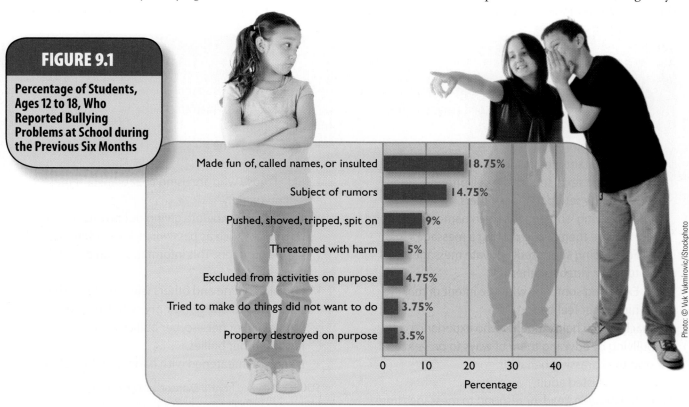

FIGURE 9.1

Percentage of Students, Ages 12 to 18, Who Reported Bullying Problems at School during the Previous Six Months

Made fun of, called names, or insulted — 18.75%
Subject of rumors — 14.75%
Pushed, shoved, tripped, spit on — 9%
Threatened with harm — 5%
Excluded from activities on purpose — 4.75%
Tried to make do things did not want to do — 3.75%
Property destroyed on purpose — 3.5%

Percentage

Photo: © Vuk Vukmirovic/iStockphoto

SOURCE: Data from Dinkes, R., Cataldi, E. F., Kena, G., Baum, K., & Snyder, T. D. (2006). *Indicators of School Crime and Safety: 2006.* NCES 2007-003/NCJ 214262. Washington, D.C.: U.S. Government Printing Office.

cyberbullying Bullying or harassment through electronic means such as e-mail, website postings, instant messaging, text messaging, blogs, mobile phones, or chatrooms; also called *online bullying*.

to report online solicitations. Internet crime is a crime like any other and should be reported to proper local, state, or federal authorities.

More prevalent than sexual predation, however, are nasty e-mails, texts, or website postings about an individual student. This phenomenon, known as **cyberbullying**, can constitute a computer crime if it reaches a serious level. It is a federal crime to anonymously annoy, harass, threaten, or abuse any person via the Internet or a telecommunications system. Even at a less-than-criminal level, cyberbullying can lead to the same traumatic effects as physical bullying.

Bullying is all about power. The bully has it; the victim does not. Technology accelerates bullying as social media make it easy for bullies to enlist large, usually anonymous groups to carry out relentless attacks with text messages, e-mails, and sometimes compromising digital photos. Adults are removed from this assault and are not present electronically to intervene. Victims often feel ashamed, powerless, and fearful of retaliation if they report the bully or bullies. Cyberbullying

is a serious, behind-the-scenes, event that often occurs not only during but also after school time. It is essential that this type of bullying be addressed openly in schools and that all students understand what each of them can do to report bullying they have witnessed, or bullying where they are a victim or an unwitting collaborator. All cyberbullying interventions require a school climate of trust and caring that ensures all communications with school personnel are confidential.

The most important action a student can initiate if she or he is experiencing cyberbullying is to tell someone immediately. Many schools are promoting Internet safety programs, and a number of websites offer helpful tips for students that teachers can use to educate their students on preventing cyberbullying (see the sidebar "Tips for Students Who Are Cyberbullied"). Creating a safe and trusting classroom community extends to protecting your students from online abuse.

Classroom Community and Goodness of Fit

As we mentioned earlier, good classroom management requires that you be fully conscious in the

---

TIPS FOR STUDENTS WHO ARE CYBERBULLIED

Cyberbullying is harassment that occurs during online activities. Be aware of its many forms, such as:

- A threatening e-mail
- Nasty instant messaging session
- Repeated texts sent to the cell phone
- A website set up to mock others
- "Borrowing" someone's screen name and pretending to be them while posting a message
- Forwarding supposedly private messages, pictures, or video to others
- Excluding someone with the intent of making him or her feel bad

Teachers can help students who experience cyberbullying by advising them of ways to prevent and stop the harassing behavior:

- Tell a trusted adult.
- Never open, read, or respond to messages from people you know to be cyberbullies.

- If the problem is school-related, tell a school teacher or administrator. All schools have bullying solutions.
- Do not erase the messages. They may be needed to take action.
- Block those who are using chat or instant messaging to bully.
- Think carefully before giving out private information online such as passwords, PINs, addresses, or phone numbers. This information can be used by bullies.
- Be polite online and others will tend to do the same. If someone gets angry or bullies you, ignore him or her—cyber bullies want a reaction just like other bullies.
- If you are threatened with harm, call the police.

SOURCE: Adapted from "Beware of the Cyber Bully," iSAFE, Inc. http://www.isafe.org/imgs/pdf/education/CyberBullying.pdf, accessed April 2, 2010.

---

classroom. It requires what Jacob Kounin (1970) called "withitness," a concept sometimes interpreted as having "eyes in the back of your head" to ward off any undesirable behavior. I prefer to think of "withitness" as a broad awareness that you have about yourself and your students together. Do you have a centered presence in the classroom? Are you aware of the students' dispositions on any given day as they enter your room? At any moment, do you know whether the principles of classroom community that you and the students have developed are working?

These are important matters to take into consideration when deciding on the "goodness of fit" between yourself and the teaching profession. Think about the following concepts:

- Good teachers are usually interested in learning as much as they can about their students.
- Effective teachers are very organized and plan ahead.
- New teachers frequently imagine how they will speak and act in front of a class.
- Good teachers care deeply about listening to and valuing their students' ideas.
- Teachers need to be fully conscious or "with it" at all times, and especially in a large group of students.
- Effective teachers are often role models for their younger, less empowered students.

Concluding Thoughts

Clearly, good communication and collaboration with your students are vital for creating a classroom in which everyone feels responsible for managing the environment and working toward the common good. As a teacher, you should identify the most effective rules for your classroom and seek the students' assistance in establishing these as classroom priorities. When you involve your students in setting guidelines for everyone to follow, you help them buy into an environment where everyone can learn and occurrences like bullying and sexual harassment are stopped in their tracks.

Classroom community relates to the principles of teaching and learning we have discussed throughout this book. When you have your students work in groups, develop their own strategies for solving problems, and apply their concepts to meaningful real-world projects, you not only help them learn individually, but you also foster their sense of the classroom as a learning community. When you honor diversity and use culturally relevant pedagogy, you create the same effect. All of these practices are good teaching methods *and* good classroom management strategies.

Finally, your ability to be honest with your students and to show your interest in their lives will go a long way toward earning their trust and turning the classroom into a safe place and a genuine learning community.

RESOURCES FOR FURTHER EXPLORATION

Online Resources

Bullying: Facts for Schools and Parents

http://www.naspcenter.org/factsheets/bullying_fs.html

Sponsored by the National Association of School Psychologists, this page offers an overview of bullying and strategies for responding to bullying incidents. Also see the section of the site called "Behavior & Discipline."

Controlling a Classroom Isn't as Easy as ABC

http://articles.latimes.com/2009/dec/14/local/la-me-classroom-control14-2009dec14

This article, written by Seema Mehta, discusses what teachers and principals in one middle school do to maintain classrooms where behavioral disruptions are at a minimum.

Kidscape: Staying Safe Online

http://www.kidscape.org.uk/cyberbullying/cyberbullyingchildrenyoungpeople.shtml

This website provides important tips for staying safe in chatrooms, when using e-mail, and when text or video messaging.

Responsive Classroom

http://www.responsiveclassroom.org/

This website describes the Responsive Classroom model and provides access to a number of other resources to foster social and academic learning.

CHAPTER 10

MAKING THE DECISION TO BECOME A TEACHER

© Jack Hollingsworth/photodisc/Getty Images

> *The mediocre teacher tells. The good teacher explains. The superior teacher demonstrates. The great teacher inspires.*
> —William Arthur Ward, American educator, 1921–1994

A t this point in your journey, you would be correct to conclude that modern classrooms are complex places, that teaching is a highly sophisticated activity, and that a career in education requires careful planning, the capacity for spontaneous decision making, and actions based on careful personal reflection.

In this final chapter, we examine some ways of thinking about teaching as a profession in the hopes that it will inform your decision-making process. Moments of absolute certainty are rare, but there are signs that can help you make your choice.

LEARNING OUTCOMES

After reading this chapter, you should be thinking about the following ideas:

LO1 Public education is vital to a thriving democracy, and teachers in the 21st century need to foster critical thinking, creativity, collaboration, and communication.

LO2 Teaching is about building relationships with students and acknowledging the many ways in which people learn.

LO3 Good teachers have specific personal attributes that make them well suited for the profession. You can demonstrate some of your talents in your teaching portfolio.

LO4 Your responsibility is to understand who you are, where your strengths and weaknesses lie, and what your next steps should be in your journey to become a teacher.

Goodness of Fit

> *"You have to love kids and want to connect with them—because if you don't connect with the kids, you will never be able to convey the materials; if you cannot feel the music, you cannot play the music.... I can teach anyone about pedagogical strategies but I cannot teach a person to love kids. And you can feel it in a classroom as soon as you walk in."* —**Christopher Day (2004)**

As you learned in Chapter 1, *goodness of fit* is a term used in descriptive statistics to mean a match between a theory and a set of observations. By using the term to refer to the match between a teacher candidate's attributes and the job of a teacher, this book has invited you to consider your own suitability for the teaching profession.

Think about what you have learned about teaching and what you have recognized about your personal attributes. Remember that there is no one definition of a "good" or "successful" teacher. The power of a teacher cannot be overestimated. You will be responsible for the education of tomorrow's thinkers and leaders, and you will learn the joy of making a contribution to other people's growth and development.

Research has found that people are often happier when they are making a contribution to others (Seligman, 2002), and that is certainly true of teaching. But considerable evidence also shows that people are more successful when they are engaged in work that plays to their strengths. If teaching does not play to your own strengths, perhaps it is not the best profession for you. An article written for the *New Yorker* magazine (2008) discussed how difficult it was for professional sports scouts to determine, based on observing college athletes at play, who would be the best draft pick for particular positions, in this case, in football. Titled "Most Likely to Succeed," the article emphasized how difficult it is to predict how someone will do in a position once he or she is hired, no matter how much you learn about the person beforehand (Gladwell, 2008). Nowhere is this as serious an issue as when hiring a new teacher. This is mainly because research tells us that really good teachers have profound effects on student learning and, unfortunately, the converse is true. In fact, some research indicates that a student would be more likely to succeed with a terrific teacher in a lower-performing school than with a terrible teacher in a high-performing school (Hanushek et al., 2005).

This is a good time to consider how you may be able to tell if you are a good fit for teaching. These are some attributes of good teachers that form only the beginning of a list. You probably have others and can make this list even longer. Many individuals who succeed as teachers have:

- A centered presence in the classroom
- A sensitivity to the classroom setting
- An ability to respond thoughtfully to each student
- A personal capacity for juggling lots of balls in the air
- An appreciation of how children and young adults grow and change
- An understanding of the ways our students bring their outside worlds into the classroom
- A desire to help students feel capable and competent

THE IMPORTANCE OF OBSERVING IN THE FIELD

As we mentioned in Chapter 1, visiting a school and spending time in classrooms can provide a sense of the school culture and the school climate. This is important

Q: *What is your most memorable field experience so far?*

in order to gain a real-time, current look at the life of teachers and students. Your first formal experience in a classroom will probably be through your field placement. The field placement is an opportunity for you to serve as an apprentice and learn from the regular classroom teacher and from your own experience of working with the students.

In some formal field experiences, you begin by making observations. Keep some of the attributes just mentioned in mind as you observe in the classroom setting. In other placements, you may be considered a *participant-observer*. While participating in the life of the classroom, you make careful observations and study the classroom environment to learn about child and adolescent development and teaching methods. Usually, participant-observers are not required to spend the entire school day in the field placement; rather, they must be immersed in the school for a specific number of hours each week.

In other field placements, you are considered a *student teacher*. In this arrangement, you are assigned to a teacher, usually called the "cooperating teacher," on a daily basis for a specified period of time, such as ten to twelve weeks. Student teachers at the secondary level often receive two placements, one in a middle school and the other in a high school. At the elementary level, depending on your state's requirements, you may receive one placement in grades K–2 and another in grades 3–5.

As a student teacher, you will be expected to teach the class at prearranged times. During some of these teaching experiences, you will be formally observed by a supervisor assigned by your institution. Student teaching is a special time when you develop a clear idea of what the life of a classroom teacher is all about. It is a very important part of your professional preparation.

Before you start your field experience, it is important to learn as much as possible about the school and classroom to which you have been assigned. Be certain that you understand your role in the classroom and that you are aware of the dress code for teachers in the school. Ask questions. Be gracious, and be sure to thank the teacher in whose classroom you are gaining experience.

TEACHSOURCE VIDEO CASE

Effective Teaching

Find the TeachSource Video Case "Teaching as a Profession: What Defines Effective Teaching?" on the student website to learn about what makes an effective teacher from the perspective of several teachers and administrators. After watching the video, consider the following question:

Terms like flexible, thoughtful, spontaneous, caring, *and* knowledge-able *emerge as significant attributes of teachers. How would you rank these in order of importance?*

LO1 THE PURPOSES OF PUBLIC EDUCATION AND THE ROLE OF THE TEACHER

"Above all things, I hope that the education of the common people will be attended to, convinced that on their good sense we may rely with the most security for the preservation of a due degree of liberty." —Thomas Jefferson, in a letter to James Madison, 1787

Chapter 3 described the vital role public education has played in American democratic society since the early days of the nation. As the preceding quotation from Thomas Jefferson indicates, American public schools have always been expected to fulfill certain public missions that go beyond the purely academic.

Today, as you have seen throughout this book, **public education** serves the basic function of preparing young people to lead productive lives by increasing their academic achievement and improving their readiness to secure jobs in an increasingly global economy. In addition, however, public education helps equip our youth to become responsible and active citizens in a democratic society. In other words, it prepares them to participate in decisions that contribute to the social good (Center on Education Policy, 2007).

Although the current era of standards-based assessments emphasizes quantifiable academic achievement, it is useful to envision your career in education as serving a broader purpose. The Center for Education Policy (2007) describes the mission of public education in terms of six main themes:

1. To provide universal access to free education
2. To guarantee equal opportunities for all children
3. To unify a diverse population
4. To prepare people for citizenship in a democratic society
5. To prepare people to become economically self-sufficient
6. To improve social conditions

In Chapter 9, we explored how classrooms can create a sense of community, a social group mindful of the needs of each of its members. In this sense, creating a classroom community becomes more than a tool for effective teaching and learning; it becomes a model for social justice and social participation in the microcosm of the classroom. Clearly, the important goals of education include helping students develop their abilities to think critically, appreciate diverse cultures, maintain curiosity about the world, and show confidence in expressing their own ideas.

In Chapter 1, we described teaching as an essential profession and reviewed a code of ethics developed by the National Education Association. Now that we have come to the end of this text, I invite you to think about the profession of teaching as requiring an overriding commitment by its members to the well-being of their students. Teaching is not an ordinary job. It is a profession that establishes our identities and reveals our values.

Most important, the functions and responsibilities of teachers are not confined to the classroom. Central to your work as a teacher is devoting time and energy to professional communities, activities, conferences, and workshops. Teaching is an opportunity for intellectual development, both through professional teacher

public education
Education that is publicly financed, tuition-free, accountable to public authorities, and accessible to all students. The term covers various types of public schools, including traditional schools, charter and magnet schools, vocational schools, and alternative schools.

Communication, collaboration, and connection are the hallmarks of 21st-century teaching and learning.

© Comstock/Photolibrary

development courses and through your own intimate contact with new books, ideas, and technologies. Actually, few teachers who are not also intellectually curious are successful.

Further, as you have seen in this text, teaching in the 21st century requires guiding students through the huge quantity of information that enters their lives on a daily basis. It is your job to help them understand what is valid and what needs to be discarded. These contemporary teaching needs make the teacher's role more complex and ever-changing than in any previous era. Luckily, you can find support through various professional organizations and on many online sites, in chat rooms, and on blogs.

ONE SIZE DOES NOT FIT ALL

In Chapter 3, when we explored the history of American public education and the many reform movements that have dotted the landscape of teaching and learning, we saw that American education is a large mosaic. Methods are varied, and successes and failures weave their way through each successive period of history. There is no one right way to teach; there are many right ways—and many incorrect ways as well. Just as there are multiple learning styles and learning profiles, teaching is as variable as the types and personalities of teachers.

The challenge is to imagine you are on a journey of both inward and outward exploration. You will explore your own personality traits, subject areas of expertise, capacity for generosity, and schooling stories. Try to remember the special moments that made you feel like school was the best place in the world. Also recall those times when being a student was painful or you were victimized by a teacher, knowingly or unknowingly.

One of your most useful tools is your capacity for reflection, along with your humility. It is profoundly moving to affect the lives of young people. It is also an extraordinary responsibility.

Find a way to connect with colleagues or classmates with whom you can have a conversation about teaching. Learning to teach is very much about having conversations and exchanging stories with willing colleagues. These discussions will help you discover the ways teaching will be a personal expression of yourself.

LO2 CREATING A CULTURE OF CARING

Many teachers talk about the importance of caring about students so that they see themselves as valuable and capable of learning. Creating a caring environment has a deep effect on you as well. Katy Ridnouer tells the following story, illustrating how an ethic of caring contributes to the life of a middle school teacher.

Did You Know?

Up to one-third of new U.S. teachers leave the profession within the first few years.

Although the United States trains more than enough teachers to meet its needs, the attrition rate for educators is higher than for any other professional occupation. According to a report from the National Commission for Teaching and America's Future, up to one-third of new U.S. teachers leave the profession within the first few years. I was one of them. In my second year, I taught eighth-grade language arts in a school full of challenges. I felt isolated, unsafe, and incapable, but I trudged on. I met with parents, I brainstormed with colleagues, and I discussed issues with members of the administration. Nothing changed. At the end of the year, I decided to leave teaching for the quiet solitude of the bookseller's life.

For six months or so, I convinced myself that I had made a good choice. Then the dreams about my classroom started. I was in front of my eighth graders, leading a grammar lesson. I saw their willing faces. I saw *them*. I then realized that I had expected everyone else to change while I remained the same. I expected the surly child to be pleasant, but I did nothing to encourage this behavior. I expected the underachieving child to work to his potential, but I did nothing to bring this about. I even expected the motivated child to stay motivated but did nothing to contribute to that end. My eyes opened, I returned to teaching, and I have never looked back.

I identify as a teacher. It's what I am meant to do, and it is as rewarding to me as art is to the artist, a great play is to the athlete, and the correct diagnosis is to the doctor. When I see students grapple with a concept and come away with new understanding of the material and a new respect for themselves, the long hours I invest hardly matter.' . . .

Today, my guiding maxim as a teacher is to create a learning community within the four walls of the classroom. I define a learning community as a group of people who come together with a willing spirit to learn and support one another despite racial, economic, religious, and achievement differences. Learning communities promote curiosity, higher-level thinking, enhanced interpersonal skills, and confidence in both students and teachers. I have found that the key to creating a learning community is to *manage your classroom with heart*—and by that, I mean permeate the classroom atmosphere with caring concern. This involves care in interactions with students, lesson planning, seating chart decisions, discipline concerns, grading, and more. Putting care for your students first creates a learning community that inspires them to be their best selves, both in school and out in the world.

When I went back to the classroom, I changed the way I perceived my job. . . . Most significantly, I had to care about my students, which was something I hadn't really allowed myself to do before. Sure, I was friendly to them and I wanted them to succeed, but I can't say I was a caring teacher. Frankly, I saw caring as a risky venture. I worried that my feelings might be hurt if my students mocked my concern for them or if they didn't reciprocate it. I worried that I might get caught up in my students' personal concerns and neglect their academic achievement. I worried that the administration would think I had "gone soft." But on my second go-round, I decided to take the risk: to allow myself to care about my students—to nurture them and their learning. I am a happier teacher, a better teacher, and a richer human being because of it. My great hope is that by welcoming my students into my heart, I have enriched their lives.

SOURCE: From *Managing Your Classroom with Heart: A Guide for Nurturing Adolescent Learners* (pp. 1–3), by Katy Ridnouer, Alexandria, VA: ASCD. © 2006 by ASCD. Reprinted with permission. Learn more about ASCD at www.ascd.org.

Katy Ridnouer's story is one of hope and resolve. She returned to the middle school classroom because she instinctively knew that was where she was meant to be. That intangible quality, that inner knowing, cannot be taught; it must be felt. She needed to revisit her desire to teach because, on the first go-around, she was not meeting with a sense of personal success.

Her story is a reminder that the early years of teaching confront us with many challenges. Working with young people is often unpredictable and can shake one's confidence. Feelings of frustration are not uncommon; however, they are often counterbalanced by a sense of profound accomplishment when students have that "aha" moment and demonstrate that they really "get it." This story reminds us that becoming proficient in our chosen profession takes time. Being patient with yourself as you begin is an important attribute.

The next story offers another perspective on a new teacher and the culture of caring she has created.

Jaime Barron started teaching the fourth grade in an urban area where poverty is commonplace, most children are from minority backgrounds, and more than ninety percent have lived all or some of their lives in homeless shelters. The students come to school with very little social capital. Many are from single-parent families where their responsibilities include the care of younger siblings. All of the students receive free breakfast and lunch daily.

Since Jaime's experience with these fourth-grade students was very positive, she asked if she could "loop" with this class to fifth grade. (*Looping* is the process of sending an entire class together into the next grade level with the same teacher. In some school districts, it requires parental approval.) When I visited her and her class, it was the middle of the fifth grade, and the twenty-nine students were working in seven groups on projects that involved designing model ecosystems for different animals around the world.

Jaime's room is covered with print; student work hangs everywhere. There are posters hanging from clotheslines strung across the room. The posters explain group-work rules that include taking turns, listening to others, and offering ideas. For these students, working independently is a challenge, but they enjoy working on projects and accessing information on the computer, and they tell me they really like Ms. Barron.

The classroom is small and crowded, and there are not enough resources. The students have little knowledge about environments beyond their urban apartments and shelters. Doing group projects that construct environments far beyond their streets is a new experience for them. To aid their imagination, a world map hangs in the classroom. Their city is circled in red.

All the students, who range in age from ten to thirteen, appear to have a fundamental understanding that Ms. Barron cares about them. They respond to this. Each morning they bring her enormous plan book to her and ask, "What are we doing today?" They understand that she prepares for them. She is very calm and very firm; she never yells; she never takes unacceptable behavior personally. Jaime knows that the students with whom she works struggle in their environment. She reminds them of rules and structures they have developed to keep the class running smoothly and to maximize learning. The students tell me they feel safe in her class and are lucky to be with her. "She never yells." Jaime tells me there is little truancy in her class.

I ask Jaime if she will remain in this school next year, when her current students move on to middle school. Yes, she will stay, she explains, because she feels she is making a difference and she is needed here.

It will come as no surprise to you that, to Jaime Barron, teaching is much more than a job. It is an authentic commitment to working on behalf of her students. Her clarity about her purpose finds its way into the classroom community that she and her students have created. The students trust her and know she will not harm them, demean them, scream at them, or use her power over them. Her calm voice and caring manner are accompanied by

WRITING & REFLECTION

Demonstrating Understanding

One way to reflect on what becoming a teacher means to you is to complete an "I am" poem. "I am" poems ask the poet to state five different descriptions of the self. Focus on your understanding of choosing to become a teacher by completing the following statements:

I wonder . . . (two things you wonder about).

I hear . . . (your inner voice).

I see . . . (your vision for your professional self).

I want . . . (what you hope for).

I AM . . . a Future Teacher.

classroom structures that keep the students productive and safe.

Jaime is extremely well prepared all the time. She consistently has a creative, activity-oriented experience in which to engage the class. She takes the students on field trips, monitors their homework, and works with them one-on-one during lunchtime.

Jaime also actively reflects on her teaching. She has some days that are worse than others, some days that are better, but throughout the ups and downs she loves her work and cannot imagine doing anything else.

> She is very calm and very firm; she never yells; she never takes unacceptable behavior personally.

LOOKING AGAIN AT MULTIPLE WAYS OF TEACHING AND LEARNING

"*Now that my five-year-old niece, Maren, has entered kindergarten, we have an ongoing philosophical discussion about education. 'Teachers know everything,' she says. 'No,' I say. 'Teachers know some things. Nobody knows everything. There are some things you know that your teacher doesn't know.' 'Like what?' 'Like*

what it feels like to be your Mommy and Daddy's oldest child, to be Gary's good friend, to be my five-year-old niece.' **99**
—Judy Logan (1999)

Throughout this text, we have visited different types of classrooms with varying approaches to teaching. As we have seen, studies in neuroscience show that, for a concept to get hooked into their prior knowledge, individuals need to construct meaning for themselves. We have explored project-based and problem-based learning as ways to place the students' own construction of knowledge at the center of their learning experience.

Many educators see "student-centered learning" as an "anything goes" method. On the contrary, student-centered environments seek to draw out students' ideas in order to deal with the misconceptions that often accompany the learning of something new. Unless we understand what students are thinking about the material in which we engage them, we cannot know if they "get it."

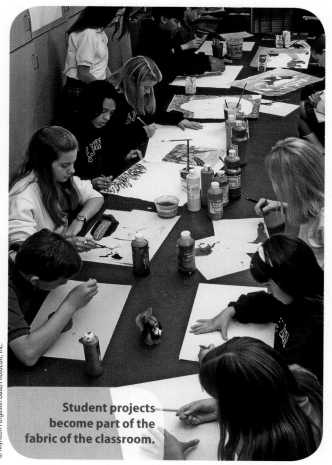

© Myrleen Ferguson Cate/PhotoEdit, Inc.

Student projects become part of the fabric of the classroom.

Do remember, however, that student-centered environments use multiple teaching strategies, ranging from direct explanations to problem-based and project-based learning. The successful teacher learns how to adapt the materials to the class in a way that reaches the individual students and asks them to do something to demonstrate their understanding. Hence, student-centered classrooms invite learners to create explanations, demonstrate meaning, and come up with their own ideas and questions related to the content area.

USING CURRENT TECHNOLOGIES

Today, making connections to students' lived experiences means accessing the wired world of cyberspace in ways that enhance students' critical thinking and their abilities to understand a concept. In earlier chapters, we emphasized the growing effect of technology on education. Connect, communicate, and collaborate—these are the three Cs of the newest wave of technology use in the classroom. Teaching can involve creating a class website for which all of the students collaborate to determine the content . Students may use the website to publish digital videos related to a topic of study. With Web 2.0 technology, such as blogs and wikis, the user can readily add to the content.

Technology offers two more benefits that are not always appreciated:

1. Learning is more powerful when students are prompted to take information presented to them in one form and "represent" it in an alternative way. The technology now available for teaching and learning helps students do just that. When students create their own representations of information, they provide clues about their thinking and give teachers a view of the accuracy of their conceptions.
2. You have seen the importance of recognizing that there are multiple intelligences and different learning styles. Technology can help students integrate information from multiple modalities, ensuring that all students, no matter what their learning style, have the opportunity to grasp key concepts.

Consider your teaching role in a "flat" world and take an interest in other languages and the global community. Explore possibilities for linking your class with classes in different regions of the country or in foreign countries. The opportunity to engage your students in communication on a global scale is one of the most exciting teaching challenges of the 21st century.

Google sponsors a site called Google for Educators (http://www .google.com/educators/) that includes a number of online tools such as blog software and collaborative word-processing applications. The section on Google Earth, a satellite-mapping resource, includes suggestions for use in the classroom. Rip Van Winkle would not recognize these tools!

Get a head start and investigate technologies such as these. Look into the technological capacities of the schools or districts in which you find yourself observing and practice-teaching—and do the same when you get your first teaching job. Remember that your students will be deluged with data and that one of your critical roles will be helping them assess the value of the information to which they are exposed.

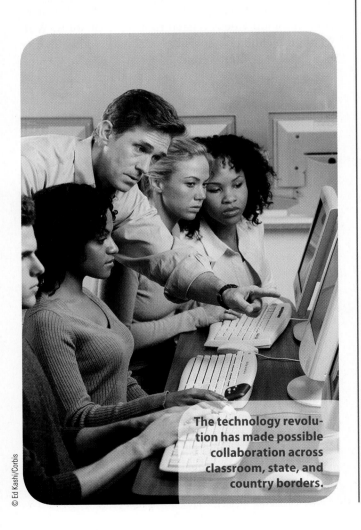

The technology revolution has made possible collaboration across classroom, state, and country borders.

© Ed Kashi/Corbis

Getting Started in the Teaching Profession

If you follow a traditional path toward becoming a teacher, you'll receive guidance along the way and help in finding the full list of requirements for your state. As mentioned earlier, field experiences play an important role in teacher preparation. Many states require professional certification, and although the exact process for becoming a teacher varies from state to state, there are some common requirements.

CERTIFICATION AND STANDARDS

Becoming a teacher in the public schools requires **certification** by your state. A state teaching certificate or license shows that you have met the state's requirements for becoming a teacher at specific grade levels and (especially for higher grades) in a certain subject area. For instance, your certificate might be for elementary education (grades K–6), for middle school social studies, or for middle school and high school biology.

Your state's Department of Education (DOE) website will describe the range of areas for which you can be licensed. Requirements for teacher certificates or licenses vary from state to state. Some states are relatively compatible with other states in their certification requirements; some states are more individualistic. Of course, your teacher education program will go a long way toward preparing you for state certification, but it is important to understand the certification requirements *beyond* completing your program.

The Praxis Tests

❝*Praxis is the doctrine that when actions are based on sound theory and values, they can make a real difference in the world.*❞ —Paulo Freire (1970)

Most states require that future teachers pass a state exam or series of exams. The Educational Testing Service has developed **The Praxis Series** of professional assessments for beginning teachers. (As used by social scientists, the term *praxis* relates to action based on principles and theories that have a sound basis in research and experience.) A large number of states use this series of tests to assess your knowledge of subject matter and pedagogy.

The Praxis Series consists of three separate kinds of tests:

1. The Praxis I tests measure basic academic skills in reading, mathematics, and writing. Usually you

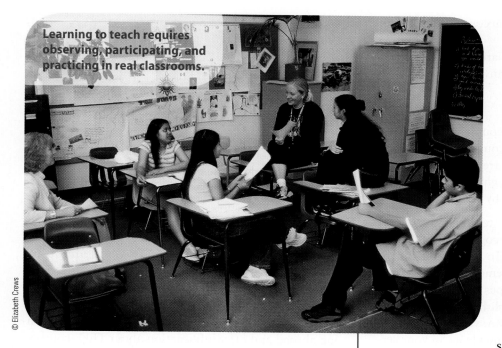
Learning to teach requires observing, participating, and practicing in real classrooms.

© Elizabeth Crews

Interstate New Teacher Assessment and Support Consortium (INTASC) An organization that develops standards and principles to guide the preparation, licensing, and professional development of teachers. INTASC's members are state education agencies and national educational organizations.

take these tests before entering your teacher education program or before your student teaching or internship.

2. The Praxis II tests measure knowledge about specific subject areas and about principles of learning and teaching. Generally you take these tests when you complete your teacher preparation program.

3. The Praxis III assessment focuses on actual classroom performance. If your state requires Praxis III, the assessment usually takes place in your first year of teaching and leads to a higher level of certification. It includes direct observation of your classroom practice, review of a video or other documentation you send in, and interviews.

Several states offer their own assessments for certification and licensing, but these tests are typically similar to the Praxis tests. See the Review Card at the back of the book for sample test questions, and visit the Praxis website (http://www.ets.org/praxis/) to find out whether the state in which you hope to teach requires the Praxis tests.

The INTASC Standards

Many of the requirements for certification are based on standards and principles developed by a national organization, the **Interstate New Teacher Assessment and Support Consortium (INTASC)**. Established in 1987, INTASC represents a combined effort by numerous state education agencies and national educational organizations to reform the preparation, licensing,

and professional development of teachers. The consortium works from the premise that "an effective teacher must be able to integrate content knowledge with the specific strengths and needs of students to assure that *all* students learn and perform at high levels" (Council of Chief State School Officers, 2007).

The National Board for Professional Teaching Standards

As mentioned in Chapter 1, the National Board for Professional Teaching Standards (http://www.nbpts.org/) offers a national system for certifying teachers who meet rigorous standards. These standards are relevant to what you have already explored about teaching and learning. National Board Certified Teachers (NBCTs) embody these "Five Core Propositions":

- **Proposition 1:** Teachers are committed to students and learning.
- **Proposition 2:** Teachers know the subjects they teach and how to teach those subjects to students.
- **Proposition 3:** Teachers are responsible for managing and monitoring student learning.
- **Proposition 4:** Teachers think systematically about their practice and learn from experience.
- **Proposition 5:** Teachers are members of learning communities. (National Board for Professional Teaching Standards, 2002)

These are themes familiar to all those who are preparing to become teachers. The National Board has used these general propositions to establish standards for certification in many areas of teaching, from early-childhood education through middle-childhood education to the various academic specialties in secondary education. National Board standards are created by committees of educators who are accomplished professionals in their fields.

The process of becoming a National Board Certified Teacher is arduous and has many steps. To seek this certification, you must:

- Hold a bachelor's degree.
- Have three full years of teaching/counseling experience.
- Possess a valid state teaching/counseling license for that period of time, or, if you are teaching where a license is not required, have taught in schools recognized and approved to operate by the state.

Compared with an ordinary teaching certificate, National Board Certification is recognized in all states as a higher level of achievement. To obtain this certification, you must meet the requirements of a portfolio assessment that includes videotapes of your teaching, student work, and your accomplishments outside of your school experience. In addition, you must take an exam that assesses your content knowledge in your certificate area; test centers are located across the country.

TEACHING POSITIONS HERE AND ABROAD

Teachers are in demand throughout the United States and all over the world. In the United States, the teaching areas in shortest supply include, but are not limited to, special education, bilingual education, earth science, chemistry, physics, mathematics and computer science, and foreign languages. Of course, these shortages vary by particular location and with population trends.

As Chapter 8 indicated, though, the world has shrunk tremendously because of technology. You may want to challenge your thinking by going to a foreign country and gaining firsthand experience teaching there. If you decide to do this, it is wise to find others who have traveled this path before you and learn from them what the experience was like. There are groups of teachers who have taught abroad and can serve as resources for you. You can access these groups through teaching-abroad websites, such as the ones listed in the Resources for Further Exploration section at the end of this chapter.

What kinds of positions are available in foreign countries? Although there are teaching opportunities in all disciplines and languages, the majority of positions available are for native English speakers teaching English as a foreign language. To be eligible for these positions, you usually must hold a certificate for Teaching English as a Foreign Language (TEFL). Native English speakers may take an online course to become certified in TEFL. A number of websites, such as the one shown in Figure 10.1, list opportunities for teaching abroad and offer information about TEFL courses.

In addition, there are more than 300 American International Schools overseas. These are typically private, nonprofit schools based on an American or a British model. Often, the schooling they provide leads to the International Baccalaureate diploma, an international credential that is offered at some schools in this country as well. To explore American International Schools, visit the International Schools Services website (http://www.iss.edu/). Half of the staff members at these schools are from North America.

TIPS FOR NEW TEACHERS

As you begin your field work or your work in your own classroom, remember that as a teacher, you are an

Figure 10.1

Part of a Screen from the Teach Abroad Website
Teach Abroad is one of a number of websites that offer information about overseas teaching positions and certification.

WHAT COUNTRY DO YOU WANT TO TEACH IN?

any country ▾ GO
text list of countries
POPULAR SEARCHES: China, South Korea, Taiwan, Thailand, Mexico, Japan, England, Spain, United Arab Emirates, India

Begin your search for a TEFL Certification Program

Most Recent Teach Abroad Opportunities

Most recent World Wide postings
Most recent Korean postings
Most recent Taiwanese postings
Most recent Chinese postings

RSS Feeds

SOURCE: From http://www.teachabroad.com/. Reprinted by permission of GoAbroad.com.

educational leader. Your teaching is as much a product of *who you are* as of how you implement strategies. The following list offers some tips as you get started.

- **Learn as much as you can about your school environment.** Do your homework. Be prepared. By that I mean learn everything you can about the school in which you will be doing your field placement work or getting your first teaching job.
  - How long has the school been in this community?
  - How many students and teachers are there?
  - How many administrators are there?
  - Who are the students? What types of homes, apartments, or other forms of housing arrangements do they live in?
  - Can you expect a student body that is diverse ethnically? Socially? Economically? How many inclusion classrooms are there?
  - How many networked computers are in each classroom?
  - What does the school website have to say? Is this school or district known for any particular achievements?
  - Do classes have their own websites?
  - How do the students perform on mandated assessments? These scores are a matter of public record.
  - If this is your field placement, from whom do you need permission?
  - Are visitors and invited guests required to sign in? What is the correct protocol?
- **Keep a journal.**
  - Record your experiences as you begin. Include your fears and your questions. If you have a smartphone, an iPad, a netbook, or another small electronic device, save these journal entries and look back upon them as you continue.
  - Be fully conscious in the classroom. Journaling can help you stay conscious so you do not "shoot from the hip."
- **Join a collegial group, and find a friend.** Become part of a new-teacher group, either in your school or college or in your community. If you cannot find one that meets face-to-face, check for responsible groups online. In the most trying of times, it is often your colleagues who offer the most support and help you move forward. This point was made clearly by the teachers who shared their stories in Chapter 2.

  If you are lucky, you will find one particular person in your new school with whom you can connect

Your teaching is as much a product of who you are as of how you implement strategies.

and share your experiences of teaching. This kind of relationship often builds into a lasting friendship.
- **Find a mentor.** Connect with an experienced teacher whom you trust, and communicate your hopes and fears to this person. Being a teacher means you are always a learner: learning about yourself, your content area, and your students. There is much to learn from mentors, so seek out a person who can fill this role for you.
- **Remember that teaching is not telling.** Teaching is not about you; it is about the students. Your focus should be on them. How will you engage them? What will you do on behalf of their learning?
- **Plan for creative experiences and activities.** Prepare lessons in which the students' active engagement is at the center, and listen to their ideas. Showing your students that you value what they think is priceless.
- **To create a safe environment, show that you are human.** Do not believe that you have to know everything and do everything right. Model vulnerability for your students; show them that you can laugh at your own mistakes. Students will feel more comfortable when you show that you are learning as well. This does not mean that you are not credible; it simply means that as humans we all make mistakes.
- **Be passionate.** Teachers express their passion for teaching in different ways, but being delighted to be with your students, coming in well prepared, and having a specific plan in mind are all ways to show the students that you care.

- **Differentiate instruction.** Remember that treating all students equally does not ensure equality of outcomes. Equitable and fair-minded teaching considers the ways all of our students, in all their diversity, learn best.

Educational Associations

Dozens of professional organizations provide continuing support of one kind or another for teachers. These range from national associations that offer professional development resources to local union affiliates that may negotiate your next contract with the school district.

Professional organizations have the potential to create learning communities among their members. They offer rich resources for you to use in planning lessons and expanding your professional knowledge. Some of them also help improve your salary and working conditions and protect your professional rights.

Here we review two of the most prominent organizations, the American Federation of Teachers and the National Education Association. There are also many subject- and grade-level–specific groups that provide resources, grants, and guidance for you as you begin your professional career; see the Resources for Further Exploration section in Chapter 2 for a list.

THE AMERICAN FEDERATION OF TEACHERS

The American Federation of Teachers, a union affiliated with the American Federation of Labor and Congress of Industrial Organizations (AFL-CIO), was founded in 1916 to represent the interests of classroom teachers. Its first member, John Dewey, recognized the importance of teachers' having their own organization. Today, one visit to the organization's website (http://www.aft.org/) reveals a wealth of resources for the classroom teacher and for other education personnel as well. For example, the site provides information about professional development opportunities and grants.

In addition to being a valuable resource, the AFT directly represents teachers in many school districts around the country. The organization has 43 state affiliates, more than 3,000 local affiliates, and more than 1.3 million members. You may find, particularly if you teach in a large urban school system, that the AFT negotiates contracts for the teachers and other school employees in your district. If so, you will probably become a member of the union, and you may want to take an active role in the local affiliate.

THE NATIONAL EDUCATION ASSOCIATION

The National Education Association, founded in 1857, now has approximately 3 million members and more than 14,000 local affiliates. In addition to its Code of Ethics, described in Chapter 1, the NEA provides job searches, teaching tips and tools, important resources for your professional development, and activities and workshops of interest in your state. The organization's website (http://www.nea.org/) is a valuable point of entry to these resources.

Since the 1960s, the NEA has functioned as a union, conducting collective bargaining on behalf of teachers and working to protect teachers' rights as employees of a school district. It also acts as a lobbying organization on educational issues, and it helps set professional standards for the teaching profession.

THE VISION OF THE AFT

The following passage helps explain the AFT's overall goals and principles.

As a community of professionals in unison with all working people, we are committed collectively to advancing human rights, opportunity, social and economic justice, freedom of conscience and expression, unfettered civic and political participation, fairness at work, tolerance, democracy, and security at home and abroad. The AFT stands for the right of individuals everywhere to form and participate in voluntary democratic, civic, cultural, religious, and fraternal institutions for self-help, worship, advocacy, and mutual support.

SOURCE: 2007 AFT Vision Statement. Reprinted by permission of AFT. AFT is a union of professionals, which represents educators in school districts across the country.

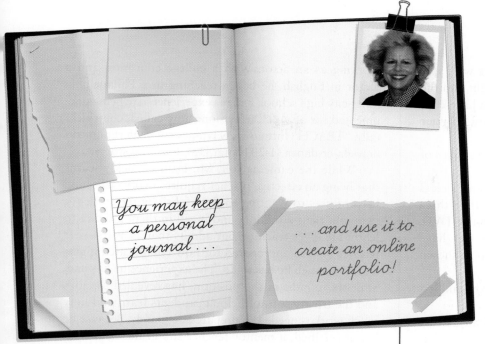

© Dar Yang Yan/iStockphoto

You may keep a personal journal . . .

. . . and use it to create an online portfolio!

- Include a table of contents so that viewers can skip to parts that particularly concern them.
- Begin with a short essay introducing yourself. In a few paragraphs, describe your interest in teaching and learning and what you have accomplished. See the sidebar for a sample introductory essay.
- Describe your educational philosophy; that is, what you believe a good teacher needs to understand about teaching and learning.
- Discuss your classroom management theory. If your focus is on building community in the classroom, be specific about how you plan to do that.

Most teachers belong to either the AFT or the NEA, and some belong to both. Your decision about membership may be governed in part by local conditions, such as which organization represents the teachers at your school. Remember that an important benefit of membership is that it provides links to other teachers for professional collaboration.

LO3 Build Your Teaching Portfolio

Developing a portfolio is an excellent way to organize your thinking about teaching and to display some of your accomplishments on this journey. You should continue to update the portfolio each year you teach. It is your professional and personal record, and it demonstrates your knowledge and beliefs as well as your accomplishments. What you choose to include in your portfolio is a statement of what you think is important.

When you begin to look for a job, you will need a version of your portfolio to present to prospective employers, either in the form of a website URL or a printed version, depending on the circumstances of the interview. The portfolio you show others should be concise, clear, readable, and well organized.

Here are some suggestions for preparing your portfolio:

- Your portfolio should be easily accessible online, either as a PowerPoint file, a Word document with appropriate images, or a PDF.

A SAMPLE INTRODUCTORY ESSAY FOR A PORTFOLIO

I have just graduated from Hofstra University, where I majored in biology and secondary education. I have always loved science and enjoy sharing it with others. I have had experience student teaching in grades 7–9 and 10–11. My certification area in biology and general science prepares me to teach grades 7–12 in New York State. I have passed all the exams and requirements for this initial certification.

For my field experience, I have been a participant-observer in grades 8 and 11, and I feel equally comfortable in the middle school and the high school. I have also spent two summers as a counselor at an environmental education camp in Maine, where I enjoyed working with teenagers in a natural setting. I believe my organizational skills, my ability to plan, my understanding of the content area, and my passion for teaching will enable me to be a successful new teacher.

- Describe your student teaching experience with specific mention of the grade levels you taught and the lessons and activities you prepared. If you have copies of supervisors' observations that attest to your abilities, include them.
- Include photos or electronic files of a few samples of student work from your field experience.
- If you have approved photos of yourself and a class in action, or even a brief video (no more than three minutes long) that you have burned on a DVD, include them. ("Approved" means that you have received consent forms from the other people shown in the photos or video.)
- Include your resume, certifications, awards, and letters of reference.
- Have all the material available electronically, either on a personal professional website or on a CD that you give to the interviewer.
- Do not overdo it. We live in a fast-paced culture, and people do not have a great deal of time to read your portfolio. Be concise and to the point.

See the Review Card at the back of the book for additional ideas on building your teaching portfolio.

LO4 Concluding Thoughts

TURNING TO TEACHING

As we explored in Chapter 1, people often think that because of their many years as students in classrooms, they can also teach. Such was the case for actor Tony Danza who expressed a desire to teach after many years working as an actor. With a college education and a major in English, he began teaching in a Philadelphia inner-city high school, and his experiences are being documented for an A&E television show called, coincidentally, "TEACH" (http://www.latimes.com/entertainment/news/la-et-danza31-2010mar31,0,3952980.story).

While the cameras roll, Mr. Danza quickly learns that being an effective teacher requires many skills, and he professes to wanting to do "right" by the students, maintain their attention, and instill in them a desire to learn. He loves teaching but admits that as a first-year teacher he was unprepared for how complicated it gets and how much he has to do. The experience he has had, after six months in the position, has revealed the joys and the frustrations of helping students learn and how much work is needed to prepare adequately. Because he is not certified, a mentor teacher sits in the class with him. He certainly seems to have some of the attributes described in the beginning of the chapter—a centered presence in the classroom, a sensitivity to the classroom setting, an ability to respond thoughtfully to each student, and a desire to help students feel capable and competent. If you watch the videos of his experience, you can also appreciate the expression "teachers can never be over-prepared" and how your plan to become a teacher is serving you.

PASSION QUOTIENT

A noted author (Friedman, 2006) talks about something he calls the "passion quotient" for teaching. He tells the story of a young child who receives his or her first fire truck or doctor's kit and wants to be a fireman or a

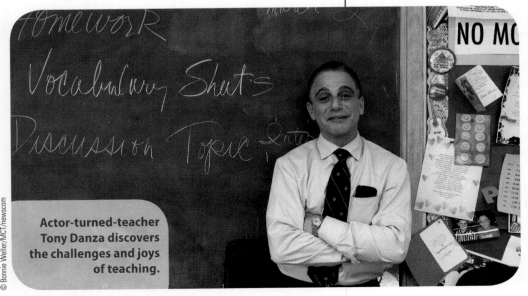

doctor. That innocent passion for a certain job, without knowing the salary or the working hours or the preparation required, is what you need to get back in touch with. You need to discover your inner passion, and when you find it, you will know it.

You may already know that your passion is teaching, in which case you will be eager to explore the professional organizations described in this chapter. Or you

Actor-turned-teacher Tony Danza discovers the challenges and joys of teaching.

may still be searching and wondering. If we are going to be successful, what we select as our life's work must bring us joy, especially if it is teaching. Remember, it is fine to change your mind and say, "I thought this was for me, but now I see I'm better suited to another career."

I want to remind you, though, that teaching is wonderfully satisfying work. The feeling you get when you realize that you have made a contribution on behalf of someone else's development is indescribable. I remember my first year of teaching like it was yesterday. I was nervous, over-prepared, and in the end overjoyed. Although I needed the paycheck (which in 1966 was quite meager), I'd forget to pick it up at the main office of the junior high where I taught science. The school secretary used to tease me, but one day she gave me a wonderful compliment. She said, "Judging by the smile I always see on your face, I can tell that you get paid for this job in other ways." I was touched by this statement (although my landlord, of course, needed payment in cash).

© RonTech2000/iStockphoto

Becoming a teacher is a commitment to a life of service that has the potential to bring you great joy and personal satisfaction. My best wishes to you on this journey.

RESOURCES FOR FURTHER EXPLORATION

Online Resources

A Candidate's Guide to National Board Certification
http://www.nea.org/ or http:www.aft.org

Available at both the AFT website and the NEA website, this booklet complements the resource materials provided by the National Board for Professional Teaching Standards.

Electronic Portfolios
http://www.electronicportfolios.org

This website gives important information about the application and development of electronic portfolios for interviewing, teaching, and continued professional development.

Google for Educators
http://www.google.com/educators/

You will find a links to Google Earth, teacher blogs, and much more on this useful website.

Teach Abroad
http://www.teachabroad.com

This site lists specific job opportunities abroad as well as training programs and other opportunities.

Teacher Leaders Network
http://www.teacherleaders.org/

This network supports teachers as they explore professional development through meaningful conversations with educators from around the country. It is sponsored by the Center for Teaching Quality in Hillsborough, North Carolina.

Print Resources

Karen A. Bosch and Katharine C. Kersey, *The First-Year Teacher: Teaching with Confidence*, revised edition (New York: National Education Association, 2000).
Available from the NEA's online bookstore (http://store.nea.org/), this book helps answer many questions for first-year teachers who are moving from the college campus to their own classrooms.

Katy Ridnouer, *Managing Your Classroom with Heart: A Guide for Nurturing Adolescent Learners* (Alexandria, VA: Association for Supervision and Curriculum Development, 2006).
This is a fine book that discusses topics like "balancing care and discipline," "handling common challenges," and "expectations and accountability."

References

AAUW Educational Foundation. (2001). *Hostile Hallways: Bullying, Teasing, and Sexual Harassment in School.* Washington, D.C.: American Association of University Women Educational Foundation.

AAUW Educational Foundation. (2004). *Harassment-Free Hallways: How to Stop Sexual Harassment in School.* Washington, D.C.: American Association of University Women Educational Foundation.

Aleman, A. M. (2006). Latino demographic, democratic individuality, and educational accountability: A pragmatist's view. *Educational Researcher,* 35(7): 25–35.

American Educational Research Association. (2004). English language learners: Boosting academic achievement. *Research Points,* 2:1 (Winter).

American Federation of Teachers. (2003). *Where We Stand: Teacher Quality.* AFT Teachers Educational Issues Department, Item Number 39–0230. Washington, D.C.: Author.

American Federation of Teachers. (2007). A vision that endures. http://www.aft.org/about/vision.htm; retrieved February 7, 2007.

Anderson, B. C. (2000). An A for home schooling. *City Journal,* 10(3), Summer. New York: Manhattan Institute for Policy Research.

Annie E. Casey Foundation. (2001). *Where Kids Count, Place Matters: Trends in the Well-Being of Iowa Children.* Des Moines, IA: Iowa Kids Count.

Annie E. Casey Foundation. (2006a). 2000 Census data: Key facts for United States. Kids Count Census Data Online, http://www.aecf.org/; retrieved February 10, 2010.

Annie E. Casey Foundation. (2006b). *2006 Kids Count Data Book: State Profiles of Child Well-Being.* Washington, D.C.: Author.

Annie E. Casey Foundation. (2007). Children in immigrant families: Percent: 2005. Kids Count State-Level Data Online, http://www.kidscount.org/sld/compare_results .jsp?i=750; retrieved March 20, 2010.

Annie E. Casey Foundation. (2009a). Children in single-parent families: Percent: 2008. Kids Count State-Level data Online, http://www.kidscount.org/sld/compare_ results.jsp?i=721; retrieved April 20, 2010.

Annie E. Casey Foundation. (2009b). *Kids Count Indicator Brief: Reducing the High School Dropout Rate.* Baltimore, MD: Author. Available: http://www.aecf.org/ KnowledgeCenter/Publications.aspx.

Ashford, E. (2009). Technology facilitates learning in small groups. *eSchool News,* November 1. Available: http:// www.eschoolnews.com/2009/11/01/esn-special-report-small-group-collaboration/.

Ball, A. (2003). Geo-literacy: Forging new ground. Edutopia-online, http://www.edutopia.org/geo-literacy-forging-new-ground; retrieved May 11, 2010.

Ball, A. (2004). Innovative techniques provide a well rounded education. Edutopia-online, http://www .edutopia.org/landry; retrieved April 5, 2010.

Bavelier, D. & Green, C. S. (2009). Increasing speed of processing with action video games. *Current Directions in Psychological Science* 18(6): 321–326.

Bennett-Goleman, T. (2001). *Emotional Alchemy: How the Mind Can Heal the Heart.* London: Harmony Books.

Bickart, T., Jablon, J., & Dodge, D. T. (2000). *Building the Primary Classroom: A Complete Guide to Teaching and Learning.* Washington, D.C.: Teaching Strategies, Inc.

Bielick, S., Chandler, K., & Broughman, S. P. (2001). *Home-schooling in the United States: 1999* (NCES 2001–033). Washington, D.C.: U.S. Department of Education, National Center for Education Statistics.

Bolton, M. M. (2009). Their words, unleashed by wiki: Web tool opens brave new world for young writers. *The Boston Globe,* December 3. Available: http://www.boston .com/news/local/articles/2009/12/03/young_writers_in_ westwood_unleash_their_best_words_with_web_tool/ ?page=2.

The Boston Historical Society and Museum. (2010). Who were the Puritans? http://www.bostonhistory.org/?s= librarymuseum&p=researchguide; retrieved July 10, 2010.

Bransford, J., Brown, A. L., & Cocking, R. (Eds.). (2000). *How People Learn: Brain, Mind, Experience, and School.* Washington, D.C.: National Academy Press.

Bransford, J. & Donovan, S. (2004). *How Students Learn.* Washington, D.C.: National Academy Press.

Braun, H., Jenkins, F., & Grigg, W. (2006). *A Closer Look at Charter Schools Using Hierarchical Linear Modeling* (NCES 2006–460). Washington, D.C.: U.S. Department of Education.

Brooks, J. G. (2002). *Schooling for Life: Reclaiming the Essence of Learning.* Reston, VA: Association for Supervision and Curriculum Development.

Brooks, J. G. & Brooks, M. (1999). *In Search of Understanding: The Case for Constructivist Classrooms.* Reston, VA: Association for Supervision and Curriculum Development.

Brooks-Gunn, J., Duncan, G. J., & Aber, J. L. (Eds.). (2000). *Neighborhood Poverty. Volume 1: Context and Consequences for Children.* New York: Russell Sage Foundation.

Brown, J. (2000). *The Sea Accepts All Rivers & Other Poems.* Alexandria, VA: Miles River Press.

Brown-Chidsey, R. (2007). No More "Waiting to Fail." *Educational Leadership* 65(2): 40–46.

Bruner, J. S. (1960). *The Process of Education.* Cambridge, MA: Harvard University Press.

Bruner, J. S. (1966). *Toward a Theory of Instruction.* Cambridge, MA: Harvard University Press.

Bullough, R. V. & Gitlin, A. D. (2001). *Becoming a Student: Linking Knowledge Production and Practice of Teaching.* New York, NY: Routledge Falmer.

Carnegie Forum on Education and the Economy. (1986). *A Nation Prepared: Teachers for the 21st Century.* New York: Carnegie Corporation.

Carter, G. (2006). Supporting the whole child. *ASCD Education Update* 48(12): 2, 8. Alexandria, VA: Association for Supervision and Curriculum Development.

Cawelti, G. (2006). The side effects of NCLB. *Educational Leadership* 64(3): 64–88.

Center on Education Policy. (2007). *Why We Still Need Public Schools: Public Education for the Common Good.* Washington, D.C.: Nancy Kober. http://www.cep-D.C .org/; retrieved February 1, 2010.

Center for Education Reform. (2005). *All About Charter Schools.* Washington, D.C.: Center for Education Reform.

Centers for Disease Control and Prevention (CDC). (2010). Youth Risk Behavior Surveillance—United States, 2009. *Morbidity and Mortality Weekly Report* 59(SS-05), June 4.

Chana High School. (2010). A California model continuation high school. http://www.puhsd.k12.ca.us/chana/; retrieved January 25, 2010.

Christenson, S. L. & Thurlow, M. L. (2004). Keeping kids in school: Efficacy of check & connect for dropout prevention. *NASP Communiqué* 32(6): 37–40.

Cohen, J. (2006). Social, emotional, ethical, and academic education: Creating a climate for learning, participation in democracy, and well-being. *Harvard Educational Review* 76(2): 201–237.

Collaborative for Academic, Social, and Emotional Learning (CASEL). (2010). http://www.casel.org/; retrieved April 9, 2010.

Condliffe Lagemann, E. (2007). Public rhetoric, public responsibility, and the public schools. *Education Week* 26(37): 30, 40.

Corcoran, K. (2002). Bullying slurs are rampant, nationwide survey finds. *San Jose Mercury News,* December 13.

Council of Chief State School Officers. (2007). Interstate New Teacher Assessment and Support Consortium (INTASC). http://www.ccsso.org/Projects/interstate_new_ teacher_assessment_and_support _consortium/780.cfm; retrieved February 13, 2007.

Davis, G. A. & Rimm, S. B. (2004). *Education of the Gifted and Talented.* (5th ed.) Boston: Allyn & Bacon.

Day, C. (2004). *A Passion for Teaching.* New York: Routledge.

DeBell, M. & Chapman, C. (2003). *Computer and Internet Use by Children and Adolescents in 2001* (NCES 2004– 014). Washington, D.C.: U.S. Department of Education, National Center for Education Statistics.

Dee, T. S. (2005). A teacher like me: Does race, ethnicity, or gender matter? *American Economic Review* 95(2): 158–165.

Dee, T. S. (2006). The why chromosome. *Education Next,* no. 4 (Fall): 68–75.

Dewey, J. (1916/2004). *Democracy and Education.* New York: Dover.

Dewey, J. (1938). *Experience and Education.* New York: Collier Macmillan.

Dinkes, R., Cataldi, E. F., & Lin-Kelly, W. (2007). *Indicators of School Crime and Safety: 2007* (NCES 2008-021/NCJ 219553). Washington, D.C.: U.S. Department of Education, National Center for Education Statistics.

Downes, S. (2004). Educational blogging. *Educause Review,* September/October: 14–26.

Duckworth, E. (1991). Twenty-four, forty-two, and I love you: Keeping it complex. *Harvard Educational Review* 61:1 (February): 1–24.

Eccles, J. S., Lord, S., & Midgley, C. (1991). What are we doing to adolescents? The impact of educational contexts on early adolescents. *American Journal of Education* 99: 521–542.

Eccles, J. S. & Midgley, C. (1989). Stage/environment fit: Developmentally appropriate classrooms for early adolescents. In R. Ames & C. Ames (Eds.), *Research on Motivation in Education,* Vol. 3. San Diego, CA: Academic, pp. 139–186.

Education Commission of the States. (2007a). Charter schools: Quick facts. http://www.ecs.org/clearing-house/76/44/7644.pdf; retrieved May 13, 2010.

Education Commission of the States. (2007b). StateNotes: Charter school teacher certification. http://mb2.ecs.org/ reports/Report.aspx?id=93; retrieved November 13, 2009.

Evans, S. (1989). *Born for Liberty: A History of Women in America.* New York: Free Press Publications.

Farber, B. A. (1991). *Crisis in Education: Stress and Burnout in the American Teacher.* San Francisco: Jossey-Bass.

Fein, R. A., Vossekuil, B., Pollack, W. S., Borum, R., Modzeleski, W., & Reddy, M. (2002). *Threat Assessment in Schools: A Guide to Managing Threatening Situations and to Creating Safe School Climates.* Washington, D.C.: United States Secret Service and United States Department of Education.

Felder, R. M. & Brent, R. (2005). Understanding student differences. *Journal of Engineering Education* 94(1): 57–72.

Felder, R. M. & Silverman, L. K. (1988, 2002). Learning and teaching styles in engineering education. *Journal of Engineering Education* 78(7): 674–681. Author's Preface by R. M. Felder, written in 2002, http://www4.ncsu.edu/ unity/lockers/users/f/felder/public/Papers/LS-1988.pdf; retrieved June 30, 2010.

Fisch, K. (2006). This is not education as usual. http://the fischbowl.blogspot.com/2006/12/this-is-not-education-as-usual.html; posted December 15, 2006, retrieved December 18, 2006.

Fisch, K. (2009). The Fischbowl: Did you know? http:// thefischbowl.blogspot.com/2009/09/did-you-know-40-economist-media.html; retrieved March 29, 2010.

Freire, P. (1970). *Pedagogy of the Oppressed.* M. B. Ramos (Trans.). New York: Continuum.

Friedman, T. (2006). *The World Is Flat: A Brief History of the Twenty-First Century.* (Updated and expanded ed.) New York: Farrar, Straus and Giroux.

Fry, R. (2006). *The Changing Landscape of American Public Education: New Students, New Schools.* Washington, D.C.: Pew Hispanic Center Research Report.

Ganley, B. (2009). Teaching and learning with technology. Presentation at the University of British Columbia. http://vimeo.com/3008955/; retrieved June 12, 2010.

Gardner, H. (1993). *Frames of Mind: The Theory of Multiple Intelligences.* New York: Basic Books.

Gardner, H. (2003). *Intelligence Reframed: Multiple Intelligences for the 21st Century.* New York: Basic Books.

Gardner, H. (2006). *Multiple Intelligences: New Horizons.* New York: Basic Books.

Gladwell, M. (2008). Most likely to succeed: How can we hire when we can't tell who is right for the job? *The New Yorker Magazine,* December 15. Available: http://www.newyorker.com/reporting/2008/12/15/081215fa_fact_gladwell?currentPage=all.

Goleman, D. (2006). *Emotional Intelligence: Why It Can Matter More than IQ.* New York: Bantam.

Graham, K. A. (2010). Tony Danza goes back to school. *Los Angeles Times,* March 31. Available: http://articles.latimes.com/2010/mar/31/entertainment/la-et-danza31-2010mar31.

Greene, J. P., Forster, G., & Winters, M. (2003, July). Education Working Paper No. 1. New York: The Manhattan Institute for Policy Research.

Greene, M. (1978). *Landscapes of Learning.* New York: Teachers College Press.

Greene, M. (1995). *Releasing the Imagination: Essays on Education, the Arts, and Social Change.* San Francisco: Jossey-Bass.

Guilfoyle, C. (2006). NCLB: Is there life beyond testing? *Educational Leadership* 64(3): 8–13.

Hammerness, K. (2006). *Seeing Through Teachers' Eyes: Professional Ideals and Classroom Practices.* New York: Teachers College Press.

Hanushek, E., Kain, J. F., O'Brien, D. M., & Rivkin, S. G. (2005). The market for teacher quality. NBER Working Paper Series, Vol. w11154. Available: http://ssrn.com/abstract=669453.

Hart, B. & Risley, T. R. (1995). *Meaningful Differences in the Everyday Experience of Young American Children.* Baltimore, MD: Brookes Publishing Co.

Hinchcliffe, D. (2006). The state of Web 2.0. http://web2.wsj2.com/the_state_of_web_20.htm; retrieved December 10, 2006.

Hittie, M. (2000). Building community in the classroom. Paper presented at the International Education Summit, Detroit, Michigan, June 26, 2006.

Hoffman, N. (1981). *Woman's True Profession: Voices from the History of Teaching.* New York: The Feminist Press and McGraw Hill.

Humphreys, T. (1998). *A Different Kind of Discipline.* Dublin, Ireland: Gill & Macmillan, Ltd.

Information Please Database. (2006). State compulsory school attendance laws. http://www.infoplease.com/ipa/A0112617.html; retrieved February 22, 2010.

Initiative on Educational Excellence for Hispanic Americans. (2002). Ten reasons to become a teacher. http://www.yic.gov/publications/tenreasons/; retrieved January 25, 2010.

International Society for Technology in Education. (2002). *National Educational Technology Standards for Teachers: Preparing Teachers to Use Technology.* Washington, D.C.: Author.

Intrator, S. (2003). Tuned In and Fired Up: How Teaching Can Inspire Real Learning in the Classroom. New Haven, CT: Yale University Press.

Jackson, P., Corey, S., Kleibard, H., & Gage, N. L. (1968). *The Way Teaching Is.* Reston, VA: Association for Supervision and Curriculum Development.

Joubert, J. (2005). *The Notebooks of Joseph Joubert.* Paul Auster (Trans.). New York: The New York Review of Books.

Jukes, I. (2006). From Gutenberg to Gates to Google (and beyond . . .): Education for the online world. http://ibo.org/ibap/conference/documents/IanJukes-FromGutenbergtoGatestoGoogleandBeyond1.pdf; retrieved December 2, 2009.

Juvonen, J., Le, V., Kaganoff, T., Augustine, C. H., & Constant, L. (2004). *Focus on the Wonder Years: Challenges Facing the American Middle School.* Santa Monica, CA: Rand Corporation.

Kaiser Family Foundation. (2010). Generation M2: Media in the lives of 8- to 18-year-olds. http://www.kff.org/entmedia/upload/8010.pdf; retrieved February 1, 2010.

Kashen, S. (1994). Bilingual education and second-language acquisition theory. In C. F. Lebya (Ed.), *Schooling and Language Minority Students.* Los Angeles: California State University, pp. 61–63.

Kelley, T. (2006). Talk in class turns to God, setting off public debate on rights. *New York Times,* December 18. Available: http://www.nytimes.com/2006/12/18/nyregion.

Kim, S. H. & Bagaka, J. (2005). The digital divide in students' usage of technology tools: A multilevel analysis of the role of teacher practices and classroom characteristics. *Contemporary Issues in Technology and Teacher Education* 5(3/4): 318–329.

Klein, S., Ortman, P., & Friedman, B. (2002). What is the field of gender equity in education? In J. Koch & B. Irby (Eds.), *Defining and Redefining Gender Equity in Education.* Greenwich, CT: Information Age Publishing.

Kliewer, C. (1998). The meaning of inclusion. *Mental Retardation* 36: 317.

Klopfer, E., Osterweil, S., & Salen, K. (2009). Moving learning games forward. An MIT Education Arcade paper. Available: http://education.mit.edu/papers/MovingLearningGamesForward_EdArcade.pdf.

Koch, J. (2002). Gender issues in the classroom. In W. R. Reynolds & G. E. Miller (Eds.), *Educational Psychology.* Volume 7 of the *Comprehensive Handbook of Psychology.* Editor-in-Chief: I. B. Weiner. New York: Wiley.

Kohn, A. (1999). *Punished by Rewards: The Trouble with Gold Stars, Incentive Plans, A's, Praise, and Other Bribes.* Boston: Houghton Mifflin.

Kosciw, J. G., Diaz, E. M., & Greytak, E. A. (2008). *The 2007 National School Climate Survey: The Experiences of Lesbian, Gay, Bisexual and Transgender Youth in Our Nation's Schools*. New York: Gay, Lesbian and Straight Education Network.

Kounin, J. S. (1970). *Discipline and Group Management in Classrooms*. New York: Holt, Rinehart and Winston.

Krug, E. A. (1964). *The Shaping of the American High School, 1880–1920*. New York: Harper & Row.

Kyraciou, C. (2001). *Essential Teaching Skills*. Cheltenham, United Kingdom: Nelson Thornes LTD.

Lareau, A. (2003). *Unequal Childhoods: Class, Race, and Family Life*. Berkeley and Los Angeles: University of California Press.

Levine, M. (2007). The essential cognitive backpack. *Educational Leadership* 64(7): 16–22.

Lionni, L. (1970). *Fish is Fish*. New York: Scholastic Books.

Lofing, N. (2007). Chana named model school. *Sacramento Bee*, April 5. Available: http://www.sacbee.com/293/v-print/story/148899.html.

Logan, J. (1999). *Teaching Stories*. New York: Kodansha America.

Lowe, C. (2002). Why weblogs? http://kairosnews.org/why-weblogs; posted July 27, 2002, retrieved December 20, 2009.

Lowes, S. (2005). Online teaching and classroom change: The impact of virtual high school on its teachers and their schools. Teachers College, Columbia University: Institute for Learning Technologies. http://www.ilt.columbia.edu/publications/lowes_final.pdf; retrieved January 16, 2010.

Maker, J. & Nielson, A. (1996). *Curriculum Development and Teaching Strategies for Gifted Learners*. (2nd ed.) Austin, TX: PRO-ED.

Manning, M. L. (2000). A brief history of the middle school. *The Clearing House* 73(4): 288–301.

Markoff, J. (2006). For $150, third-world laptop stirs big debate. *The New York Times*, November 30.

McBrien, J. L. & Brandt, R. S. (1997). *The Language of Learning: A Guide to Education Terms*. Alexandria, VA: Association for Supervision and Curriculum Development.

McGuire, W., Ed. (1954). *Collected Works of C. J. Jung*, Vol. 17. Princeton, NJ: Princeton University Press.

McGuirk, J. (2001). *"Youth at Risk": Is Technology the Answer?* Brisbane, AU: Australian National Training Authority. Available: http://www.eric.ed.gov/PDFS/ED480395.pdf.

Mehta, S. (2009). Controlling a classroom isn't as easy as ABC. *Los Angeles Times*, December 14, p. A1.

Miller, L. (2004). 12 tips for new teachers. In K. D. Salas, R. Tenorio, S. Walters, & D. Weiss (Eds.), *The New Teacher Book: Finding Purpose, Balance, and Hope During Your First Years in the Classroom*. Milwaukee, WI: Rethinking Schools, Ltd.

Minority Teacher Recruitment Project (2010). University of Louisville College of Education and Human Development. http://louisville.edu/education/research/special-projects/mtrp/; retrieved March 3, 2010.

Mitchell, S. (2004). *Charter Schools, Still Making Waves*. Washington, D.C.: Center for Education Reform.

Moe, T. M. (2001). *A Primer on America's Schools*. Stanford: Hoover Institution Press.

Moos, R. H. (1979). *Evaluating Educational Environments: Procedures, Measures, Findings, and Policy Implications*. San Francisco: Jossey-Bass.

Moran, S., Kornhaber, M., & Gardner, H. (2006). Orchestrating multiple intelligences. *Educational Leadership* 64(1): 23–27.

National Assessment of Educational Progress. (2005). *America's Charter Schools: Results from the NAEP 2003 Pilot Study* (NCES 2005–456). Washington, D.C.: U.S. Department of Education.

National Association for Gifted Children. (2010). What is gifted? http://www.nagc.org; retrieved October 14, 2010.

National Board for Professional Teaching Standards. (2002). *What Teachers Should Know and Be Able to Do*. Arlington, VA: Author. http://www.nbpts.org/UserFiles/File/what_teachers.pdf; retrieved January 5, 2010.

National Center for Education Statistics. (2006). *The Condition of Education 2006* (NCES 2006–071). Washington, D.C.: U.S. Government Printing Office.

National Center for Education Statistics. (2009). Fast facts: Enrollment trends. http://nces.ed.gov/fastfacts/; retrieved February 17, 2010.

National Center on Education and the Economy. (2006). *Tough Choices or Tough Times: The Report of the New Commission on the Skills of the American Workforce*. San Francisco: Jossey-Bass.

National Collaborative on Diversity in the Teaching Force. (2004). *Assessment of Diversity in America's Teaching Force: A Call to Action*. Washington, D.C.: National Education Association.

National Commission on Excellence in Education. (1983). *A Nation at Risk: The Imperative for Educational Reform*. Washington, D.C.: U.S. Department of Education.

National Education Association. (1899). Report of the Committee on College Entrance Requirements. *Journal of the Proceedings and Addresses of the Thirty-Eighth Annual Meeting, Los Angeles*, pp. 632–817.

National Education Association. (1975). Code of ethics of the education profession. http://www.nea.org/aboutnea/code.html; retrieved July 14, 2006.

National Education Association. (2003). Status of the American Public School Teacher 2000–2001. Washington, D.C.: Author.

National Education Association. (2006a, May 2). National Teacher Day spotlights key issues facing profession. http://www.nea.org/newsreleases/2006/nr060502.html; retrieved July 14, 2006.

National Education Association. (2006b). *Rankings and Estimates: Rankings of the States 2005 and Estimates of School Statistics 2006*. Washington, D.C.: Author.

National Education Association. (2007). Issues in education: Charter schools. http://www.nea.org/charter/index.html; retrieved May 13, 2007.

National Education Association. (2009). *Status of the American Public School Teacher 2005–2006*. Washington, D.C.: Author.

National School Boards Foundation. (2007). Safe and smart: Research and guidelines for children's use of the Internet.

http://www.nsbf.org/safe-smart/index.html; retrieved
May 30, 2007.

Nelson, C. & Wilson, K. (1998). *Seeding the Process of
Multicultural Education*. Plymouth, MN: Minnesota
Inclusiveness Program.

New Commission on the Skills of the American Workforce.
(2006). *Tough Choices or Tough Times*. Washington,
D.C.: National Center on Education and the Economy.

Northeast Foundation for Children. (2007). What is the
Responsive Classroom approach? http://www. responsive
classroom.org/about/aboutrc.html; retrieved May 29,
2007.

Oakes, J. (1985). *Keeping Track*. New Haven: Yale University Press.

Office for Civil Rights. (1997). *Sexual Harassment: It's
Not Academic*. Washington, D.C.: U.S. Department of
Education.

Office for Civil Rights. (2001). *Revised Sexual Harassment
Guidance: Harassment of Students by School Employees,
Other Students, or Third Parties*. Washington, D.C.: U.S.
Department of Education.

Olweus, D. (2003, March). A profile of bullying at school.
Educational Leadership 60(6): 12–17.

O'Neal, C. (2007). How Online Simulations Work in the
Classroom. Available online at: http://www.edutopia.org/
online-simulations-classroom; retrieved February 3, 2010.

Orenstein, P. (2009). Stop your search engines. *New York
Times Magazine*, October 25.

Osterman, K. (2000). Students' need for belongingness in the
school community. *Review of Educational Research* 70:
323–367.

Oxendine, L. (1989). *Dick and Jane are Dead: Basal Reader
Takes a Back Seat to Student Writing*. Charleston, WV:
Appalachia Educational Laboratory, Inc.

Palmer, P. (1998). *The Courage to Teach: Exploring the
Inner Landscape of a Teacher's Life*. San Francisco, CA:
Jossey-Bass.

Pape, L., Adams, R., & Ribiero, C. (2005). The virtual high
school: Collaboration and online professional development. In Z. L. Berge & T. Clark (Eds.), *Virtual Schools:
Planning for Success*. New York: Teachers College Press.

Parsad, B. & Jones, J. (2005). *Internet Access in U.S. Public
Schools and Classrooms: 1994–2003* (NCES 2005–015).
Washington, D.C.: U.S. Department of Education,
National Center for Education Statistics.

Perkins, D. (1993). Teaching for understanding. *American
Educator* 17(3): 28–35.

The Pew Forum on Religion and Public Life. (2002). *Americans Struggle with Religion's Role at Home and Abroad*.
Washington, D.C.: Author.

The Pew Forum on Religion and Public Life. (2010). U.S.
Religious Landscape Survey. http://religions.pewforum
.org/reports/; retrieved March 3, 2010.

Prensky, M. (2001, October). Digital natives, digital immigrants. *On the Horizon* 9(5).

Princiotta, D. & Bielick, S. (2006). *Homeschooling in the
United States: 2003* (NCES 2006–042). Washington,
D.C.: U.S. Department of Education, National Center for
Education Statistics.

Project Tomorrow. (2007). Speak up 2006: Snapshot of
selected national findings from teachers. http://www
.tomorrow.org/docs/Speak%20Up%202006%20National
%20Snapshot_Teacher.pdf; retrieved May 26, 2007.

Rasmussen, K. (1997). Using real-life problems to make
real-world connections. *Curriculum Update*, Summer.
Alexandria, VA: Association for Supervision and Curriculum Development.

Ray, B. (2004). *Home Educated and Now Adults*. Salem,
OR: National Home Education Research Institute.

Rimm-Kaufman, S. (2006). *Social and Academic Learning
Study on the Contribution of the Responsive Classroom
Approach*. Turners Falls, MA: Northeast Foundation for
Children.

Robinson, K. (2006). Do schools kill creativity? Invited talk
at the Technology, Entertainment, Design (TED) Conference, Monterey, CA. http://www.ted.com/index.php/talks/
view/id/66; retrieved May 24, 2009.

Rogers, C. R. (1983). *Freedom to Learn for the 80s*. Columbus, OH: Charles Merrill.

Ryan, K. & Cooper, J. M. (2007). *Those Who Can, Teach*.
(11th ed.) Boston: Houghton Mifflin.

Ryan, M. (2010). iPods touch Salem-Keizer schools. *States-
man Journal*, March 31, p. 1.

Sadker, D. M. & Zittleman, K. R. (2007). *Teachers, Schools,
and Society: A Brief Introduction to Education*. New
York: McGraw-Hill.

Sadker, D. M. & Zittleman, K. R. (2009). *Still Failing at Fairness: How Gender Bias Cheats Girls and Boys and What
We Can Do About It*. New York: Scribner.

Sadker, M. & Sadker, D. (1995). *Failing at Fairness: How
Our Schools Cheat Girls*. New York: Touchstone/Simon
& Schuster.

Sampson, R. (2002). *Bullying in Schools*. Problem-Oriented
Guides for Police Series, Guide No. 12. Washington, D.C.:
Office of Community Oriented Policing Services, U.S.
Department of Justice. http://www.popcenter.org/
problems/PDFs/Bullying_in_Schools.pdf; retrieved Janu-
ary 10, 2010.

Schaffhauser, D. (2010). Realityworks teaches business ed
with online simulation games. THE Journal, April 2.
Available: http://thejournal.com/articles/2010/04/02/
realityworks-teaches-business-ed-with-online-simulation-
games.aspx.

Schön, D. A. (1983). *The Reflective Practitioner:
How Professionals Think in Action*. New York: Basic
Books.

Scott, A. O.(2000). Sense and nonsense. *New York Times
Magazine*, November 26. http://partners.nytimes.com/
library/magazine/home/20001126mag-seuss.html;
retrieved July 28, 2010.

Searls, D. (2005). Getting flat, part 2. *Linux Journal*. http://
www.linuxjournal.com/article/8280; retrieved April 29,
2010.

Sears, J. (1991). Teaching for diversity: Student sexual identities. *Educational Leadership* 49(1): 54–57.

Seligman, M. E. P. (2002). *Authentic Happiness*. New York:
Free Press.

Seligman, M. E. P., Steen, T. A., Park, N., & Peterson, C. (2005). Positive psychology progress: Empirical validation of interventions. *American Psychologist* 60: 410–421.

Selingo, J. (2004). In the classroom, web logs are the new bulletin boards. *New York Times,* Circuits, August 19.

Shulman, L. (1987). Knowledge and teaching: Foundations of the new reform. *Harvard Educational Review* 57(1):1–22.

Slavin, R. E. & Madden, N. A. (2006). *Success for All: 2006 Summary of Research on Achievement Outcomes.* Baltimore: Johns Hopkins University, Center for Data-Driven Reform in Education.

Smith, T. W. & Lambie, G. W. (2005). Teachers' responsibilities when adolescent abuse and neglect are suspected. *Middle School Journal* 36(3): 33–40.

Snyder, T. & Dillow, S. (2010). *Digest of Education Statistics 2009* (NCES 2010–013). Washington, D.C.: U.S. Department of Education, National Center for Education Statistics.

Snyder, T. D., ed. (1993). *120 Years of American Education: A Statistical Portrait.* Washington, D.C.: U.S. Department of Education, National Center for Education Statistics.

Snyder, T. D., Tan, A. G., & Hoffman, C. M. (2006). *Digest of Education Statistics 2005* (NCES 2006–030). Washington, D.C.: U.S. Department of Education, National Center for Education Statistics, U.S. Government Printing Office.

Stansbury, M. (2009). Can gaming change education? New research on gaming design and brain plasticity offers more perspectives on educational gaming. *eSchool News,* December 9. Available: http://www.eschoolnews .com/2009/12/09/can-gaming-change-education/.

Style, E. (1996). Curriculum as window and mirror. Available: http://www.wcwonline.org/seed/curriculum.html. Originally published in 1988 in *Listening for All Voices: Gender Balancing the School Curriculum.* Summit, NJ: Oak Knoll School Monograph, pp. 6–12.

Thorpe, R. (2003). Getting the center to hold: A funder's perspective. Chapter 5 in N. Dickard (Ed.), *The Sustainability Challenge: Taking Edtech to the Next Level.* Washington, D.C.: Benton Foundation and the Education Development Center.

Toh, K-A., Ho, B-T., Chew, C. M. K., & Riley, J. (2003). Teaching, teacher knowledge, and constructivism. *Educational Research for Policy and Practice* 3: 195–204.

Tomlinson, C. (2000). Reconcilable differences? Standards-based teaching and differentiation. *Educational Leadership* 58(1): 6–11.

Torp, L. & Sage, S. (2002). *Problems as Possibilities: Problem-Based Learning for K–16 Education.* (2nd ed.) Alexandria, VA: Association of Supervision and Curriculum Development.

Tough, P. (2006). What makes a student? *New York Times Sunday Magazine,* November 26.

U.S. Census Bureau. (2007). *Statistical Abstract of the United States: 2007.* Washington, D.C.: Author.

U.S. Department of Education. (1998). Achieving excellence in the teaching profession. In *Promising Practices: New Ways to Improve Teacher Quality.* Washington, D.C.: U.S. Government Printing Office. http://www.ed.gov/pubs/ PromPractice/chapter1.html; retrieved January 4, 2010.

U.S. Department of Education, National Center for Education Statistics. (2009). *The Condition of Education 2006* (NCES 2006–071). Washington, D.C.: U.S. Government Printing Office. http://nces.ed.gov/pubsearch/pubsinfo .asp?pubid=2009081/; retrieved January 15, 2010.

U.S. Department of Education, Office of Special Education and Rehabilitative Services, Office of Special Education Programs. (2005). *25th Annual Report to Congress on the Implementation of the Individuals with Disabilities Education Act.* Washington, D.C.: U.S. Government Printing Office.

Vacca, R. S. (2004, May). Student records 2004: Issues and policy considerations. *CEPI Education Law Newsletter.* Richmond, VA: Commonwealth Educational Policy Institute. Available: http://www.cepionline.org/newsletter/ 2003–2004/2004_May_stud_records.html.

Vygotsky, L. (1962). *Thought and Language.* Cambridge, MA: MIT Press.

Wallis, C. & Steptoe, S. (2006). How to bring our schools out of the 20th century. *Time Magazine,* December 18.

Weaver, R. (2004). Diverse educators critical to quality teaching. President's Viewpoint, National Education Association, Nov. 10. http://www.nea.org/columns/rw041110. html; retrieved April 17, 2007.

Wells, J. & Lewis, L. (2006). *Internet Access in U.S. Public Schools and Classrooms: 1994–2005* (NCES 2007–020). Washington, D.C.: U.S. Department of Education, National Center for Education Statistics.

Winebrenner, S. (2000). Gifted students need an education, too. *Educational Leadership* 58(1): 52–56.

Wisconsin Education Association Council. (2006). Great schools issue paper: The common school movement. http://www.weac.org/professional_resources/great_ schools/issues_papers/index.aspx; retrieved March 8, 2010.

Wood, T. & McCarthy, C. (2002). Understanding and preventing teacher burnout. Washington, D.C.: ERIC Clearinghouse on Teaching and Teacher Education, ED477726.

Zins, J., Weissberg, R., Wang, M., & Wahlberg, H., Eds. (2004). *Building Academic Success on Social and Emotional Learning: What Does the Research Say?* New York: Teachers College Press.

Zuckerbrod, K. (2007). 9 States united on test, standards for high school math. *Philadelphia Inquirer,* April 11.

Index

A

Abuse
    child, 102, 145, 193
    emotional, 145
    online, 194 (*See also* Cyberbullying)
    sexual, 145
    substance, 102, 103
    teen, 193
Academic choice, 188
Academic curriculum, 188
Academic freedom, 144
Academic proficiency, 181
Academy, defined, 50
Acceleration/accelerated programs,
    defined, 122
Accountability, 129, 132–139, 174
Achievement, technology and, 152
Achievement gap, NCLB and, 130, 132
Adler, Mortimer, 58
Advanced placement (AP) courses, 122, 123
Advertising, Internet, 158
Aesthetic education, defined, 60–62
AFL-CIO. *See* American Federation of
    Labor and Congress of Industrial
    Organizations (AFL-CIO)
African Americans, education of, 55, 63
AFT. *See* American Federation of Teachers
    (AFT)
After-school centers, 64
Alice and Jerry Books, The, 84
American Federation of Labor and
    Congress of Industrial Organizations
    (AFL-CIO), 208
American Federation of Teachers (AFT),
    16–17, 19, 41, 208, 209
American International Schools, 206
American public education
    colonial education in, 47–50
    common schools in, 50–51, 52, 55
    expansion of, 52–54
    funding of, 62–67
    goals of, 47
    goodness of fit and, 200
    history of, 47–55
    immigration in, 51
    important events in, 53
    minorities in, 55
    new nation and, 50–54
    normal schools in, 54–55
    priorities of, 62–67
    reform in, 55–67
    rethinking, 55–62
    social capital in, 48
    standards for, 62–67
    teacher education in, 54–55
Annie E. Casey Foundation, 101
Anthony, Susan B., 55
AP courses. *See* Advanced placement
    (AP) courses
Apprenticeship, 48
Assertion, 188
Assessments
    authentic, 86, 88–89, 131
    defined, 85
    embedded, 86
    performance, 86, 131 (*See also*
      Authentic assessments)
    portfolio, 206
    The Praxis Series as, 204–205
    rubric as, 87–88
    standardized, 84, 88–89
    standardized testing as, 88–89
    standards-based, 199
Assistive technology (AT), 161–162
Asynchronous distance learning, 173
Attendance, 158
Attitudes, about sexual orientation, 100
Attributes
    of good teachers, 11, 210
    personal, 16, 197, 198
    of teaching, 13
Auditory learners, defined, 111
Authentic assessments, 86, 88–89, 131
Autobiography, educational, 7–8, 20
Autonomy, 187

B

Bagley, William, 57
Basal readers, 84–85
Beecher, Catherine, 55
Behaviorism, 73, 79
Belonging
    classroom safety and, 187
    defined, 179
Bennett-Goleman, Tara, 121
Bethel School District No. 403 v. Fraser, 142
Bias, 100, 107
Bilingual education, defined, 97–99
Bilingual Education Act, 63
Bisexual, defined, 99
Blind students, 161
Blocking technologies, 159
Blogs/blogging, 155, 156–157, 203
*Board of Curators of the University of
    Missouri, Papish v.,* 142
*Board of Education of Topeka, Kansas,
    Brown v.,* 63
Boarding schools, 49
Bodily-kinesthetic intelligence, 109
Boys. *See also* Males; Men
    gender-fair education and, 105–107, 123
    hidden curriculum and, 38–39
    public education and, 48, 49, 50, 64–65
Braille, 161
Brooks, Jacqueline Grennon, 30, 37, 71, 72,
    76, 78, 79, 80, 105
*Brown v. Board of Education of Topeka,
    Kansas,* 63
Bruett, Karen, 168
Bruner, Jerome, 74, 75
Buckley Amendment, 140
Bullying, 100, 145, 190–195
Burnout, 33–34, 40
Bush, George W., 129
Business Game, 171

C

*Cardinal Principles of Secondary
    Education,* 56
Caring, culture of, 200–202
Carter, Gene, 112
Case study, Russell Byers Charter School,
    134–135
CASEL. *See* Collaborative for Academic,
    Social, and Emotional Learning
    (CASEL)
Caucasians, in teaching force, 26
CCSSO. *See* Council of Chief State Officers
    (CCSSO)
Center for Education Policy, 199
Centered communication, 155
Certification, 204–206
Challenges, 31, 33, 34–37
Charter schools, 106, 133–135
Child abuse, 102, 145, 193
Choices
    academic, 188
    for alternatives to traditional schools,
      132–139
Christians, 99
Civil Rights Act, 63, 64, 65, 144
Clarity, 190
Classes, virtual, 172–174
Classroom community. *See also* Classroom
    environments; Community
    building, 181–190
    bullying and, 190–194

Classroom community (*continued*)
  classroom management and, 181–184
  cyberbullying and, 193–194
  defined, 182
  goodness of fit and, 194–195
  harassment and, 190–194
  multicultural education and, 104
  noise and, 184–185
  procedures and, 184
  public education and, 199
  Responsive Classroom approach to,
    187–188
  routines and, 184, 188, 190
  rules and, 184, 190
  safety in, 186–190
  in secondary classroom, 189–190
  silence and, 184–185
  teasing and, 192–193
  tips for creating, 188–189
  well-managed classroom and, 184–185
Classroom environments, 179, 191. *See also*
  Classroom community
Classroom management, 181–184, 188,
  194–195
Classroom(s)
  connected, 150–151
  flat, 150, 162, 166
  global, 168–175
  inclusion, 116–121
  online, 181
  responsive, 187–188
  as safe place, 139, 140, 186–189
  student-centered, 203
  technology in, 150–151, 152
  virtual, 172–174, 181 (*See also* Online
    education)
  well-managed, 184–185
Climate
  emotional, 140
  school, 20–21, 139, 140, 186, 194, 198
    (*See also* School environment)
Clinton, Bill, 12, 107
Code of ethics, 13–16, 199, 208
Cognitive learning theories, 73–75, 79
Collaboration, 165, 167, 168, 170, 175,
  195, 203
Collaborative for Academic, Social, and
  Emotional Learning (CASEL), 124
Collaborative learning environments, 172
Colleagues, 39
Collegial group, 207
Colonial education, 47–50
Columbine High School shooting, 141
Commitment, emotional/intellectual, 25
Committee of Ten, 56
Common goals, 36
Common schools, 50–51, 52, 55
Communication
  centered, 155
  collaboration and, 175, 195
  connectivity and, 175
  cyberbullying and, 194
  early-childhood education and, 27
  global, 169, 203
  global collaboration and, 167

  online, 158
  people skills and, 168
  risk-free, 192
  sexual harassment and, 192
  socially acceptable, 175
  student-student, 174
  teacher-student, 174
  ThinkQuest and, 173
  tracking student progress and, 158
  wireless, 157
Communication skills, 171, 190
Community
  classroom (*See* Classroom community)
  global, 203
  of learners, 154–155
  learning, 36, 40, 154–155, 183, 192
  new teachers and, 207
  safety and, 139, 140
  support for teachers and, 39
Competence, 187
Computer labs, 64
Computer resources, 160
Concrete operational stage of
  development, 74
Conflict resolution, 175
Connected classroom, 150–151
Connectedness, 140, 203
Connectivity, 175
Consistency, 190
Constructivism, 75–82
Contemporary trends, 115–116. *See
  also* Issues
Context
  neuroscience and, 79–81
  social, 101
Contracts, 19
Cooperating teacher, defined, 198
Cooperation, 188, 190
Cooperative learning, defined, 125
Council of Chief State Officers
  (CCSSO), 131
Counseling programs, 103
Creative thinking, 170
Creative thinking skills, 127
Critical theory, 59, 60
Critical thinking, 167, 203
Critical thinking skills, 127
Cultural diversity, 131
Cultural referents, 104
Culturally relevant pedagogy, 104,
  105, 195
Culture(s)
  of caring, 200–202
  global classroom and, 169
  religion and, 99
  school, 20–21, 198
Curriculum
  academic, 188
  adapting, 85
  for blind students, 161
  in common schools, 51
  covering, 83
  defined, 37, 82
  Dewey and, 57
  early-childhood education and, 27

  of essentialists, 57
  formal, 82–83
  games and, 171
  gifted and talented students and, 122
  hidden, 38–39, 82–83, 135–136
  high school, 56–57
  homeschooling and, 135–136
  informal, 82–83
  Internet technology and, 153
  national standards and, 83–84
  NCLB Act, 66–67, 129
  of perennialism, 58
  project-based learning and, 126
  SEL and, 124
  social, 188
  standardized assessment and, 84
  state frameworks and, 83–84
  teachers and, 12
  as window/mirror, 84–85
Cyberbullying, 158–159, 193–194
Cyberstalking, 158

D

Dame schools, defined, 48
Danza, Tony, 210
Day, Christopher, 197
De facto segregation, 63, 96
De jure segregation, 63
Decisions
  to become teachers, 3–21, 27–31,
    71–72, 197–211
  regarding educational associations,
    208–209
  regarding goodness of fit, 197–204
  regarding passion quotient, 210–211
  regarding school climate, 20–21
  regarding school culture, 20–21
  regarding talking about teaching, 6–11
  regarding teaching portfolio, 209–210
  regarding teaching profession, 12–20,
    204–208
Democracy, education and, 181
Department of Education (DOE), 204
Depression, 102
Des Moines, Tinker v., 142
Development
  early-childhood education and, 26, 27
  professional, 40–41, 42, 64
  stages of, 74
Dewey, John, 5, 38, 57–58, 60, 61, 79, 181,
  208
Dick and Jane basal readers, 84
Differences, defined, 101
Different Kind fo Discipline, A
  (Humphreys), 144
Differentiated instruction, 121,
  123–124, 208
Differentiation, defined 123
Digital divide, 159–161
Digital learning environment, 167
Digital media, 170–172
Digital natives, defined, 150

Digital Renaissance, 149. *See also* Information technology revolution
Digital technology, 150, 159. *See also* Information technology revolution
Disabilities. *See also* Disabled students
  children with, 65–66
  gifted and talented students and, 122
  inclusion and, 116–117
  learning, 118, 161
  types of, 118
Disabled students, 161-162. *See also* Disabilities
Discipline, behaviorism and, 73
Discovery learning, 74–75
Discrimination
  employment, 65
  racial, 144
  religious, 144
  sexual, 144
  sexual orientation and, 100
  Title IV and, 65
  Title IX and, 64, 105, 106
  Title VII and, 65
Discussion forum, 155
Dismissal, 144
Distance learning, 173
Diverse learning environments, 104
Diverse students, 112. *See also* Student diversity
Diversity
  cultural, 131
  differentiated instruction and, 208
  ethnic, 96–97
  honoring, 16, 195
  religious, 99
  student, 25, 96–97, 101, 103–108, 123
DOE. *See* Department of Education (DOE)
Doe, Santa Fe Independent School District v., 143
Dover Area School District, et al., Tammy Kitzmiller, et al. v., 107
Downes, Stephen, 155, 156
Dr. Seuss, 95
Dress codes, 143, 198
Dropout prevention services, 64
Dropout rate, 102, 103
Drug abuse counseling programs, 103
Du Bois, W. E. B., 55
Dual-language programs, 97–98
Duckworth, Eleanor, 27
Due process, defined, 144

E

Early-childhood education, 26–27, 64
Early-learning programs, 26
eBay, 160
Education
  aesthetic, 60–62
  aim of, 181
  bilingual, 97–99
  colonial, 47–50

  contemporary trends in (*See* Contemporary trends)
  democracy and, 181
  early-childhood, 26–27, 64
  efforts to reform/rethink, 55–67
  gender-fair, 103, 105–107, 123
  of gifted and talented students, 121–123
  globalization and (*See* Globalization)
  issues in (*See* Issues)
  multicultural, 103, 104–105
  online, 3 (*See also* Virtual classes/classrooms)
  parental, 64
  public (*See* Public education)
  secondary, 49
  sex, 103
  social capital in, 48
  special, 117
  teacher, 54–55
Education Amendments of 1972, 64
Education games, 171
Educational associations, 208–209
Educational autobiography, 7–8, 20
Educational blogging, 156–157
Educational philosophy
  aesthetics as, 60–62
  critical theory as, 59, 60
  essentialism as, 57, 60
  existentialism as, 59, 60
  perennialism as, 58, 60
  pragmatism as, 57 (*See also* Progressivism)
  progressivism as, 57–58, 60
  social reconstructionism as, 59, 60
  vision and, 38
Educational reform, 55–67
Elementary and Secondary Education Act (ESEA), 64, 129. *See also* No Child Left Behind (NCLB) Act
Eliot, Charles, 56
ELLs. *See* English-language learners (ELLs)
ELS. *See* Expeditionary Learning Schools Outward Bound (ELS)
E-mail, 158
Embedded assessments, defined, 86
Emotional abuse, 145
Emotional climate, 140
Emotional commitment, 25
Emotional goals, 181
Emotional Intelligence (Goleman), 124
Emotions, teaching and, 25
Empathy, 188
Employment discrimination, 65
English as a Second Language (ESL), 97
English-language learners (ELLs), 97, 98–99, 101
Enrichment activities, 122, 123
Enrollment
  private school, 96
  public school, 95–96
  of students, 95–101
Entrepreneurship Game, 171
Environment
  caring, 200

  classroom, 179, 191 (*See also* Classroom community)
  cognitive learning theory and, 74
  digital learning, 167
  diverse learning, 104
  global, 40
  homeschooling and, 135
  learning, 104, 124, 167, 172, 186
  least restrictive, 117
  LGBT students and, 100
  online, 172, 173, 174
  safe, 207 (*See also* Safety)
  school, 36, 207 (*See also* School climate)
  sexual harassment and, 192
  social, 75
  social cognitive learning theories and, 75
  student-centered, 203
ePals Global Community, 169
Equal Educational Opportunities Act of 1974, 63
Equality, public education and, 55
Equity
  defined, 107
  reason for, 123–124
ESEA. *See* Elementary and Secondary Education Act (ESEA)
ESL. *See* English as a Second Language (ESL)
Essentialism, 57, 58, 60
Ethnic diversity, 96–97
Evans, Sara, 47
Exceptional learners, defined, 116
Existential intelligence, 109
Existentialism, 59, 60
Expectations, 190
Expeditionary Learning Schools Outward Bound (ELS), 134
Experiential learning, 134

F

Facebook, 155
Facilitation, 167
Fairness, 190
Family Educational Rights and Privacy Act (FERPA), 140–141
Family risk index, defined, 102
FAPE. *See* Free and appropriate public education (FAPE)
Female teachers, 54
Females, 26. *See also* Girls; Women
Ferguson, Plessy v., 63
FERPA. *See* Family Educational Rights and Privacy Act (FERPA)
Field placement/experiences, 198
Filtering technologies, 159
Finance Game, 171
First Amendment Center, 108
First Amendment rights, 142–143, 144
Fish is Fish (Lionni), 81–82
Flat classroom, 150, 162, 166
Flat world, 165–166, 175
Foresight, 190
Formal curriculum, defined, 82–83

Formal operational stage of development, 74
Formal schools, 50
Fourteenth Amendment, 144
Franklin Academy, 50
Franklin, Benjamin, 50
Fraser, Bethel School District No. 403 v., 142
Free and appropriate public education (FAPE), 117
Freedom, academic, 144
Freedom from discrimination, 144
Freedom of expression, 144
Freedom of religion, 143
Freire, Paulo, 59, 204
French Creole, 97
Friedman, Thomas, 150, 165, 166, 168, 175, 210
Full inclusion, defined, 117
Funds/funding, 49, 62–67

G

Games/gaming, 170, 171–172
Gardner, Howard, 108, 110
Gardner, Lew, 16
Gay-Straight Alliances (GSAs), 100
Gender, schooling and, 38
Gender roles, 54–55
Gender-fair education, 103, 105–107, 123
Geographical divide, 159
Gifted and talented students, 116, 121–123
Gifted inclusion, 123
Girls. *See also* Females; Women
    gender-fair education and, 105–107, 123
    hidden curriculum and, 38–39
    public education and, 48, 49, 50, 64–65
Global classroom, 168–175
Global collaboration, 167, 169
Global communication, 169, 203
Global community, 203
Global environment, 40
Global student, 166–168
Globalization
    digital media and, 170–172
    flat world and, 165–166
    global classroom and, 168–175
    global student and, 166–168
    knowledge economy and, 165–168
    virtual classes and, 172–174
Goals
    of AFT, 208
    of American public education, 47
    for classroom community, 181
    common, 36
    of education, 181, 199
    emotional, 181
    IEPs and, 118
    of NCLB, 132
    social, 181
    of teacher preparation programs, 37
    teaching, 10, 25

Goleman, Daniel, 124
Goodness of fit, 11, 16, 194–195, 197–204
Google, 160, 204
Google Earth, 204
Google for Educators, 204
Grade books, 158
Grading/grades, 141, 158
Greene, Maxine, 60–62
Grooming, 143
Group learning, 175
Grunwald Associates LLC, 172
GSAs. *See* Gay-Straight Alliances (GSAs)
Guided discovery, 188

H

Handheld wireless devices, 157
Harassment
    hostile environment, 192
    peer, 159
    preventing, 190–195
    sexual, 145, 191–192
    sexual orientation and, 100
Hartford Female Seminary, 55
Hazelwood School District v. Kuhlmeier, 142
Head Start, 64
Heterosexual, defined, 99
Hidden curriculum
    defined, 38–39, 82–83
    homeschooling and, 135–136
High school curriculum, 56–57
High school virtual classes, 172–174
High schools, 52
Hinchcliffe, Dion, 155
Hispanic students, 96
Hispanics, in public education, 55
Homelessness, 102
Homeschooling, 133, 135–136
Homework completion, 158
Homophobia, 100
Homosexual, defined, 99
Hook, Sidney, 5
Hostile environment harassment, 192
Humphreys, Tony, 144
Hunger, 102

I

IB program. *See* International Baccalaureate (IB) program
IDEA. *See* Individuals with Disabilities Education Act (IDEA)
IEP. *See* Individualized education programs (IEP)
Ill-structured problem, defined, 127
Immigration, 51, 96, 98
Inclusion
    controversy about, 117
    defined, 66
    full, 117

    gifted, 123
    partial, 66, 117
Inclusion classroom, 116–121
Individualized education programs (IEP), 118, 119–120, 142
Individuals with Disabilities Education Act (IDEA), 65–66, 116, 118, 142
Informal curriculum, defined, 82–83
Information
    assessing value of, 204
    knowledge *vs.,* 166–168
    managing, 168
Information Age, 165, 166, 176
Information overload, 151–152
Information technology revolution. *See also* Technology
    AT and, 161–162
    classroom and, 150–152
    digital divide and, 159–161
    explanation for, 149–150
    information overload in, 151–152
    Internet safety and, 158–159
    learning and, 152–157, 162
    lifelong learners and, 40
    technology and, 150–151, 152–157, 162
    tracking student progress and, 158
    Web 2.0 and, 155–157
Injustice, social, 191
Inquiry, defined, 62
Instruction
    defined, 72
    differentiated, 121, 123–124, 208
Instructional methods, defined, 72
INTASC. *See* Interstate New Teacher Assessment and Support Consortium (INTASC)
Intellectual commitment, 25
Intelligence profile, defined, 110
Intelligence(s)
    bodily-kinesthetic, 109
    existential, 109
    interpersonal, 109
    intrapersonal, 109
    linguistic, 109, 110
    logical-mathematical, 109, 110
    moral, 109
    multiple, 108–111, 126, 131, 203
    musical, 109
    naturalist, 109
    spatial, 109
    spiritual, 109
Interaction
    social, 188
Interactive whiteboard, defined, 161
Interdisciplinary learning, in middle schools, 52
International Baccalaureate (IB) program, 122–123, 206
International Schools Services website, 206
Internet
    connected classroom and, 150–151
    cyberbullying and, 193–194
    flat classrooms and, 150

homeschooling and, 135
    videoconferencing on, 170
Internet advertising, 158
Internet cafés, 160
Internet crime, 194
Internet research, 152
Internet safety, 158–159, 193, 194
Internet technology, 153–155
Interpersonal intelligence, 109
Interstate New Teacher Assessment and
    Support Consortium (INTASC), 205
Intrapersonal intelligence, 109
iPod touch, 157
Issues
    regarding alternatives to traditional
        schools, 132–136
    regarding charter schools, 133–135
    regarding differentiated instruction,
        123–124
    explanation of, 115–116
    regarding gifted and talented students,
        121–123
    regarding homeschooling, 133, 135–136
    regarding inclusion classrooms,
        116–121
    regarding middle schools, 136–139
    regarding NCLB, 129–132
    regarding problem-based learning, 125,
        126–129, 131
    regarding project-based learning,
        125–126, 127, 128, 129, 131
    regarding protecting rights of students,
        139–143
    regarding protecting rights of teachers,
        143–145
    regarding safe school climate, 139
    regarding SEL, 124
    regarding violence, 139

J

Jackson, Phillip, 38
Jefferson, Thomas, 50, 56, 99, 199
Job training, 64
Jobs, classroom, 188
Johnson, Lyndon, 64
Jones, John E., 108
Joubert, Joseph, 72
Journal, 207
Jung, Carl, 19
Junior high school, 52

K

Kaiser Family Foundation, 162
Kevorkian, Jack, 87
Kierkegaard, Søren, 59
Kindergarten, 26
Kinesthetic learners, defined, 111
Kingston, Maxine Hong, 31

Kliewer, Chris, 116
Knezek, Don, 168
Knowledge
    cognitive learning theory and, 74
    educational associations and, 208
    information *vs.*, 166–168
    learning and, 203
    pedagogical content, 72
    prior, 77
    scholarly, 38
    self, 38
Knowledge economy, 165–166
Kounin, Jacob, 195
*Kuhlmeier, Hazelwood School
    District v.*, 142
Kurshan, Barbara, 175

L

Lagemann, Ellen Condliffe, 132
Land Ordinance Act of 1785, 50
Language-minority students, 97–99
Laptop project, 160
Latin grammar schools, 48–49, 50
Latino, 101
Latino immigration, 98
Learners
    auditory, 111
    communities of, 154–155 (*See also*
        Learning communities)
    exceptional, 116
    experience as, 112
    kinesthetic, 111
    lifelong, 40–42
    visual, 111
Learning
    aesthetics and, 62
    asynchronous distance, 173
    becoming teachers and, 30
    burnout and, 33–34
    caring culture and, 200
    classroom safety and, 187
    cooperative, 125
    discovery, 74–75
    distance, 173
    early-childhood education and, 27
    experiential, 134
    global classroom and, 168
    good teachers and, 198
    group, 175
    information technology revolution and,
        152–157, 162
    interdisciplinary, 52
    Internet technology and, 153–155
    lifelong, 98
    multiple ways of, 202–203
    principles of, 70–89
    problem-based, 125, 126–129, 131,
        151, 188, 203
    progressivism and, 57
    project-based, 125–129, 131, 151, 170,
        188, 203

safe enfironment and, 207
    service, 189
    silence and, 185
    social and emotional, 124
    student-centered, 59, 75–82, 203
    synchronous distance, 173
    to teach, 89, 200
    technology and, 152–155, 162, 203
    video games for, 171
    working relationships and, 188
Learning communities, 36, 40, 154–155,
    183, 192
Learning disabilities, 118, 161
Learning environments, 104, 124, 167,
    172, 186
Learning how to learn, 166–167
Learning objectives, 190
Learning profiles, 200
Learning styles, 111, 200, 203
Learning theories
    behaviorism as, 73, 79
    cognitive, 73–75, 79
    constructivism as, 75–82
    defined, 73
    social cognitive, 75, 79
Least restrictive environment, defined, 117
Legal responsibilities, of teachers, 145
Lesbian, gay, bisexual, and transgender
    (LGBT), 99, 100
Libraries, 160
Lifelong learners/learning, 40–42, 98
Lifestyle, global classroom and, 169
Linguistic intelligence, 109, 110
Lionni, Leo, 81–82
Logan, Judy, 203
Logical-mathematical intelligence, 109, 110

M

Madison, James, 199
Mainstreaming, 117
Males, 25, 31. *See also* Boys; Men
Management
    classroom, 181–184, 188, 194–195
    defined, 181
    time, 167
Mann, Horace, 50, 54
Marketing, online, 158
Maxine Greene Foundation for Social
    Imagination, the Arts, and
    Education, 61
McGuffey Readers, 84
Media, digital, 170–172
Men, 54. *See also* Boys; Males
Mental schemes
    defined, 76–77
    role of, 77
    understanding, 85
    at work, 77–78
Mentoring/mentors, 39, 40, 207
Metacognition, defined, 167

Metaphor, for teaching, 8–10
Middle schools, 52, 136–139
Minority Teacher Recruitment Project
 (MTRP), 55
MIT Media Lab, 160
MIVA, defined, 168
Modeling/models, defined, 75, 153–154
Moral intelligence, 109
More, Thomas, 115
Morning Meeting, 187, 188, 192
MTRP. *See* Minority Teacher Recruitment
 Project (MTRP)
Multicultural education, 103, 104–105
Multiple intelligences, 108–111, 126,
 131, 203
Multitasking, 175
Musical intelligence, 109

N

NAEYC. *See* National Association for
 the Education of Young Children
 (NAEYC)
NAGC. *See* National Association for Gifted
 Children (NAGC)
NASA CONNECT, 170
NASA Digital Learning Network, 171
*Nation at Risk: The Imperative for
 Educational Reform, A,* 65,
 66, 101
*Nation Prepared: Teachers for the 21st
 Century, A,* 19
National Assessment of Educational
 Progress, 133
National Association for Gifted Children
 (NAGC), 123
National Association for the Education of
 Young Children (NAEYC), 17–18,
 26, 41
National Board Certification, 206
National Board Certified Teachers
 (NBCTs), 205–206
National Board for Professional Teaching
 Standards (NBPTS), 19, 205–206
National Center for Education
 Statistics, 135
National Center on Response to
 Intervention, 121
National Commission on Excellence in
 Education, 65
National Council for the Social Studies
 (NCSS), 42
National Council of Teachers of English
 (NCTE), 42
National Council of Teachers of
 Mathematics (NCTM), 42, 66, 83
National Education Association (NEA),
 13–16, 19, 41, 56, 134, 136, 199,
 208–209
National Governors Association, 131
National Middle School Association, 138
National School Climate Survey, 100

National Science Teachers Association
 (NSTA), 42
National Spelling Bee, 135
National standards, 83–84
National Youth Risk Behavior Survey
 (YRBS), 102
Naturalist intelligence, 109
NBCTs. *See* National Board Certified
 Teachers (NBCTs)
NBPTS. *See* National Board for Professional
 Teaching Standards (NBPTS)
NCLB Act. *See* No Child Left Behind
 (NCLB) Act
NCSS. *See* National Council for the Social
 Studies (NCSS)
NCTE. *See* National Council of Teachers of
 English (NCTE)
NCTM. *See* National Council of Teachers
 of Mathematics (NCTM)
NEA. *See* National Education Association
 (NEA)
NEFC. *See* Northeast Foundation for
 Children (NEFC)
Neglect, 145
Negligence, 145
Negroponte, Nicholas, 160
Neill, A. S., 59
Neuroscience
 defined, 71
 perspectives from, 79–81
New Commision on the Skills of the
 American Workforce, 167
New teachers, 40, 206–208
New York Times, 95
News Corporation, 160
No Child Left Behind (NCLB) Act, 39,
 64, 66, 83, 88, 98, 101, 117,
 129–132, 142
Noise, in classroom, 184–185
Normal schools, 54–55
Northeast Foundation for Children
 (NEFC), 187–188
Northwest Ordinance of 1787, 50
NSTA. *See* National Science Teachers
 Association (NSTA)

O

Obama, Barack, 129
Observing/observations, 198
Office for Civil Rights, 191, 192
"Old Deluder Satan" Act, 49
One Laptop Per Child Project (OLPC), 160
Online abuse, 194. *See also* Cyberbullying
Online classrooms, 181
Online communication, 158
Online courses, 172, 173
Online discussion boards, 155
Online education, 3. *See also* Virtual
 classes/classrooms
Online environments, 172, 173, 174
Online marketing, 158

Operant conditioning, defined, 73
Opportunities, 34–37
Outsourcing, defined, 166

P

Paideia Proposal (Adler), 58
Palmer, Parker, 25
Paper grade books, 158
*Papish v. the Board of Curators of the
 University of Missouri,* 142
Parental education, 64
Parochial schools, defined, 51
Partial inclusion, 66, 117
Participant-observer, defined, 198
Partnership for 21st Century Skills, 168
Passion, 207
Passion quotient, 210–211
"Pauper's Oath," 49–50
PBS, 171, 172
PCK. *See* Pedagogical content knowledge
 (PCK)
Pedagogical content knowledge
 (PCK), 72
Pedagogy
 culturally relevant, 104, 105, 195
 defined, 72
 SDAIE, 98
Pedagogy of the Oppressed (Freire), 59
Peer grading, 141
Peer harassment, 159
People skills, 168
Perennialism, 58, 60
Performance, student, 86, 87
Performance assessment, 86, 131. *See also*
 Authentic assessments
Performances of understanding, 86–87
Personal attributes, 16, 197, 198
Personal reflection, 3
Phillips Academy, 50
Phillips Exeter Academy, 50
Philosophy of teaching statement,
 defined, 10
Piaget, Jean, 74, 75
Play-based activities, 27
Plessy v. Ferguson, 63
Portfolio, teaching, 10, 86, 209–210
Portfolio assessment, 206
Poverty, 100, 101–102, 159, 160
Powell, Lawrence Clark, 149
Pragmatism, 57. *See also* Progressivism
Praxis Series, The, defined, 204–205
Pregnancy, teen, 102, 103
Pre-kindergarten, 26
Prensky, Marc, 150
Preoperational stage of development, 74
Pre-school, 26
*Principles and Standards for School
 Mathematics,* 66
Prior knowledge, 77
Priorities, educational reform and, 62–67
Privacy, technology and, 158

Privacy rights, 140, 141–142, 144
Private academies, 49
Private school enrollment, 96
Private schools, 49, 133, 144
Problem solving, 165
Problem-based learning, 125, 126–129,
    131, 151, 188, 203
Problem-solving skills, 170
Procedures, classroom, 184
Profession, teaching as, 12–20
Professional development, 40–41, 42, 64
Proficiency
    academic, 181
    NCLB and, 131
Progress reports, 158
Progressivism, 57–58, 60
Project Zero, 86
Project-based learning, 125–129, 131, 151,
    170, 188, 203
*Promising Practices: New Ways to Improve
    Teacher Quality,* 12
Protestants, 99
Public education
    American (*See* American public education)
    defined, 199
    free and appropriate, 117
    mission of, 199
    purposes of, 199–200
Public funds, 49
Public libraries, 160
Public school enrollment, 95–96
Public schools, 133, 144
Punishments, behaviorism and, 73
Puritans, 47–49

Q

Qualities, for good teachers, 11
Quid pro quo sexual harassment, 192
Quinn, Donald D., 71

R

Racial discrimination, 144
Rand Corporation, 138
Rasmussen, Karen, 127
Readers, basal, 84–85
Reflection, personal, 3
Reflective practitioner, defined, 5–6
Reform, 19, 55–67, 101
Relationships
    global classroom and, 169
    learning and, 188
    new teachers and, 207
    teaching about, 179, 188
    working, 188
Religion
    freedom of, 143
    schools and, 103, 107–108
Religious discrimination, 144

Religious diversity, 99
Religious schools, 49
Research
    on classroom safety, 187
    on effective teachers, 5
    on gaming, 171
    on gifted and talented students, 122
    on good teachers, 197–198
    Internet, 152
    on learning, 75
    on learning styles, 111
    on male teachers, 31
    on multiple intelligences, 111
    on online courses, 173–174
    on teaching/vision, 37
Resources
    computer, 160
    teaching, 42
Respect, sexual harassment and, 192
Response to Intervention (RTI), 115, 118,
    121, 123
Responsive Classroom, 187–188
Revolution
    defined, 149
    Information technology (*See*
        Information technology revolution)
Rewards
    behaviorism and, 73
    of teaching life, 32–33
Rights
    of students, 139–143
    of teachers, 143–145, 208
Risk, students at, 101–103
Robinson, Ken, 167, 168
Rogers, Carl, 75
Routines, classroom, 184, 188, 190
RTI. *See* Response to Intervention (RTI)
Rubric, defined, 87–88
Rules, classroom, 184, 190
Russell Byers Charter School, 134–135

S

Safe environment, 207
Safety
    classroom and, 139, 140, 186–190
    Internet, 158–159, 193, 194
Salaries, 34, 41
*Santa Fe Independent School District v.
    Doe,* 143
Sartre, Jean Paul, 59
Scholarly knowledge, 38
Schön, Donald, 5
School climate, 20–21, 139, 140, 186, 194,
    198. *See also* School environment
School culture, 20–21, 198
School environment, 36, 207. *See also*
    School climate
School reform, 19
Scott, A. O., 95
SDAIE. *See* Specially Designed Academic
    Instruction in English (SDAIE)

Sealfon, Rebecca, 135
Searls, Doc, 166
Secondary classroom
    community building in, 189–190
    consistency and, 190
Secondary education, 49
Secondary school, 50, 52, 136
Secret Service, 140
Segregation, 63, 96
SEL. *See* Social and emotional
    learning (SEL)
Self-contained class, 66
Self-control, 188
Self-exploration, 3
Self-knowledge, 38
Service learning, defined, 189
SES. *See* Socioeconomic status (SES)
Sex discrimination, 65
Sex education, 103
Sexual abuse, 145
Sexual discrimination, 144
Sexual harassment, 145, 191–192
Sexual orientation, 99–100
Silence, in classroom, 184–185
Simulations, 153–154, 171
Single-sex schooling, 106
Skinner, B. F., 73
Smart Board, 161
Social and emotional learning (SEL), 124
Social capital
    defined, 48
    socioeconomic disparities and, 101
Social classes, 159
Social cognitive learning theories, 75, 79
Social context, 101
Social curriculum, 188
Social environment, 75
Social goals, 181
Social injustice, 191
Social interaction, 188
Social networking, 158, 172
Social networking sites, 155
Social reconstructionism, 59, 60
Socialization, homeschooling and, 135–136
Socially acceptable communication, 175
Socioeconomic disparities, 100–101
Socioeconomic status (SES), defined, 100
Socratic method, 58
Spatial intelligence, 109
Special education, defined, 117
Special education students, 66
Specially Designed Academic Instruction in
    English (SDAIE), 98
Spiraling, defined, 74–75
Spiritual intelligence, 109
Stages of cognitive development, defined, 74
Standardized assessment, 84, 88–89
Standardized testing/tests, 88–89, 129,
    135, 187
Standards
    for American public education, 62–67
    certification and, 204–206
    educational reform and, 62–67
    INTASC, 205

Standards *(continued)*
  national, 83–84
  NCLB and, 131–132
Standards movement, 83–84
Standards-based assessments, 199
Standards-based educational reform,
  66–67
Standards-based tests, 181
Stanton, Elizabeth Cady, 55
Starry Night, The (van Gogh), 62
State frameworks, for curriculum, 83–84
Stereotyping, 106, 107
Student diversity, 25, 96–97, 101,
  103–108, 123
Student performance, 86, 87
Student teacher/teaching, defined, 198
Student-centered classrooms/
  environment, 203
Student-centered learning, 59, 75–82, 203
Students
  adapting curriculum to, 85
  aesthetics and, 60
  bilingual education and, 97–98
  blind, 161
  Dewey and, 57
  with disabilities, 116–117, 118 (*See also*
    Disabled students)
  disabled, 161 (*See also* Disabilities)
  diverse, 112 (*See also* Student diversity)
  English-language learners and, 98–99
  enrollment for, 95–101
  essentialists and, 57
  ethnic diversity and, 96–97
  experiences as, 7
  First Amendment rights of, 142–143
  gender-fair education of, 103,
    105–107
  gifted and talented, 116, 121–123
  global, 166–168
  Hispanic, 96
  language-minority, 97–99
  learning styles and, 111
  male teachers and, 31
  multicultural education of, 103,
    104–105
  multiple intelligences of, 108–111
  religion and, 103, 107–108
  religious diversity and, 99
  rights of, 139–143
  sexual orientation and, 99–100
  social context and, 101
  socioeconomic disparities and,
    100–101
  special education, 66
  Title IX and, 105–107
  white, 96, 97
Students at risk, 101–103
Student-student communication, 174
Style, Emily, 84, 104
Substance abuse, 102, 103
Sullivan, Anne, 181
Support, for teachers, 27, 39–40
Surveys, on dropout rate, 102–103
Synchronous distance learning, 173

T

Tammy Kitzmiller, et al. v. Dover Area
  School District, et al., 107
Taxes, funding schools through, 62
Teacher burnout, 33–34. *See also* Burnout
Teacher education, 54–55
Teachers
  aesthetics and, 60
  African American, 55
  challenges for, 31, 33, 34–37
  cooperating, 198
  decisions to become (*See* Decisions)
  essentialists and, 57
  expert, 72
  favorite, 10–11
  female, 54
  good, 11, 197–198
  legal responsibilities of, 145
  as lifelong learners, 40–42
  new, 40, 206–208
  opportunities for, 34–37
  progressivism and, 57
  rights of, 143–145
  role of, 199–200
  student, 198
  support for, 39–40
Teacher-student communication, 174
Teaching
  code of ethics for, 13–16
  constructivism and, 78–79
  with digital media, 170–172
  educational associations for,
    208–209
  exciting aspects of, 31–32
  with games, 170–172
  gender roles in, 54–55
  getting started in, 204–208
  in global classroom, 168–175
  metaphor for, 8–10
  multiple ways of, 202–203
  preparing for, 3
  principles of, 70–89
  profession of, 12–20
  progressivism and, 57
  rewards of, 32–33
  school climate for, 20–21
  school culture for, 20–21
  student, 198
  talking about, 6–11
  team, 52
  with videoconferencing, 170–172
  vision and, 37–39
Teaching English as a Foreign Language
  (TEFL), 206
Teaching journal, 35
Teaching philosophy, 10
Teaching portfolio, 10, 86, 209–210
Teaching positions, 206
Teaching resources, 42
Teaching stories
  about becoming a teacher, 27–31
  about burnout, 33–34

  about challenges in teaching, 31, 33,
    34–37
  early-childhood education, 26–27
  exciting, 31–32
  regarding hidden curriculum, 38–39
  introduction to, 25
  about learning, 33–34
  about opportunities in teaching, 34–37
  about rewards of teaching, 32–33
  regarding support for teachers, 39–40
  regarding teachers as lifelong learners,
    40–42
  regarding teaching/vision, 37–39
"Teaching to the test," 89
Team teaching, in middle schools, 52
Teamwork, 167
Teasing, 192–193
Technological fluency, defined, 159
Technology. *See also* Information
  technology revolution
  assistive, 161–162
  blocking, 159
  changes in, 3, 40
  in classroom, 150–151, 152
  digital, 150, 159
  filtering, 159
  Internet, 153–155
  learning and, 3, 152–155, 162
  teaching positions and, 206
  using current, 203–204
Teen abuse, 193
Teen pregnancy, 102, 103
TEFL. *See* Teaching English as a Foreign
  Language (TEFL)
Tenure, defined, 144
Tests/testing. *See also* Assessments
  NCLB and, 129–132
  The Praxis Series, 204–205
  standardized, 88–89, 129, 135, 187
  standards-based, 181
Texting, 156–157, 159
Theories, learning. *See* Learning theories
Theory of multiple intelligences,
  108–111, 126
Thinking
  creative, 170
  critical, 167, 203
Thinking skills
  creative, 127
  critical, 127
ThinkQuest, 170, 173
This We Believe: Successful Schools for
  Young Adolescents, 138
Thorpe, Ronald, 175
Time management, 167
Tinker v. Des Moines, 142
Title 1, 64
Title IV, 65
Title IX, 64–65, 105, 106, 191
Title VI, 64
Title VII, 65
Tomlinson, Carol, 124
Tracking student progress, 158
Tracking system, defined, 56–57

Traditional schools, alternatives to, 132–136
Transgender, defined, 99
Tuitions, 49
Tuskegee Normal School, 55
Tutoring, 64
Twitter, 155
Two-way programs, 97

U

Understanding performances, 86–87
Uniforms, 142
Unions, 19, 208
U.S. Department of Commerce, 159
U.S. Department of Education, 102, 106,
    116, 130, 140, 141, 192
USA PATRIOT Act, 142

V

van Gogh, Vincent, 62
Video games, 171

Videoconferencing, 167, 170–172
Violence, 139, 171
Virtual classes/classrooms, 172–174, 181.
    See also Online education
Virtual field trips, 170
Virtual schools, defined, 173
Vision
    of essentialists, 57
    teaching and, 37–39
Visual learners, defined, 111
Vygotsky, Lev, 75

W

War on Poverty, 64
Ward, William Arthur, 197
Washington, Booker T., 55
Web 2.0, 155–157, 203
Web-based grade books, 158
Websites
    for educational associations, 208
    for global classroom, 169
    International Schools Services, 206
    tracking student progress and, 158

White students, 96, 97
Wikipedia, 156
Wikis, 155, 156–157, 203
Wireless communication, 157
Wireless devices, 157
Wireless tablet, 165
"Withitness," 195
Women. *See also* Females; Girls
    dropout rate and, 103
    public education and, 48, 54, 55
Working relationships, 188
World Is Flat, The (Friedman), 150, 165

Y

Young Women's Leadership School of East
    Harlem, 106
YRBS. *See* National Youth Risk Behavior
    Survey (YRBS)

SPEAK UP!
SHE DID

TEACH was built on a simple principle: to create a new teaching and learning solution that reflects the way today's faculty teach and the way you learn.

Through conversations, focus groups, surveys, and interviews, we collected data that drove the creation of the current version of TEACH that you are using today. But it doesn't stop there – in order to make TEACH an even better learning experience, we'd like you to SPEAK UP and tell us how TEACH worked for you.

What did you like about it? What would you change? Are there additional ideas you have that would help us build a better product for next semester's students?

At **www.cengagebrain.com** you'll find all of the resources you need to succeed – **videos, flash cards, interactive games, quizzes** and more!

Speak Up! Go to **CourseMate** for TEACH. Access at **login.cengagebrain.com**.

Learning Outcomes

LO1 Reflecting on your educational autobiography and teaching metaphor may help to clarify your thinking around what it means to be a teacher. It will also influence your personal philosophy and goals as a future educator.

LO2 A teacher of your own may have had a profound impact on your life and your desire to become a teacher yourself, and may serve as a role model.

LO3 Good teachers usually have common attributes; as you consider becoming a teacher, you must reflect on the goodness of fit between your qualities as a person and the demands of the profession.

LO4 Your understanding of teaching as "the essential profession" will be enhanced by your knowledge of the history and standards of several professional organizations that offer support to educators in settings from early childhood through university-level instruction.

LO5 Teachers must be committed to pursuing a school climate and a school culture that have a positive impact on students' ability to learn; the quality of the teacher in the classroom extends throughout the entire school and makes all the difference.

LO6 Being a reflective practitioner means looking forward and backward and realizing that we teach who we are.

Chapter Outline

LO1 Looking Backward: Talking about Teaching 6
Your Educational Autobiography 7
What Is Your Metaphor for Teaching? 8
LO2 A Favorite Teacher 10
LO3 What Qualities Are Needed to Be a Good Teacher? 11
LO4 Looking Forward: The Profession 12
An Essential Profession 12
A Code of Ethics 13
An Organized Profession 16
Starting Early 17
A National Board 19
More Than a Profession 19
LO5 The Workplace: School Climate and School Culture 20
LO6 Concluding Thoughts 21

Teaching Suggestions and Resources

Reflection Questions

Beginning Your Educational Autobiography

Encourage your students to begin their educational autobiography by describing their early school experiences, starting with some basic facts: where they went to school, how they traveled there, how it felt to be in the classroom, and when (if at all) they thought about becoming a teacher themselves. You may wish to share your own story. For example:

I remember walking to school with my older sister, and after getting used to kindergarten I loved first grade. I remember starting to read and loving my first-grade teacher. I thought school was neat. My elementary school was a wonderful old building in the Bronx in New York City. There was a swimming pool in the school, and every week we had swimming lessons with Mrs. Doyle. I felt special because my school had a swimming pool.

Ask your students to start their educational autobiography with some similar facts.

- How old were you when you started school?
- Did you attend a nursery school or preschool?
- Where did you live?
- Was the school within walking distance, did you take a bus, or did someone drive you? What is your earliest memory of being in a classroom?
- What grade were you in?

Your Favorite Teacher

Have your students describe a teacher or teachers who had a profound influence on them. These questions will help focus their thinking:

- What was the nature of this teacher's influence? How did he or she change your thinking about yourself, school, or learning?
- In what grade did you have your favorite teacher? What was special about that year?
- Construct a list of attributes the teacher had. What particular qualities made him or her your favorite?
- How can this memory serve you as you explore the field of education?

Key Terms

reflective practitioner 5

educational autobiography 7

philosophy of teaching statement 10

goodness of fit 11

National Education Association (NEA) 13

American Federation of Teachers (ATF) 16

National Association for the Education of Young Children (NAEYC) 17

National Board for Professional Teaching Standards (NBPTS) 19

school climate and **school culture** 20

Thinking about Your Strengths and Weaknesses

When students begin to think about a career in teaching, one of their tasks is to analyze their own strengths and weaknesses. Guide them with these questions:

- What are some of your strengths as a person? As a student? As a future professional?
- How do these strengths serve you as you look forward to becoming a teacher?
- What are some of your weaknesses? Will they be problematic if you choose teaching as a profession?

Teaching as a Profession

The question of teaching's status as a profession dates back at least as far as Myron Lieberman's 1956 book *Education as a Profession*. Using Lieberman as a source, Robin Ann Martin (2000) discusses several attributes of a profession. Share these three key ones with your students:

- A profession offers a unique, definite, and essential service.
- A profession places an emphasis on intellectual techniques in performing its service.
- A profession requires a long period of specialized training.

Then ask them to think about these attributes and explain how they apply to teaching:

- In teaching, what is the unique and essential "service"?
- For teaching, what do you think the "intellectual techniques" are?
- Though Lieberman and Martin say a profession requires a long period of specialized training, just how much time is needed to prepare teachers is a hotly debated topic. What do *you* think?

Discussion Questions

1. Did anything about your personal educational autobiography surprise you? Share it here with other beginning education students.
2. For you, what is the most intimidating aspect of becoming a teacher?

TeachSource Video Case

Advice from the Field

Find the TeachSource Video Case "Becoming a Teacher: Voices and Advice from the Field" on the student website. This video showcases several teachers, some new to the field and some who have been teaching for years. Pay special attention to their ideas about what is needed to be a successful teacher. After the main video, view the bonus video called "Essential Qualities That Teachers Must Possess." Ask your students these questions:

- Jot down the various qualities the teachers mention as essential. How many of them overlap with the attributes listed in the sidebar "Attributes of Good Teachers"? How many are new?
- Begin thinking about whether you have these qualities. Are there some you don't have currently but could work to develop?

Learning Outcomes

LO1 Teachers enter the profession for a variety of reasons, but they often cite a love of children and a love of learning as common factors in their decision.

LO2 The nature of teaching makes it both a challenging and rewarding career.

LO3 Teachers reveal themselves in their classrooms; being conscious of this can help you use your strengths to create a hidden curriculum with positive messages for students.

LO4 Many avenues of support will be available to you as a new teacher, such as your colleagues, a mentor, professional organizations, and professional development programs.

Chapter Outline

LO1 Who Are Our Teachers? 25
Early-Childhood Education 26
Deciding to Become a Teacher 27
LO2 Excitement and Challenges in Teaching 31
What Are the Most Exciting Aspects of Teaching? 31
Rewards of a Teaching Life 32
What Are the Most Difficult Challenges for Teachers? 33
Teaching, Learning, and Burnout 33
Challenges and Opportunities 34
LO3 Teaching and Vision 37
Hidden Curriculum 38
LO4 Support for Teachers 39
Who Provides the Most Support to Teachers? 39
Mentoring New Teachers 40
Teachers as Lifelong Learners 40
How Do Teachers Continue Professional Development? 41
Benefits of Lifelong Learning 41
Concluding Thoughts 42

Teaching Suggestions and Resources

Reflection Questions

Feelings about Teaching and Learning

Ask your students to think about these questions:

- Was there a time when you felt you were intellectually engaged to a high degree? Was that a result of an in-school or out-of-school experience?
- Can you describe a "learning experience"? What was the subject or topic? What did you learn? Why does it stand out in your memory? Who functioned as your teacher in this experience?
- What is the major appeal of teaching for you?
- Which of the foregoing stories, if any, resonates best with your story?
- Why is it important to understand your own thinking about this career?

The Most Exciting Moments

Ask your students to think about these questions:

- Do you remember an "aha" moment as a student? Can you describe it?
- What do *you* anticipate will be the most exciting part of teaching?

The Challenges of Teaching

Ask your students to think about these questions:

- Meaningful learning takes time. So how do teachers reconcile the pressure to "get through" the curriculum with meaningful learning? Do you have any ideas?
- Jane believes that, given time, her students can find "personal meaning" in the math topics she teaches. Can you think of a math topic that has personal meaning for you?
- Do you remember a teacher who made connections between topics in the curriculum and your life outside of school? How did those connections help you find personal meaning in the subject you were studying?
- How do you feel about the number of hours you will need to spend preparing to teach effective lessons? Will that time be a burden or what Pearl calls a "source of pleasure"?

Key Terms

teacher burnout 33

hidden curriculum 38

learning community 40

professional development 40

• Knowing that you will have to deal with lots of paperwork, and possibly with unhelpful administrators and difficult parents, do you still believe firmly that the rewards of teaching outweigh the troubles? If so, why?

Learning from Others

Ask your students to think about these questions:

• As Amanda discovered, being a good listener is often a good way to learn about a school's environment. How are your listening skills?
• As you enter teaching, what do you think are the benefits of jumping right into school committees as Amanda did?
• Have you ever kept a personal journal or diary? Have you thought about keeping a teaching journal like Amanda's as you begin your career—writing down your reflections on the day or the week?

Discussion Questions

1. Whose teaching story in this chapter did you most relate to? Why?
2. Which story did you find the most instructive for your own teaching philosophy?
3. How do you think you will avoid burnout?

TeachSource Video Case

Surprises of the First Year

There is another story about the challenges and excitement of teaching in the TeachSource Video Cases section of the student website. Watch the video "The First Year of Teaching: One Colleague's Story," in which Will Starner talks about his initial year in a classroom. "I've had a lot of situations that I really didn't know would come up," he says. In the bonus video, "Mr. Starner Reflects on the First Year of Teaching," he mentions that he had "all these different theories running through my head," and it felt overwhelming to select the best approach for the context. Ask your students these questions:

• What are the main challenges Will Starner identifies?
• What ways did he find to cope with these difficulties?
• What is your impression of Mr. Starner? Discuss your reaction to his candid description of his first year of teaching. What attributes do you think make him potentially a very successful teacher?

Learning Outcomes

LO1 The earliest schools in America were both different from and similar to today's schools.

LO2 Early pioneers of public schooling, including Thomas Jefferson, Benjamin Franklin, and Horace Mann, shaped the history of American public education.

LO3 Philosophies influencing education include essentialism, progressivism, perennialism, social reconstructionism, critical theory, and existentialism.

LO4 Public school funding in America has historically been the responsibility of the states (and has fallen to localities), but federal government legislation, publications, and court cases have changed the course of public education.

LO5 Inclusive education integrates students with special needs and general education students in the same blended classroom.

LO6 Standards-based educational reform supports strict benchmarks for student learning that are assessed by state tests in specified content areas.

Chapter Outline

LO1 A Brief History of American Public Education 47
The Colonies 47
Latin Grammar Schools 48
Geographical Differences in Colonial Education 49
The Late Colonial Period 49

LO2 A New Nation 50
The Academy 50
Rise of the Common School 50
Expansion of Public Schools 52
Teacher Education and the Development
  of Normal Schools 54
Normal Schools and Female Teachers 54
Gender Roles in Teaching 54
*The Tuskegee Normal School and the Education
  of African Americans 55*

**LO3 Competing Visions: Efforts to Rethink
  and Reform Education 55**
The High School Curriculum 56
The Emergence of Essentialism 57
Progressivism and John Dewey 57
Enduring Ideas: The Influence of Perennialism 58
Radical Reform Philosophies: Social Reconstructionism,
  Critical Theory, and Existentialism 59
Aesthetics and Maxine Greene 60

Teaching Suggestions and Resources

Reflection Questions

The School as Social Control?

Horace Mann believed that all children should learn together in common schools. He lived at a time of tremendous social change when immigrants were pouring into the northeastern states, farmers were leaving rural areas to work in factories, and cities were growing rapidly, with crime and poverty on the rise. Some historians believe that Mann and other reformers, alarmed by the upheaval, promoted state-regulated public education mainly as a way to bring order and discipline to the working class. According to this interpretation, Mann and his fellow reformers felt threatened by the growing population of urban poor, and for this reason they placed a major emphasis on "moral training," standardization, and classroom drill. Have your students reflect on the idea of school as social control.

- Do you think that today's schools still function as institutions for social control?
- What messages do you believe are sent to children through public schooling today?
- Remember the hidden curriculum mentioned in Chapter 2. The *hidden curriculum* involves messages from the teacher and the school about how the classroom and school function: the rules, the expectations, and the goals. Does this promote the kind of social control Mann envisioned? How and why?

Experiences with Tracking

Ask your students to consider their own high school education. Was there evidence of tracking—different courses available for different types of students? Ask students to describe how tracking was used in their high school and how they recall feeling about it.

Progressivism and Essentialism Today

It is often said that Dewey's progressivism is alive and well in 21st-century classrooms. Ask students to cite specific examples of how his philosophy influences classroom work today. If they are observing in the field, have them look for the attributes of progressive education in the classrooms they visit. If they are not in the field, they can reflect on their own school years. What are the hints of Dewey's progressivism evident in today's classrooms?

LO4 Federal and State Efforts at Educational Reform: Funding, Priorities, and Standards 62
Separate but Equal? 63
The Elementary and Secondary Education Act 64
Title IX 64
A Nation at Risk 65
LO5 The Individuals with Disabilities Education Act 65
LO6 Standards-Based Educational Reform 66
Concluding Thoughts 67

Key Terms

dame school 48

Latin grammar school 49

academy 50

common school 50

parochial school 51

normal school 54

tracking 56

essentialism 57

progressivism 57

perennialism 58

aesthetic education 60

inquiry 62

Brown v. Board of Education of Topeka, Kansas 63

Title 1 64

Title IX 64

A Nation at Risk: The Imperative for Educational Reform 65

Individuals with Disabilities Education Act (IDEA) 65

inclusion 66

Likewise, threads of essentialism are found in many schools and classrooms. Many people believe that today's standards-oriented reform movement has a "back-to-basics," essentialist feel about it. This teacher-centered model of education may be evident in your students' classroom observations or in their recollections of their own schooling. What evidence is there of an essentialist approach in today's classrooms?

The Arts

Ask your students to think about these questions:

- What is your own educational experience with the arts? Have you personally experienced an engagement with the arts that allowed you to think about another area of learning in a different way?
- In what ways do you think education in the arts can free students to be more personally expressive?

Maxine Greene and Teaching

Maxine Greene believes that people who choose to become teachers should ideally be "those who have learned the importance of becoming reflective enough to think about their own thinking and become conscious of their own consciousness" (Greene, 1995). Ask your students what they think that means.

Your Experience with Student Diversity

Ask your students to think about these questions:

- What was your schooling like in terms of student diversity?
- Does it surprise you that there was a time when black children and white children were required to attend different schools in some parts of the country?
- What is the downside of a segregated education for all parties involved? In what ways can students of various backgrounds suffer from an absence of diversity?

Discussion Questions

1. Why is it important to diversify the teaching workforce? Why does it matter, for example, that a typical kindergarten teacher is a white female?
2. How would you characterize your personal teaching philosophy at this point? Are you an essentialist? a progressive? a social reconstructionist? a mix of several types? How and why?

TeachSource Video Case

Educational Philosophies in the Classroom

How does perennialism or progressivism operate in an actual classroom? Can you see the difference between them? Find the TeachSource Video Case "Philosophical Foundations of American Education: Four Philosophies in Action" on the student website. The video has four segments, each exploring a different philosophy in a classroom setting. The philosophies shown are essentialism, progressivism, perennialism, and critical theory. Ask your students these questions:

- If I followed this philosophy strictly in the classroom, how would I behave?
- What learning materials would I typically use? (Textbooks, classic works of literature, original source materials, contemporary writings)

Learning Outcomes

LO1 Many people think that they can teach because they have spent many years in classrooms.

LO2 Pedagogy is both an art and a science and is expressed through instructional practice.

LO3 By studying the human brain and development, scientists and educators have acquired a lot of knowledge about how people learn; it makes sense to use this understanding of how people learn as we think about how to become better teachers.

LO4 While the term "curriculum" is used often in schools, most people do not recognize that a curriculum is a course of study in a given subject area. National and state standards define topics to be addressed in a given subject area at each grade level.

LO5 Evidence of learning takes many forms, but the best way to understand what students know may be to ask them.

LO6 The expression "one size fits all" does not apply to teaching—teachers must learn about their students and find ways to teach to their special needs and talents.

Chapter Outline

LO1 Anyone Can Teach? 71

LO2 Pedagogy and Instruction 72

LO3 Learning Theories 73
Behaviorism: A Teacher-Centered Approach 73
Cognitive Learning Theories: The Role of Mental Processing 73
Social Cognitive Theories: The Role of Social Interactions 75
Constructivism: Student-Centered Learning 75
The Essence of Constructivism: Building Mental Schemes 76
Mental Schemes at Work 77
Constructivism and Teaching 78
Perspectives from Neuroscience: The Importance of Context 79
Fish Is Fish 81

LO4 What Is a Curriculum? 82
Formal, Informal, and Hidden Curricula 82
The Role of National Standards and State Frameworks 83
Curriculum and Standardized Assessment 84
Curriculum as Window and Mirror 84

Teaching Suggestions and Resources

Reflection Questions

Life as a Student

Remember, we tend to teach as we have been taught, but that may not be the best approach for our future students!

- In what ways, if any, do your experiences as a student reflect the ideas of behaviorism?
- Do you remember one or more teachers who relied heavily on external rewards or punishments?

The Context of Learning

Specific school memories or anecdotes often stay with us as we grow older. Ask your students to recall an experience in which the context of a lesson or activity became attached to the memory of the lasting idea or concept you learned. Have them describe that experience and indicate how you think the context—or, as Jackie Grennon Brooks refers to it, the "palette"—made a difference.

Curriculum and Standardized Assessment

In what ways, if any, do local schools' curricula suffer as a result of the inflexibility imposed by standardized assessment? Have your students consider this story, and respond to the questions that follow it.

> Several years ago, an elementary school in a northeastern suburb began an initiative to build a pond on its school property. The pond would attract birds and insects, the teachers and administrators thought, and they could build an elementary science curriculum around it. They had the pond installed and "seeded" it with a few small koi (similar to goldfish) and water plants.
>
> Grade-level classes took responsibility for monitoring the temperature and turbidity of the pond as well as carefully noticing the life in and around it. The science curriculum in that school grew, with exploration of the properties of the pond being the centerpiece.

- Do you think it is acceptable to address the science curriculum through a study of a pond, even though standardized tests have no questions about ponds? Why or why not?

Adapting the Curriculum to Your Students 85

LO5 Assessment: How Do We Know What They Know? 85
Standardized Testing: A Challenge for Authentic Assessment 88

LO6 Learning to Teach 89
Concluding Thoughts 89

Key Terms

pedagogy 72

instruction 72

pedagogical content knowledge (PCK) 72

learning theory 73

behaviorism 73

cognitive learning theories 73

social cognitive learning theories 75

constructivism 75

mental scheme 76

curriculum 82

informal curriculum 82

assessment 85

embedded assessments 86

authentic (performance) assessment 86

rubric 87

- If exploring a pond makes it difficult to "cover" all of the standards-based curriculum on which your students would be tested, how do you decide what to do?
- Do you think a curriculum can be both innovative and standards-based?
- Overall, would this pond-centered curriculum still be possible today, given the dominance of standards-driven assessments and state frameworks? Why or why not?
- How is this pond curriculum reflective of a progressive philosophy?

Discussion Questions

1. What did you think about the mailbox story?
2. Did you find that you had naïve conceptions of your own as you were growing up—misconceptions about how things really worked? Talk about them. How did you begin to revise these notions?

TeachSource Video Cases

A High School Debate

When constructivism informs pedagogy, teachers can develop instructional methods known as constructivist teaching. As you can imagine, this type of teaching places a lot of responsibility for learning on the students. It asks them to be actively engaged in creating meaning through experiences in which they take part. Find the TeachSource Video Case "Constructivist Teaching in Action: A High School Classroom Debate" on the student website. Ask your students these questions:

- In what ways is the teacher, Ms. Levy-Brightman, promoting the tenets of constructivist learning theory?
- How does she structure the learning experience?
- How does the carefully structured debate provide the students with a way to really learn the material?
- What information does the teacher gather from the student debates?

Performance Assessment

Find the TeachSource Video Case "Performance Assessment: Student Presentations in a High School English Class" on the student website. Ask your students these questions:

- When students make a poster about the writer they are studying, how does that represent a constructivist experience?
- Why do you think the students wanted their peers' feedback on their creativity?
- How did the teacher include the students in deciding how to assess this activity?
- What role did peer assessment play in these performances?

Learning Outcomes

LO1 Your own elementary, middle, and high schools may have undergone a shift in student population and a major change in curriculum.

LO2 Today's classrooms may be multi-lingual, multi-ethnic, or multi-age.

LO3 Students arrive at the classroom door from a wide range of social, economic, and emotional contexts.

LO4 Teachers recognize the importance of understanding their students' cultural experiences.

LO5 Students have a large variety of learning styles.

LO6 The mental image you have of yourself as a teacher is frequently based on your own experiences as a student.

LO7 Honoring the learner is the primary task of the teacher.

Chapter Outline

LO1 **The Students: A Changing Landscape 95**

LO2 Ethnic Diversity 96
Language-Minority Students 97
Bilingual Education 97
Teaching English-Language Learners 98
Religious Diversity 99
Sexual Orientation 99
Socioeconomic Disparities 100
Overlapping Attributes: The Social Context 101

LO3 **Students Who Are at Risk 101**

LO4 **Contemporary Issues Relating to Student Diversity 103**
Multicultural Education 104
Educating Girls and Boys: Separate or Together? 105
Religion and Schools 107

LO5 **Multiple Intelligences: What Does It Mean to Be "Smart"? 108**
Learning Styles 111

LO6 **Teaching the Broad Range of Diverse Students 112**

LO7 **Concluding Thoughts 112**

Teaching Suggestions and Resources

Reflection Questions

Religious Diversity

Ask your students to consider the possible extent of religious diversity in their future classrooms. In this context, they should think about the teachings of their own religion that have influenced their lives personally. Then reflect on this question: How does understanding your own religious beliefs help you better serve your students?

Assessing Your Own Demographics

Ask your students to think about these questions:

- Demographics is a general term for the kind of statistics we have been discussing so far in this chapter—the characteristics of human populations. How would you describe your demographics?
- Did you attend a neighborhood school? If so, how did it reflect the composition of your neighborhood? What do you think are the advantages of attending the local neighborhood school?
- Why might a diverse student body make a greater contribution to the entire group's learning than would a homogeneous group?

Students at Risk

Ask your students to think about these questions:

- Judging from your experience, which of the risk factors we have been discussing is (are) most likely to affect students in your community?
- Of the dropout-prevention strategies described in the chapter, which do you find most relevant for your future classroom?

Connections between Gender and Learning

Ask your students to think about these questions:

- Did you attend a same-sex school for any part of your education? In what ways, if any, was that a positive or negative experience?

Key Terms

bilingual education 97

sexual orientation 99

LGBT 99

socioeconomic status (SES) 100

students at risk 101

dropout rate 102

multicultural education 104

culturally relevant pedagogy 104

gender-fair education 106

equity 107

theory of multiple intelligences 108

intelligence profile 110

learning style 111

- Research tells us that teachers often address girls and boys differently in the classroom. Without meaning to, they tend to call on boys more frequently than girls and often, in the lower grades, use this tactic as a means of maintaining control in the classroom. Can you remember a time when you were treated in a certain way in school because you were male or female? What was that like for you? What did you think about it? What do you think now?

Teaching Values

Though schools may not teach religious doctrine, they may teach civic values, including honesty, good citizenship, and respect for others. Schools may even teach sexual abstinence or contraception. Since most religions also teach such values, why is it not unlawful to teach them? How can we draw the distinction between civic values and religious values?

Discussion Questions

1. Which areas of student diversity pose the most challenges for you as a future teacher?
2. How will you meet those challenges?

TeachSource Video Cases

Bilingual Education in Fourth Grade

To see how a two-way language immersion program can function, find the TeachSource Video Case "Bilingual Education: An Elementary Two-Way Immersion Program" on the student website. As you begin watching the video, note whether all the students are English-language learners. Ask your students these questions:

- Would you have liked to have been a student in this program? Why or why not?
- In what ways, if any, does the two-way program level the playing field for English-language learners?
- How, if at all, were you able to tell which students were native English speakers?
- Why is communication between the Spanish and English teachers essential?

Teaching to Students' Strengths

To explore how one teacher accounts for his students' varying intelligence profiles and styles of learning, find the TeachSource Video Case "Multiple Intelligences: Elementary School Instruction" on the student website. The video examines a class writing assignment about the passengers' experience during the ocean voyage of the *Mayflower*.

This traditional social studies lesson is transformed by Mr. Won Park as he asks fourth-grade students to think about the voyage in many different ways and then to write a first-person account from a passenger's point of view. Ask your students these questions:

- In what ways is this lesson informed by multiple intelligences theory?
- If you did not know about multiple intelligences and different learning styles, what would you think of this lesson?
- Why do you think Mr. Won Park asked the students to touch their faces and their clothes and to smell their clothes? What do you think he was hoping for?
- What aspects of this lesson used intrapersonal intelligence? Interpersonal intelligence? Kinesthetic learning?

Learning Outcomes

LO1 Inclusion classrooms offer all students significant possibilities. They look no different from mainstream classrooms.

LO2 Education for the gifted and talented targets students who give evidence of high achievement in areas such as intellectual, creative, artistic, or leadership capacities. Inclusion students can also be gifted and talented!

LO3 Differentiated instruction requires that teachers learn a great deal about who their students are, what their lives are like, and how they can best learn.

LO4 Problem- and project-based learning experiences engage students in realistic questions that require planning and collaboration before a solution can be found.

LO5 The No Child Left Behind Act has impacted the way teachers design and implement curriculum.

LO6 Many alternative school models have been developed that are unlike traditional public and private schools.

LO7 Teachers and students have legal rights and responsibilities guaranteed by the Family Educational Rights and Privacy Act and the U.S. Constitution.

Chapter Outline

LO1 The Inclusion Classroom 116
Types of Disabilities 118
Individualized Education Programs 118
Response to Intervention 118
LO2 The Education of Gifted and Talented Students 121
LO3 Differentiated Instruction 123
Social and Emotional Learning 124
LO4 The Power of Projects and Problems for Student Learning 125
Project-Based Learning 125
Problem-Based Learning 126
LO5 No Child Left Behind and Its Successor 129
Teaching to the Test? 129
Does One Size Fit All? 131
Variation among States: Are the Standards Really Standard? 131
The Achievement Gap 132
LO6 Alternatives to Traditional Schools: More Choices in an Era of Accountability 132
The Rise of Charter Schools 133
Who Teaches in Charter Schools? 134
A Case Study: The Russell Byers Charter School 134

Teaching Suggestions and Resources

Reflection Questions

Attributes of a Successful Inclusion Teacher

Ask students to make a list of attributes that people seeking to become inclusion teachers need to have to be successful with students with special needs.

Labels, Labels, Everywhere

This chapter has explored some ways students in today's classrooms are classified or "labeled": Students can have gifts, talents, learning disabilities, speech or language impairments, and so on.

- In what ways are labels helpful in education?
- Where, if at all, do labels cause harm?
- Were you labeled in any way? How did that affect your life at school?
- What famous people were labeled as having learning, physical, or speech disabilities in school?

Your Beliefs about Homeschooling

Supporters of homeschooling describe the movement as designed to enable students to learn freely, meaning that they are free from the constraints of teachers' plans, school schedules, peer abilities, and school disruptions. Many homeschooling groups help families support each other and network socially. Still, critics worry that homeschooling deprives children of vital learning experiences.

- Do you believe students miss important experiences by not attending a public or private school? What experiences in particular?
- Can you name one specific area of study that you believe cannot be managed successfully at home? Explain your choice.

Safe Schools

Ask your students to think about these questions:

- Was there ever a time in your school experience when you did not feel safe? Describe what that was like and how you handled it. What was the outcome?
- Imagine a sixth-grade student coming to you to report that a classmate has been very depressed since the death of her dog. The informant describes a conversation in which this student said she wanted to kill herself. What would you do?

Homeschooling: Another
Nontraditional Option 135

**Middle School: A Movement
in Transition 136**

Critiques of the Middle School
Model 137

A Framework for Effective
Middle Schools 138

**Creating a Safe School Climate:
The Concern about Violence
in Schools 139**

**LO7 Protecting the Rights of
Students 139**

The Right to Privacy 139

*Recent Challenges to
FERPA 141*

Compromises on Privacy 141

*First Amendment Rights
of Students 142*

**The Rights and Responsibilities
of Teachers 143**

Teachers' Rights 144

Teachers' Legal
Responsibilities 145

Concluding Thoughts 145

Key Terms

exceptional learners 116

least restrictive 116

inclusion 116

special education 116

**learning disability (or specific
learning disability)** 118

**individualized education
program (IEP)** 118

**Response to Intervention
(RTI)** 118

differentiated instruction or
differentiation 123

cooperative learning 125

project-based learning 126

problem-based learning 126

ill-structured problem 127

charter schools 133

homeschooling 135

**Family Educational Rights
and Privacy Act (FERPA)** or
the **Buckley Amendment** 140

due process 144

tenure 144

Discussion Questions

1. Do you think you would like to teach in an inclusion classroom, either as the general education teacher or the inclusion specialist? Why or why not?
2. The charter school movement and the home school movement are both gaining students. Why do you think that is so? What might be done to stem the exodus from conventional public education?

TeachSource Video Cases

Teaching Strategies for the Inclusion Classroom

Find the TeachSource Video Case "Inclusion: Grouping Strategies for Inclusive Classrooms" on the student website. Ask your students these questions:

- In what ways does the general education teacher, Sheryl Cebula, employ teaching strategies that use multiple intelligences theory?
- Which teacher is in charge? How can you tell?
- How would you describe Ms. Cebula's personal pedagogy in her role as the general education teacher?
- The inclusion specialist, Ms. Jordan, intervenes in many ways. How would you describe her role in the classroom?

Collaboration between the General Education Teacher and the Inclusion Specialist

Find the TeachSource Video Case "Inclusion: Classroom Implications for the General and Special Educator" on the student website. Ask your students these questions:

- How does the general education teacher help the students with diverse abilities in this inclusion classroom?
- What interventions are implemented for students with apparent hyperactivity disorders?
- In what ways was the general education teacher's preparation insufficient for her current position?
- What types of students are helped by occupational therapists?
- What is the best way for teachers to learn about the nature of their students' learning disabilities?

Educators Discuss IDEA and NCLB

Find the TeachSource Video Case "Foundations: Aligning Instruction with Federal Legislation" on the student website. Ask your students these questions:

- What is the best advice for a new teacher who finds himself or herself in an inclusion classroom as a general education teacher?
- How does the inclusion specialist express the sentiments behind this chapter's idea that one size does not fit all?

Teachers Discuss Their Ethical and Legal Responsibilities

Find the TeachSource Video Case "Legal and Ethical Dimensions of Teaching: Reflections from Today's Educators" on the student website. Ask your students these questions:

- In the video, one administrator says, "If you don't know, ask. If you're not sure, don't." What does this mean?
- What did you think of the teacher who reported "disturbing things" she heard during after-school conversations among students? Would you have done the same thing? Why? Why not?

Learning Outcomes

LO1 Most school-age children do not know a time when they did not use a computer at least once a week, or even daily, and are engaged by technology in the classroom.

LO2 Because technology is part of many students' daily lives, it makes sense to use it for more than gathering information and social networking—it can be used as a tool that fosters interactive, real-world learning.

LO3 Communication is becoming increasingly open with the rise of Web 2.0; many teachers today participate in blogs or start their own blog as a way to share ideas about teaching and learning.

LO4 Technology in the classroom can benefit disadvantaged and disabled students.

LO5 Because of all the data available online, teachers have often had to rethink their role because all the information we could ever want to know about a topic is a few mouse clicks away.

Chapter Outline

LO1 What Does Technology Mean for the Classroom? 150
The Flat Classroom 150
The Connected Classroom 150
The Problem of Information Overload 151

LO2 Technology and Learning 152
Ways That Internet Technology Supports Learning 153
Real-World Problems 153
Simulations and Modeling 153
Communities of Learners 154

LO3 Web 2.0 155
Blogs 155
Wikis 156
Implications of Web 2.0 157
Using Handheld Wireless Devices for Assessment 157
Tracking Student Progress from Home 158
Internet Safety 158

LO4 The Digital Divide 159
Assistive Technology 161

LO5 Concluding Thoughts 162

Teaching Suggestions and Resources

Reflection Questions

The Role of Education in the Information Revolution

Citing former Secretary of Education Richard Riley, a book declared in 2004 that "none of the top 10 jobs that will exist in 2010 exist today" (Gunderson, Jones, & Scanland, 2004). The point is that technology is changing so rapidly that many new jobs will appear while many old ones disappear. As teachers, we must prepare students for jobs that do not yet exist—jobs in which they will use technologies that have not been invented in order to solve problems that we don't even know are problems yet (Gunderson, Jones, & Scanland, 2004). Ask your students: What should the role of education become in this age of the Information Revolution? (Hint: Think about skills, abilities, and dispositions.)

Beliefs about Computers in Education

Reflecting on their own computer use and their beliefs about its role in their education is a good way for your students to start formulating a personal approach to integrating technology in their teaching.

- What would your life be like if you did not have ready access to the Internet?
- What is the most important use you make of the computer and the Internet?
- How much of your time is spent on social networking sites such as Facebook?
- In your view, what are the most important reasons for integrating technology in schools?

Discussion Questions

1. Are you a digital native? a digital immigrant (someone who did *not* grow up with technology)?
2. In your opinion, what is the greatest promise of technology for teaching and learning?

TeachSource Video Cases

Teaching with Technology

Find the TeachSource Video Case "Expanding the Definition of Literacy: Meaningful Ways to Use Technology" on the student website. This video provides glimpses of classrooms in which

Key Terms

digital natives 150

flat classroom 150

simulation 153

model 155

blog (short for weblog) 155

wiki 156

technological fluency 159

digital divide 159

assistive technology (AT) 161

interactive whiteboard 161

teachers at varying grade levels are using technology to enhance the literacy skills of their students. Ask your students these questions:

- What methods do these teachers use to keep their students "on track" during their Internet research?
- What is Ms. Sweeney, the high school history teacher, hoping her students will gain through the use of technology? What are some of the skills she hopes students will acquire?
- In what ways does the approach of the elementary school teacher, Ms. Cebula, differ from that of Ms. Sweeney?
- How does the middle school language arts teacher, Ms. Brion-Meisels, express her pedagogy through the use of technology?
- How does the integration of technology foster critical thinking skills?

Integrating Technology to Teach Literacy in Middle School

Find the TeachSource Video Case "Middle School Reading Instruction: Integrating Technology" on the student website. In the classroom shown in the video, Mr. Lawrence is exploring a Greek myth with his inner-city students. Ask your students these questions:

- Mr. Lawrence talks about creating a community in the classroom. How do you think he does that through his interactions with the students?
- How does the students' use of technology—an online discussion forum where they post their thoughts about the question of the day—help create community?
- How does the online discussion forum foster literacy skills?

Active Learning in High School Social Studies

Find the TeachSource Video Case "Integrating Internet Research: High School Social Studies" on the student website. This class is exploring the civil rights movement. Ask your students these questions:

- How does technology allow students to take ownership of their own learning in this classroom?
- Why does the teacher believe it is useful for students to learn about the civil rights movement by using Internet resources?
- How would you describe the role of the teacher in this social studies unit? Is the teacher imparting information or acting as a guide and facilitator?
- In this unit, what is the role of primary sources on the Internet?
- How does the teacher deal with the disparity between her own level of computer knowledge and that of the students?

Computers and Classrooms

Find the TeachSource Video Case "Educational Technology: Issues of Equity and Access" on the student website. This Video Case explores some of the complexities a school district faces in attempting to provide equitable access to technology for all of its students. Ask your students these questions:

- In this school district, what is the educational technology coordinator's main challenge in providing equity?
- How can new teachers gain the technological knowledge they need?
- What is the advantage of having a computer lab in the school? How do you think that facilitates learning?

Learning Outcomes

LO1 The "global" classroom is a reality, with technology making it possible for classrooms all over the world to connect, collaborating on projects and learning from one another.

LO2 Today's students must possess 21st-century skills: to go beyond understanding core concepts and memorizing facts in academic subjects, and to think creatively and critically about a problem, work collaboratively with others to find solutions, and see themselves as problem solvers who communicate their ideas clearly.

LO3 Today's teachers must demonstrate a passion for learning, seek opportunities created by globalization to enhance classroom learning, and help students navigate their ever-expanding world and develop 21st-century skills.

Chapter Outline

LO1 **Education in the Knowledge Economy** 165
The Flat World 165
LO2 The Global Student: Having Information vs. Constructing Knowledge 166
Learning How to Learn 166
Global Collaboration 167
Skills for the 21st Century 167
LO3 **Teaching in the Global Classroom** 168
Teaching with Digital Media: Videoconferencing, Games, and More 170
Digitally Inclined 172
Virtual Classes in High School 172
The Teacher's Role in a Global Classroom 174
Concluding Thoughts 175

Teaching Suggestions and Resources

Reflection Questions

21st-Century Skills

Imagine how differently we live now than did teachers in the first decade of the 20th century!

- Reflecting on your own education, inside and outside the classroom, describe your exposure to world geography and foreign cultures.
- Describe a time when an interdisciplinary unit prompted you to "think outside the box."
- Describe strategies you have developed for managing, interpreting, validating, and acting on the many pieces of information that come your way on a daily basis.
- In what ways do you take responsibility for your own learning?

The Online Community

Chapter 9 explores the important concept of the classroom as a learning community. To be effective, teachers need to build a sense of community in the classroom. Ask your students to take a moment to think about their own experience with online communities, either in coursework or in other areas such as chatrooms, blogs, social networking sites (Facebook), and the like.

- What factors help an online group function as a real community?
- In what ways is an online community similar to a classroom community? How is it different?

Discussion Question

At this point in the text, how, if at all, has your image of teaching and learning changed? Be specific!

Key Terms

knowledge economy 165

globalization 165

Information Age 166

metacognition 167

videoconferencing 167

MIVA 168

gaming 171

digital media 172

virtual school 173

TeachSource Video Cases

Learning How to Learn

Find the TeachSource Video Case "Metacognition: Helping Students Become Strategic Learners" on the student website. This video shows a middle school class trying to make sense of a newspaper article about China. The way the teacher, Ms. Craven, asks students to think about the words they encounter in the newspaper provides a glimpse into metacognition. To get the full benefit of the video, watch it more than once! Ask your students these questions:

- Ms. Craven requires the students to make personal comments about what they are reading, right on the paper itself. How is this helpful for learning?
- How does writing a comment like "What does this mean?" on the newspaper article represent metacognition?
- What metacognitive strategies, if any, do you employ when reading this textbook?

A Global Classroom

Find the TeachSource Video Case "Diversity: Teaching in a Multiethnic Classroom" on the student website. In this video, a Japanese language teacher, a classroom teacher, and all the students in a second-grade class learn an ancient Japanese art form. Students in the class hail from the United States, Japan, Russia, New Zealand, and Africa. Although they are not using the Internet, this lesson has many attributes of appropriate education for the global classroom. Ask your students these questions:

- In what ways does this American classroom feel like a global classroom?
- Think back to what we said in Chapter 4 about curriculum as both a window and a mirror for students. How does this activity act as a window and a mirror for the students in the class?
- Why might some people criticize the use of an ancient Japanese art form for storytelling?
- How does this activity foster an appreciation of global differences?

Learning Outcomes

LO1 A classroom becomes a community when the participants share an understanding of the beliefs, values, and goals that form the basis for the group.

LO2 Classroom management is the term typically used when referring to the prevention of disruptive behaviors and the fostering of a smooth-running class.

LO3 Belongingness in school communities refers to the expressed feeling that individuals are part of a group and of something larger than themselves.

LO4 Formal classroom meetings are a venue for sharing feelings and goals and are a way to establish community with a classroom.

LO5 Sexual harassment and bullying, both in class and in cyberspace, refer to abusive behaviors perpetrated by individuals with power over others who feel powerless.

Chapter Outline

LO1 Building Community in the Classroom 181

LO2 Classroom Management and Classroom Community 181

LO3 Rules, Procedures, and Routines: A Collaborative Effort 184
Is a Well-Managed Classroom Silent? 184
Being Fully Conscious 185

LO4 The Classroom as a Safe Place 186
The Responsive Classroom Approach to Community
   Building 187
Tips for Creating a Classroom Community 188
Community Building in the Secondary Classroom 189
   Consistency 190
   Clarity 190
   Fairness 190
   Foresight 190

LO5 Preventing Harassment and Bullying 190
Sexual Harassment in School 191
Bullying and Teasing 192
Cyberbullying 193
Classroom Community and Goodness of Fit 194
Concluding Thoughts 195

Teaching Suggestions and Resources

Reflection Questions

The Teacher as the Adult in the Classroom

Teachers are also life-long learners; we learn constantly about ourselves, our students, and our content areas. As we return to the theme of "we teach who we are," it is important that we seek the inner understanding that is a hallmark of really wonderful teachers. Ask your students to think about these questions:

- What does it mean to act like an adult in the classroom? What attributes does that involve?
- What behaviors are inappropriate for teachers?
- Do you remember teachers who were ineffective because of behaviors that were not responsible?
- How can you curb a tendency to speak without thinking?
- Even though you are well meaning, has there been a time when you hurt somebody's feelings because you were overly blunt?

Student Roles and Responsibilities

Ask your students to think back to their own middle and high school experiences with fulfilling roles in the classroom community.

- In what ways, if any, did students contribute to the management of the daily classroom routines and protocols?
- Did you have any service learning experiences? If so, reflect on what those experiences taught you.

Harassment and Bullying in the Classroom

Reflecting on personal experiences or views on these serious topics can help your students handle these issues in their own classrooms.

- Do you remember a time when you or someone you knew was bullied or sexually harassed in school? What was the experience like? How did you or your acquaintance deal with it?
- How would you recognize bullying or sexual harassment in your own classroom?
- Females sometimes bully in less physical ways than do males. How would you describe and identify female bullying?

Key Terms

classroom management 181

classroom community 182

Responsive Classroom 188

service learning 189

sexual harassment 191

bullying 192

cyberbullying 194

Discussion Questions

1. How does a new teacher establish a sense of authority in the classroom?
2. In your judgment, what is the most important thing you can do to establish classroom community?

TeachSource Video Cases

Teachers Building Community

Find the TeachSource Video Case "Classroom Management: Best Practices" on the student website. In this video, several teachers demonstrate and talk about the ways they conduct their classrooms. Notice that, in the first segment, the elementary teacher talks about investing time in helping the children understand the routines of the classroom. The middle school teacher explicitly addresses the building of a community with shared expectations. The seventh-grade student reminds us that the teacher must be a "listener" before he or she jumps to judgment, and the guidance counselor reminds teachers that if a student is acting up, it is usually not a personal response to the teacher. Ask your students these questions:

- What do you think the elementary school teacher means when she says that she waits at least six weeks before giving her young students independent activities?
- How does the middle school drama teacher create community?
- Why do you suppose the seventh-grade student urges his teachers not to react first but to listen first?
- Why do you think Ms. Miller spends two hours on grouping students? How does that effort contribute to classroom community?

Using Classroom Meetings to Create Community

Find the TeachSource Video Case "Elementary Classroom Management: Basic Strategies" on the student website. The teacher in this video, Ms. Moylan, uses Morning Meeting to create community in her classroom. In particular, the video shows a meeting in which she helps prepare students for a busy field trip the following week. Ask your students these questions:

- How does Ms. Moylan use the "fair crayon can" with names inside it? How does this device promote fairness?
- How does she engage students in community problem solving?
- When she engages her students in role playing, what is she trying to accomplish?
- After viewing this teacher in action for a few minutes, how would you describe her classroom management style?
- What is the significance of consistency and fairness, especially for the new teacher?

Learning Outcomes

LO1 Public education is vital to a thriving democracy, and teachers in the 21st century need to foster critical thinking, creativity, collaboration, and communication.

LO2 Teaching is about building relationships with students and acknowledging the many ways in which people learn.

LO3 Good teachers have specific personal attributes that make them well suited for the profession. You can demonstrate some of your talents in your teaching portfolio.

LO4 Your responsibility is to understand who you are, where your strengths and weaknesses lie, and what your next steps should be in your journey to become a teacher.

Chapter Outline

Goodness of Fit 197
The Importance of Observing in the Field 198
LO1 The Purposes of Public Education and the Role
    of the Teacher 199
One Size Does Not Fit All 200
LO2 Creating a Culture of Caring 200
Looking Again at Multiple Ways of Teaching
    and Learning 202
Using Current Technologies 203
Getting Started in the Teaching Profession 204
Certification and Standards 204
  The Praxis Tests 204
  The INTASC Standards 205
  *The National Board for Professional
    Teaching Standards 205*
Teaching Positions Here and Abroad 206
Tips for New Teachers 206
Educational Associations 208
The American Federation of Teachers 208
The National Education Association 208
LO3 Build Your Teaching Portfolio 209
LO4 Concluding Thoughts 210
Turning to Teaching 210
Passion Quotient 210

Teaching Suggestions and Resources

Reflection Questions

Demonstrating Understanding

One way for your students to reflect on what becoming a teacher means to them is to complete an "I am" poem. "I am" poems ask the poet to state five different descriptions of the self. Ask students to focus on their understanding of choosing to become a teacher by completing the following statements:

I wonder . . . (two things you wonder about).
I hear . . . (your inner voice).
I see . . . (your vision for your professional self).
I want . . . (what you hope for).
I AM . . . a Future Teacher.

Discussion Questions

1. What do you think of the "Five Core Propositions" of the National Board for Professional Teaching Standards? Which one(s) are you most confident that you have already achieved?
2. Which "Tips for New Teachers" do you think are the most important and why?

TeachSource Video Case

Effective Teaching

Find the TeachSource Video Case "Teaching as a Profession: What Defines Effective Teaching?" on the student website. Terms like *flexible, thoughtful, spontaneous, caring,* and *knowledgeable* emerge as significant attributes of teachers. Ask your students: How would you rank these in order of importance?

Key Terms

public education 199

certification 204

The Praxis Series 204

Interstate New Teacher Assessment and Support Consortium (INTASC) 205

Wrap-Up Questions

1. Describe a time when you experienced a classroom as a community. How did the teacher create it? How did it feel to belong to this community?
2. What are the greatest personal challenges you need to overcome to build community in your classroom?
3. What is the meaning behind the statement "Good teaching leads to good classroom management"?
4. How can you become a "centered presence" in your classroom?
4. What level of passion do you feel about teaching? Why is that important?
5. What would be your greatest challenge in teaching abroad? How appealing is the possibility of teaching abroad for you?
6. What have you concluded from your evaluation of your "goodness of fit" with the teaching profession?

To the instructor: Use the following Learning Projects to further your students' exploration and understanding of the topics presented in the chapter.

1 Becoming a Teacher: Looking Forward and Backward at the Same Time

Gaining Entry to the Profession: Developing a Timeline

Becoming a teacher requires at least a bachelor's degree, usually related to the field in which you plan to teach. Beyond that, however, requirements for becoming a teacher vary from state to state. In most states, some form of advanced training is also needed. If you are seriously considering teaching as a career, it is important to find out exactly what you need in order to become a teacher in the state in which you want to work. As a start, visit this webpage provided by the AFT: http://www.aft.org/teachers/jft/becoming.htm. As you do your research, look for answers to the following questions:

- In your state, can you begin teaching with just a bachelor's degree?
- Do you have to take and pass tests to gain a teaching certificate or license? How many tests? In which areas of study?
- Are you required to obtain a master's degree? If so, what disciplines are accepted as leading to certification?
- Some states require attendance at special seminars in addition to completing the requirements for your academic degree. Is that the case in your state? If so, what seminars are required?

Finally, develop a timeline for your professional preparation. What courses will you take and when will you take them? When will you complete your requirements? Make a checklist of tests, seminars, courses, and application dates for gaining entry into teaching in your state.

Observing a School: Culture and Climate

Now that you have developed a feeling for your own educational history and taken a peek at the profession of teaching, it is time to visit a school of your choice and shadow one or more teachers for part of the school day.

Before you visit, you will need to secure permission from the principal or head of school. Schedule your visit on a day that is convenient for the teacher or teachers you will be shadowing. It is probably best to visit more than one teacher's class. Be sure to select a school that houses the grade or grades you are interested in teaching. Dress appropriately and professionally: no jeans or T-shirts; no very short skirts; no recreational or casual attire.

During your visit you will notice many things, but pay particular attention to the school's culture and climate. Write an essay about this experience. How do you feel about pursuing a teaching career as a result of this visit? What, if anything, has changed for you?

2 Teaching Stories

The Induction Phase

About 40 percent of teachers leave the profession within the first five years on the job (Baldacci et al., 2006). Well-designed teacher induction programs are successful in reducing this turnover rate. Beyond assigning a mentor, many induction programs offer weekly meetings for new teachers during which participants share stories, gain insights, and keep journals on the period of transition from novice to more experienced teacher. The goal of induction programs is not only to assist new teachers as they enter the teaching profession but also to develop reflective teachers who are responsive to the diverse cultural, social, and linguistic backgrounds of all their students.

Imagine that you are a teacher new to a school. What might be some strategies and tools an induction program could offer that would help you? Check local school districts to see if such programs are indeed available.

Interviewing a Classroom Teacher

By now, you may have an idea of the grade or grade level you are interested in teaching. Are you a future elementary, middle, or secondary school teacher? What is the subject area in which you specialize? Are you a future social studies, mathematics, English, science, or foreign language teacher? (Elementary school teachers can say "yes" to most of these subject categories!) Will you be specializing in music, art, physical education, or another area? Are you interested in special education or gifted education?

It is important to interview a classroom teacher who is working in a way you envision for yourself. Suppose you are a future social studies teacher; in that case, you will want to interview someone who has been teaching social studies for some time. Also try to choose a person who teaches at the grade level you currently aspire to.

How can you find a teacher to interview? You can request a name from a local school district. Or your teacher education program may have a field placement office that can suggest school districts with which your college or university has a relationship. Further, if your institution offers graduate programs for teachers already in the classroom, these classroom teachers can be excellent candidates for interviews. Finally, you may have a relative who is currently teaching in a context like the one you are heading for.

Be sure to thank these individuals for their time and to place a limit on the time you spend with them. Generally 30 minutes should be sufficient. Here are some suggestions for interview questions. They include those answered by the teachers quoted in this chapter.

- How did you decide to enter teaching?
- For you, what are the most exciting aspects of the work?
- What do you think are the most difficult challenges for teachers?
- Who has given you the most support?
- How do you continue your professional development?
- How do you know you are successful?
- How would you define teaching?
- What advice would you give to a future teacher?

You will have your own questions to add to the list. For instance, you may be curious to know whether the teachers you interview are interested in National Board certification. Or you may want to learn about their personal interests or hobbies that are manifested in their teaching style. When you complete your interview, write about it in your journal. Respond to the following questions:

- What was the interview experience like?
- What did you learn about teaching that was new to you?
- What, if any, attributes did this teacher have that you could identify with?
- In what way(s) was this teacher different from you?

3 An Overview of Schooling in America

Separation of Church and State

Embedded in the Constitution of the United States is the guarantee of religious freedom for all citizens. The expression "separation of church and state" was coined by Thomas Jefferson, who opposed the use of public funds for the teaching of religion in public schools. Today the expression is often used to resist the infusion of religion into public schools. Many believe that the principle of separation of church and state is a part of our historical, legal, and political heritage, and that it helps to preserve and protect our religious liberty. The Supreme Court ruled in 1963 that prayers and Bible readings were no longer allowed in tax-supported public schools, a decision that respected the diverse religions represented by the students.

Yet the issue is far from settled. There has been much recent debate about the extent to which religious beliefs find their way into public schools. Research some of the controversies that have emerged. Some examples include the Pledge of Allegiance requirement, school prayer, and the conflicts in the state of Kansas and in Dover, Pennsylvania, about the teaching of evolution.

After reading about the different viewpoints, what do you think? Should public schools provide a forum for the opinions of religious groups? Why or why not?

Then and Now

Many of today's educational practices began when the country was young. For example, local control, compulsory education, and tax-supported schools are premises of today's public schools, and you have seen in this chapter how early they originated.

Many of the early conflicts exist today as well. Issues concerning race, social class, and gender inequities are evident in the disparities between today's urban, suburban, and rural schools. Select one issue that dates back to America's early years and describe the ways in which it is reflected in the differences among modern-day urban, suburban, and rural schools.

Reading Dewey

John Dewey thought and wrote a great deal about education. To gain greater insight into his educational philosophy, read his article "My Pedagogic Creed," written in 1897. In this article he talks about what education is and his beliefs about schools, curriculum, and pedagogy. You can find it by searching online for the article title. In what ways does Dewey's philosophy manifest itself in what you know about schools and schooling today?

4 Principles of Teaching and Learning: Exploring Pedagogy, Curriculum, and Instruction

Examining a School's Language Curriculum

Visit an elementary school close to your university or college and explain that, for a course project, you would like to examine the school's language arts basal reader and/or its literature series for the first through the third grade.

- What is your impression of the reading material being used for these early readers?
- Knowing what you do about the children who attend this school, in what ways do you think this reading material may act as a window? As a mirror?

Developing a Curriculum

Select a hobby or an area of personal interest about which you can develop a curriculum—that is, a logical sequence of topics and concepts to be addressed in teaching a group of youngsters about this interest area. For example, if your hobby is figure skating and your imaginary students are in seventh grade, you may want to explore with them the history of figure skating and some biographical data about figure skaters. You may also want to provide diagrams and explanations of various skating techniques, the best skates to buy, and, of course, some cautions and guiding principles.

Your curriculum should address as many aspects of your interest area as possible, but it should also hold the attention of the chosen grade level of students for more than a few days. Use the following guide to assist you in this challenge:

- What is your area of special interest? It can be a hobby, an academic interest, or a visual or performing art.
- What are the most important things you would want young people to know about this area? Make a list.
- Organize your list of topics, starting from the most basic and moving to the most complex.
- Explain each of the topics from the perspective of someone who knows very little about your special area.
- What do you think are the most prevalent misconceptions about your area? Write them down. (For instance, some people may think figure skating is dangerous.)
- How will you help students who hold these misconceptions to reconstruct their mental schemes?

5 Who Are Today's Students?

"English-only" vs. Bilingual Education

A 1998 initiative in California, known as Proposition 227, banned native-language instruction in the state. California has had a particularly high influx of Spanish-speaking students. What do you think motivated voters to approve this extreme measure?

Explore the research that explains this phenomenon, and consider the issues from the standpoint of a future teacher. Did the initiative result from prejudice against Latinos and linguistic minorities, or was there a misunderstanding of bilingual education?

Developing a Multiple Intelligences Survey

Imagine you want to learn more about your students. What types of questions could you include in a survey to give you an indication of each student's intelligence profile? Choose an approximate age level for your imaginary class, and develop a survey that will help you learn more about your students.

6 Contemporary Trends and Pressing Issues in Education

The Controversy Surrounding Inclusion

Inclusion has brought with it a lot of controversy. For this project, you will need to do some additional research on the education of students with special needs. Imagine that you are the parent of a child with a learning disability, and think about the following questions:

- What type of person would make the ideal teacher for your child?
- Would you want your child in an inclusion classroom or a segregated setting with special services? Why?
- What do you believe are the pros and cons of inclusion? Of a segregated setting?

The Achievement Gap

Examine the work of sociologists and psychologists who have studied the effects of social class, family structure, and race on the achievement gap between poor children and wealthier children. Identify three causes for the differences in achievement results and suggest research-supported remedies that can help close the achievement gap. See the Resources for Further Exploration section at the end of the chapter for sources that will help you get started.

Charter Schools

Explore the charter school movement and describe the ways in which it holds promise for remedying the achievement gap. Specifically, investigate one of the following charter schools and describe the qualifications required to teach there.

The KIPP TRUTH Academy in Dallas, Texas: http://www.kipptruth.org/

The CHIME charter schools in Los Angeles County, California: http://www.chimeinstitute.org/

Compass Montessori Charter School in Jefferson County, Colorado: http://www.compassmontessori.org/

The Charter School of Wilmington in Delaware: http://www.charterschool.org/

- What unique instructional strategies are found in the charter school you explored?
- In what ways are these schools designing their goals for curriculum and instruction by taking into account the nature of their specific student bodies?
- Describe the "up" side and "down" side of charter schools.

7 The Information Technology Revolution in the 21st Century

Computers in the Classroom

Arrange an interview in a local school with either the technology specialist or an assistant principal. This can be an elementary, middle, or secondary school. Explain that you are doing a college or university project designed to help you more fully understand the ways schools integrate technology and learning. Here are some suggested questions for your interview. You may have many more.

- Does the school have computers in every classroom? Does it also have a separate computer lab?
- How many networked computers are there in the average classroom?
- Do the computers access the Internet via a wired or wireless connection?
- Who oversees the maintenance and upgrade of the computers and software?
- Does the school have a philosophy or list of guidelines governing the use of the computers in the classroom?
- In what ways are the networked computers used by teachers in the school to promote learning?
- What do you think the next step is for this school to become a more technologically current environment?

After the interview, reflect on what you have learned. What uses for computers in this school most impressed you? What are some of the glaring problems associated with technology integration—in this school and elsewhere?

8 Globalization and Education

Globalization: Arguments For and Against

Globalization used to be widely celebrated as a new birth of freedom. The inference was that better connections in a more open world would improve people's lives by making new products and ideas universally available, breaking down barriers to trade and democratic institutions, resolving tensions between old adversaries, and empowering more and more people (Friedman, 1999). Now, however, globalization is itself a topic of global debate. As someone seeking a career in education, you may want to examine some of the causes of this debate. One place to start is the website of the International Monetary Fund (http://www.imf.org/), where you can find an article called "Globalization: Threat or Opportunity?" You may have your own ideas about whether globalization is a "good thing." As you read and think about this subject, consider the following questions:

- Who benefits most from globalization?
- Why are some people suspicious of globalization?
- How might this debate find its way into the classroom?
- How can schools reflect a global marketplace?

Creating an Online Course

Imagine you are teaching this chapter of the book in an online environment. You have 17 students, all of whom are high school seniors taking an elective course in globalization. The students come from seven different high schools in various regions of the United States as well as in India, Belarus, and China.

- How will you organize the materials for this course?
- What "big ideas" or major concepts will you want the students to learn?
- Provide examples of four topics that would stimulate discussion and get the participants to reflect on the material.
- How will you assess the students' discourse?
- How will you foster a learning community online?
- Are you currently part of an online learning community?

9 The Classroom as Community

Supreme Court Decisions and Sexual Harassment

Explore the following Supreme Court cases: *Franklin v. Gwinnett* (1992), *Gebser v. Lago Vista Independent School District* (1998), and *Davis v. Monroe* (1999). (You can find information online.) For each case, ask yourself:

- What were the circumstances of the case?
- What decision was reached by the High Court?
- What are the damages to be paid by the school or district?

What are the implications of this case for sexual harassment in schools?

An Ideal Classroom Community

Think of a classroom environment in which you would feel comfortable and respected, encouraged to learn and to participate. Make a list of the attributes of that classroom. Next to each attribute, indicate the role the teacher would play in creating the environment.

- Do you think your teaching style and personality will affect your success in creating this kind of community? Why or why not?
- What physical structure do you imagine your classroom will have? How will it be arranged? How will that structure help you build community?
- What strategies will you employ to promote respect among your students?

10 Making the Decision to Become a Teacher

Your Decision about Teaching

Write a 400-word essay describing why you believe your decision to become a teacher represents a "good fit" with the profession—or not.